MICHELIN

EATING OUT IN PUBS 2015

the MICHELIN guide

DEAR READER,

We are delighted to present the 2015 edition of the Michelin guide to Eating Out in Pubs – our guide to the best dining pubs in the UK & Ireland.

The standard of pub cooking continues to reach new heights, and there is now an enormous amount of choice available. Some pubs offer British classics beside the fire in the bar, while others offer creative international cooking in smart dining rooms; some showcase homemade or organic ingredients from small local producers, while others import a diverse range of ingredients from abroad. Whatever the style, the quality and consistency required to be in the guide remain the same.

→ *All of the pubs within these pages have been selected by our team of famous Michelin inspectors, who are the eyes and ears of our readers. They always pay their own bills and their anonymity is key to ensuring that they receive the same treatment as any other guest. Each year, they search for new establishments to add – and only the best make it through! The 'best of the best' are then recognised with awards.*

Our famous Stars ✿ are awarded to places serving top class cuisine – taking into account the quality of ingredients, the mastery of techniques and flavours, the levels of creativity and, of course, consistency.

As you flick through this year's guide you'll notice more colour and greater clarity: we wanted the 2015 edition to be more enjoyable to read and to make your search for establishments easier and faster! This is because our commitment, for over a century, has been to help you make the best choices when it comes to your travels.

These are not our only awards; look out too for the Bib Gourmands ☺, which highlight places offering good food at moderate prices.

Many of our modern day pubs started life as coaching inns, providing refreshment and a place to stay for weary travellers and their horses. The car may have replaced the horse and carriage but the trend for pubs offering accommodation continues – you'll find that many of our recommended pubs also have bedrooms.

Michelin Travel Partner is committed to remaining at the forefront of the culinary world and to meeting the needs of our readers. Please don't hesitate to contact us – we'd love to hear your opinions on the establishments listed within these pages, as well as those you feel could be of interest for future editions.

We hope you enjoy your dining and accommodation experiences – happy travelling with the 2015 edition of the Michelin Eating Out in Pubs guide!

Awards
Stars and Bib Gourmand

✿✿	Excellent cooking, worth a detour
✿	Very good cooking in its category
☺ Bib Gourmand	Good cooking at moderate prices: less than £28 / €40 for a starter, main course and dessert

CONTENTS

MICHELIN

GREAT BRITAIN & IRELAND

REGIONAL MAPS OF...

SCOTLAND
North East
North West
hern
nd
Isle of Man
Yorkshire & the Humber
East Midlands
ENGLAND
West Midlands
East of England
WALES
London
South East
South West
Isle of Wight

THE **PUB** OF **THE YEAR**

The Wild Rabbit

Church St, Kingham
Oxfordshire OX7 6YA

Tel: 01608 658389

www.thewildrabbit.co.uk

➔ See page 333 for more details

Our team of full-time inspectors has spent the last year travelling across Great Britain and Ireland, looking for pubs worthy of inclusion in this year's Michelin Eating Out In Pubs guide.

Every year, we choose one pub to be our 'Pub of the Year'. This pub stands out from the rest, offering all you would expect from the best of British pubs - plus a little bit more.

The Wild Rabbit is owned by Lady Bamford, who was an advocate for organic farming long before it became fashionable. As interest in all things organic grew, so did her empire, starting with the first Daylesford Organic farm shop and followed by several more shops, a restaurant, a spa and a clothing range; all with the same 'self-sufficient, sustainable and organic' ethos at their heart.

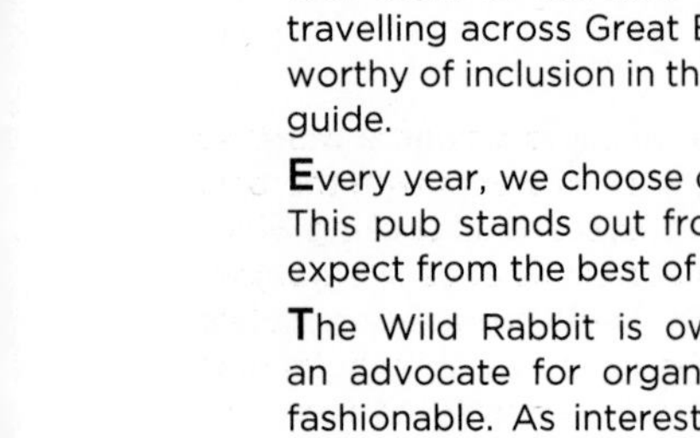

Wild Rabbit, Kingham

Lady Bamford's latest venture is this creeper-clad chocolate box pub, situated in a charming Cotswold village. It's been given a top-to-toe makeover and the result is an understated, rustic-looking but ultra-contemporary inn with flagged floors, log fires, leather sofas and vast expanses of wood and stone. Floor to ceiling windows give the dining room a bright, airy feel; there's an open kitchen to one side and a central table with appealing displays of bread, cheese and dried ham. The atmosphere is animated and service, cheery and efficient; ask for a seat on the suntrap terrace when the weather allows.

THE FOOD

The Daylesford influence is obvious, and nowhere more so than with the food. The capable kitchen works with the best organic ingredients to produce rustic, seasonal cooking which is British at heart and full of flavour. Light bites like goujons of sole, potted rabbit or crisp pig's head croquette populate the bar menu, while dishes on the main menu might include satisfying hare ravioli or a substantial Gloucester Old Spot for two. The smell from the Josper oven tempts many a hungry diner into choosing a juicy steak, and comforting puddings range from a rich chocolate mousse to a creamy rice pudding with prunes soaked in Armagnac.

NATURAL PRODUCTS

Cotton robes hang ready in the bedrooms; settle in with an espresso from your coffee machine and a homemade biscuit or two. The rustic-chic theme continues here with a preponderance of natural products: expect rugged wood flooring, stone walls, exposed beams and maybe a chestnut four-poster. Most of the rooms are in the main house, but there are also four garden rooms, ideal for those who've brought their dogs. All are named after woodland animals and 'Rabbit' is naturally the best.

HOW TO **FIND** A **PUB**

COUNTRY, REGION AND COUNTY NAMES

Coloured tab:

- ENGLAND
  - East Midlands
  - East of England
  - London
  - North East
  - North West
  - South East
  - South West
  - West Midlands
  - Yorkshire & the Humber
- SCOTLAND
- WALES
- IRELAND
  - Northern Ireland
  - Republic of Ireland

ADDRESS, TELEPHONE & WEBSITE

How to get there.

FACILITIES & SERVICES

- Meals served in garden or on terrace
- A particularly interesting wine list
- Wifi
- No dogs allowed • Dog friendly
- Credit cards not accepted

PRICES & CLOSING TIMES

Approximate range of prices for a three-course meal, plus information on booking and annual closures.

Prices are given in £ sterling, and in €uro for the Republic of Ireland.

There are 3 ways to search for a pub in this guide:

- → use the regional maps that precede each section,
- → use the alphabetical list of pubs at the end,
- → use the alphabetical list of place names at the end.

CROSS AT KENILWORTH

Dishes not only look impressive but taste good too

NEW PUB OR INN IN THE GUIDE

ENGLAND • West Midlands • Warwickshire

When you first catch sight of this pub's smart exterior, you'll just know that they take things seriously here and when an eager member of staff greets you, settles you in and explains the menu, this first impression is confirmed. Further proof comes on your plate: skilfully executed, classical cooking uses prime seasonal ingredients, and dishes not only look impressive but taste good too. If you're seated in the back room, which opens onto the terrace, you get to watch the kitchen in action. The bright and airy room next door used to be a classroom – a fact alluded to by the eye-catching wall lamps shaped like hand bells. The front bar, with its adjoining snug and wood burning stove, makes a cosy place for a beer and a homemade sausage roll.

16 New St,
KENILWORTH, CV8 2EZ
Tel.: (01926)853840
Website: www.thecrosskenilworth.co.uk

On northwestern side of town on A 429, Coventry Road. Parking.

ONE OF OUR FAVOURITES

PRICES
Meals: £ 25 (lunch) and a la carte £ 30/45

MAP: 20

NUMBER ON THE REGIONAL MAP

CLOSING TIMES
Closed Sunday dinner, Monday and bank holidays

Wells Bombardier and Hook Norton Old Hooky

BEERS SERVED

513

PUBS WITH BEDROOMS

Room prices range from the lowest-priced single to the most expensive double or twin.

Breakfast is usually included in the price. Marked in blue on the map

INSPECTORS' **FAVOURITES**

All the pubs in this guide have been selected for the quality of their cooking. However, we feel that several of them deserve additional consideration as they boast at least one extra quality which makes them particularly special.

It may be the delightful setting, the charm and character of the pub, the general atmosphere, the pleasant service, the overall value for money or the exceptional cooking.

To distinguish these pubs, we point them out with our "Inspectors' favourites" Bibendum stamp.

We are sure you will enjoy these pubs as much as we have.

ENGLAND

EAST MIDLANDS

EAST OF ENGLAND

LONDON

NORTH EAST

NORTH WEST

SOUTH EAST

BEER
IN THE **U.K.** & **IRELAND**

It's easy to think of beer as just bitter or lager. But that doesn't tell half the story. Between the two there's a whole range of styles and tastes, including pale ales, beers flavoured with spices, fruits and herbs, and wheat beers. It's all down to the skill of the brewer who'll juggle art, craft and a modicum of science to create the perfect pint.

Grist and wort may sound like medieval hangover cures, but they're actually crucial to the brewing process. Malted barley is crushed into grist, a coarse powder which is mashed with hot water in a large vessel called a mash tun. Depending on what sort of recipe's required, the brewer will add different cereals at this stage, such as darker malt for stout. The malt's natural sugars dissolve and the result is wort: a sweet brown liquid, which is boiled with hops in large coppers. Then comes the most important process of all: fermentation, when the hopped wort is cooled and run into fermentation vessels. The final addition is yeast, which converts the natural sugars into alcohol, carbon dioxide and a host of subtle flavours.

Finally, a beer has to be conditioned before it leaves the brewery, and in the case of cask conditioned real ales, the beer goes directly into the cask, barrel or bottle. The yeast is still active in there, fermenting the beer for a second time, often in a pub cellar.

Beer's as natural a product as you can get. This is what's in your pint:

BARLEY
It's the main ingredient in beer and rich in starch. Malted before brewing to begin the release of sugars.

HOPS
Contain resins and essential oils, and used at varying times to give beer its distinctive flavour. Early on they add bitterness, later on they provide a spicy or citrus zest.

YEAST
Converts the sugars from the barley into alcohol and carbon dioxide during fermentation. It produces compounds that affect the flavour of the beer.

WATER
Burton and Tadcaster have excellent local water, and that's why they became great ale brewing centres. Meanwhile, the water of London and Dublin is just right for the production of stouts and porters.

All the time there's a delicate process going on as the beer is vulnerable to attack from micro-biological organisms. But as long as the publican cares about his beer, you should get a tasty, full-flavoured pint.

REAL QUALITY

The modern taste for real ale took off over thirty years ago when it looked like the lager industry was in the process of killing off traditional "warm ale". There are several styles, but the most popular in England and Wales is bitter, which boasts a seemingly inexhaustible variety of appearance, scent and flavour. You can have your bitter gold or copper of colour, hoppy or malty of aroma, dry or sweet of flavour (sweet flavoured bitter? This is where the term "bitter" is at its loosest). Sometimes it has a creamy head; sometimes no head at all. Typically, go to a Yorkshire pub for the former, a London pub for the latter.

Mild developed its popularity in Wales and the north west of England in Victorian times. Often dark, it's a weaker alternative to bitter, with a sweetish taste based on its hop characteristics.

In Scotland, the near equivalent of bitter is heavy, and the most popular draught ales are known as 80 shilling (export) or 70 shilling (special). And, yes, they have a heavy quality to them, though 60 shilling ale - or Light - is akin to English mild.

Full-bodied and rich, stouts (and their rarer porter relatives) are almost a meal in themselves. They're famously black in colour with hints of chocolate and caramel, but it's the highly roasted yeast flavour that leaves the strong after taste.

Michelin is committed to improving the mobility of travellers

ON EVERY ROAD AND BY EVERY MEANS

Since the company came into being - over a century ago - Michelin has had a single objective: to offer people a better way forward. A technological challenge first, to create increasingly efficient tyres, but also an ongoing commitment to travellers, to help them travel in the best way. This is why Michelin is developing a whole collection of products and services: from maps, atlases, travel guides and auto accessories, to mobile apps, route planners and online assistance: Michelin is doing everything it can to make travelling more pleasurable!

A tyre...
→ *what is it?*

Round, black, supple yet solid, the tyre is to the wheel what the shoe is to the foot. But what is it made of? First and foremost, rubber, but also various textile and/or metallic materials... and then it's filled with air! It is the skilful assembly of all these components that ensures tyres have the qualities they should: grip to the road, shock absorption, in two words: 'comfort' and 'safety'.

1 *TREAD*
The tread ensures the tyre performs correctly, by dispersing water, providing grip and increasing longevity.

2 *CROWN PLIES*
This reinforced double or triple belt combines vertical suppleness with transversal rigidity, enabling the tyre to remain flat to the road.

3 *SIDEWALLS*
These link all the component parts and provide symmetry. They enable the tyre to absorb shock, thus giving a smooth ride.

4 *BEADS*
The bead wires ensure that the tyre is fixed securely to the wheel to ensure safety.

5 *INNER LINER*
The inner liner creates an airtight seal between the wheel rim and the tyre.

  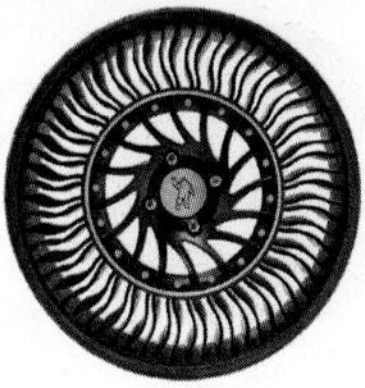

Michelin
→ *innovation in movement*

Created and patented by Michelin in 1946, the belted radial-ply tyre revolutionised the world of tyres. But Michelin did not stop there: over the years other new and original solutions came out, confirming Michelin's position as a leader in research and innovation.

→ *the right pressure!*

One of Michelin's priorities is safer mobility. In short, innovating for a better way forward. This is the challenge for researchers, who are working to perfect tyres capable of shorter braking distances and offering the best possible traction to the road. And so, to support motorists, Michelin organises road safety awareness campaigns all over the world: «Fill up with air» initiatives remind everyone that the right tyre pressure is a crucial factor in safety and fuel economy.

The Michelin strategy:
→ *multi-performance tyres*

Michelin is synonymous with safety, fuel saving and the capacity to cover thousands of miles. A MICHELIN tyre is the embodiment of all these things – thanks to our engineers, who work with the very latest technology.

Their challenge: to equip every tyre – whatever the vehicle (car, truck, tractor, bulldozer, plane, motorbike, bicycle or train!) – with the best possible combination of qualities, for optimal overall performance.

Slowing down wear, reducing energy expenditure (and therefore CO_2 emissions), improving safety through enhanced road handling and braking: there are so many qualities in just one tyre – that's Michelin Total Performance.

MICHELIN Total Performance

Every day, **Michelin** is working towards sustainable mobility

OVER TIME, WHILE RESPECTING THE PLANET

Sustainable mobility

➜ *is clean mobility... and mobility for everyone*

Sustainable mobility means enabling people to get around in a way that is cleaner, safer, more economical and more accessible to everyone, wherever they might live. Every day, Michelin's 113 000 employees worldwide are innovating:

- by creating tyres and services that meet society's new needs,
- by raising young people's awareness of road safety,
- by inventing new transport solutions that consume less energy and emit less CO_2.

➜ *Michelin Challenge Bibendum*

Sustainable mobility means allowing the transport of goods and people to continue, while promoting responsible economic, social and societal development. Faced with the increasing scarcity of raw materials and global warming, Michelin is standing up for the environment and public health.

Michelin regularly organises 'Michelin Challenge Bibendum', the only event in the world which focuses on sustainable road travel.

ENGLAND

1

2

1 © Jason Friend / LoopImages / Photononstop

2 D. Pearson / Agency Jon Arnold Images / age fotostock

3 Funkystock / age fotostock

3

A vision of England sweeps across a range of historic buildings, monuments and rolling landscapes. This image, taking in wild natural borders extending from the rugged splendour of Cornwall's cliffs to pounding Northumbrian shores, seeks parity with a newer picture of Albion: redefined cities and towns whose industrial past is being reshaped by a shiny, steel-and glass, interactive reality. The country's geographical bones and bumps are a reassuring constant: the windswept moors of the south west and the craggy peaks of the Pennines, the summery orchards of the Kentish Weald, the "flat earth" constancy of East Anglian skies and the mirrored calm of Cumbria's lakes. The pubs of England have made good use of the land's natural bounty over the past decade; streamlined establishments have stripped out the soggy carpets and soggier menus and replaced them with crisp décor and fresh, inventive cooking. England's multi-ethnic culture has borne fruit in the kitchens of your local...

EAST MIDLANDS

England

An area that combines the grace of a bygone age with the speed of the 21C. To the east (Chatsworth House, Haddon Hall and Burghley House) is where Pride and Prejudice came to life, while Silverstone to the south hosts the Grand Prix. Market towns are dotted all around: Spalding's cultivation of tulips rivals that of Holland, Oakham boasts its stunning Castle and Great Hall, and the legendary "Boston Stump" oversees the bustle of a 450 year-old market. The brooding beauty of the Peak District makes it the second most visited National Park in the world. Izaak Walton popularised the river Dove's trout-filled waters in "The Compleat Angler" and its surrounding hills are a rambler's dream, as are the wildlife habitats of the National Forest and the wind-swept acres of the pancake-flat fens.

Above it all looms Lincoln Cathedral's ancient spire, while in the pubs, local ale – typically brewed in Bakewell, Dovedale or Rutland – slips down a treat alongside the ubiquitous Melton Mowbray pie.

North West
Yorkshire & the Humber
West Midlands
Peak District National Park
MANCHESTER
SHEFFIELD
HUDDERSFIELD
STOKE-ON-TRENT
DERBY
BIRMINGHAM
WOLVERHAMPTON
COVENTRY
NOTTING
LEICES
Darwen
Chorley
Bury
Rochdale
Bolton
Wigan
Oldham
Holmfirth
Leigh
Brighouse
Dewsbury
Wakefield
Pontefract
Barnsley
Conisbrough
Rotherham
Ashton-under-Lyne
Glossop
Stocksbridge
St. Helens
Altrincham
Hyde
Stockport
Widnes
Runcorn
Northwich
Wilmslow
Whaley Bridge
Chapel-en-le-Frith
Castleton
HighPeak
Dronfield
Staveley
Worksop
Maltby
Buxton
Baslow
Chesterfield
Macclesfield
Bakewell
Chatsworth House
Haddon Hall
Hardwick Hall
Mansfield
Winsford
Middlewich
Tarporley
Congleton
Clay Cross
Matlock
Sandbach
Crewe
Kidsgrove
Leek
Dovedale Site
Alfreton
Sutton-in-Ashfield
Ripley
Heanor
Hucknall
Nantwich
Ashbourne
Belper
Newcastle-under-Lyme
Audlem
Ilkeston
Whitchurch
West Bridgford
Stone
Uttoxeter
Sudbury
Market Drayton
Long Eaton
Eccleshall
Abbots Bromley
Burton-upon-Trent
Rempstone
Hodnet
Stafford
Loughborough
Newport
Rugeley
Swadlincote
Crudgington
Weston Park
Cannock
Ashby de la Zouch
Shepshed
Coalville
Gailey
Lichfield
Telford
Tamworth
Brownhills
Walsall
Ironbridge
Much Wenlock
Sutton Coldfield
Atherstone
Hinckley
Bridgnorth
Dudley
Nuneaton
Bedworth
Lutterworth
Halesowen
Stourbridge
Kidderminster
Solihull
Rugby
Kenilworth
Tenbury Wells
Stourport
Bromsgrove
Redditch
Royal Leamington Spa
Henley
Daventry
Warwick
Southam
Leominster
Worcester
Droitwich
Alcester
Bromyard
Stratford-upon-Avon
Ettington
Pershore
Hidcote Garden
Newtown
Great Malvern
Upton
Evesham
Shipston-on-Stour
Banbury
Ledbury
Chipping Campden
Broadway
Brackley
Tewkesbury
Moreton
Chastleton House
Ross-on-Wye
Winchcombe
Cheltenham
Stow-on-the-Wold
Chipping Norton
Bicester

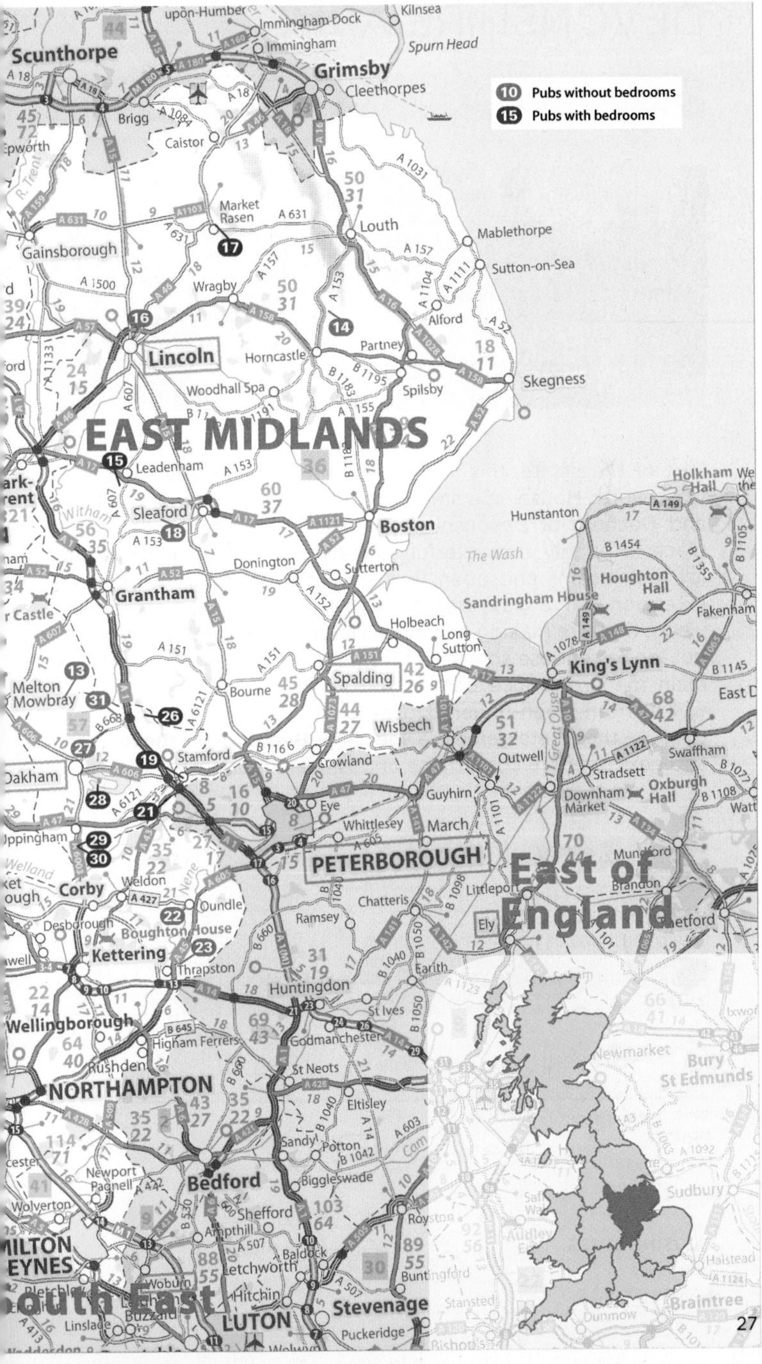

Pubs without bedrooms
Pubs with bedrooms
EAST MIDLANDS
East of England
South East
Scunthorpe
Grimsby
Cleethorpes
Immingham Dock
Immingham
Kilnsea
Spurn Head
Brigg
Caistor
Epworth
Market Rasen
Louth
Mablethorpe
Sutton-on-Sea
Gainsborough
Wragby
Alford
Lincoln
Horncastle
Partney
Spilsby
Skegness
Woodhall Spa
Leadenham
Sleaford
Boston
Donington
Sutterton
The Wash
Grantham
Holbeach
Long Sutton
Spalding
Bourne
Melton Mowbray
Stamford
Crowland
Wisbech
Outwell
Oakham
Uppingham
Eye
Guyhirn
Whittlesey
March
PETERBOROUGH
Corby
Weldon
Oundle
Chatteris
Littleport
Ely
Desborough
Boughton House
Kettering
Thrapston
Ramsey
Earith
Huntingdon
St Ives
Wellingborough
Higham Ferrers
Rushden
Godmanchester
NORTHAMPTON
St Neots
Eltisley
Sandy
Potton
Newport Pagnell
Bedford
Biggleswade
Wolverton
MILTON KEYNES
Ampthill
Shefford
Royston
Letchworth
Baldock
Buntingford
Woburn
Hitchin
Stevenage
Linslade
LUTON
Puckeridge
Hunstanton
Holkham Hall
Houghton Hall
Sandringham House
Fakenham
King's Lynn
Swaffham
Stradsett
Downham Market
Oxburgh Hall
Mundford
Brandon
Thetford
Newmarket
Bury St Edmunds
Sudbury
Halstead
Braintree
Dunmow
Stansted

DEVONSHIRE ARMS

Hugely characterful bar and contemporary brasserie

Part of the estate, this inn is just minutes down the road from Chatsworth House, in a small hamlet largely owned by the Duke and Duchess of Devonshire. There are two clear parts to the place: a hugely characterful, homely bar with exposed stone, low oak beams and open fires, and a bright modern brasserie extension with a glass-fronted wine cave and village and stream views. If you're making a flying visit, have afternoon tea; if you've got longer, choose something from the lengthy, classically based main menu. Produce comes from the surrounding villages, as well as from green-fingered locals who swap their wares for beer tokens – the estate game is a speciality. Bedrooms in the main inn and next door are cosy; those opposite are more modern.

Devonshire Sq,
BEELEY, DE4 2NR
Tel.: (01629)733259
Website: www.devonshirebeeley.co.uk

5 mi southeast of Bakewell by A 6 and B 6012. Parking.

PRICES
Meals: a la carte £ 28/49

14 rooms:
£ 99/189

MAP: 1

CLOSING TIMES
Open daily
booking advisable

Peak Ales

SAMUEL FOX COUNTRY INN

Classic cooking with modern and Spanish twists

The dramatic landscape of the Hope Valley will be the first thing to catch your eye, and the curious pub sign depicting a fox beneath an umbrella, the next - it makes sense, however, when you discover that famed local businessman, Samuel Fox, was the inventor of the steel-ribbed umbrella! The attractive light-stone building dates back over 200 years and conceals a cosy room with tables arranged around the semi-circular bar. Classic cooking has modern touches; at lunch, choose from specials such as homemade terrine with chutney and brioche, and at dinner, slow-cooked local pork belly with chorizo - a nod to the chef's time spent in Andalucia. On Friday nights, try the popular 'secret supper' small plates. Smart modern bedrooms have good extras.

Stretfield Rd,
BRADWELL, S33 9JT
Tel.: (01433)621562
Website: www.samuelfox.co.uk

12 mi northwest of Baslow by A 623 and B 6049. Parking.

PRICES
Meals: £ 20 (early dinner) and
a la carte £ 26/42

4 rooms:
£ 70/130

MAP: 2

CLOSING TIMES
Closed 5-15 January

Bradfield Ales, Kelham Island Pale Rider and Pennine Best Bitter

DEVONSHIRE ARMS

Stout, satisfying dishes use local produce

Be sure to admire the views as you make your way over to the South Yorkshire and Derbyshire border, where you'll find this smart inn. In summer, fight for a spot on the small terrace; otherwise, choose from one of several modern rooms - including the private dining area, 'Tom's Kitchen', which is perfect for a special occasion. Fresh, seasonal ingredients are at the core of the menu, with the likes of thick gammon and double-fried eggs or steak and ale suet pie with triple-cooked chips - and you may well struggle to make it through to dessert! They like to keep things local and their suppliers are acknowledged on a blackboard above the fire, with eggs coming from just down the road and much of the meat, from the butcher who lives opposite.

Lightwood Ln,
MIDDLE HANDLEY, Eckington, S21 5RN
Tel.: (01246)434800
Website: www.devonshirearmsmiddlehandley.com

8.5 mi southeast of Sheffield by A 61 and B 6056 (Eckington Rd), turning at traffic light in village onto B 6052 then Middle Handley rd. Parking.

PRICES
Meals: a la carte £ 27/43

MAP: 3

CLOSING TIMES
Closed Monday except bank holiday lunch and Sunday dinner

Bradfield Farmers Blonde, Kelham Island Easy Rider and Welbeck Red Feather

INN AT TROWAY

Hearty portions and regional ales

This early Victorian pub is set in a picturesque location and offers delightful views out over the rolling countryside; make the most of these by grabbing a seat either on the terrace or in the airy rear dining room. This is an area popular with walkers and the food is satisfyingly hearty; perfect for refuelling after a brisk morning hike. Among the options on the extensive menu might be a ploughman's platter, a gourmet handmade burger or a steak supper for two; desserts often include playful elements, so you might find dishes containing doughnuts or marshmallows. There's a good value set menu served from 12-7pm and a fine selection of regional ales on offer 24/7. Unusually, the menu makes recommendations as to which dishes go well with beer.

Snowdon Ln,
TROWAY, Eckington, S21 5RU
Tel.: (01246)417666
Website: www.relaxeatanddrink.co.uk

7.5 mi southeast of Sheffield by A 61 and B 6056 (Eckington Rd). Parking.

PRICES
Meals: a la carte £ 19/33

MAP: 4

CLOSING TIMES
Open daily

Thornbridge Ales

ELM TREE

Most ingredients are sourced from within 10 miles

This 18C stone building takes its name from an elm tree which used to stand on the village green. It was once a wheelwright's by day and a pub by night, and the fact that it's now wholly a pub evidently pleases the loyal band of locals sitting at the brightly lit bar. Head left for a seat by the wood-burning stove or through to the rear for a more intimate experience - or in summer, dine on the terrace. The menu reads like a roll call of pub classics, with the likes of liver and bacon, gammon steak with Ted's egg and chips, homemade Derbyshire steak burger, and specials that could include mushroom and wild garlic ravioli. Dishes are good value and presented in a modern manner, and most ingredients are sourced from within 10 miles.

ELMTON, S80 4LS
Tel.: (01909)721261
Website: www.elmtreeelmton.co.uk

4 mi northeast of Bolsover by A 632 signed off B 6417. In centre of village. Parking.

PRICES
Meals: £ 11 (weekday lunch) and a la carte £ 18/38

MAP: 5

CLOSING TIMES
Closed Tuesday and Sunday dinner

Black Sheep Best Bitter and Golden Sheep, Kelham Island Easy Rider and Robinsons Dizzy Blonde

CHEQUERS INN

Built into the stone boulders of Froggat Edge

This 16C inn is built right into the stone boulders of Froggatt Edge and even has a direct path from its garden up to the peak. As traditional inside as out, it's a comfortingly no-nonsense sort of place, boasting an open fire, gleaming brass, a large bar and a quieter, cosier room across the hall. The majority of diners are walkers, but the jolly team welcome one and all as if they were locals. Cooking is unfussy and wholesome, with classical dishes that always include fish and chips, bangers and mash and a pie, as well as more imaginative specials such as roast partridge or seared scallops and black pudding on the blackboard. No.1, to the rear, is the quietest of the comfy bedrooms; hampers of homemade produce are a popular take-home purchase.

Hope Valley,
FROGGATT, S32 3ZJ
Tel.: (01433)630231
Website: www.chequers-froggatt.com

3 mi north of Baslow on A 625. Situated on the edge of the village. Parking.

PRICES
Meals: a la carte £ 25/33

6 rooms:
£ 85/115

MAP: 6

CLOSING TIMES
Closed 25 December

Peak Ales Bakewell Best, Kelham Island Easy Rider and Bradfield Brewery Farmers Blonde

DEVONSHIRE ARMS (N)

Produce from farms on the Chatsworth Estate

Another inn from the Devonshire Group and, as with the others, it comes with bedrooms, making it an ideal choice if you're looking to book a weekend away in the Peak District. Designed by none other than the Duchess herself, the stylish rooms are appealingly contemporary and, with the popular Chatsworth Farm shop in the very same village, you'll want to stock up on supplies to take home. Traditional pub dishes get a makeover on the menu and, as in the shop, much of the produce on your plate will have come directly from farms on the Chatsworth Estate. Servings are generous and dishes like suet pudding or lamb hotpot, satisfyingly filling, so you'll do well to get through three courses. Order at the bar; staff are friendly and efficient.

PILSLEY, DE45 1UL
Tel.: (01246)583258
Website: www.devonshirepilsley.co.uk

3 mi northeast of Bakewell off A 619. In centre of village. Parking

PRICES
Meals: a la carte £ 19/32

13 rooms:
£ 75/165

MAP: 7

CLOSING TIMES
Open daily
booking advisable

Peak Ales Swift Nick and Bakewell Best, Thornbridge Jaipur

SARACEN'S HEAD

With portions this large, you won't leave hungry

Set opposite a pretty church in a remote, picturesque village, the Saracen's Head may not seem like the kind of place where you need to book, but arrive without a reservation and you could be disappointed. Pass the chefs hard at work in the kitchen and you'll arrive in a bright bar with rustic furnishings, which leads through to a high-ceilinged room with exposed beams and another open-fired room filled with local art. The large, frequently changing menu is chalked up on a blackboard over the fireplace and lists good old pub and restaurant favourites such as prawn cocktail, pressed ham hock or crisp roast duck with orange syrup; consider your options carefully, as with portions this large, it's unlikely you'll make it through three courses!

Church Ln,
SHIRLEY, DE6 3AS
Tel.: (01335)360330
Website: www.saracens-head-shirley.co.uk

Between Ashbourne and Brailsford off A 52. Parking.

PRICES
Meals: a la carte £ 20/40

MAP: 8

CLOSING TIMES
Open daily

Greene King IPA, Morland Old Speckled Hen and Timothy Taylor Landlord

THREE HORSESHOES INN

You can buy their homemade produce

This large, whitewashed building may not look much like a pub but open the door and you can rest assured you're in the right place. It's more of a dining pub than your typical village local but it's still characterful - full of books, artefacts and paintings. Numerous interlinking rooms allow you to create a different experience every time you come: choose an antique table beside the exposed brick fireplace, an intimate corner in one of the smaller rooms, or in summer, a pleasant alfresco spot. A friendly, efficient team point out the blackboards that are scattered about the place, displaying classical, seasonal dishes which prove robust and flavoursome. If 3 courses is too much, don't worry - you can buy something from the shop to take home.

44-46 Main St,
BREEDON ON THE HILL, DE73 8AN
Tel.: (01332)695129
Website: www.thehorseshoes.com

Signposted off A 42 between Castle Donington and Ashby de la Zouch. Parking.

PRICES
Meals: a la carte £ 20/40

MAP: 9

CLOSING TIMES
Closed 25-26 December, 1 January, Sunday dinner and Monday

Marston's Pedigree and Shardlow Narrowboat

THE JOINERS

Manages to make simple things taste great

You can't help but feel that the locals had a part to play in the naming of this pub, which started life as the Joiners Arms and has since been renamed 'The Joiners'. Set in a small rural village, this neat, whitewashed building dates back to the 17C and boasts characterful wood floors and low beams. Run by an enthusiastic husband and wife team, it's more of a dining pub than a place for a casual drink; although the group of regulars crowded round the pine-fitted bar would probably tell you otherwise. Menus display a mix of refined pub classics and more brasserie-style dishes, all cooked and presented in a straightforward yet effective manner. There's a good value set lunch and a wide selection of wines by the glass; Thursday is 'fish night'.

Church Walk,
BRUNTINGTHORPE, LE17 5QH
Tel.: (0116)2478258
Website: www.thejoinersarms.co.uk

Between Leicester and Husbands Bosworth off A 5199. Parking.

PRICES
Meals: £ 17/22 and a la carte £ 25/39

MAP: 10

CLOSING TIMES
Closed Sunday dinner and Monday
booking essential

Sharp's Doom Bar

ROYAL OAK

Appealing dishes with the occasional quirky touch

This pub may no longer boast the majestic oak tree it was once named after but its spacious grounds still remain a draw; where, from June to August, a large marquee plays host to summer weddings. Set at the heart of a sleepy village, it's owned by two brothers who have totally modernised the place, creating a spacious yet cosy bar and a more intimate dining room. Menus offer plenty of choice, from sandwiches and soup through to sharing platters, old pub favourites and appealing main courses, with many dishes displaying a quirky touch – such as the deconstructed scotch egg with homemade piccalilli or the home-cured salmon with beetroot horseradish slaw. Well-equipped, up-to-date bedrooms are in an adjacent block; one has a whirlpool bath.

The Green,
LONG WHATTON, LE12 5BD
Tel.: (01509)843694
Website: www.theroyaloaklongwhatton.co.uk

4 mi northwest of Loughborough by A 6 and B 5324. In the centre of the village. Parking.

PRICES
Meals: £ 16 (weekday dinner) and a la carte £ 21/39

7 rooms:
£ 79/105

MAP: 11

CLOSING TIMES
Open daily

St Austell Tribute, Sharp's Doom Bar and Dancing Duck Nice Weather

RED LION INN

Produce from the kitchen garden guides the menu

Set in the village centre, this spacious creamwashed pub with its rustic bar and characterful dining rooms is very much part of the community. Whilst it maintains a healthy drinking trade, it's the food here that's the main attraction. The latest produce from the kitchen garden informs the menu and the à la carte has a map of suppliers' locations on the back - and it's reassuring that they don't stray too far from the doorstep; you'll find sausages from the village butcher, game from the Belvoir Estate and cheese from the nearby dairies. Cooking is straightforward and unfussy, resulting in a pleasing mix of refined pub classics with the odd local or global twist, and dishes with more of a restaurant style. Service is friendly and attentive.

2 Red Lion St,
STATHERN, LE14 4HS
Tel.: (01949)860868
Website: www.theredlioninn.co.uk

8 mi north of Melton Mowbray by A 607. Parking.

PRICES
Meals: £ 18 (weekdays) and
a la carte £ 22/41

MAP: 12

CLOSING TIMES
Closed Sunday dinner and Monday
booking essential

Grainstore Ales, Fuller's London Pride, Milestone Shine On and Brewster's Ales

BERKELEY ARMS

Daily changing bar snacks and modern dishes

This attractive village pub dates back to the 16C and is currently under the control of an enthusiastic local couple, who have plenty of experience in the hospitality industry. As you enter, a roaring fire greets you; turn left for the low-beamed bar with its tiled floor and pine tables or right for a slightly more formal dining room. The relaxed, personable service is overseen by charming owner Louise, while her husband, Neil, is hard at work behind the scenes, preparing an appealing seasonal menu of locally sourced produce. Dishes are gutsy and satisfying - there's a daily changing selection of bar snacks and a balanced à la carte of slightly more adventurous, modern offerings, such as braised pig cheek or sea bass with fennel and chorizo.

59 Main St,
WYMONDHAM, LE14 2AG
Tel.: (01572)787587
Website: www.theberkeleyarms.co.uk

7 mi east of Melton Mowbray off B 676. In centre of village. Parking.

PRICES
Meals: £ 15 (weekdays)/19 and
a la carte £ 21/44

MAP: 13

CLOSING TIMES
Closed first 2 weeks
January, 2 weeks summer,
Sunday dinner and Monday

Marston's Pedigree,
Castle Rock Harvest Pale,
Batemans XB and guest ales

BLUE BELL INN

Home-cooked meals for ramblers

Set in a tiny village at the heart of the Lincolnshire Wolds, this welcoming whitewashed pub is a popular stop-off point for ramblers navigating the Viking Way. It was originally named after the bluebell flower but a previous landlord was unhappy with the moniker, so he split the word in two and hung a big blue fibreglass bell outside. You enter into a traditional bar with a copper counter and comfy sofas, which in turn leads through to a bright red dining room - a popular spot come evening time. Menus cover all bases, offering honest, home-cooked dishes which are big on flavour; maybe devilled whitebait or potted shrimps, followed by corned beef hash, twice-baked cheddar soufflé or whole locally smoked trout. Comforting nursery puddings follow.

1 Main Rd,
BELCHFORD, LN9 6LQ
Tel.: (01507)533602
Website: www.bluebellbelchford.co.uk

4 mi north of Horncastle by A 153 and right hand turn east. Parking.

PRICES
Meals: a la carte £ 20/34

MAP: 14

CLOSING TIMES
Closed 12-26 January

Batemans XB and weekly guest ales

HARE & HOUNDS

Simple classics done well

Built in 1680 as a house, the Hare & Hounds has not long been a pub but ever since the current owners (who also have the Brownlow Arms at Hough-on-the-Hill) took over and spent some money on the place, it has been enthusiastically adopted by the locals. The owners' ethos of 'simple pub classics done well' goes down a storm – the menus are refreshingly concise and local produce is to the fore. There's a soup, pie and pasta of the day and steaks from the chargrill are the choice of many. Service is cheerful and the pub is charmingly decorated; you can eat wherever you like – in the bar or in either of the dining rooms. There are smart, comfortable bedrooms in the old stables and the pub also hosts popular jazz evenings.

The Green,
FULBECK, NG32 3JJ
Tel.: (01400)273322
Website: www.hareandhoundsfulbeck.com

7.5 mi northwest of Sleaford signed off A 17. In the village centre. Parking.

PRICES
Meals: a la carte £ 19/36

8 rooms:
£ 60/80

MAP: 15

CLOSING TIMES
Closed 25 December and Sunday dinner

Marston's Pedigree and EPA

WIG & MITRE

Come at 9am for a hearty, homemade breakfast

Nestled among period shops on a steep hill, this well-established, part-14C pub is something of a Lincoln institution; standing midway between the castle, used as a court - hence the 'Wig' - and the cathedral - hence the 'Mitre'. There's a cosy bar downstairs, and two period dining rooms and a light, airy beamed restaurant above. The menu changes quarterly, displaying largely classical dishes with the odd Mediterranean or Asian influence. There's a blackboard of daily specials, a good value weekday set selection and, for those who enjoy a hearty homemade breakfast, they open at 9am. With wine books and maps dotted about the place and over 20 wines by the glass, it comes as no surprise to find that they own the next door wine shop too.

30-32 Steep Hill
LINCOLN, LN2 1LU
Tel.: (01522)535190
Website: www.wigandmitre.com

Close to the Cathedral. Lincoln Castle car parks adjacent.

PRICES
Meals: £ 15 (lunch and early dinner)
and a la carte £ 21/33

MAP: 16

CLOSING TIMES
Closed 25 December

Black Sheep Best Bitter
and Oakham JHB

ADVOCATE ARMS

Smart modern pub offering afternoon tea

This building started life in the early 19C as the Gordon Arms Hotel and is located just a few steps away from the main market square. Apart from the original revolving door, there's not much of its past to be seen nowadays as, courtesy of a top-to-toe refit, it's now smart and modern, with large etched glass walls dividing the place into a large bar and two dining areas. It's open from early in the morning to late at night, so you can pop in and start your day with a bacon sandwich or break up your shopping with afternoon tea. Lunch sticks to good old pub classics, while at dinner, mature local steaks are a speciality. Puddings are satisfyingly traditional and tasty regional cheeses are a feature. Bedrooms are spacious and well-equipped.

2 Queen St,
MARKET RASEN, LN8 3EH
Tel.: (01673)842364
Website: www.advocatearms.co.uk

In town centre, opposite the main market square.
Free car parks around the town.

PRICES
Meals: a la carte £ 13/44

10 rooms:
£ 55/90

MAP: 17

CLOSING TIMES
Closed Sunday dinner except in December

Adnams Southwold Bitter, Greene King IPA and Wells Bombardier

BUSTARD INN

Enjoy a pint of 'Cheeky Bustard' beer!

From the outside it resembles a schoolhouse, but The Bustard Inn is hardly bookish. Its flag-floored bar is simple and uncluttered while the spacious, beamed restaurant, with its cream-tiled floor and exposed brick, has a touch of the Mediterranean about it. There's a great value set lunch menu available Tues-Sat (also offered at dinner Tues-Thurs), while the more ambitious à la carte shows the chef's talents off to the full. Dishes might include fillet of Lincolnshire beef, pan-fried sea trout or homemade venison sausages, and satisfying desserts like sticky toffee pudding. Wine isn't overlooked, with reasonable mark-ups and a fine selection of clarets – or you can slay your thirst with a pint of specially brewed 'Cheeky Bustard' beer.

44 Main St,
SOUTH RAUCEBY, NG34 8QG
Tel.: (01529)488250
Website: www.thebustardinn.co.uk

4 mi west of Sleaford by A 17 and minor road south. Parking.

PRICES
Meals: £ 13 (weekday lunch) and
a la carte £ 22/46

MAP: 18

CLOSING TIMES
Closed 1 January, Sunday dinner
and Monday except bank holidays

Batemans Yella Belly Gold,
Cheeky Bustard and guest ales

BULL & SWAN

On a Sunday, try the roasting pot for four

This stone-built pub started life as a medieval hall house, and was converted into a travellers' inn during the late 1600s. It changed name several times, settling on the Bull & Swan in 1739, when it was taken over by Walter Robinson, a former coachman to the Earl of Exeter, and it remains the only public house south of the river. One side of the pub houses the characterful, lively beamed bar and the other, a more formal dining room. The menu offers something to suit all tastes, from sharing slates to classics such as Lincoln Red rib-eye steak or haslet with free range fried eggs and bacon; on Sundays try the roasting pot for four with all the trimmings. Stylish, individually designed bedrooms are named after members of a historic drinking club.

St Martins,
STAMFORD, PE9 2LJ
Tel.: (01780)766412
Website: www.thebullandswan.co.uk

0.5 mi south of the town centre on B 1081. Parking on London Rd.

PRICES
Meals: a la carte £ 22/44

7 rooms:
£ 75/140

MAP: 19

CLOSING TIMES
Open daily

Nene Valley BSA, Grainstore Rutland Bitter and Adnams Southwold Bitter

RED LION

Cookery classes held in the barn

This thatched honey-stone inn is located right in the heart of the attractive village of East Haddon, and boasts a terrace to the front, along with pretty gardens to the rear. It was originally a farmhouse but has been sympathetically extended, resulting in a pleasing mix of wood panelling, exposed bricks and beams, and wood and slate flooring. Although there are always plenty of local drinkers, it's the food that's the main focus here: menus offer upgraded pub classics, such as a mutton cottage pie or a venison and duck burger, and for those who like a hands-on approach, they offer cookery classes in the adjacent barn. Service is enthusiastic and attentive, and bedrooms are warm and welcoming – one even has a roll-top bath in the room.

Main St,
EAST HADDON, NN6 8BU
Tel.: (01604)770223
Website: www.redlioneasthaddon.co.uk

8.5 mi northwest of Northampton off A 428. Parking.

PRICES
Meals: a la carte £ 22/38

7 rooms:
£ 80/110

MAP: 20

CLOSING TIMES
Closed 25 December

Wells Bombardier, Young's Special and Young's Bitter

EXETER ARMS

Owned by a local sheep farmer

This 18C inn has been sympathetically yet stylishly restored by its owner, a local sheep farmer with a passion for good food. The interior has a unique charm and is adorned with copper pans, enamel signs, old hop sacks and hop bines, as well as an antique mangle and a clothes horse. The bar is kept exclusively for drinkers - for dining there's a snug candlelit restaurant and a stylish Lloyd Loom furnished conservatory which opens out onto the terrace. An array of menus offer everything from retro sandwiches and tasty pizzas to 'home comforts' and the chef's signature dishes (classics given a modern twist); in winter you'll find venison, partridge and pheasant from the local shoots. Stylish, well-appointed bedrooms have smart, modern bathrooms.

21 Stamford Rd,
EASTON-ON-THE-HILL, PE9 3NS
Tel.: (01780)756321
Website: www.theexeterarms.net

2.5 mi southwest of Stamford on A 43. Parking.

PRICES
Meals: a la carte £ 23/37

6 rooms:
£ 70/110

MAP: 21

CLOSING TIMES
Closed Sunday dinner

Black Sheep Ale and
Castle Rock Harvest Pale

FALCON INN

Appealing modern interpretations of classic dishes

In the pretty village of Fotheringhay – the birthplace of Richard III and the deathplace of Mary Queen of Scots – under the shadow of a large church, sits the attractive, stone-built Falcon Inn. It boasts a neat garden and a small paved terrace, a pleasant private dining annexe and a beamed bar with an unusual display of 15C bell clappers. You'll find the regulars playing darts and drinking real ales in the small tap bar, and the diners in the conservatory restaurant with its wicker chairs, formally laid tables and garden outlook. Good-sized menus include unusual combinations and some interesting modern takes on traditional dishes; you might find purple sprouting broccoli in your stilton soup or red pepper and dandelion dressing on your crab.

FOTHERINGHAY, PE8 5HZ
Tel.: (01832)226254
Website: www.thefalcon-inn.co.uk

3.5 mi north of Oundle by A 427 off A 605. In the centre of the village. Parking.

PRICES
Meals: £ 14 (weekdays) and
a la carte £ 21/34

MAP: 22

CLOSING TIMES
Open daily

Fuller's London Pride, Greene King IPA and Digfield Fool's Nook

WHEATSHEAF

Local Aylesbury duck is often a highlight

Sitting in the middle of the delightful village of Titchmarsh is this charming honey-stone inn, which dates from 1640. It's run by a husband and wife team who have successfully given it a modern makeover whilst also keeping the pub's inherent character. Decorated with striking wildlife photographs, the main bar has a lovely warm and welcoming feel, helped along by a wood-burning stove; of the two more formal dining rooms, the Garden Room is the most popular. The seasons are sufficiently reflected in the menu and all of the breads and ice creams are homemade. Local Aylesbury duck is often a highlight, as are dishes like braised feather blade of beef. Puddings have more of a continental feel and could feature panna cotta or crème brûlée.

1 North St,
TITCHMARSH, NN14 3DH
Tel.: (01832)732203
Website: www.thewheatsheafattitchmarsh.co.uk

2 mi northeast of Thrapston by A 605. In the centre of the village. Parking.

PRICES
Meals: £ 19 (weekday lunch) and
a la carte £ 18/37

MAP: 23

CLOSING TIMES
Closed Sunday dinner

Sharp's Doom Bar,
Fuller's London Pride and
Butcombe Bitter

THE MARTINS ARMS

Lots of character and wholesome, gutsy cooking

Blazing log fires cast a welcoming glow in this creeper-clad pub; full of feminine touches like fresh flowers, comfy cushions and gleaming copperware. Originally a farmhouse on the Martin family estate, it contains several articles salvaged from the original manor house, including the carved Jacobean fireplace and the old library shelves - now used to hold drinks in the bar. Said bar is the place for an impromptu lunch, while the period furnished dining rooms, adorned with hunting pictures, are more suited to a formal dinner - but do book. The menu has a meaty, masculine base with a mix of classical and more modern dishes; portions are hearty and there's plenty of game in season. Unsurprisingly, Colston Bassett Stilton is always available too!

School Ln,
COLSTON BASSETT, NG12 3FD
Tel.: (01949)81361
Website: www.themartinsarms.co.uk

East of Cotgrave off A 46. Parking.

PRICES
Meals: a la carte £ 22/52

MAP: 24

CLOSING TIMES
Closed dinner 25 December and 1 January

Greene King IPA, Marston's Pedigree and Timothy Taylor Landlord

REINDEER INN

Buy your drinks through the hatch in summer

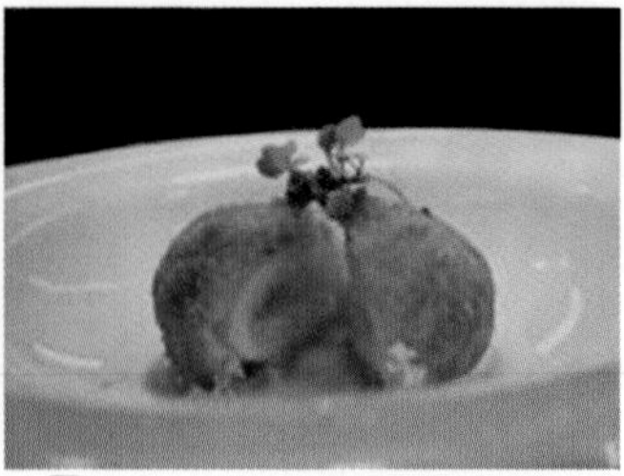

It would win no prizes in a beauty contest and its interior is infinitely more shabby than it is chic, but this hub-of-the-village pub serves such tasty, good value food that you simply won't care. In winter everyone appreciates the blazing log fire and the cosy, relaxed atmosphere, while in summer, the cricket pitch behind the pub becomes the focal point, with drinks delivered through a hatch when a game is in full swing. Reasonably priced menus offer pub classics like home-cured gammon steak or fish and chips alongside dishes such as smoked haddock scotch egg or fillets of red mullet, with steaks a perennial favourite. Themed evenings like fish and lobster night go down a storm - and they even provide a takeaway service.

Main St,
HOVERINGHAM, NG14 7JR
Tel.: (01159)663629
Website: www.thereindeerinn.com

5 mi south of Southwell by A 612. Parking.

PRICES
Meals: £ 11/29 and a la carte £ 29/38

MAP: 25

CLOSING TIMES
Closed Tuesday lunch, Sunday dinner and Monday
booking essential at lunch

Black Sheep Best Bitter, Castle Rock Harvest Pale and Woodeforde's Wherry

OLIVE BRANCH & BEECH HOUSE

Charming in every way possible

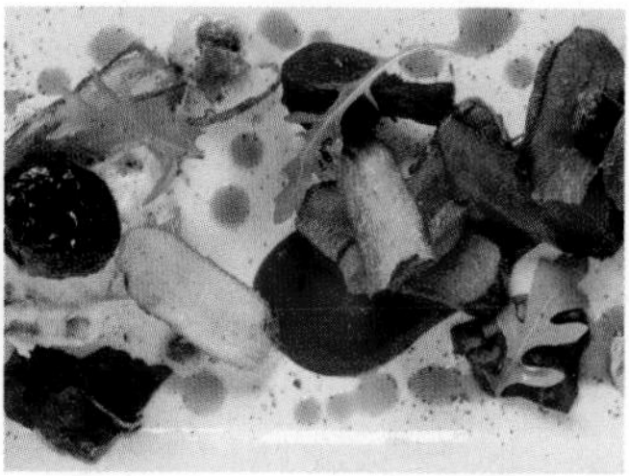

If it's the bucolic character of a proper country inn you're after, then the Olive Branch is a good bet, with its charmingly understated bar and dining rooms. It has the heart and soul of a real community pub and you'll find local farmers here enjoying a pint, as visitors locate their table thanks to the little blackboards that bear their name. There's a delightful garden, a friendly, informative serving team and a chef who gives regular cookery demonstrations in the old barn. Classic dishes might include ham hock terrine, roast chump of lamb or sausage and mash; the provenance of ingredients is listed on the menu, pasta dishes feature heavily and there's plenty of game in season. Stylish bedrooms include a host of extras.

Main St,
CLIPSHAM, LE15 7SH
Tel.: (01780)410355
Website: www.theolivebranchpub.com

9.5 mi northwest of Stamford by B 1081 off A 1. Parking.

PRICES
Meals: £ 17/30 and
a la carte £ 28/49

6 rooms:
£ 98/195

MAP: 26

CLOSING TIMES
Open daily
booking essential

Grainstone Olive Ale and
Timothy Taylor Landlord

WHEATSHEAF INN

The aroma of freshly baked bread fills the air

If you're on your way to Rutland Water, it's well worth diverting via this little village for a visit to the Wheatsheaf - but be careful not to overshoot the parking space as you pull up or you'll end up in the stream. The first thing you notice as you walk through the door is the aroma of freshly baked bread, which sits tantalisingly on the bar and often contains onion on Sundays. The owners may have experience in London but they've wisely kept this as a family-friendly country pub complete with a pool table and a dartboard. Where they do use their experience is in the kitchen: robust, modern British cooking comes with hints of the Med and cleverly uses cheaper cuts to keep the prices down. Sunday lunch is a steal and desserts are a must.

1 Stretton Rd,
GREETHAM, LE15 7NP
Tel.: (01572)812325
Website: www.wheatsheaf-greetham.co.uk

Just off the A1 on the B 668 to Cottesmore and Oakham. Parking.

PRICES
Meals: a la carte £ 20/33

MAP: 27

CLOSING TIMES
Closed first 2 weeks January, Monday except bank holidays and Sunday dinner

Brewster's Hop a doodle doo, Oldershaw Old Boy and Oakham Inferno

FINCH'S ARMS

Delightful terrace with views over Rutland Water

Cross the threshold of this pretty stone inn and you're transported to a different world, where'll you find a quaint bar, a small anteroom with huge flowers stencilled on the walls, two very stylish dining rooms with vast windows overlooking Rutland Water, and a delightful terrace which shares the view. Assured, seasonal dishes use local lamb, beef and game, and range from appealing sharing boards on the 'Bar and Terrace' menu through to partridge breast with Lincolnshire Poacher salad or loin of lamb with buttered cabbage on the good value set and à la carte menus. Desserts are satisfyingly old school, featuring the likes of rice pudding with homemade plum jam, and afternoon tea is also an option. Ultra-modern bedrooms complete the picture.

Oakham Rd,
HAMBLETON, LE15 8TL
Tel.: (01572)756575
Website: www.finchsarms.co.uk

3 mi east of Oakham by A 606. Parking.

PRICES
Meals: £ 14/20 and
a la carte £ 20/41

10 rooms:
£ 80/130

MAP: 28

CLOSING TIMES
Open daily

Grainstore Rutland Bitter and
Castle Rock Harvest Pale

MARQUESS OF EXETER

They keep chickens and pigs & grow their own veg

This attractive 16C thatched pub is located in a pleasant village in the heart of the Rutland countryside. Locals gather in the cosy, flag-floored bar, beside inglenook fireplaces and under characterful exposed beams; while further on through, there's a relaxed, rustic dining room with chunky scrubbed tables, old leather chairs and a range. The daily menu offers tasty, classical combinations that let good quality ingredients stand out; they even grow their own vegetables and keep chickens and pigs at the bottom of the garden. There's an appealing 'Lunch for Less' menu and specials written up on gilt mirrors, while the sharing plates - maybe rib of beef or shoulder of lamb - are firm favourites too. Comfy bedrooms are found across the car park.

52 Main St,
LYDDINGTON, LE15 9LT
Tel.: (01572)822477
Website: www.marquessexeter.co.uk

Just south of Uppingham, signposted off A 6003; in the middle of the village. Parking.

PRICES
Meals: £ 16 (weekday lunch) and a la carte £ 24/37

17 rooms:
£ 80/135

MAP: 29

CLOSING TIMES
Closed 25 December

Marston's Pedigree and Brakspear Bitter

OLD WHITE HART

Sit in the garden and watch the petanque team

This pub offers all you'd expect from a traditional 17C coaching inn - and a lot more besides. It's got the chocolate box village setting, the open fires, the comfy corners and the seasonally changing menu of hearty, classic dishes; but it also has a cosy, relaxing ambience, charming service led by the lovely owner, a 10-piste petanque pitch (plus a petanque team), and stylish, individually decorated bedrooms with excellent bathrooms and homely extras. It will come as no surprise to hear they're usually busy, but there's plenty of space for everyone, whether that be in one of the two beamed bars, in the split-level restaurant, out at a picnic table in the neat garden or on the smart, canopy-covered front terrace.

51 Main St,
LYDDINGTON, LE15 9LR
Tel.: (01572)821703
Website: www.oldwhitehart.co.uk

Just south of Uppingham signposted off A 6003; opposite the village green. Parking.

PRICES
Meals: a la carte £ 22/31

10 rooms:
£ 65/100

MAP: 30

CLOSING TIMES
Closed 25 December and Sunday dinner in winter

Greene King IPA, Nene Valley NVB, Gun Dog Ales Jack's Spaniels and Great Oakley Wot's Occurring

JACKSON STOPS INN

Price-conscious cooking with interesting touches

This lovely stone and thatch pub started life as The White Horse but was later jokingly renamed by the locals when the 'Jackson-Stops' estate agent sign stood outside for so long. Inside it's divided into several areas, each with its own unique feel, including a small open-fired bar, a cosy barn and a two-roomed restaurant. Dishes are largely rooted in tradition but a few display some interesting touches, so you might find a starter like chicken liver pâté with redcurrant and Earl Grey consommé, followed by a main course of beef and venison casserole with stilton and herb dumplings, or confit duck leg with parsnip mash and pancetta cassoulet. Cooking is pleasingly price-conscious and features locally reared meats and produce smoked nearby.

Rookery La,
STRETTON, LE15 7RA
Tel.: (01780)410237
Website: www.thejacksonstops.com

8 mi northwest of Stamford by B 1081 off A 1. Parking.

PRICES
Meals: £ 15 (lunch) and a la carte £ 24/41

MAP: 31

CLOSING TIMES
Closed Monday except bank holidays and Sunday dinner

Grainstore Ales

EAST OF ENGLAND

England

© D. Potter / Design Pics / Photononstop

Wide lowland landscapes and huge skies, timber-framed houses, a frowning North Sea canvas: these are the abiding images of England's east. This region has its roots embedded in the earth and its taste buds whetted by local seafood. Some of the most renowned ales are brewed in Norfolk and Suffolk. East Anglia sees crumbling cliffs, superb mudflats and saltmarshes or enchanting medieval wool towns such as Lavenham. Areas of Outstanding Natural Beauty abound, in the Chilterns of Bedfordshire and Hertfordshire, and in Dedham Vale, life-long inspiration of Constable. Religious buildings are everywhere, from Ely Cathedral, "the Ship of the Fens", to the fine structure of Long Melford church. The ghosts of great men haunt Cambridge: Newton, Darwin, Pepys and Byron studied here, doubtless deep in thought as they tramped the wide-open spaces of Midsummer Common or Parker's Piece.

Look out for Cromer crab, samphire, grilled herring, Suffolk pork casserole and the hearty Bedfordshire Clanger.

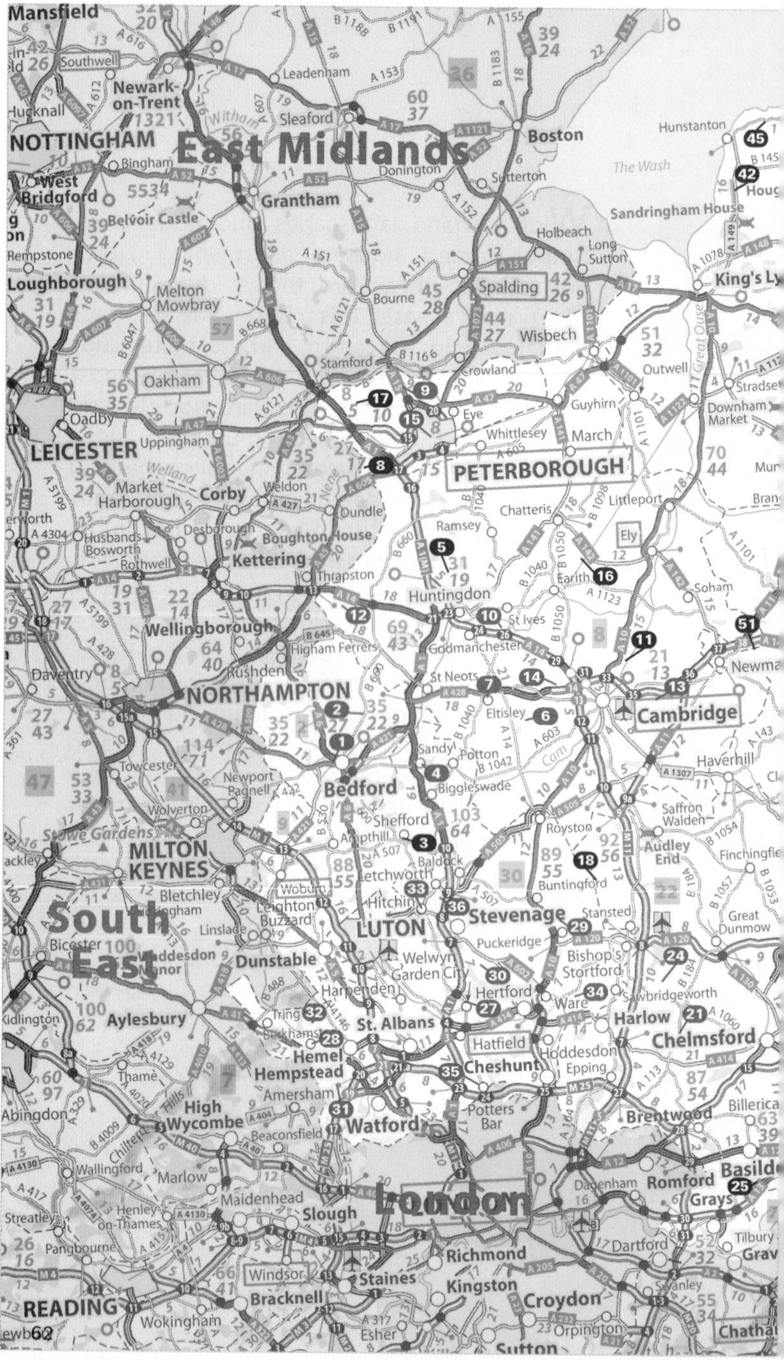
East Midlands
South East
Mansfield
Southwell
Newark-on-Trent
Hucknall
NOTTINGHAM
West Bridgford
Bingham
Belvoir Castle
Rempstone
Loughborough
Melton Mowbray
Leadenham
Sleaford
Witham
Grantham
Boston
Donington
Sutterton
The Wash
Hunstanton
Sandringham House
Holbeach
Long Sutton
Spalding
Bourne
King's Lynn
Wisbech
Outwell
Stamford
Crowland
Oakham
Oadby
LEICESTER
Uppingham
Eye
Guyhirn
Downham Market
Stradsett
Whittlesey
March
PETERBOROUGH
Welland
Market Harborough
Corby
Weldon
Oundle
Nene
Chatteris
Littleport
Ely
Ramsey
Husbands Bosworth
Desborough
Boughton House
Rothwell
Kettering
Thrapston
Huntingdon
Earith
Soham
St Ives
Godmanchester
Wellingborough
Higham Ferrers
Rushden
Daventry
NORTHAMPTON
St Neots
Eltisley
Cambridge
Newmarket
Great Ouse
Cam
Towcester
Newport Pagnell
Bedford
Sandy
Potton
Biggleswade
Haverhill
Saffron Walden
Wolverton
Stowe Gardens
MILTON KEYNES
Shefford
Ampthill
Royston
Audley End
Finchingfield
Letchworth
Baldock
Buntingford
Bletchley
Woburn
Leighton Buzzard
Linslade
Hitchin
Stevenage
Stansted
Great Dunmow
Bicester
Waddesdon Manor
LUTON
Dunstable
Welwyn Garden City
Puckeridge
Bishop's Stortford
Harpenden
Hertford
Ware
Sawbridgeworth
Kidlington
Aylesbury
Tring
St. Albans
Berkhamsted
Harlow
Chelmsford
Hemel Hempstead
Hatfield
Hoddesdon
Epping
Thame
Cheshunt
Abingdon
Chiltern Hills
High Wycombe
Amersham
Watford
Potters Bar
Brentwood
Billericay
Beaconsfield
Basildon
Wallingford
Marlow
London
Dagenham
Romford
Grays
Maidenhead
Streatley
Henley-on-Thames
Slough
Tilbury
Pangbourne
Dartford
Richmond
Windsor
Staines
Kingston
Swanley
READING
Bracknell
Croydon
Wokingham
Esher
Orpington
Sutton
Chatham

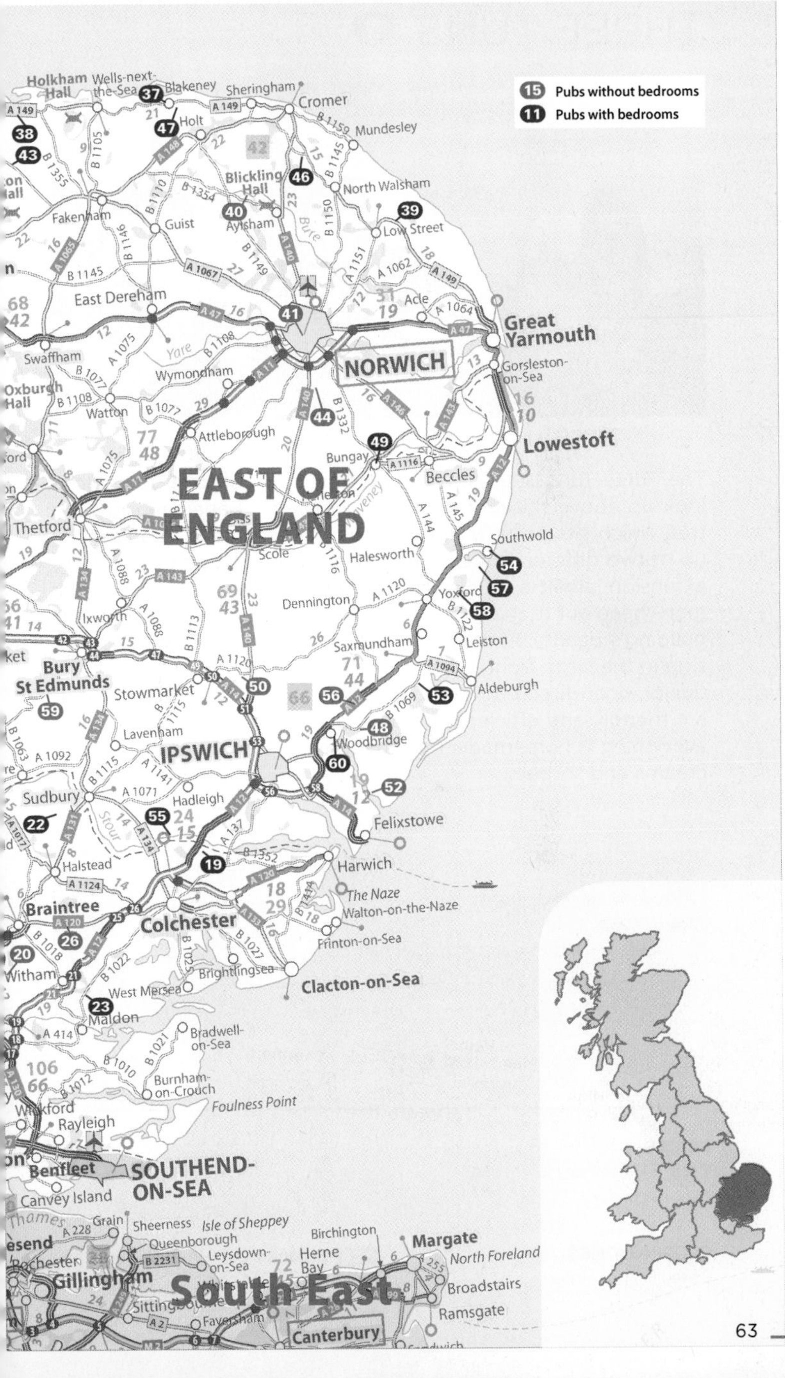

15 Pubs without bedrooms
11 Pubs with bedrooms
EAST OF ENGLAND
NORWICH
IPSWICH
SOUTHEND-ON-SEA
South East
Holkham Hall
Wells-next-the-Sea
Blakeney
Sheringham
Cromer
Mundesley
Holt
Blickling Hall
North Walsham
Fakenham
Guist
Aylsham
Low Street
East Dereham
Acle
Great Yarmouth
Gorsleston-on-Sea
Swaffham
Wymondham
Oxburgh Hall
Watton
Attleborough
Lowestoft
Bungay
Beccles
Thetford
Scole
Halesworth
Southwold
Dennington
Yoxford
Leiston
Saxmundham
Aldeburgh
Ixworth
Bury St Edmunds
Stowmarket
Lavenham
Woodbridge
Sudbury
Hadleigh
Felixstowe
Harwich
Halstead
The Naze
Walton-on-the-Naze
Braintree
Colchester
Frinton-on-Sea
Witham
Brightlingsea
Clacton-on-Sea
West Mersea
Maldon
Bradwell-on-Sea
Burnham-on-Crouch
Foulness Point
Wickford
Rayleigh
Benfleet
Canvey Island
Thames
Grain
Sheerness
Isle of Sheppey
Queenborough
Leysdown-on-Sea
Rochester
Gillingham
Sittingbourne
Faversham
Birchington
Herne Bay
Margate
North Foreland
Broadstairs
Ramsgate
Canterbury

THREE TUNS N

An interesting mix of the old and the new

The Three Tuns is set in a leafy residential suburb; if you're lost, look up above the rooftops for the majestic Canadian redwood tree which sits proudly in the garden. The place is clearly made up of two different parts: a 16C thatched building and a late 19C extension; albeit a little back-to-front with the older part to the rear - head out to the lovely terrace to fully appreciate the original building's beauty. In case you were in any doubt, there's a 'New' sign in the large front bar and an 'Old' sign, leading through to a quaint, open-fired bar with low seating and exposed beams. Staff are friendly and efficient and the classically trained chef ensures everything is homemade, from the breads and brioche to the ice creams and sorbets.

57 Main Rd,
BIDDENHAM, MK40 4BD
Tel.: (01234)354847
Website: www.thethreetunsbiddenham.co.uk

2 mi northwest of Bedford by A 4280. Parking.

PRICES
Meals: £ 17 (weekday lunch) and
a la carte £ 24/41

MAP: 1

CLOSING TIMES
Closed Sunday dinner

Greene King IPA and Thwaites Magic Sponge

PLOUGH AT BOLNHURST

Go for dishes with a Mediterranean slant

This charming pub has 15C origins and is a hit with locals and visitors alike, who frequent the place come rain or shine. The garden, with its trickling stream, is the place to be in summer, while on colder days there's the choice of the bar or restaurant; both with cosy low beams and fires - the latter a little smarter, with its modern wallpaper and upholstered chairs. The same seasonal menu is served throughout, with many dishes displaying strong Mediterranean influences; you might find roast chorizo or sweet Spanish pickles, followed by 28-day aged Aberdeenshire steaks - including côte de boeuf for two - and other dishes containing Sicilian olive oil or black olive purée. There's also a great selection of cheeses and wines by the glass.

Kimbolton Rd,
BOLNHURST, MK44 2EX
Tel.: (01234)376274
Website: www.bolnhurst.com

On B 660, 7 mi north of Bedford. Parking.

PRICES

Meals: £ 13 (weekday lunch)/20
and a la carte £ 30/48

MAP: 2

CLOSING TIMES

Closed 2 weeks January, Sunday dinner and Monday

Adnams Southwold Bitter, Hopping Mad Brainstorm and Nethergates Growler

BLACK HORSE

Surprisingly stylish and modern inside

Don't be deceived by the picture perfect exterior; if you're looking for a quaint country inn, you're in the wrong place. It may appear traditional from the outside, but inside it's as stylish and modern as you can get. Contemporary light fittings are set amongst marble-style flooring and a granite-topped counter, and there's a walled courtyard complete with mirrors and fairy lights. The friendly staff serve an equally eclectic mix of generously portioned dishes. Lunch could include anything from 'pie of the day' to a smoked salmon scotch egg, while dinner might offer potted beef cheeks followed by suprême of arctic char or four bone rack of lamb on summer vegetable tagine. Accessed via a meandering garden path, the bedrooms are comfy and cosy.

Ireland,
SHEFFORD, SG17 5QL
Tel.: (01462)811398
Website: www.blackhorseireland.com

1.5 mi northwest of Shefford by B 658 and Ireland rd. Parking.

PRICES
Meals: £ 15 (weekday lunch) and a la carte £ 24/41

2 rooms: £ 75

MAP: 3

CLOSING TIMES
Closed 25-26 December and 1 January

Fuller's London Pride, Adnams Southwold Bitter and Sharp's Doom Bar

JOHN O'GAUNT INN (N)

Beautiful gardens overlooking the wheat fields

This cosy, honest village inn is located on the edge of a pretty village and its delightful gardens overlook the wheat fields behind. It started life as three 18C cottages; was first licenced in 1835; and is named after the 1st Duke of Lancaster, who held the manor of Sutton in the 14C. The current owners have plenty of experience when it comes to running pubs and it now has a welcoming open-fired bar - complete with a skittle game owned by the villagers themselves - and a smart dining room with a plush feel. Everything on the menu is homemade, from the fresh crisps with zingy pesto dip to the chicken liver parfait with onion marmalade or the cheddar tart with roasted local asparagus - and they also serve some tasty 'Crumps Butchers' steaks.

30 High St,
SUTTON, SG19 2NE
Tel.: (01767)260377
Website: www.johnogauntsutton.co.uk

5 mi northeast of Biggleswade by B 1040. Parking.

PRICES
Meals: a la carte £ 26/38

MAP: 4

CLOSING TIMES
Closed Monday except bank holidays and Sunday dinner

Woodforde's Wherry, Adnams Broadside and Fat Sprat

ABBOT'S ELM

Passionately compiled wine list

It's hard to believe this attractive thatched inn is actually a reconstruction of its 17C predecessor; part destroyed by fire in 2010, now only the elegant brick fireplace remains from its former days. Inside it's surprisingly modern, with an open-plan layout and a vaulted, oak-beamed roof. The bar offers light bites, hot plates such as smoked haddock with bubble and squeak, and a 'menu du jour'; while later in the week there's also an à la carte and a tasting menu served in the formal dining room, where you'll find appealing dishes such as honey-roast duck breast. Cooking is hearty and flavoursome and the passionately compiled wine list offers most choices by the glass or carafe. Cosy bedrooms come with free wi-fi and fluffy bathrobes.

Moat Ln,
ABBOTS RIPTON, PE28 2PA
Tel.: (01487)773773
Website: www.theabbotselm.co.uk

6 mi north of Huntingdon by B 1514, A 141 and B 1090. Parking.

PRICES
Meals: £ 14 (weekday lunch) and a la carte £ 19/39

3 rooms: £ 60/85

MAP: 5

CLOSING TIMES
Closed Sunday dinner

Oakham Ales JHB, Sharp's Doom Bar and Lord Conrad's Slap N' Tickle

WILLOW TREE

A quirky look and adventurous cooking

It may be named after a majestic British tree - the likes of which you'll find blowing elegantly in the wind as you enter the car park - but this pub is far from your usual affair. The life-sized cow model in the garden is the first clue as to the quirky nature of the place, followed inside by the feeling of being in a 'House and Home' magazine, courtesy of chandeliers, gilt mirrors and Louis XV style furniture dotted about the place. Menus offer everything from old pub classics to more ambitious dishes such as scotch duck egg, rabbit terrine or venison haunch Rossini, and they offer a 'Summer Deckchair' menu and afternoon tea from May-September. These are accompanied by an appealing wine list, with most selections available by the glass.

29 High St,
BOURN, CB23 2SQ
Tel.: (01954)719775
Website: www.thewillowtreebourn.com

3 mi south of Cambourne by A 1198 off B 1046, in the centre of the village. Parking.

PRICES
Meals: a la carte £ 13/46

MAP: 6

CLOSING TIMES
Open daily

Milton Brewery Pegasus and Lord Conrad's Ales

ELTISLEY

Chic, stylish pub serving unfussy dishes

You might imagine that this chic, stylish gastropub is a strictly dining affair, but the contemporary bar is equally as welcoming to drinkers as diners; the latter can sit and watch their meal being prepared from the windows in the snug. For a more formal occasion head through to the restaurant, where grey walls meet wood and tile flooring, and bold designs are offset by swanky chandeliers. Large parties should ask for the 'Wurlitzer', a stylish high-backed semi-circular banquette, while for summer dining the terrace is ideal. Cooking is simple, unfussy and relies on quality local ingredients: meat is from nearby farms and vegetables, from their allotment. Everything from the bread and pasta to the desserts and ice cream is homemade.

2 The Green,
ELTISLEY, PE19 6TG
Tel.: (01480)880308
Website: www.theeltisley.co.uk

Between St Neots and Cambridge, signposted off A 428. Parking.

PRICES
Meals: a la carte £ 22/36

MAP: 7

CLOSING TIMES
Closed Monday in winter
and Sunday dinner

Wells Eagle IPA and guest ales

CROWN INN

A good old English inn set in a delightful parish

With its 17C honey-stone walls, charming thatched roof and lovely location in a delightful country parish, the Crown Inn really is a good old English pub. Sup a cask ale or two beside the characterful inglenook fireplace in the bar, then head through to the cosy dining room, the large decagonal conservatory or out onto the spacious decked terrace. The same seasonally changing menu is served throughout, featuring old British favourites such as steak and ale pie, homemade cider and apple sausages or lamb with bubble and squeak. Bedrooms are smart, modern and individually designed - some have four-posters, sleigh beds or roll-top baths - and if you fancy treating yourself in the morning, you can order a hamper and enjoy breakfast in your PJs.

8 Duck St,
ELTON, PE8 6RQ
Tel.: (01832)280232
Website: www.thecrowninn.org

Midway between Oundle and Peterborough signposted off A 605.
Parking.

PRICES
Meals: £ 15 (weekdays) and
a la carte £ 25/38

8 rooms:
£ 65/150

MAP: 8

CLOSING TIMES
Open daily

Tydd Steam Golden Crown Ale

BLUE BELL

Don't leave before trying their tasty desserts

The pretty village of Glinton is home to the Blue Bell and also to its experienced owners who, after some time away, have returned to their roots. A pretty flower display greets you at the front and there's a pleasant terrace round the back; while inside there are plenty of nooks and crannies in which to hide yourself away. In true pub style, there's plenty of space beneath the old 18C beams for the local drinkers, and the atmosphere is suitably warm and welcoming. Lunch offers pub favourites, generously filled sandwiches and tempting salads in a choice of sizes, while dinner steps things up a gear with some more modern dishes like maple-glazed duck breast with confit leg croquette... and be sure to save room for one of their tasty desserts.

10 High St,
GLINTON, PE6 7LS
Tel.: (01733)252285
Website: www.thebluebellglinton.co.uk

5 mi north of Peterborough off A 15 in centre of village. Parking.

PRICES
Meals: a la carte £ 22/40

MAP: 9

CLOSING TIMES
Closed Sunday dinner

Greene King IPA and Old Speckled Hen

THE COCK

Extensive list of daily fish specials

As you approach this 17C country pub you'll come across two doors: one marked 'Pub', leading to a split-level bar, and the other marked 'Restaurant', leading to a spacious dining room. Run by an experienced team, it has a homely feel, with warm fabrics, comfy seating and attractively papered walls. In winter, the best spot is beside the fire, while in summer, it's by the French windows. Cooking rests firmly on the tried-and-tested side of things, with classic pub staples such as lamb shank and belly pork, good value set lunches and an extensive list of daily changing fish specials. A tempting sausage board offers an appealing mix of homemade sausages from their 75+ recipes, along with different sauces and several varieties of mashed potato.

47 High St,
HEMINGFORD GREY, PE28 9BJ
Tel.: (01480)463609
Website: www.cambscuisine.com

The village is 5 mi east of Huntingdon signposted off A 14. Parking.

PRICES
Meals: £ 13 (weekday lunch) and
a la carte £ 22/37

MAP: 10

CLOSING TIMES
Open daily
booking essential

Nethergate IPA, Nene Valley Bitter and Tydd Steam Barn Ale

CROWN AND PUNCHBOWL

Sophisticated food and friendly service

The clue that this is more of a dining than a drinking establishment lies in the fact that there's no real bar; however, the Crown and Punchbowl still delivers on pubby character thanks to its beams, open fires and chunky wood tables. When it comes to dining, there's plenty of choice, with a seasonally changing à la carte, daily specials and a popular 'sausage board'. The kitchen does traditional - such as a delicious blade of beef or sticky toffee pudding - as well as modern, with dishes like fish terrine and horseradish sorbet or deconstructed millionaire's shortbread. The seared scallops are a permanent feature and there's a sophisticated element to all of the cooking. Relax on the pleasant terrace then head for one of the simple bedrooms.

High St,
HORNINGSEA, CB25 9JG
Tel.: (01223)860643
Website: www.thecrownandpunchbowl.com

Just off the A 14, northeast of Cambridge. Parking.

PRICES
Meals: a la carte £ 26/43

5 rooms:
£ 80

MAP: 11

CLOSING TIMES
Closed 26 December-1 January, dinner Sunday and bank holiday Monday

Thwaites Original

PHEASANT

A lovely country feel and a great value set menu

Recently returned to its former owners, this picture postcard pub is quite simply delightful. Hidden away in a sleepy hamlet, it has a lovely countryside feel, with exposed beams and hunting scenes galore; John Bull wallpaper features and, in the dining room, bread is carved under the watchful eye of a stuffed albino pheasant. The wide-ranging seasonal menu has something for everyone, from nibbles like salted almonds or crispy squid through to tasty dishes like venison terrine or sea trout with shrimp butter. There's a classic section for the more traditional diner and an incredible value set menu too. An excellent selection of wines comes courtesy of the owner, who is a Master of Wine, and staff are warm, gracious and attentive.

Village Loop Rd,
KEYSTON, PE28 0RE
Tel.: (01832)710241
Website: www.thepheasant-keyston.co.uk

Signposted off junction 15 of A 14. Parking.

PRICES
Meals: £ 16 (lunch and early dinner)
and a la carte £ 24/39

MAP: 12

CLOSING TIMES
Closed 2-15 January, Sunday dinner
and Monday booking essential

Nene Valley NVB, Adnams Southwold Bitter and Digfield Barnwell Bitter

HOLE IN THE WALL

Run with passion by a young team

Local workers used to leave their empty tankards in a hole in this charming 16C pub's wall; these would then be filled, ready for them to pick up on their way home. The hole may have long since been closed up, but you can still sup a pint in the pub's cosy beamed bar. Better still, enjoy a meal prepared with zeal by the young chefs; one of whom was a past MasterChef finalist. The regularly changing seasonal menu offers starters like sardines on toast or lamb koftas, with main courses such as Blythburgh pork chop or Barbury duck breast and heartwarming, classical desserts like rice pudding or marmalade and almond cake. Lunch is a steal, homemade bread is baked twice a day and they are partial to a bit of meat curing and smoking too.

2 High St,
LITTLE WILBRAHAM, CB21 5JY
Tel.: (01223)812282
Website: www.holeinthewallcambridge.com

Just off the A 14 east of Cambridge, the Wilbrahams are signposted off A 1303. Parking.

PRICES
Meals: £ 16 (lunch) and a la carte £ 24/44

MAP: 13

CLOSING TIMES
Closed 2 weeks January, Sunday dinner, Monday and Tuesday lunch
booking advisable

Milton Justinian and Lacons Encore

THREE HORSESHOES

Adventurous cooking and a lively bar

Set in a pretty village, famous for its stunning hall, this appealing pub with its whitewashed walls and attractive thatched roof fits right in. To the front, scrubbed wooden tables are set beside a small bar and a welcoming fireplace; to the rear, a more formal conservatory with Lloyd Loom chairs looks out over the garden. The interesting bar menu offers modern dishes such as truffled mac and cheese, slow-cooked egg with onion soubise or hanger steak with kimchi purée; the daily changing à la carte follows suit, featuring the likes of smoked eel with green tea and wasabi cotta or haunch of venison with cime di rapa and morcilla crumb. The bar is a lively place, so if you're looking for a romantic table for two, make for the conservatory.

High St,
MADINGLEY, CB23 8AB
Tel.: (01954)210221
Website: www.threehorseshoesmadingley.com

West of Cambridge signposted off A 1303. Parking.

PRICES
Meals: a la carte £ 25/46

MAP: 14

CLOSING TIMES
Open daily
booking advisable

Adnams Southwold Bitter and guest ales

BEEHIVE

A great spot for weary shoppers

Just off the city centre ring road might not be your first choice of location for a pub but it's close at hand for shoppers and has stood here long enough to have built up a steady group of regulars. Owners James and Sharon have lived in the area all their lives and, remembering the pub in its heyday, jumped at the chance to get the place up and running again when it was closed and put on the market. It now has a smart modern interior with stripped floorboards, a zinc-topped bar and a mix of high stools, armchairs and banquettes. When it comes to the food, it's well-presented, flavoursome and satisfying; the house pâté with chutney is a must, followed by a classic like slow-cooked shoulder of lamb or a pub favourite such as toad in the hole.

62 Albert Pl,
PETERBOROUGH, PE1 1DD
Tel.: (01733)310600
Website: www.beehivepub.co.uk

In the centre of the city just off Bourges Boulevard. Pay and display parking across the road.

PRICES
Meals: a la carte £ 21/40

MAP: 15

CLOSING TIMES
Closed 1 January and Sunday dinner

Star Brewing Co Meteor, Lacons Encore and Castor Ales Nector

ANCHOR INN

Tempting dishes and river views

It may seem like a strange name for a pub that's nowhere near the coast - but it does have some watery connections. Built in 1650, this building was originally used to house the workers who created the Hundred Foot Wash in order to alleviate flooding in the fens. If you fancy a river view, head for the wood-panelled rooms to the front of the bar, where you'll discover a pleasant outlook and a tempting menu, which might include smoked eel, pork loin in Parma ham, tea-infused duck or the house speciality of grilled dates wrapped in bacon. There are always some fish specials chalked on the board, while others occasionally use produce from the nearby Denham Estate. Neat, pine-furnished bedrooms include two suites; one boasts river views.

SUTTON GAULT, CB6 2BD
Tel.: (01353)778537
Website: www.anchor-inn-restaurant.co.uk

Off B 1381; from Sutton village follow signs to Sutton Gault; pub is beside the New Bedford River. Parking.

PRICES
Meals: £ 14 (weekday lunch) and a la carte £ 23/42

4 rooms:
£ 60/155

MAP: 16

CLOSING TIMES
Open daily

Nethergate Growler, Buntingford Twitchell and Black Bar Bitter

WHITE HART

Memorabilia-filled interior and a sun-trap terrace

This delightful 17C inn stands at the centre of the charming village of Ufford. Outside, there's a super sun-trap of a terrace and garden, while inside, there's a cosy bar housing an interesting collection of railway signs, farm implements and chamber pots - as well as a pleasant beamed restaurant with exposed stone walls and a lovely little conservatory. The menu offers a broad range of dishes, from simple sandwiches to starters of beetroot cured salmon or seared scallops with wild mushroom cream, followed by Thai-style fish casserole or creamy rabbit pie; and much of the meat comes from their farm. Sweet, country bedrooms each have their own florally inspired style; one boasts a four-poster and the two twin rooms outside allow dogs to stay.

Main St,
UFFORD, PE9 3BH
Tel.: (01780)740250
Website: www.whitehartufford.co.uk

Ufford is signposted off B 660 northwest of Peterborough. Parking.

PRICES
Meals: a la carte £ 23/38

6 rooms:
£ 75/120

MAP: 17

CLOSING TIMES
Open daily

Adnams Southwold Bitter, St Austell Tribute, Castle Rock Harvest Pale

CRICKETERS

Go for the wood-fired specialities

This deceptively spacious pub sits opposite the cricket pitch in a sleepy village and is popular with locals and visitors alike - with plenty of cosy, welcoming bedrooms for the latter. The blackboard menu above the fire in the bar informs you of the dishes of the day; head to the dining room with its exposed beams, horse harnesses and polished brass for more of a 'restauranty' feel. The menu offers Italian dishes with the occasional global influence: expect tasty homemade pasta and wood-fired specialities alongside Thai-style mussels or chicken Kiev stuffed with wild mushroom and truffle butter. Bread is baked daily and produce is sourced as locally as possible; the owners' son, Jamie Oliver, provides fruit, veg and herbs from his organic garden.

CLAVERING, CB11 4QT
Tel.: (01799)550442
Website: www.thecricketers.co.uk

On the main road through the village close to the cricket pitch.
Parking.

PRICES
Meals: a la carte £ 21/37

20 rooms:
£ 68/120

MAP: 18

CLOSING TIMES
Closed 25-26 December
booking essential

Adnams Ales, Sharp's Doom Bar and Nethergate Jamie's Tipple

SUN INN

Who can resist a just-made sausage roll?

Despite its bright, modern exterior, this is a pub that's rooted in history. It's located in the heart of a picturesque village, opposite a delightful church, and dates back to the 15C. The interior is just the right side of shabby, with a large panelled area and a beautiful wooden bar stocked with real ales and topped with homemade sausage rolls. There's also a relaxed, art-filled dining room. Cooking has an Italian slant: the weekly set menu offers two simple choices, along with wines; while the main menu features hearty, rustic dishes in two sizes – including a large selection of antipasti, followed by the likes of bollito misto, braised cuttlefish with squid ink or lemon sole with radicchio. Bedrooms are snug; two have a Scandic feel.

High St,
DEDHAM, CO7 6DF
Tel.: (01206)323351
Website: www.thesuninndedham.com

In the centre of the village. Parking.

PRICES
Meals: £ 19 (weekdays) and
a la carte £ 24/29

7 rooms:
£ 85/160

MAP: 19

CLOSING TIMES
Closed 25-26 December

Adnams Broadside and Crouch Vale Brewers Gold

SQUARE & COMPASSES

Genuine hospitality from hands-on owners

This pub is hidden deep in the Essex countryside, down a labyrinth of lanes, so you might just need that compass after all. A charming little pub with low beams, wood burning stoves and cosy character aplenty, this is a place that offers genuine hospitality from its hands-on owners and friendly team. It has a small locals bar with gravity fed casks and a dining room displaying numerous certificates and menus from the owners' pasts on its exposed brick walls. Unfussy menus offer the usual pub classics like home-cooked gammon or Stokers Ale pie, while the daily changing blackboards might list terrines of locally shot game or pan-fried fish caught nearby. Unashamedly traditional puddings feature the likes of spotted dick or rhubarb crumble.

FULLER STREET, CM3 2BB
Tel.: (01245)361477
Website: www.thesquareandcompasses.co.uk

Between Braintree and Chelmsford off the A 131. Parking.

PRICES
Meals: a la carte £ 20/36

MAP: 20

CLOSING TIMES
Closed Sunday dinner
booking essential

Wibblers Dengie IPA, Maldon Farmers IPA and Colchester No 1

QUEENS HEAD

Sit outside, looking down to the river

Don't make the mistake of trying to go in the front door - you have to enter to the side or rear of this characterful 16C pub. It's located in the heart of the village and has a pretty garden which leads down to the banks of the river. The interior is just as inviting though, with its original beams, inglenook fireplaces and galleried upper level. The extensive menu changes every two months and is supplemented by blackboard specials. Dishes take on more of a restaurant than a pub style, offering the likes of English asparagus with a crispy quail's egg, prosciutto and hollandaise, followed by soy-glazed salmon with spiced crab linguine and shellfish consommé. They hold regular Garrett sessions (folk, roots and acoustic dinner concerts).

Queen St,
FYFIELD, CM5 0RY
Tel.: (01277)899231
Website: www.thequeensheadfyfield.co.uk

3 mi northeast of Chipping Ongar on B 184 in centre of village. Parking.

PRICES
Meals: £ 16 (lunch) and a la carte £ 22/45

MAP: 21

CLOSING TIMES
Closed 1-7 January, Sunday dinner and Monday

Adnams Ales and Crouch Vale Ales

PHEASANT

They grow their own veg and keep chickens and bees

Set on the edge of a pretty little village, this 16C pub is every bit a true country inn. Run by a former landscape gardener and his wife, it centres around sustainability, with a one acre garden over the road where they grow vegetables and keep chickens and bees. The hub of the pub is a very inviting low-beamed bar and the locals come in their droves for biweekly 'Thirsty Thursday'. The cooking keeps things simple, offering heartwarming dishes in traditional combinations; maybe a prawn cocktail, followed by belly pork or local venison, finished off with an apple crumble. To keep the regulars happy, they also serve takeaway fish & chips. Modern bedrooms are across the car park and feature good quality bedding and views over rolling fields.

GESTINGTHORPE, CO9 3AU
Tel.: (01787)465010
Website: www.thepheasant.net

Between Sudbury and Castle Hedingham off B1058. Parking.

PRICES
Meals: a la carte £ 23/36

5 rooms:
£ 85/165

MAP: 22

CLOSING TIMES
Closed first 2 weeks January

Adnams Southwold Bitter, Woodeforde's Wherry and regular guest ales

THE BULL

Contemporary bedrooms and a beautiful garden

This attractive roadside pub dates back to the 1500s and boasts a beautifully landscaped rear garden and terrace, as well as distant views of West Mersea from the picnic tables in front. There are lots of different rooms inside, including a beamed bar and a snug frequented by the locals; it's been modernised but it still retains the pubby character you'd expect of a building its age. Seasonal dishes look to Europe for their inspiration, so you might find crayfish Niçoise salad or linguine; there are also some great British classics like Barnsley pork chop or beer-battered haddock with triple-cooked chips, and a good value lunch menu too. Individually decorated, contemporary bedrooms are located in a cottage and named after local villages.

2 Maldon Rd,
GREAT TOTHAM, CM9 8NH
Tel.: (01621)893385
Website: www.thebullatgreattotham.co.uk

Between Tiptree and Maldon on B 1022. Parking.

PRICES
Meals: £ 15 (weekday lunch) and a la carte £ 19/44

4 rooms:
£ 75/85

MAP: 23

CLOSING TIMES
Open daily

Adnams Southwold Bitter & Greene King IPA

DUKE'S HEAD

Hosts many of the village's community events

Run by an enthusiastic couple who help support nearby sports clubs and host plenty of community events, this spacious 17C pub is the very definition of a proper village local. It features a large terrace and a pleasant garden with a children's tree house, and behind its smart modern façade, has a bright, relaxed feel. When it comes to the food, dishes are tasty, well-crafted and of a good size; you might find omelette Arnold Bennett or bubble and squeak, followed by chicken Kiev, king prawn spaghetti or pumpkin and chestnut gnocchi. These can be eaten in a laid-back, pine-furnished room or in the more formal, pre-laid dining room. If you're just after some nibbles, the bar, with its open fire and low level seating, is always a good bet.

High St,
HATFIELD BROAD OAK, CM22 7HH
Tel.: (01279)718598
Website: www.thedukeshead.co.uk

In the centre of the village. Parking.

PRICES
Meals: a la carte £ 22/36

MAP: 24

CLOSING TIMES
Closed 25-26 December

Greene King IPA, Sharp's Doom Bar and Timothy Taylor Landlord

BELL INN

Run by the same family for the last 70 years

If you're wondering about the hot cross buns, the story goes that past landlord Jack Turnell took over the pub on Good Friday, whereupon he nailed a bun to one of the beams; since then, a bun has been added every year - the cement version marking the wartime rationing. The Bell has been run by the same family for the last 70 years, although dates back nearly 12 times that. Drinkers will find themselves at home in the wood-panelled bar, while diners can choose from a beamed area or more formal restaurant. Cooking uses quality produce to create classically based dishes with a modern touch; maybe apple tart with a glass of malted milkshake. Bedrooms are styled after famous Victorian mistresses; those in Hill House display thoughtful extras.

High Rd,
HORNDON ON THE HILL, SS17 8LD
Tel.: (01375)642463
Website: www.bell-inn.co.uk

In the centre of the village. Parking.

PRICES
Meals: £ 19 (dinner) and a la carte £ 20/46

27 rooms: £ 65/145

MAP: 25

CLOSING TIMES
Closed 25-26 December and bank holidays

Greene King IPA and Crouch Vale Brewers Gold

COMPASSES AT PATTISWICK

Great views and local game

This remote pub started life as two estate workers' cottages, and its name comes from its far-reaching, 360 degree countryside views. Large gardens with plenty of seating make the most of this panorama, while the mini playground ensures any kids in your party will be kept happy. Inside, it's smart and spacious, with open fires, chatty local staff and a warm, relaxing feel. Lunch sees the likes of sandwiches, a ploughman's or a Melton Mowbray pork pie with piccalilli, while the wide-ranging à la carte keeps things traditional with potted shrimps, ox cheek or a hearty roast mutton shepherd's pie. Food is laudably local, with game from the surrounding estate. Nursery puddings might include warm treacle tart or a fruit crumble with custard.

Compasses Rd,
PATTISWICK, CM77 8BG
Tel.: (01376)561322
Website: www.thecompassesatpattiswick.co.uk

Between Braintree and Coggeshall signposted off A 120. Parking.

PRICES
Meals: a la carte £ 20/34

MAP: 26

CLOSING TIMES
Open daily

Bishop Nick's Hersey, Adnams Southwold and Woodeforde's Wherry

WAGGONERS

A little piece of France in a charming setting

Set on the edge of the Brocket Hall Estate, this 17C pub was once a popular stop-off point for stagecoaches and a favourite haunt of the estate workers. It has plenty of charm, with a delightfully simple open-fired bar providing a pleasant spot for weary walkers, locals and their dogs, and a very formal linen-laid dining room adding a more serious tone. The bar menu provides a list of unfussy snacks, while the à la carte presents much more ambitious offerings, with prices to match. Both the owner and chef are French, so dishes might include sautéed frogs legs or foie gras ballotine, followed by duck leg confit or veal roulade with caramelised onion tart. Daily specials are often presented on gueridon trolleys and usually feature a fish dish.

Brickwall Close,
AYOT GREEN, AL6 9AA
Tel.: (01707)324241
Website: www.thewaggoners.co.uk

2.5 mi south of Welwyn off B 197. Parking.

PRICES
Meals: £ 18 (weekday lunch) and
a la carte £ 27/38

MAP: 27

CLOSING TIMES
Open daily
booking advisable

Sharp's Doom Bar, Greene King IPA and Abbot Ale, Adnams Broadside and Ghost Ship.

OLD MILL Ⓝ

All-encompassing menus by the Grand Union Canal

With its imposing red brick and its smart clipped hedges, this pub looks more like a former schoolhouse than an old mill, but its position on the Grand Union Canal and its still-turning waterwheel are a testament to its industrial past. It has Georgian and Victorian origins, but now boasts a smart, homely style, with a rustic bar, a stylish dining room and a small courtyard garden. All-encompassing menus move with seasons and offer flavourful dishes ranging from a superfood salad or a pork pie through to sausage and mash or seared calves' liver with sauté potatoes. Deli boards are a feature, as are grass-fed, dry-aged British steaks and there are various events in the pub's calendar; from gourmet burger nights to a cheese and port evening.

London Rd,
BERKHAMSTED, HP4 2NB
Tel.: (01442)879590
Website: www.theoldmillberkhamsted.co.uk

On A 4251 as you enter the town. Parking

PRICES
Meals: £ 12 (lunch and early dinner)
and a la carte £ 23/59

MAP: 28

CLOSING TIMES
Closed 25 December

Sharp's Doom Bar,
Red Squirrel and Tring Side
Pocket for a Toad

GOLDEN FLEECE

The Golden Fleece Smokey is a speciality

This part-16C property was left to go to rack and ruin for ten long years, so when it finally found a buyer, it was in need of some real TLC. Who better to take on the challenge than a couple who grew up in the village: one of whom had their first job - aged 13 - at this very pub? It's not hard to see why they - and their many regulars - are so fond of it, with its spacious garden, pretty terrace overlooking the village and period features like a vast inglenook fireplace. Food is tasty and comforting, with popular dishes including Millionaire's bun (fillet steak in a bread roll), suet pudding and the Golden Fleece smokey. Old-school puddings might include a warming blackberry sponge with custard. Gluten and dairy free options are available.

20 Green End,
BRAUGHING, SG11 2PG
Tel.: (01920)823555
Website: www.goldenfleecebraughing.co.uk

In the middle of the village, on B 1368. Parking.

PRICES
Meals: a la carte £ 21/37

MAP: 29

CLOSING TIMES
Closed 25-26 December and Sunday dinner

Adnams Southwold Bitter and Broadside, Churchend Vicars Ruin and Innis & Gunn Original

TILBURY

Charming 18C inn offering something for everyone

This charming 18C inn is found just off the green of an equally delightful village. It's had many names over the years but has now reverted back to its original; the logo providing a clue as to its meaning - a two-wheeled horse-drawn carriage. There's a lovely heated terrace and a mature garden where they grow herbs and, inside, three rustic rooms with exposed beams and brick floors. It's owned by two brothers and heavily supported by the villagers, and there's something on offer here for one and all. Pub classics please traditionalists, while more creative dishes such as potted rabbit with carrot cake or maple-roasted guinea fowl really showcase the kitchen's skills. Add to this a selection of Brakspear's ales and everyone is happy.

1 Watton Rd,
DATCHWORTH, SG3 6TB
Tel.: (01483)815550
Website: www.thetilbury.co.uk

4 mi southeast of Stevenage signposted off A 602. Parking.

PRICES
Meals: £ 18/21 and a la carte £ 23/40

MAP: 30

CLOSING TIMES
Closed Monday and Sunday dinner

Brakspear's Ales

BRICKLAYERS ARMS

Good old-fashioned French-inspired dishes

This pub is tucked away by itself on the outer reaches of a small hamlet, so you'll need a good navigator when trying to find it. Part-built in 1722, it was originally two cottages before becoming a butcher's, a blacksmith's and later, an alehouse. Inside it's rather smart, with polished tables and fresh flowers everywhere; the areas to the side of the bar being more formally laid than those in front. This isn't the place for a quick snack (a glance at the menu will show there are none), but somewhere serving good old-fashioned, French-inspired dishes. Sunday lunch is a real family affair and if you've only time for a fleeting visit, have a hearty pudding on the terrace. The wine list is a labour of love, featuring boutique Australian wines.

Hogpits Bottom,
FLAUNDEN, HP3 0PH
Tel.: (01442)833322
Website: www.bricklayersarms.com

5 mi northeast of Amersham signposted off the A 404. Parking.

PRICES
Meals: £ 17 (weekdays) and
a la carte £ 24/46

MAP: 31

CLOSING TIMES
Closed 25 December

Tring Bring Me Sunshine, Sharp's Doom Bar and Rebellion IPA

ALFORD ARMS

Busy, rural and popular with hikers

Set among the network of paths that run across the Chilterns, this attractive Victorian pub is a popular destination for hikers - and when you're trying to squeeze your car into a tight space on the narrow country lane, arriving by foot may suddenly seem the better option. The pleasant garden flanks the peaceful village green - where you might spot the odd Morris dancer or two - and the warm bar welcomes four-legged friends as equally as their owners. The traditional menu has a strong British stamp and follows the seasons closely, so you're likely to find salads and fish in summer and comforting meat or game dishes in winter; these might include belly pork with sticky parsnips, a lamb and rabbit shepherd's pie or a tempting blackboard special.

FRITHSDEN, HP1 3DD
Tel.: (01442)864480
Website: www.alfordarmsfrithsden.co.uk

4.5 mi northwest of Hemel Hempstead signposted off A 4146. Parking.

PRICES
Meals: a la carte £ 21/37

MAP: 32

CLOSING TIMES
Closed 25-26 December

Tring Side Pocket for a Toad, Chilton Beechwood Bitter and Sharp's Doom Bar

RADCLIFFE ARMS

True neighbourhood pub, open for breakfast

Named after a renowned local family, the Radcliffe Arms enjoys its position as a true neighbourhood pub. It might have been modernised but this is still a friendly, relaxed place for the town's drinkers to gather, supping on gravity fed real ales or debating which of the 13 varieties of gin or 28 wines by the glass are best. The central bar is surrounded by a mix of wooden tables and chairs, and there's a small conservatory to the rear. Tasty cooking includes a few pub classics but it's more about well-presented, restaurant-style dishes here; you might find beetroot risotto, daube of beef or the locals' favourite, tiger prawns with chilli sauce. If you fancy it, you can even visit both before and after work, as they open at 8am for breakfast.

31 Walsworth Rd,
HITCHIN, SG4 9ST
Tel.: (01462)456111
Website: www.radcliffearms.com

A short walk from the High St. in the direction of the station.
Limited parking.

PRICES
Meals: a la carte £ 21/42

MAP: 33

CLOSING TIMES
Open daily

Buntingford Twitchell, Polar Star and Royston Red

FOX AND HOUNDS

Come in summer for the outdoor seafood bar

London to Hertfordshire isn't the biggest of moves but swapping the hustle and bustle of crowded streets for the peace and quiet of the countryside is a move that childhood sweethearts James and Bianca - now husband and wife - believe was well worth making. If the weather's good, sit in the garden or on the terrace; if not, find a spot in the pleasant bar or dining room. Menus are concise, offering tasty, unfussy dishes that display a clear understanding of flavours. There are a few pub classics alongside more restaurant-style dishes such as salt and pepper squid or scallops with herb butter, and there's a popular seafood bar outside in the summer too. All of the pastas are homemade, they smoke their own fish and desserts are not to be missed.

2 High St,
HUNSDON, SG12 8NH
Tel.: (01279)843999
Website: www.foxandhounds-hunsdon.co.uk

Between Hertford and Harlow signposted off A 414, in the village centre. Parking.

PRICES
Meals: £ 14 (weekdays) and
a la carte £ 24/40

MAP: 34

CLOSING TIMES
Closed 26 December, Sunday dinner and Monday

Adnams Southwold Bitter and Broadside, Tring Brewery Ales

SUN AT NORTHAW

Ingredients are sourced from the East of England

This restored, part-16C pub sits by the village green. It's deceptively spacious, with a contemporary style and a traditional edge. Cooking is original, so expect a wide range of dishes like crispy pigs' ears, spiced lamb pie, red gurnard or maybe even sea urchin. There's a strong regional slant here too: ingredients are sourced from the East of England, there are local ales and ciders behind the bar - as well as some English bottles on the wine list - and the toilet walls are even papered with Ordnance Survey maps of the area. Look out for wooden crates of veg scattered about the place and expect to see a chef coming to grab an onion or two. Service is friendly and the pub's affectionate dog, Smudge, may well wander over to welcome you too.

1 Judges Hill,
NORTHAW, EN6 4NL
Tel.: (01707)655507
Website: www.thesunatnorthaw.co.uk

Beside village green on main road through the village. Parking.

PRICES
Meals: £ 13 (weekday lunch) and
a la carte £ 27/48

MAP: 35

CLOSING TIMES
Closed Sunday dinner and Monday except bank holidays when closed Tuesday

Buntingford Golden Plover, Adnams Broadside, Nethergate Old Growler and Grain Harvest Moon

FOX

Can't decide? Try 'The Fox Slate' for two

Set right in the heart of the village, opposite the green, is this smart, bright pub, which is proving extremely popular. Drinkers and diners vie for tables in the modern bar but there's also a contemporary, slightly colonial-style dining room and a sheltered terrace to choose from. Light wood floors and matching furniture feature throughout and the keener eye will notice a host of subtle references to Norfolk - home to the owner's other pubs. Dishes are modern with some Asian influences and there's a good choice of game in season; they also take their seafood seriously here, with the likes of herb-crusted Cromer crab and pan-fried golden ray on the menu. For those who just can't decide, 'The Fox Slate' for two provides the perfect solution.

WILLIAN, SG6 2AE
Tel.: (01462)480233
Website: www.foxatwillian.co.uk

3 mi northeast of Hitchin by A 505 and side road. Parking.

PRICES
Meals: a la carte £ 23/37

MAP: 36

CLOSING TIMES
Open daily

Brancaster Best, Woodeforde's Wherry, Adnams Southwold Bitter and Sharp's Doom Bar

WHITE HORSE

Hearty dishes and homely bedrooms by the harbour

Maybe you've spent the afternoon bird-spotting along the beautiful north Norfolk coastline, or boating out to Blakeney Point to see the seals basking on the sandbanks. The invigorating sea air will no doubt have stoked your appetite, so head for something hearty to eat at this brick and flint former coaching inn. The same menu is served in all areas and changes according to what's freshly available and in season. Dishes might include pigeon breast, local mussels or a vast portion of tasty fish and chips, with tapas boards and seafood platters to share and desserts like a delicious chocolate and griottine cherry torte. The homely bedrooms come in various shapes and sizes and there is a lovely enclosed courtyard and a suntrap of a terrace.

4 High St,
BLAKENEY, NR25 7AL
Tel.: (01263)740574
Website: www.blakeneywhitehorse.co.uk

Just off the quay. Parking.

PRICES
Meals: a la carte £ 23/30

9 rooms:
£ 55/170

MAP: 37

CLOSING TIMES
Closed 25 December
booking advisable

Adnams Broadside, Southwold Bitter and Lighthouse

WHITE HORSE

Great views over the marshes

There's no denying that when sitting on the rear terrace or in the spacious conservatory, the views over the Brancaster Marshes and Scolt Head Island really make this pub. If you can't get a seat in either, panic not, as there's still the bar or the landscaped front terrace complete with its pleasant southerly aspect and patio heaters. On the all-day bar menu you'll find old favourites, a selection of tapas-style dishes and a few more ambitious offerings; while on the seasonally changing à la carte and daily specials, there'll be dishes such as dressed Cromer crab, confit Norfolk pork belly or marinated slow-cooked veal breast. Bedrooms have a crisp New England style; go for one of the Garden Rooms, as each comes with a private terrace.

BRANCASTER STAITHE, PE31 8BY
Tel.: (01485)210262
Website: www.whitehorsebrancaster.co.uk

On A 149 Hunstanton to Wells Rd. Parking.

PRICES
Meals: a la carte £ 25/35

15 rooms:
£ 100/220

MAP: 38

CLOSING TIMES
Open daily
booking essential

Brancaster Best and Oyster Catcher, Woodeforde's Wherry and Adnams Ghost Ship

INGHAM SWAN

Thatched 14C inn with smart, modern bedrooms

This attractive thatched pub, dating from the 14C and sitting in the shadow of a fine 11C church, lies in a small hamlet known for its delightful cricket field - all in all, a charming scene of English pastoral splendour. The cosy beamed interior is equally characterful and while this is clearly more of a dining pub, drinkers are still welcome. The one area which does break with tradition is the cooking, which is far from straightforward but clearly skilled; dishes are made up of many ingredients, albeit in classic combinations, and presentation adopts a contemporary style; even the fillet of beef is elevated to something a lot more interesting. Wine dinners and cookery classes are popular events; smart, modern bedrooms complete the picture.

Sea Palling Rd,
INGHAM, NR12 9AB
Tel.: (01692)581099
Website: www.theinghamswan.co.uk

In the centre of the village. Parking.

PRICES
Meals: £ 15/27 and a la carte £ 27/44

4 rooms:
£ 75/119

MAP: 39

CLOSING TIMES
Closed 25-26 December, Sunday dinner and Monday in winter
booking essential at dinner

Woodforde's Ales

WALPOLE ARMS

The owners are farmers and use their own produce

This pretty 18C inn with carefully manicured gardens is set in a sleepy little village not far from Oulton, where the owners' family have been farming since the 1930s. The interior is surprisingly modern, yet in keeping with the building's age: the beamed bar with its wood-burning stove provides a warm welcome and leads through to a more formal room with mock-bookshelf wallpaper. The menu champions local, seasonal ingredients, featuring produce from their farm and from just down the road, with rare breed beef a speciality. The steaks, sea bass and herring roes are all surefire hits; you'll also find influences from further afield, with the likes of taleggio and herb arancini or seeded halloumi with spiced couscous. Service is bright and bubbly.

The Common,
ITTERINGHAM, NR11 7AR
Tel.: (01263)587258
Website: www.thewalpolearms.co.uk

In the centre of the village. Parking.

PRICES
Meals: a la carte £ 20/39

MAP: 40

CLOSING TIMES
Closed 25 December and Sunday dinner in winter

Woodforde's Wherry, Adnams Broadside and Southwold Bitter

REINDEER

Proudly British cooking uses lesser-known cuts

Despite being located on a busy main street just west of the ring road, the Reindeer's young owners seem to have found a niche for themselves and they have been steadily building up a keen local following. Inside, the pub has a good old rustic feel and, satisfyingly, plenty of space is kept aside for drinkers, who have 10 real ales and 12 keg beers, lagers and ciders to choose from. Cooking is straightforward and proudly British, employing lesser-used cuts in many of the dishes; bar snacks might include potted rabbit and duck hearts or beef dripping on toast, while the main menu features plenty of dishes for sharing. The old brewing room is now a venue for private groups and makes the perfect place for a celebration. Service is friendly.

10 Dereham Rd,
NORWICH, NR2 4AY
Tel.: (01603)612995
Website: www.thereindeerpub.co.uk

On A 1074 west of the city centre. Parking.

PRICES
Meals: a la carte £ 19/35

MAP: 41

CLOSING TIMES
Closed 25-26 December and Monday

Thornbridge Jaipur, Elgood's Cambridge Bitter and Magic Rock High Wire

ROSE AND CROWN

14C inn with honest, hearty cooking

Its warren of rooms and passageways, uneven floors and low beamed ceilings place the Rose and Crown squarely into the quintessentially English bracket of inns; and the bright dining rooms, the paved terrace and the impressive pirate ship for children in the garden add some 21C zing to the pub's 14C roots. Cooking is gutsy by nature and makes good use of local produce, with neatly presented dishes such as pan-fried hake fillet alongside trusty classics like steak and chips, and local mussels in season. Service is efficient, they are well used to being busy and a crowd of locals from the village can often be found enjoying a tipple at the bar. Bedrooms are quite a contrast to the rustic pub, being light and modern in style.

Old Church Rd,
SNETTISHAM, PE31 7LX
Tel.: (01485)541382
Website: www.roseandcrownsnettisham.co.uk

In the middle of the village. Parking.

PRICES
Meals: a la carte £ 20/33

16 rooms:
£ 80/130

MAP: 42

CLOSING TIMES
Open daily

Greene King IPA, Fuller's London Pride and Woodeforde's Wherry

DUCK INN N

Thick, juicy local steaks are a highlight

Fairy lights decorate the picket fence which fringes the garden and a flock of ducks waddle over from their pond around the corner: this is the Duck Inn, in the pretty village of Stanhoe. In the buzzy, slate-floored bar, you'll find locals enjoying Elgood's ales: check out the blackboard for bar bites like scotch quail's egg. Lunch sees open sandwiches like 'Perfick Pork' bangers, mustard and onions and dishes such as confit smoked salmon with roasted beetroot. At dinner there's plenty of fresh fish, but the mature meats are what you should go for with thick, juicy local steaks a highlight. The three dining rooms have a rustic, relaxed feel; their walls adorned with local art and vintage kitchen utensils. Bedrooms are cosy and well-kept.

Burnham Rd,
STANHOE, PE31 8QD
Tel.: (01485)518330
Website: www.duckinn.co.uk

3 mi southwest of Burnham Market on B 1155. Parking.

PRICES
Meals: a la carte £ 16/37

2 rooms:
£ 75/125

MAP: 43

CLOSING TIMES
Open daily

Elgood's Cambridge Bitter and Golden Newt, Joseph Holt Two Hoots

WILDEBEEST

Unusually themed after an African savannah

If you can't afford a safari, then a trip to the Wildebeest might be your next best bet, as it's unusually decked out in the style of an African savannah, with yellow walls, wooden wild animals and thick tree trunk tables. The young serving team are dressed in smart black dresses and act more as hostesses than waitresses, and the array of menus offer something a little bit different too. Cooking focuses mainly on modern British dishes but there are also some European influences to be found, with the likes of stone bass with parmentier potatoes, samphire, tomato fondue and salsa verde. Wednesday is steak night, when they offer various cuts from their own herd of cattle; the fore-rib presented on a wooden board is their signature dish.

82-86 Norwich Rd,
STOKE HOLY CROSS, NR14 8QJ
Tel.: (01508)492497
Website: www.animalinns.co.uk

Just off the A 140, 5.5 mi south of Norwich. Parking.

PRICES
Meals: £ 15 (weekday lunch)/23
and a la carte £ 25/42

MAP: 44

CLOSING TIMES
Open daily
booking essential

Adnams Southwold Bitter, Ringwood Best Bitter and Marston's Burton Bitter

ORANGE TREE

Be sure to save room for dessert

You're guaranteed a warm welcome at this popular 17C inn, as is your pooch, who can sit with you in the relaxed, open-fired bar while gnawing on a 'Scooby Snack'. If you fancy a more intimate affair, leave your four-legged friend at home and head for the contemporary restaurant, where wine racks temptingly adorn the walls. A vast array of menus offer everything from pub classics to restaurant-style dishes, via a list of vegetarian choices and daily specials. Flavours are vibrant and well-defined, and many dishes have an international feel, often arriving on boards or slates – you might find Brancaster crab spaghetti or garlic butter roast calves' liver. The desserts are a real highlight, and compact modern bedrooms complete the picture.

High St,
THORNHAM, PE36 6LY
Tel.: (01485)512213
Website: www.theorangetreethornham.co.uk

4.5 mi northeast of Hunstanton on A 149. Parking.

PRICES
Meals: a la carte £ 24/38

10 rooms:
£ 79/140

MAP: 45

CLOSING TIMES
Open daily

Woodforde's Wherry, Adnams Southwold Bitter and Whale Ale Pale Whale

GUNTON ARMS

Lovely views over the 18C deer park

Much of the 1,000 acre Gunton Estate has been lovingly restored over the last few decades, including the early 18C deer park, several ruined buildings and this charming pub. It has a super terrace for summer BBQs and an appealing mix of period furnishings and provocative modern art. Nibble on a venison sausage roll or Blythburgh pork crackling in the flag-floored bar - over a game of pool or darts - or head for a gnarled wood table beside the fireplace in the Elk Room. Here you can choose something cooked on the fire - such as an Aberdeen Angus steak - or from a selection of unfussy, fiercely seasonal British dishes like Barnsley lamb chop or mixed grill of Gunton fallow deer. Well-equipped bedrooms have a stylish, country house feel.

Gunton Park,
THORPE MARKET, NR11 8TZ
Tel.: (01263)832010
Website: www.theguntonarms.co.uk

5.5 mi south of Cromer on A 149. Parking on edge of the estate.

PRICES
Meals: a la carte £ 22/40

8 rooms:
£ 85/185

MAP: 46

CLOSING TIMES
Closed 25 December
booking advisable

Adnams Broadside, Woodeforde's Wherry and guest ales

WIVETON BELL

Proper pub food in a modern setting

With its lightly painted façade bearing a stylised scribble of its name, this place has all the hallmarks of a 'modernised' pub. Thankfully, this modernisation has been undertaken with style and care, so you'll find an attractive interior with beams, stripped floors, wood-burning stoves and a corner just for drinkers; as well as an airy restaurant and conservatory, a beautiful landscaped rear terrace and picnic benches out the front. The seasonal menu offers all the usual pub classics, carefully crafted from quality ingredients - many of which are locally sourced. You'll find bedrooms stylish and cosy; breakfast is continental and this could come as something of a relief considering the size of the portions served in the pub!

Blakeney Rd,
WIVETON, NR25 7TL
Tel.: (01263)740101
Website: www.wivetonbell.com

Signposted off the A 149 just south of Blakeney. Parking.

PRICES
Meals: a la carte £ 27/37

4 rooms:
£ 95/140

MAP: 47

CLOSING TIMES
Open daily
booking essential

Woodeforde's Wherry, Yetman's Blue and Adnams Broadside

BRITISH LARDER

A beacon for home-grown and Suffolk produce

Once down-at-heel, this 17C pub has been updated in its look and transformed into a beacon for Suffolk produce, courtesy of its owners who have a passion for all things local. They even encourage their customers to donate produce to the pub – a blackboard behind the bar will list what 'glut' is required and any produce brought in is weighed and an agreed price is credited against the customer's next meal. The kitchen handles these ingredients deftly and will sometimes use modern techniques such as water-baths. Deli sharing boards feature at lunch, while dinner is more structured. The pub itself is smart and contemporary but still has an appealingly rustic edge. The enthusiastic owners also hold regular wine events and cookery classes.

Orford Rd,
BROMESWELL, IP12 2PU
Tel.: (01394)460310
Website: www.britishlardersuffolk.co.uk

2.5 mi northeast of Woodbridge on the A 1152. Parking.

PRICES
Meals: £ 17 (weekday lunch) and
a la carte £ 27/48

MAP: 48

CLOSING TIMES
Closed Sunday dinner and Monday except bank holidays

Adnams Southwold Bitter, Woodforde's Wherry and Sharp's Doom Bar

CASTLE INN

Great local sausages and game in season

This sky-blue pub's open-plan interior includes dining areas and an intimate rear bar – the perfect spot for a coffee or a flick through a magazine. Cooking is fresh, simple and seasonal, and while lunch might see a burger and chips or creamy risotto verde alongside doorstop sandwiches, the evening menu might include slow-cooked salt marsh lamb shoulder or pheasant breast wrapped in Parma ham. The Innkeeper's Platter is a perennial favourite and showcases local produce, including a great pickle made by the "Rockin' Grannies" – keep an eye out for the cake stands too, with their homemade cakes and cookies. Themed evenings include 'pie and wine' night and 'film and food' night – complete with popcorn. Bedrooms are homely, warm and comfortable.

35 Earsham St,
BUNGAY, NR35 1AF
Tel.: (01986)892283
Website: www.thecastleinn.net

In the centre of town. Parking.

PRICES
Meals: £ 19 (lunch) and a la carte £ 20/33

4 rooms:
£ 70/100

MAP: 49

CLOSING TIMES
Closed 25 December, Sunday dinner and Monday in winter

Earl Soham Victoria Bitter and Cliff Quay Sea Dog

SHEPHERD & DOG (N)

Fine selection of homemade bread and butter

An unexpected find in sleepy Suffolk, this modern day good shepherd provides three for the price of one. Relax with coffee and cake on one of the cosy seats in the lounge or visit the bar for traditional pub dishes like ham hock terrine or beef pie, served between 12 and 9. Completing the trinity is the rather snazzily named 'Eaterie', which serves modern cooking in a formal style to match its smart, contemporary décor: think cauliflower with smoked eel followed by rump of lamb with toasted barley, and poached figs with polenta and pistachio. Everything, including the fine selection of breads and butters and all the ice cream, is homemade - and service doesn't let the side down either, with staff being both speedy and congenial.

EARL STONHAM, IP14 5HN
Tel.: (01449)711685
Website: www.theshepherdanddog.com

4 mi east of Stowmarket on A 1120. Parking.

PRICES
Meals: £ 11/28 and a la carte £ 26/35

MAP: 50

CLOSING TIMES
Closed 1-14 January, Sunday dinner, Monday and Tuesday

Greene King IPA

PACKHORSE INN N

Adventurous modern dishes and plush bedrooms

This smart modern pub is set in the pretty village of Moulton and named after its famous packhorse bridge, which has spanned the River Kennett since the 15C. It was bought and renovated by a former banker with a vision to put it back at the heart of the community; key to its success has been the installation of experienced couple Chris and Hayley Lee as chef and manager. There are two distinct sides to the cooking: 'Packhorse Favourites' like Suffolk rib-eye and chips for your common or garden pub fare; and more adventurous, artily presented dishes like venison pie with smoked potato, which arrives in a Kilner jar. Bedrooms are ultra-stylish with plush furnishings, roll top baths, good quality toiletries and extras like homemade biscuits.

Bridge St,
MOULTON, CB8 8SP
Tel.: (01638)751818
Website: www.thepackhorseinn.com

5 mi east of Newmarket by A 1304, B 1506 and B 1085. Parking.

PRICES
Meals: a la carte £ 28/42

8 rooms:
£ 85/175

MAP: 51

CLOSING TIMES
Open daily

Fuller's London Pride, Adnams Ghost Ship and Woodeforde's Wherry

RAMSHOLT ARMS (N)

Honest pub food and river views

The Ramsholt Arms: it may well be at the end of a long and winding road but, boy, is it worth it when you get there, as this striking inn sits against the spectacular backdrop of the River Deben. Sister to the Ufford Crown, it specialises in honest, well-priced pub food and Suffolk ales. Summer days bring hordes to the terrace but, with seating for over a hundred, there's no lack of outside space. When the weather is inclement, a window seat's the ticket: watch the pleasure boats bobbing as you eat. The menu's printed daily and might include such dishes as black pudding scotch egg, local crayfish cocktail or baked camembert to share. After come 'proper' puddings like spotted dick or plum and almond tart. Locals walk here and bring their dogs.

Dock Rd,
RAMSHOLT, IP12 3AB
Tel.: (01394)411209
Website: www.theramsholtarms.com

8 mi south of Woodbridge by A 1152 and B 1083. Parking.

PRICES
Meals: £ 10 and a la carte £ 17/29

MAP: 52

CLOSING TIMES
Closed January and Monday-Wednesday November-March

Adnams Broadside, Hellhound Dirty Blond and Cliff Quay Brewery Ales

CROWN INN

Home-reared meats and home-grown fruit and veg

These days any pub worth its salt is serving produce sourced from the local area, but there aren't many who can claim to provide most of the meat for their menus themselves, as well as the majority of the fruit and veg. The affable young owners of this characterful 15C smugglers' inn raise pigs, goats, lambs, calves, ducks, turkeys and chickens in the fields at the back. They'll show you around if you ask - although it's probably best to eat first - and you can check out the rosettes in the bar, won by their Gloucester Old Spot pigs. It's easy to find dishes which appeal on the regularly changing menu; perhaps home-reared pork terrine, braised faggots or a cured meat platter. Staying over? Rustic bedrooms have beamed ceilings and sloping floors.

Bridge Rd,
SNAPE, IP17 1SL
Tel.: (01728)688324
Website: www.snape-crown.co.uk

On B 1069, just north of Snape Maltings. Parking.

PRICES
Meals: a la carte £ 20/30

2 rooms:
£ 70/90

MAP: 53

CLOSING TIMES
Open daily

Adnams Ales

CROWN

Smart oak-panelled, nautically-themed bar

This 17C former coaching inn sits on the high street of a charming town, close to the brewery and only a hop, skip and a jump away from the sea. Its relaxed, traditionally styled bar and dining room are often buzzing with diners and the small oak-panelled, nautically-themed locals bar is a great place for a leisurely pint of Adnams of an afternoon. The same modern, seasonal menu is served throughout: choose from fresh, full-flavoured dishes like Dingley Dell ham hock terrine, Deben mussels with Broadside bacon and fries, or Emmerdale Farm Red Poll beef short rib with garlic mash. Individually designed bedrooms have a contemporary New England style and offer extras like robes and shortbread: those to the rear are the quietest; '11' is the best.

90 High St,
SOUTHWOLD, IP18 6DP
Tel.: (01502)722275
Website: www.adnams.co.uk/hotels

In the town centre. Parking.

PRICES
Meals: a la carte £ 22/35

14 rooms:
£ 135/235

MAP: 54

CLOSING TIMES
Open daily

Adnams Ales

CROWN

Large, luxurious bedrooms in a great spot

If you find the newspapers on the bar too depressing, the wine list here is a great read: a well-priced, top quality selection with over 25 available by the glass – bottles are displayed in a glass-fronted room and can also be bought to take home. Globally influenced, generously proportioned dishes feature the latest produce from local farms and estates, and might include game terrine, king prawn linguine or a locally reared rump steak, while a separate menu lists fresh seafood sourced from the east coast. Set in a great spot overlooking the Box and Stour river valleys, this smart pub also offers luxurious, ultra-spacious, superbly equipped bedrooms; all have king or super king sized beds, while some feature French windows and terraces.

STOKE-BY-NAYLAND, CO6 4SE
Tel.: (01206)262001
Website: www.crowninn.net

8 mi north of Colchester by A 134. In the centre of the village. Parking.

PRICES
Meals: a la carte £ 19/36

11 rooms: £ 95/245

MAP: 55

CLOSING TIMES
Closed 25-26 December

Adnams Southwold Bitter, Woodeforde's Wherry, Crouch Vale Brewers Gold and guest ales

UFFORD CROWN

Hearty daily menus from a family team

Close to a nursery of the same name, you'll find this freshly painted former coaching inn, offering a warm welcome to one and all. A few steps lead down to a small walled terrace and the choice of two doors - one opening into the restaurant and the other, into the bar, which consists of a series of narrow rooms. It's run by enthusiastic husband and wife team, Max and Polly, and the head chef is Polly's brother, Will. Menus change daily, with hearty dishes ranging from a crispy pork belly sandwich, lamb shank shepherd's pie or homemade beef and paprika sausages to potted crab, chargrilled duck hearts or rib of Ketley beef for 3 to share. Portions are generous and service is keen; finish with a tasty Valrhona brownie or a maple and pecan tart.

High St,
UFFORD, IP13 6EL
Tel.: (01394)461030
Website: www.theuffordcrown.com

3 mi northwest of Woodbridge on B 1348.

PRICES
Meals: a la carte £ 21/40

MAP: 56

CLOSING TIMES
Closed Tuesday

Adnams Southwold Bitter and Earl Soham Ales

ANCHOR

Global flavours punctuate the menu

The Anchor is a welcoming, relaxing place, run by an enthusiastic, friendly team. Unusually for a pub, it's housed in an Arts and Crafts building, with a pleasant terrace and a path leading directly from the garden, with its wood-fired oven, to the beach. Owners Sophie and Mark are passionate about sourcing local, seasonal produce; they grow various herbs and vegetables themselves and also bake their own bread, which is available to buy. Dishes are prepared with real care and global flavours punctuate the menu; Mrs Kirkham's White Gold cheese gives a clue as to Mark's roots. Some of the bedrooms are in the house, but ask for one of the comfy wood-clad chalet rooms in the garden – and breakfast like a king on smoked haddock and jugged kippers.

Main St,
WALBERSWICK, IP18 6UA
Tel.: (01502)722112
Website: www.anchoratwalberswick.com

In the centre of the village. Parking.

PRICES
Meals: a la carte £ 23/39

10 rooms:
£ 85/150

MAP: 57

CLOSING TIMES
Closed 25 December

Adnams Ales

WESTLETON CROWN

They cater well for gluten-free and special diets

The rustic, 17C bar of this former coaching inn welcomes you with its beams and open fires; venture a little further in, and you'll find an attractive, surprisingly modern conservatory, as well as an appealing terrace and garden. The same seasonally pertinent menu is offered throughout, so you can eat your trio of Blythburgh pork or saddle of venison wherever you choose. If you're counting the pennies, come at lunchtime, when you'll find a second menu offering the likes of sausage and mash or Suffolk lamb stew, and if you are vegetarian or have special dietary requirements, you'll find that you're also well catered for. Bedrooms have a crisp, uncluttered style and are named after birds found on the adjacent RSPB nature reserve.

The Street,
WESTLETON, IP17 3AD
Tel.: (01728)648777
Website: www.westletoncrown.co.uk

3 mi east of Yoxford signed off A 12. In the centre of the village. Parking.

PRICES
Meals: a la carte £ 28/42

34 rooms:
£ 90/215

MAP: 58

CLOSING TIMES
Open daily

Adnams Southwold Bitter

WHITE HORSE

Choose homemade sausages or fish and chips

Everyone assembles in the bar to look at the large wall menu, where each dish is displayed on a separate blackboard; this is the hub of this cheerfully run, 17C village pub, owned by a couple who established their reputation at the Beehive in Horringer. There are three further areas to choose from: to the left, a characterful beamed room which fills up quickly; to the right the brighter 'Gallery', which displays local artists' work; and a room for larger parties which leads out to the spacious garden and terrace. The kitchen's strength lies in the more conventional dishes like the pub's own homemade sausages or their superb fish and chips. The mixed hors d'oeuvres make a great starter to share, and the treacle tart is a favourite for dessert.

Rede Rd,
WHEPSTEAD, IP29 4SS
Tel.: (01284)735760
Website: www.whitehorsewhepstead.co.uk

Well signposted off the A 143, 4.5 mi south of Bury St Edmunds. Parking.

PRICES
Meals: a la carte £ 23/33

MAP: 59

CLOSING TIMES
Closed 1 week January, 25-26 December and Sunday dinner

Adnams Ales

CROWN

Modern town centre pub with minimalist bedrooms

With its farmers' markets, restaurants and cafés, the delightful riverside town of Woodbridge is up there with the best of them when it comes to foodie credentials; and all the more so since the arrival of the Crown. After a top-to-toe 21C makeover, this pub retains little evidence of its 17C roots; a glass-roofed, granite-floored bar sits at its centre, with four smart dining areas arranged around it. Bedrooms are modern, minimalistic and very cosy with good facilities; service is polite, friendly and copes well when busy. Seasonal menus are made up of modern classics - perhaps roast local partridge or Suffolk honey ham, with plenty of shellfish, including Deben oysters and mussels from the new beds - and the set menu offers terrific value.

Thoroughfare,
WOODBRIDGE, IP12 1AD
Tel.: (01394)384242
Website: www.thecrownatwoodbridge.co.uk

At town centre crossroads. Parking.

PRICES
Meals: £ 15 (weekdays) and a la carte £ 23/38

10 rooms: £ 90/200

MAP: 60

CLOSING TIMES
Open daily

Adnams and Meantime ales

LONDON

— England

© J. Arnold / hemis.fr

Twenty-first century London may truly be called the definitive world city. Time zones radiate from Greenwich, and global finances zap round the Square Mile, while a vast smorgasbord of restaurants is the equal of anywhere on the planet. A stunning diversity of population now calls the capital its home, mixing and matching its time between the urban sprawl and enviable acres of green open space. From Roman settlement to banking centre to capital of a 19C empire, London's pulse has rarely missed a beat. Along the way, expansion has gobbled up surrounding villages, a piecemeal cocktail with its ingredients stirred to create the likes of Kensington and Chelsea, Highgate and Hampstead, Twickenham and Richmond.

Apart from the great range of restaurants, London boasts over three and a half thousand pubs, many of which now see accomplished, creative cooking as an integral part of their existence and appeal. And you can find them sprinkled right the way across from zones one to five...

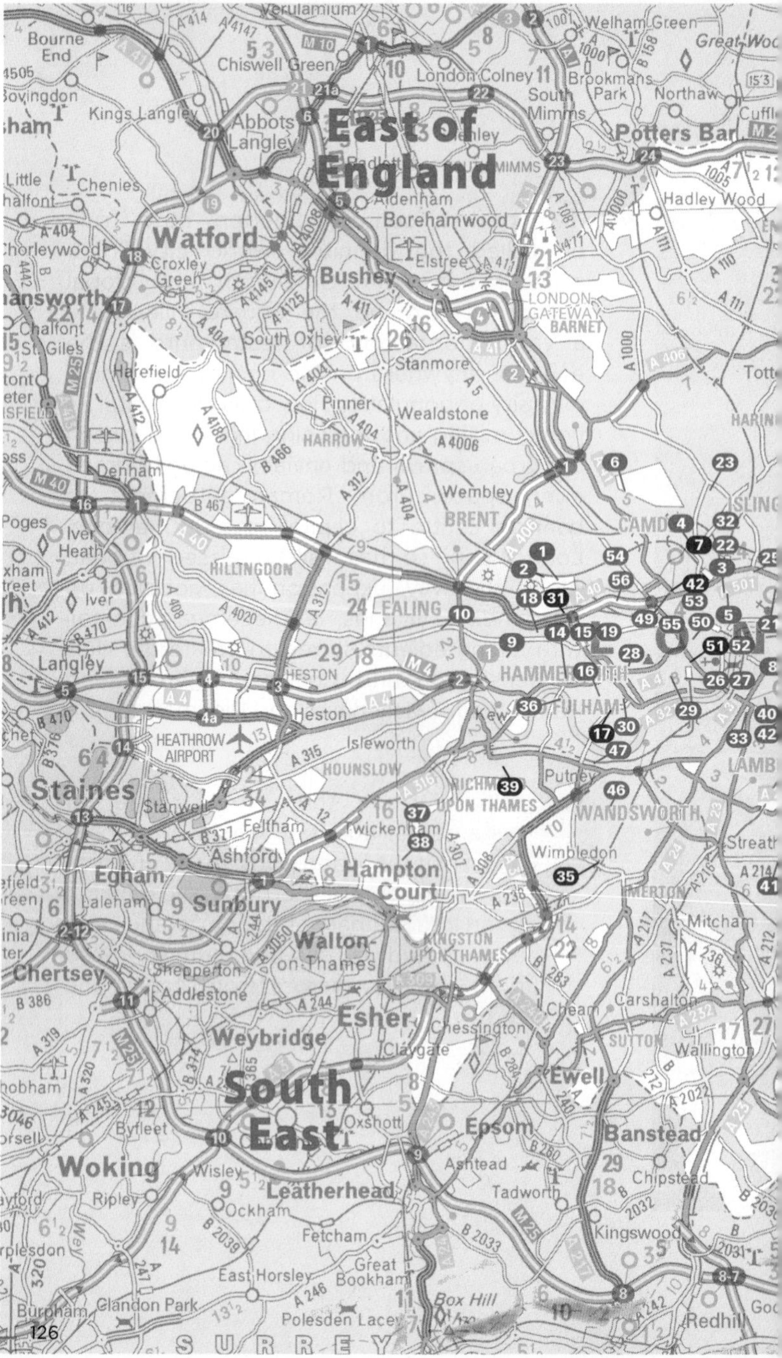
East of England
South East
SURREY
Verulamium
Bourne End
Bovingdon
Kings Langley
Chiswell Green
Abbots Langley
London Colney
South Mimms
Welham Green
Brookmans Park
Northaw
Potters Bar
Great Wood
Cuffley
Radlett
Aldenham
Borehamwood
Elstree
Hadley Wood
Little Chalfont
Chenies
Chorleywood
Watford
Croxley Green
Bushey
South Oxhey
LONDON GATEWAY
BARNET
Rickmansworth
Chalfont St Giles
Harefield
Stanmore
Pinner
Wealdstone
HARROW
Wembley
BRENT
Denham
Iver Heath
Iver
HILLINGDON
EALING
Langley
HESTON
Heston
HAMMERSMITH
FULHAM
Kew
HEATHROW AIRPORT
Isleworth
HOUNSLOW
Putney
RICHMOND UPON THAMES
WANDSWORTH
Staines
Stanwell
Feltham
Twickenham
Ashford
Hampton Court
Wimbledon
Egham
Laleham
Sunbury
Mitcham
Streatham
Chertsey
Walton-on-Thames
KINGSTON UPON THAMES
Shepperton
Addlestone
Esher
Chessington
Cheam
Carshalton
SUTTON
Wallington
Weybridge
Claygate
Ewell
Byfleet
Oxshott
Epsom
Banstead
Woking
Wisley
Ashtead
Chipstead
Leatherhead
Tadworth
Ripley
Ockham
Fetcham
Kingswood
Great Bookham
East Horsley
Burpham
Clandon Park
Box Hill
Polesden Lacey
Redhill
M 25
M 40
M 4
M 10

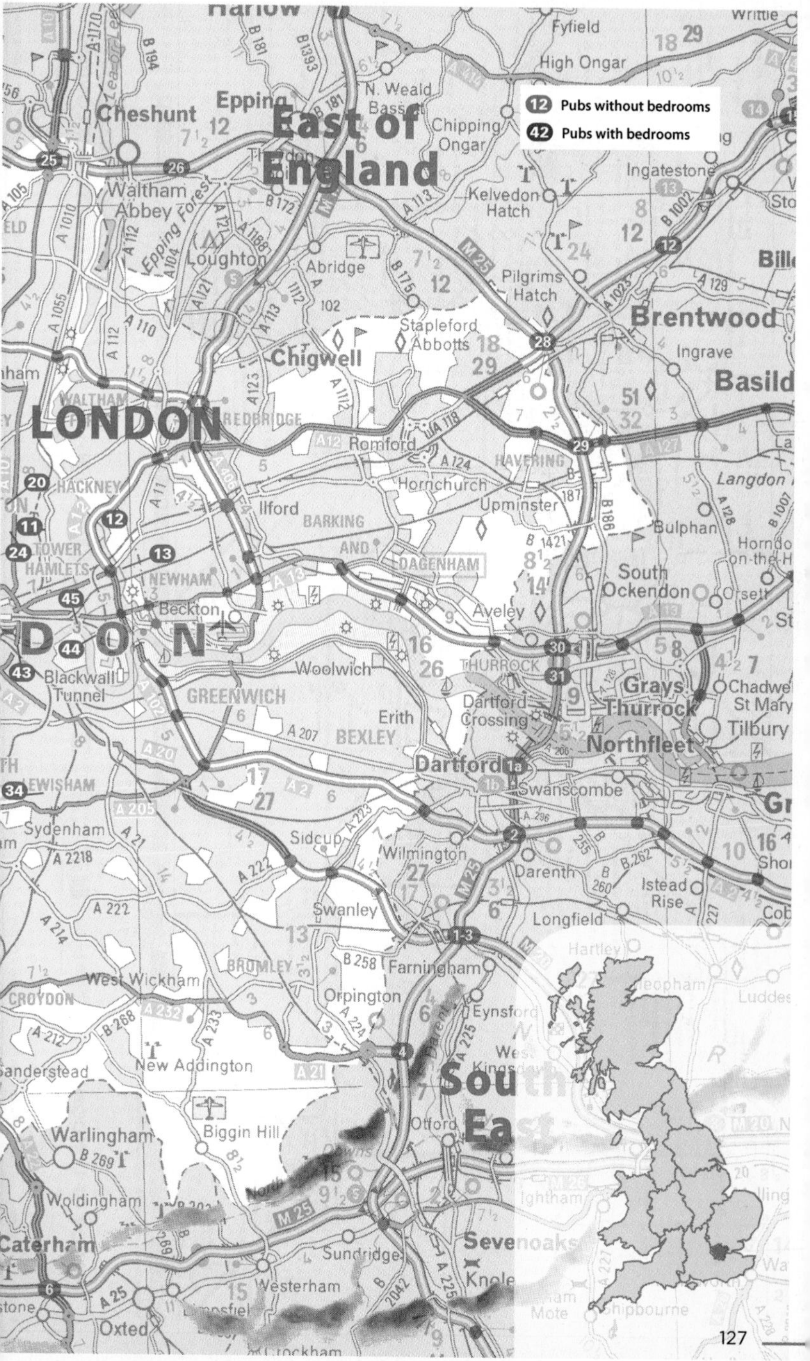

12 Pubs without bedrooms
42 Pubs with bedrooms
East of England
South East
LONDON
Harlow
Fyfield
High Ongar
Writtle
Cheshunt
Epping
N. Weald Bassett
Chipping Ongar
Theydon Bois
Waltham Abbey
Epping Forest
Loughton
Abridge
Kelvedon Hatch
Ingatestone
Pilgrims Hatch
Brentwood
Ingrave
Stapleford Abbotts
Chigwell
Basildon
WALTHAM FOREST
REDBRIDGE
Romford
HAVERING
Hornchurch
Upminster
HACKNEY
Ilford
BARKING AND DAGENHAM
TOWER HAMLETS
NEWHAM
Beckton
Bulphan
South Ockendon
Orsett
Aveley
Langdon Hills
Horndon-on-the-Hill
THURROCK
Grays Thurrock
Chadwell St Mary
Tilbury
Blackwall Tunnel
Woolwich
GREENWICH
Erith
BEXLEY
Dartford Crossing
Dartford
Northfleet
Swanscombe
LEWISHAM
Sydenham
Sidcup
Wilmington
Darenth
Istead Rise
Swanley
Longfield
Hartley
Farningham
BROMLEY
West Wickham
CROYDON
Orpington
Eynsford
New Addington
Sanderstead
West Kingsdown
Biggin Hill
Warlingham
Otford
Woldingham
Caterham
Sevenoaks
Sundridge
Knole
Westerham
Oxted
Limpsfield
Crockham
Ightham Mote
Shipbourne
Luddesdown
Meopham

Bakerloo	Central	Circle	District	Hammersmith & City	Jubilee	Metropolitan	Northern	Piccadilly	Victoria	Waterloo & City	London Overground	DLR	Emirates Air Line

† Kensington (Olympia) open weekends, public holidays and some Olympia events

MAYOR OF LONDON

tfl.gov.uk

24 hour travel information
0343 222 1234*

*Service and network charges may apply. See tfl.gov.uk/terms for details.

Sign up for email updates
tfl.gov.uk/emailupdates

@TfLTravelAlerts

UNDERGROUND

TRANSPORT FOR LONDON
EVERY JOURNEY MATTERS

 Reg. user No. 14/2681/P Version C 05.2014

Improvement works may affect your journey, please check before you travel

Correct at time of going to print

PARADISE BY WAY OF KENSAL GREEN

A quirky fun palace with something for everyone

Calling 'Paradise' a pub hardly does it justice - this is a veritable fun palace. Named after a line from a GK Chesterton poem, this gloriously bohemian place is spread over three floors and means different things to different people: some come along for comedy nights and cocktails or party nights and DJs; others pop in for drinks in the Reading room or snacks in the bar; many come to eat in the restaurant; and you can even get married here. The food is a reassuring mix of British favourites and European themed dishes, all made using good ingredients from trusted suppliers and prepared with obvious care. The surroundings are wonderfully quirky and idiosyncratic, the staff are contagiously enthusiastic and the vibe, effortlessly cool.

BRENT
19 Kilburn Ln,
KENSAL GREEN, W10 4AE
Tel.: (020)89690098
Website: www.theparadise.co.uk

⊖ **Kensal Green.** - On-street parking.

PRICES
Meals: £ 30 and a la carte £ 24/41

MAP: 1

CLOSING TIMES
Open daily
dinner only and lunch Saturday and Sunday

Greene King Golden Beech, Yard Bird and Belhaven Robert Burns

PARLOUR N

Hard not to love a place that serves cow pie

It may not quite be a pub but nor is it a restaurant so let's focus more on what Parlour actually is – a fun, warmly run and slightly quirky neighbourhood hangout. Open from breakfast until late, it has one room dominated by a large bar and the other set up for eating with an appealingly higgledy-piggledy look. They do a decent cocktail and a great range of beers and the menu is a wonderfully unabashed mix of tradition, originality and reinvention. Approaching legendary status is their cow pie which even Dan, however Desperate, would struggle to finish. The vegetable 'ravioli' is a cleverly thought-out construction and the marshmallow Wagon Wheel something for the children. On warm nights ask for one of the cabanas in the garden.

BRENT
5 Regent St,
KENSAL GREEN, NW10 5LG
Tel.: (020)89692184
Website: www.parlourkensal.com

⊖ **Kensal Green** - On-street parking.

PRICES
Meals: £ 10 (weekday lunch) and
a la carte £ 25/36

MAP: 2

CLOSING TIMES
Closed 24 December-1 January

London Fields Love Not War and Camden Pale Ale

APE & BIRD N

The Polpo people's first venture into pubs

Following the success of his ever-expanding empire of restaurants, Ape & Bird is Russell Norman's first venture into pubs. The style is stripped back and simple, but look closer and you notice the attention to detail: tin tiles shipped from the USA; chandeliers inspired by Balham tube station and a mural featuring famous Soho residents. It's a big place which at first can be a bit bewildering; go into the basement for cocktails, stay in the busy bar for snacks like sausage rolls or Welsh rarebit, or head up to the airy dining room with views over Cambridge Circus. Dishes are British, but their construction owes more to Italian principles: a few, top quality ingredients cooked with care to create plates full of flavour, aroma and appeal.

CAMDEN
142 Shaftesbury Ave,
BLOOMSBURY, WC2H 8HJ
Tel.: (020)78363119
Website: www.apeandbird.com
⊖ Leicester Square

PRICES
Meals: a la carte £ 24/34

MAP: 3

CLOSING TIMES
Closed 25 December and 1 January

Camden Brewery and Five Points Brewery Ales

BULL & LAST

Great for Sunday lunch - they know their meats

Dartmouth Park locals know a good thing when they see it and the Bull & Last, always full of character and life, is most certainly a good thing. If you haven't booked, it's still worth trying your luck as they keep the odd table back - mind you, with enticing bar snacks like pig's trotter wontons and soft shell crab tempura, you may simply find happiness at the bar ordering some of these to go with your pint. The cooking is gloriously robust and generous and the menu mainly British with some pasta dishes thrown in. The kitchen knows its way around an animal too - the charcuterie boards are very popular. Puds are traditional; cheese is in good order; and the homemade ice creams are a hit. And where else can you get marrowbone for your dog?

CAMDEN
168 Highgate Rd,
DARTMOUTH PARK, NW5 1QS
Tel.: (020)72673641
Website: www.thebullandlast.co.uk

⊖ **Tufnell Park.** - On-street parking.

PRICES
Meals: a la carte £ 23/42

MAP: 4

CLOSING TIMES
Closed 24-25 December
booking essential

Redemption Big Chief, Dark Star Partridge Best Bitter and Red Squirrel Hopfest

LADY OTTOLINE

Busy ground floor, quieter upstairs dining room

Apart from some repair work on the cornicing and the tiled floor, this substantial red-brick Victorian pub is largely unchanged from when it was called The Kings Arms. The menus in the packed and slightly chaotic ground floor bar and the Queen Anne style upstairs dining room are not hugely different: cold winter nights see dishes like braised pig cheeks with lentils or venison haunch with squash purée. The kitchen takes more care with its cooking than one expects and dishes deliver on flavour. There's also a large selection of wine by the glass. This was the second pub for this husband and wife team and a sister to the Princess of Shoreditch. It is named after the society hostess who was a friend to the Bloomsbury set.

CAMDEN
11a Northington St,
BLOOMSBURY, WC1N 2JF
Tel.: (020)78310008
Website: www.theladyottoline.com

⊖ **Chancery Lane.** - On-street parking.

PRICES
Meals: £ 28 (lunch and early dinner)
and a la carte £ 24/35

MAP: 5

CLOSING TIMES
Closed 24 December-2 January and bank holidays

Sambrook's Wandle Ale, Sharp's Doom Bar and Purity Mad Goose

WELLS

Ideal watering hole after a walk on the heath

The Wells is named after Chalybeate Well which, in 1698, was given to the poor of Hampstead - it's about 30 yards away, next to that BMW. Equidistant between Heath and High Street, this handsome pub is split in two: downstairs is the busier, more relaxed part of the operation, while upstairs you'll find a formally dressed dining room. Apart from a couple of extra grilled dishes downstairs, the two areas share a menu, which is cleverly balanced to satisfy all appetites from spirited dog walker to leisurely shopper. Salads or seared scallops can be followed by sea bass, assorted pasta or duck confit; puds are good and they do a decent crumble. Add a commendable range of ales and wines and you have a pub for all seasons.

CAMDEN
30 Well Walk,
HAMPSTEAD, NW3 1BX
Tel.: (020)77943785
Website: www.thewellshampstead.co.uk

⊖ **Hampstead.** - Parking in Well Rd.

PRICES
Meals: a la carte £ 25/35

MAP: 6

CLOSING TIMES
Open daily

Sharp's Doom Bar, Truman's Runner and Hackney Best Bitter

YORK & ALBANY

A handsome 1820s John Nash coaching inn

These days things are more egalitarian down at the York & Albany, a handsome 1820s John Nash coaching inn rescued by Gordon Ramsay after lying virtually derelict for years. Gone is the separation of bar and restaurant dining - you are now offered the same menu wherever you want to sit, whether that's in the bar, the back restaurant or downstairs next to the open kitchen. The menu has also been made a little more inclusive and offers wood-fired pizzas and pasta dishes alongside more adventurous choices like lamb shoulder with braised celery and duck with hispi cabbage. It works well because the kitchen treats a burger with the same respect as they do a rib-eye steak, although service can still wobble at times. The bedrooms have character.

CAMDEN
127-129 Parkway,
CAMDEN TOWN, NW1 7PS
Tel.: (020)73883344
Website: www.gordonramsay.com/yorkandalbany

⊖ **Camden Town.** - On-street parking.

PRICES
Meals: £ 24 (weekday lunch) and a la carte £ 31/41

10 rooms: £ 187/330

MAP: 7

CLOSING TIMES
Open daily
booking essential

Meantime Ales

JUGGED HARE

Stout British dishes for meat lovers

The famous 18C recipe created by Hannah Glasse, the UK's first domestic goddess, provided the inspiration for the renaming of this Grade II listed pub, previously known as The King's Head. It's an apt name because committed vegetarians may feel ill at ease – and not just because of the collection of glass cabinets in the bar which showcase the art of taxidermy. The atmospheric and appealingly noisy dining room, which has a large open kitchen running down one side, specialises in stout British dishes, with Denham Estate venison, Yorkshire guinea fowl and Cumbrian Longhorn steaks from the rotisserie and grill being the highlights. If the main course doesn't fill you, puddings like treacle tart or bread and butter pudding will.

CITY OF LONDON
42 Chiswell St,
CITY OF LONDON, EC1Y 4SA
Tel.: (020)76140134
Website: www.thejuggedhare.com

⊖ **Barbican.** - Limited on-street parking.

PRICES
Meals: £ 38 (dinner) and
a la carte £ 29/59

MAP: 8

CLOSING TIMES
Closed 25-26 December
booking advisable

Adnams Southwold Bitter, Sambrook's Jugged Hare Pale Ale and Harviestoun The Ridge

DUKE OF SUSSEX

Moorish cooking in a classic old gin palace

The Duke of Sussex may seem like a typical London pub, even from the front bar, but step through into the dining room and you'll find yourself in what was once a variety theatre from the time when this was a classic gin palace, complete with proscenium arch, glass ceiling and chandeliers. If that wasn't unusual enough, you could then find yourself eating cured meats or fabada, as the menu has a strong Spanish influence. Traditionalists can still get their steak pies and treacle tart but it's worth being more adventurous and trying the sardines, the paella and the crema Catalana. This is a fun, enthusiastically run and bustling pub and the kitchen's enthusiasm is palpable. On Mondays it's BYO; Sunday is quiz night.

EALING
75 South Par,
ACTON GREEN, W4 5LF
Tel.: (020)87428801
Website: www.realpubs.co.uk

⊖ **Chiswick Park.** - Parking on adjacent street.

PRICES
Meals: a la carte £ 23/36

MAP: 9

CLOSING TIMES
Open daily

St Austell Proper Job, Twickenham Brewery Naked Ladies, Itchen Valley Pure Gold

THE GROVE

A beast of a pub that's had a good makeover

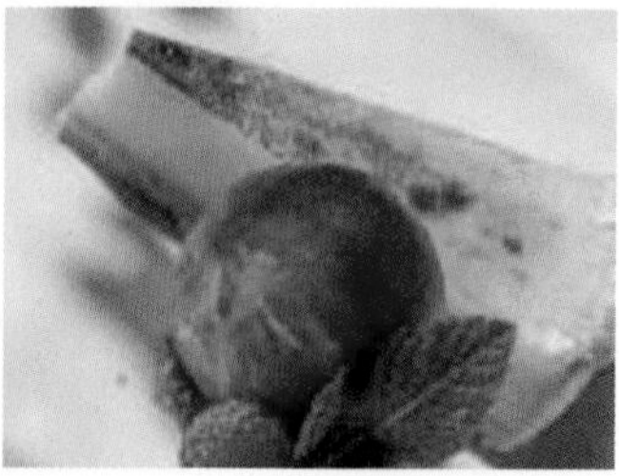

It's hard to avoid this beast of a place in central Ealing but then, why would you? It may be brewery owned and have undergone a typical London gastropub makeover, but it'll hit the spot - whether you're out with friends or after a candle-lit dinner. There's a huge front terrace dominated by drinkers but inside it's spilt into half-bar, half-restaurant; you can eat anywhere but the restaurant at the back is the quieter choice. The menus change monthly - lunch is pretty standard issue, but at dinner the skilful kitchen celebrates its classical roots. The easy-to-eat dishes add a distinctive French accent to the largely British ingredients; desserts are mostly crowd-pleasing classics and are equally satisfying.

EALING
The Green,
EALING, W5 5QX
Tel.: (020)85672439
Website: www.thegrovew5.co.uk

⊖ **Ealing Broadway.** - Free on-street parking after 7.30pm.

PRICES
Meals: £ 13 (weekday lunch) and
a la carte £ 22/36

MAP: 10

CLOSING TIMES
Open daily

Sambrook's Wandle Ale, Truman's Runner and Sharp's Doom Bar

EMPRESS

Great value seasonally inspired cooking

The name of this 1850s pub was changed from the Empress of India as some customers arrived expecting chicken tikka - information which will dishearten history teachers everywhere. Queen Victoria has been demoted to the Empress of E9 but then everything is about being 'local' these days and that includes this re-launched pub. Sourdough comes from the baker down the road and their butcher and fishmonger are within walking distance; the menu is pleasingly seasonal and the cooking is several notches above usual pub fare. Dishes like risotto made with pearl barley and feta, or lamb's liver with lentils demonstrate that this is a kitchen with confidence and ability. Prices are kept in check and Sunday lunch is a very languid affair.

HACKNEY
130 Lauriston Rd,
VICTORIA PARK, Hackney, E9 7LH
Tel.: (020)85335123
Website: www.empresse9.co.uk

⊖ **Homerton.** - On-street parking meters.

PRICES
Meals: £ 20 (weekday dinner)
and a la carte £ 23/33

MAP: 11

CLOSING TIMES
Closed 25 December and Monday lunch
except bank holidays

Camden Brewery Ales,
Sambrook's Wandle and
East London Brewing Co
Foundation Bitter

PRINCE ARTHUR

Entices with its food, not its looks

It's never wise to choose a pub on appearance alone. Whichever way you look at it, but particularly if you look at it from the street, Prince Arthur is not the most handsome place around. Inside is frankly not much more exciting, unless you're someone with a certain fondness for taxidermy in public places. But when it comes to good food and general conviviality, this Prince does just fine. Thought has gone into the bar snacks, and the menu, which changes every three months, delivers just the sort of stout, substantial dishes you want in a pub. The daily specials board is well worth a stare if you want something a touch more adventurous. Monday is quiz night and there are regular promotions that are well worth checking out.

HACKNEY
95 Forest Rd,
DALSTON, E8 3BH
Tel.: (020)72499996
Website: www.theprincearthurlondonfields.com

⊖ **Dalston Junction.** - On-street parking.

MAP: 12

PRICES
Meals: £ 10 (weekdays) and
a la carte £ 25/41

CLOSING TIMES
Closed 25 December
dinner only and lunch Saturday-Sunday

Beavertown and Sambrook's Ales

PRINCESS OF SHOREDITCH

Daily changing menu comes appealingly priced

Apparently there has been a pub on this corner site since 1742 but it is doubtful many of the previous incarnations were as busy or as pleasant as the Princess is today. The owners have always been very hands-on and their welcoming attitude has rubbed off on their friendly staff; the pub comes with an appealing buzz and, to cap it all off, the prices are more than fair. It's set over two floors and the same menu is served throughout - although you can book upstairs. The menu changes daily, and sometimes between services; the food appears quite simple but the best dishes are those that come with a satisfying rustic edge, whether that's the buttery goose rillettes, the chicken pie with terrific mash or the tender pulled pork.

HACKNEY
76-78 Paul St,
SHOREDITCH, EC2A 4NE
Tel.: (020)77299270
Website: www.theprincessofshoreditch.com

⊖ **Old Street** - On-street parking meters.

PRICES
Meals: £ 28 (lunch and early dinner)
and a la carte £ 24/34

MAP: 13

CLOSING TIMES
Closed 24-26 December
booking essential

Sambrook's Pumphouse Pale Ale, East London Brewing Co Foundation Bitter and Truman's Runner

CRABTREE

Terrific riverside terrace

On a sunny day few things in life beat being by the river in a London pub and The Crabtree certainly makes the most of its location. Its beer garden, with its barbeque-style menu, can seat over 80, while the dining room boasts its own terrace overlooking the river - and if you haven't yet booked for lunch on Boat Race day then you're probably already too late. A variety of ploys are used to fill the equally large interior of this Victorian beauty, from BYO Mondays to quiz nights on Tuesdays. For lunch the selection varies from ciabatta sarnies to shepherd's pie; the evening menu is more adventurous. The kitchen does things properly - parfaits and terrines are highlights and fish is perfectly timed - but vegetarians are also looked after.

HAMMERSMITH AND FULHAM
4 Rainville Rd,
HAMMERSMITH, W6 9HA
Tel.: (020)73853929
Website: www.thecrabtreeW6.co.uk
⊖ **Barons Court.** - On-street parking.

PRICES
Meals: a la carte £ 25/38

MAP: 14

CLOSING TIMES
Open daily

Greene King Ales

HARWOOD ARMS

Wonderful food - and game is a speciality

It may be a very handsome pub in a smart postcode and have all its tables laid up for dining but there's nothing stuck-up or snooty about this place - in fact, the only thing that's superior is the cooking. It's British to its core, with its reassuringly concise, daily changing menu resolutely governed by our country's own seasonal produce. Cornish fish, Herdwick lamb, Cumbrian chicken and Wiltshire pork can all feature and game is a real strength of the kitchen whether it's the rabbit, grouse, or Hampshire Muntjac. Dishes have real depth and flavours are bold and satisfying. Service is smooth and assured and comes courtesy of a young yet experienced team and the well-chosen wine list offers a particularly good choice of mature claret.

HAMMERSMITH AND FULHAM
Walham Grove,
FULHAM, SW6 1QP
Tel.: (020)73861847
Website: www.harwoodarms.com

⊖ **Fulham Broadway.** - On-street parking with restrictions until 8pm.

PRICES
Meals: £ 25 (weekday lunch) and
a la carte £ 38/46

MAP: 15

CLOSING TIMES
Closed 24-27 December, 1 January and
Monday lunch
booking essential

Sambrook's Wandle and
Bath Gem

HAVELOCK TAVERN

Easy-going, warm and atmospheric

The word 'gastropub' was first coined in the early '90s to describe pubs that offered great food while remaining true to their roots - and was never about pubs masquerading as restaurants. The warm and friendly Havelock Tavern was at the vanguard of this movement and little about its lived-in look has changed here over the years, which is probably why it's as busy as ever. Put your name down for a table at the bar, order a drink and then place your order from the blackboard menu which changes with each service and reflects the seasons. The food is comforting and prices fair, while the freshness is underlined by the fact that dishes often run out; there could be grilled mackerel or goujons of coley alongside a tagine or roast pork belly.

HAMMERSMITH AND FULHAM
57 Masbro Rd,
BROOK GRN, Hammersmith, W14 0LS
Tel.: (020)76035374
Website: www.havelocktavern.com

⊖ **Kensington Olympia.** - On-street pay & display parking.

PRICES
Meals: a la carte £ 19/29

MAP: 16

CLOSING TIMES
Closed 25-26 December

Sambrook's Wandle Ale, Adnams Southwold Bitter and Sharp's Doom Bar

MALT HOUSE

Dapper looking pub with friendly staff

Inside is so pristine and well-ordered, you begin to wonder if the bottles of sauce on the tables are there primarily to remind everyone that this really is still a pub. There are plenty of tables laid up for dining but there are also some sofas to add a more leisurely note and the general atmosphere is welcoming and friendly - the keen young staff help enormously in this regard. The appealing menu is all-encompassing enough to attract both the traditionalist and the more adventurous eater. Dishes are appealingly presented; meats grilled on the barbecue are something of a speciality and on Sundays three different roasts are offered. To further prove this is not your typical London boozer, there are six elegant bedrooms upstairs.

HAMMERSMITH AND FULHAM
17 Vanston Pl,
FULHAM, SW6 1AY
Tel.: (020)70846888
Website: www.malthousefulham.co.uk

⊖ **Fulham Broadway.** - On-street parking.

PRICES
Meals: a la carte £ 23/42

6 rooms:
£ 125/150

MAP: 17

CLOSING TIMES
Closed 25 December

Sharp's Doom Bar, Brakspear Bitter and Adnams Ales

PRINCESS VICTORIA

A fine-looking Victorian grande dame

London has a wealth of fine Victorian gin palaces but few are as grand as Princess Victoria. From the friezes to the etched glass, the portraits to the parquet floor, the last restoration created a terrific pub. Mind you, that's not all that impresses: there's a superb, wide-ranging wine list, with carafes and glasses providing flexibility; enticing bar snacks ranging from quail eggs to salt cod croquettes; a great menu that could include roasted skate wing or homemade pork and herb sausages; and, most importantly, cooking that's executed with no little skill. Those with proclivities for all things porcine will find much to savour - charcuterie is a passion here and the board may well include pig's cheeks and rillettes.

HAMMERSMITH AND FULHAM
217 Uxbridge Rd,
SHEPHERD'S BUSH, W12 9DH
Tel.: (020)87495886
Website: www.princessvictoria.co.uk

⊖ **Shepherd's Bush.** - On-street parking.

PRICES
Meals: £ 13 (weekday lunch) and
a la carte £ 21/45

MAP: 18

CLOSING TIMES
Closed 24-27 December

Timothy Taylor Landlord, Sharp's Doom Bar and Purity Mad Goose

SANDS END

British dishes to the fore at this cosy spot

Sands End is probably not the best known part of London, or indeed Fulham, but no doubt its residents prefer it that way so they can keep their eponymous pub to themselves. It's a cosy, warm and welcoming one, with a central bar offering some nifty homemade snacks, but try resisting because the main menu - which changes every few days - is pretty appealing itself. There's a distinct British bias which amounts to more than merely name-checking the birthplace of the ingredients. Winter dishes like braised lamb neck or roast partridge with Savoy cabbage are particularly pleasing and West Mersea oysters a good way of starting things off. There's a well-chosen and equally equitably priced wine list that sticks mostly to the Old World.

HAMMERSMITH AND FULHAM
135-137 Stephendale Rd,
FULHAM, SW6 2PR
Tel.: (020)77317823
Website: www.thesandsend.co.uk

⊖ **Fulham Broadway.** - On-street parking.

PRICES
Meals: £ 11 (weekday lunch) and
a la carte £ 28/39

MAP: 19

CLOSING TIMES
Closed 25 December
booking advisable

Upham Punter, Harveys Sussex Best Bitter and Greene King IPA

DRAPERS ARMS

Gutsy, satisfying and good value British food

Celebrating British cuisine means more than just putting a few old favourites on the menu; it's about making great use of indigenous ingredients and introducing them to a wider audience. At The Drapers Arms those unfamiliar with our own bounteous larder can see humble produce like lamb's tongues, smoked eels, blade steak and rabbit used to create dishes that are satisfying, gutsy and affordable. Locals, or those who find themselves in Islington at midday for whatever reason, can take advantage of their steal of a lunch menu. Just ignore the fact that the staff can be a little too cool for school and simply enjoy the good food, unpretentious atmosphere and shabby-chic interior of this busy Georgian pub, with its handsome façade.

ISLINGTON
44 Barnsbury St,
ISLINGTON, N1 1ER
Tel.: (020)76190348
Website: www.thedrapersarms.com

⊖ **Highbury & Islington.** - On-street parking.

PRICES
Meals: a la carte £ 22/33

MAP: 20

CLOSING TIMES
Closed 25-26 December
bookings advisable at dinner

Harveys Sussex Best Bitter, Dark Star Hophead and London Fields Hackney Hopster

PEASANT

Famed for helping spearhead the pub revolution

From the outside it may be starting to look its age, but this senior member of the gastropub movement still pulls in plenty of punters. Come evening, you have two choices: stay in the bar and compete for a spare table with the City boys having a post-work pint, or book a table in the sanctuary of the sedate upstairs dining room with its circus-themed prints and posters. Downstairs comes with an easy, eat-on-the-hoof type of menu: squid tempura and sharing boards such a cheese or meze stand out and are ideal accompaniments to a pint. In the restaurant dishes such as sea bream with capers and brown shrimps, and honey-roast duck with celeriac purée, come with a greater degree of sophistication but still deliver on flavour.

ISLINGTON, 240 St John St,
FINSBURY, EC1V 4PH
Tel.: (020)73367726
Website: www.thepeasant.co.uk

⊖ **Farringdon.** - On-street parking meters nearby; also free parking after 6.30pm and on Saturday after 1.30pm.

PRICES
Meals: £ 24 (weekday dinner) and
a la carte £ 15/28

MAP: 21

CLOSING TIMES
Closed 25 December-1 January and bank holidays except Good Friday
booking essential

Crouch Vale Brewers Gold, Meantime Brewery Pale Ale and Bath Ales Gem

PIG AND BUTCHER

Apt name - they know their way round an animal

This corner pub dates from the mid-19C when cattle drovers taking their livestock to Smithfield Market would stop for a swift one. Now sympathetically restored, it enjoys the same ownership as the Lady Ottoline and the Princess of Shoreditch. The busy bar offers an impressive number of bottled beers, while the dining room is secreted behind shelves of bric-a-brac. There's a strong British element to the daily menu and that's not just because they use words like 'Beeton' and 'Mrs'. Meat comes straight from the farm and is butchered and smoked in-house; fish comes from day boats off the south coast. Roasts take centre stage on Sundays; "just like your mother's" they claim, which presumably means something different to us all.

ISLINGTON
80 Liverpool Rd,
ISLINGTON, N1 0QD
Tel.: (020)72268304
Website: www.thepigandbutcher.co.uk

⊖ **Angel.** - Free on-street parking after 6.30pm.

PRICES
Meals: a la carte £ 26/46

MAP: 22

CLOSING TIMES
Closed 25-27 December
dinner only and lunch Friday-Sunday
booking advisable

Sambrook's Wandle Ale,
London Fields Hackney
Hopster and Bath Ales Gem

ST JOHN'S TAVERN

A shining beacon of hope on this busy thoroughfare

Having undergone an English Heritage restoration a few years back, St John's Tavern stands as something of a beacon of hope on the sluggishly smartening thoroughfare that is Junction Road. It doesn't disappoint inside either: the laid-back front bar does an appealing line in snacks like salt cod croquettes and mutton pasties, and there are few more warming spots in North London on a cold night than the large, boldly decorated rear dining room. The chefs list the provenance of their ingredients on a board next to the open kitchen, with Devon and Dorset seemingly the favoured counties. The daily menu is largely hardy and British but with nods to the Med; heartening terrines are a highlight, as is the delicious sourdough which is baked in-house.

ISLINGTON
91 Junction Rd,
ARCHWAY, N19 5QU
Tel.: (020)72721587
Website: www.stjohnstavern.com

⊖ **Archway.** - Pay & display parking; free after 6.30pm.

PRICES
Meals: a la carte £ 25/35

MAP: 23

CLOSING TIMES
Closed 25-26 December and 1 January
dinner only and lunch Friday-Sunday
booking advisable

Sambrook's Junction Ale, Bath Ales Gem and Brakspear Bitter

SMOKEHOUSE (N)

Enticing aromas rise from the wood chip smokers

If, to you , barbecuing means a burnt chicken leg, warm wine and a wet garden then a visit to Smokehouse will set you straight. You can smell the oak chips in the smoker as you approach this warm, modern pub, which was previously called The House. Meat is the mainstay of the very appealing menu - the peppered ox cheeks have understandably become a firm favourite - but whilst the flavours are undeniably gutsy, the smoking and barbecuing manages to add a little something to the ingredients without ever overpowering them. With portion sizes to appease Desperate Dan, only the committed may make it to dessert but chocolate lovers should try the Friday pie. The pub is enthusiastically run and staff are eager to recommend dishes.

ISLINGTON
63-69 Canonbury Rd,
CANONBURY, N1 2DG
Tel.: (020)73541144
Website: www.smokehouseislington.co.uk

⊖ **Highbury & Islington.** - Free on-street parking after 6.30pm.

PRICES
Meals: a la carte £ 26/37

MAP: 24

CLOSING TIMES
Closed 24-26 December
dinner only and lunch Saturday-Sunday
booking advisable

Beavertown Neck Oil, Bath Ales Gem and Vale Brewery VPA

WELL

Well-supported local; dishes cooked with care

One of the smallest pubs in the Martin brothers' portfolio is also one of the easiest to find, thanks to its wide expanse of blue canopy. This well-supported neighbourhood pub comes with the sort of food that is reassuringly familiar yet still done well, and service that instills confidence in the customer - just be sure to eat on the ground floor, rather than in the basement. Whether it's asparagus soup or veal Holstein, dishes are cooked with care and deliver on flavour. A side dish between two is needed - the macaroni cheese is worth ordering even if it doesn't necessarily match up to what you're eating - and who isn't reassured by the presence of a crumble on a menu?

ISLINGTON
180 St John St,
FINSBURY, EC1V 4JY
Tel.: (020)72519363
Website: www.downthewell.com

⊖ **Farringdon.** - On-street parking meters.

PRICES
Meals: a la carte £ 23/41

MAP: 25

CLOSING TIMES
Closed 25-26 December

Sambrook's Jugged Hare Pale Ale

ADMIRAL CODRINGTON

Great retractable roof in the dining room

If you're going to make one of your pubs the flagship of your bourgeoning organisation then it makes sense to choose the one that has 'Admiral' in its title. Cirrus Inns now run 'The Cod' and have managed to touch it all up without tampering with it too much. Lunch means some fresh fish or a club sandwich in either the front bar or the rather smart restaurant with its retractable roof; in the evening the bar sticks to just serving drinks. Start with the terrific snacks, like pork crackling with apple sauce, then head for the more familiar, tried-and-tested dishes from the monthly-changing menu. Beef is big here and is aged in-house; the burgers have become popular, with new combinations communicated by Twitter.

KENSINGTON AND CHELSEA
17 Mossop St,
CHELSEA, SW3 2LY
Tel.: (020)75810005
Website: www.theadmiralcodrington.com

⊖ **South Kensington.** - Parking in the adjacent streets.

PRICES
Meals: a la carte £ 25/45

MAP: 26

CLOSING TIMES
Closed 24-26 December

Fuller's London Pride and Upham Punter

BUILDERS ARMS

Mediterranean food to match the colourful interior

The Builders Arms is very much like a packed village local – the only difference being that, in this instance, the village is Chelsea and the villagers are all young and prosperous. The inside delivers on the promise of the smart exterior but don't expect it to be quiet as drinkers are welcomed just as much as diners. In fact, bookings are only taken for larger parties but just tell the staff that you're here to eat and they'll sort you out. The cooking reveals the effort that has gone into the sourcing of some decent ingredients; the rib of beef for two is a perennial favourite. Dishes are robust and satisfying and are not without some flair in presentation. Wine is also taken seriously and their list has been thoughtfully put together.

KENSINGTON AND CHELSEA
13 Britten St,
CHELSEA, SW3 3TY
Tel.: (020)73499040
Website: www.geronimo-inns.co.uk

⊖ **South Kensington.** - On-street parking.

PRICES
Meals: a la carte £ 26/40

MAP: 27

CLOSING TIMES
Open daily
bookings not accepted

Sharp's Doom Bar and Young's Ales

CADOGAN ARMS

How about lunch then a game of pool?

Look no further if you like pubs to feel the way they used to. Instead of turning this Victorian corner pub into a gastropub cliché, the Martin brothers - who also own the trendy Botanist at the smart end of the King's Road - respected its heritage and kept it a 'proper' pub, albeit one with decent food. Stuffed animals, antlers on the wall, original tiling and oak panelling give it a warm, unaffected feel. The best things on the menu are those that are filling, blokey and meaty, whether that's mutton with haggis, faggots or large steaks for two - and there's no let up with puds like treacle tart. In the billiard room upstairs you'll find three American 8-ball pool tables available to hire by the hour; snacks can be had up there too.

KENSINGTON AND CHELSEA
298 King's Rd,
CHELSEA, SW3 5UG
Tel.: (020)73526500
Website: www.thecadoganarmschelsea.com

⊖ **South Kensington.** - On-street parking.

PRICES
Meals: a la carte £ 23/42

MAP: 28

CLOSING TIMES
Closed 25-26 December
bookings advisable at dinner

Adnams Southwold Bitter and Sambrook's Jugged Hare Pale Ale

LOTS ROAD PUB & DINING ROOM

European menu and a great drinks list

At lunch expect to be joined by those from the nearby Design Centre; at dinner the place is colonised by good-looking locals; and at weekends it's full of folk who've been busy buying antiques. The pub may be looking a little worn around the edges but when a kitchen occupies half the bar you just know they take their food seriously. The menu may be short and at first glance rather safe but they use good produce and cook it with care and respect. Blackboards offer "season's eatings" and there's a daily recipe too. Look out too for the weekly 'wicked wines' selection where you can pick up a bargain. Steak is still a speciality and it's worth coming on Sunday for a roast and a Bloody Mary. They also have a great customer loyalty scheme.

KENSINGTON AND CHELSEA
114 Lots Rd,
CHELSEA, SW10 0RJ
Tel.: (020)73526645
Website: www.lotsroadpub.com

⊖ **Fulham Broadway.** - On-street parking.

PRICES
Meals: a la carte £ 22/35

MAP: 29

CLOSING TIMES
Closed 25 December

Sharp's Brewery Ales and guest ales

PIG'S EAR

Rustic, unfussy cooking and a laid-back vibe

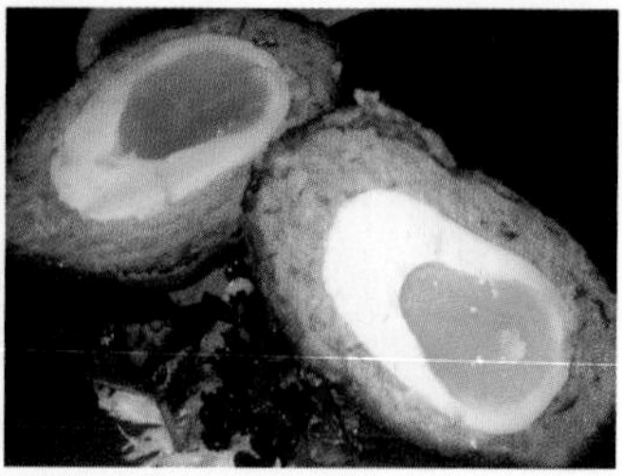

This Chelsea pub may not look much like a foodie spot from the outside, or indeed from the inside, but it does have a refreshing honesty to it. Lunch is in the rough-and-ready ground floor bar, decorated with everything from 'Tintin' pictures to covers of 'Sounds' newspaper. There's a decent choice of 5-6 main courses and a wine list on a blackboard. With its wood panelling and dressed tables, the upstairs dining room provides quite a contrast, but the atmosphere is still far from starchy. Here the menu displays a little more ambition but cooking remains similarly earthy and the wine list has plenty of bottles under £30. The kitchen knows its way around an animal: slow-cooked dishes such as pork cheeks are done particularly well.

KENSINGTON AND CHELSEA
35 Old Church St,
CHELSEA, SW3 5BS
Tel.: (020)73522908
Website: www.thepigsear.info

⊖ **South Kensington.** - On-street parking.

PRICES
Meals: a la carte £ 14/38

MAP: 30

CLOSING TIMES
Open daily

Sambrook's Junction Ale and Uley Pigs Ear

PORTOBELLO HOUSE

Once hosted The Clash but now all very smart

Whether this is a pub, bistro or hotel - or even all three - may be up for discussion but what is indisputable is that Portobello House is a great addition to this end of Ladbroke Grove. It was formerly the Earl Percy and once hosted The Clash (as, seemingly, did every boozer in these parts) but has been given a complete makeover and now has 12 smart and contemporary bedrooms. Downstairs, the bar takes up most of the space and, in a reflection of the changing local demographic, offers beers and cocktails. There are plenty of sofas to relax on; grab the one by the open fire. The menu is a combination of British stoutness and Italian flair and the cooking is bold yet comforting; it is also decently priced, especially at weekday lunches.

KENSINGTON AND CHELSEA
225 Ladbroke Grove,
NORTH KENSINGTON, W10 6HQ
Tel.: (020)31810920
Website: www.portobellohouse.com

⊖ **Ladbroke Grove.** - Free on-street parking after 6.30pm.

PRICES
Meals: a la carte £ 18/31

12 rooms:
£ 110/230

MAP: 31

CLOSING TIMES
Closed 25 December

Sharp's Doom Bar

FELLOW

Atmospheric and fun; cooking done with care

This clever Fellow established itself well before the regeneration of King's Cross finished so was all ready for the influx of new customers. Don't be fooled by its rather anonymous façade - this is a pub de nos jours, complete with a slick cocktail bar and a kitchen with worthy ingredient-sourcing credentials. Most of the action takes place on the ground floor which looks a little dark and moody but the atmosphere is brightened considerably by the staff who make a genuine effort to look after their customers. A relatively small kitchen means they keep the menu lean and clean, and influences remain largely within Europe. Fish from Cornish day boats is often a highlight; cheeses are British and puds are well worth a flutter.

KINGS CROSS ST PANCRAS
24 York Way,
ST PANCRAS, N1 9AA
Tel.: (020)78334395
Website: www.thefellow.co.uk

⊖ **King's Cross St Pancras.** - Limited on-street parking.

PRICES
Meals: a la carte £ 25/37

MAP: 32

CLOSING TIMES
Closed 25-27 December

Sharp's Doom Bar and St Austell Tribute

CANTON ARMS

Wholesome, satisfying and well-priced food

Its appreciative audience prove that the demand for fresh, honest, seasonal food is not just limited to smart squares in Chelsea or Islington. The oval-shaped bar dominates the room; the front half busy with drinkers and the back laid up for diners, although it's all very relaxed and you can eat where you want. The kitchen's experience in places like the Anchor & Hope and Great Queen Street is obvious on their menu which features rustic, earthy British food, of the sort that suits this environment so well. Lunch could be a kipper or tripe and chips; even a reinvented toasted sandwich. Dinner sees a short, no-nonsense menu offering perhaps braised venison or grilled haddock, with daily specials like steak and kidney pie for two.

LAMBETH
177 South Lambeth Rd,
STOCKWELL, SW8 1XP
Tel.: (020)75828710
Website: www.cantonarms.com

⊖ **Stockwell.** - Free parking in the evening.

PRICES
Meals: a la carte £ 19/31

MAP: 33

CLOSING TIMES
Closed Christmas-New Year, Monday lunch, Sunday dinner and bank holidays
bookings not accepted

Skinner's Betty Stogs, Timothy Taylor Golden Best and Truman's Runner

PALMERSTON

Gutsy cooking suits the lived-in look

The Palmerston has long realised that success for any pub lies in being at the heart of the local community. Since its last makeover, this Victorian pub has been popular with families - just look at all those highchairs - and local artists' work decorates the walls. It has a comfortable, lived-in feel, along with a snug, wood-panelled rear dining room with an original and quite beautiful mosaic floor. The menu is as reassuring as the service and the cooking has a satisfying, gutsy edge. There's plenty of choice, from chowders and soups to well-judged fish but it's the meat dishes that stand out, like the mature steaks or lamb chops - and if they have grouse on the menu, then forsake all others and get in quick.

LAMBETH
91 Lordship Ln,
EAST DULWICH, SE22 8EP
Tel.: (020)86931629
Website: www.thepalmerston.co.uk

⊖ **East Dulwich (Rail).** - Free on-street parking in the evening.

PRICES
Meals: £ 14 (weekday lunch) and
a la carte £ 28/64

MAP: 34

CLOSING TIMES
Closed 25-26 December and 1 January

Sharp's Doom Bar, Harveys Sussex Best Bitter and Timothy Taylor Landlord

FOX AND GRAPES

No-nonsense food in converted cottages

The Fox and Grapes is discreetly tucked away on the south side of the common, amongst a row of old workers' cottages, and is surprisingly spacious inside, with a low-ceilinged snug and a vaulted room complete with leaded windows and chandeliers. The menu is concise, offering simply cooked dishes which let the ingredients do the talking. Pies and burgers sit alongside Mediterranean-inspired dishes and the likes of Tandoori hake, while steaks cooked on the Josper grill will satisfy those with the heartiest of appetites. To start, the avocado prawn cocktail has become something of a speciality; to finish, the puddings are of the proper, no-nonsense variety and come with a port or sherry recommendation. Three modern bedrooms complete the picture.

MERTON
9 Camp Rd,
WIMBLEDON, SW19 4UN
Tel.: (020)86191300
Website: www.foxandgrapeswimbledon.co.uk

⊖ **Wimbledon.** - On-street parking.

PRICES
Meals: a la carte £ 20/46

3 rooms:
£ 100/125

MAP: 35

CLOSING TIMES
Closed 25 December

Sharp's Doom Bar and Black Sheep Best Bitter

BROWN DOG

Homely, comforting and tucked away

You really can't teach an old dog new tricks - because The Brown Dog remains a terrific neighbourhood pub and the locals clearly love it just the way it is. Mind you, this pretty Victorian pub is so well hidden in the maze of residential streets that it's a wonder any new customers ever find it anyway. The look fuses the traditional with the modern and service is bubbly and enthusiastic. Jugs of iced water arrive without prompting and the cleverly concise menu changes regularly. A lightly spiced crab salad or pint of prawns could be followed by a succulent rump of lamb, while puddings like sticky toffee date pudding or gooseberry cheesecake are also commendably priced.

RICHMOND UPON THAMES
28 Cross St,
BARNES, SW13 0AP
Tel.: (020)83922200
Website: www.thebrowndog.co.uk

⊖ **Barnes Bridge (Rail).** - On-street parking.

PRICES
Meals: a la carte £ 20/37

MAP: 36

CLOSING TIMES
Closed 25 December

Twickenham Ales, Sambrook's Wandle Ale and Hackney Brewery Best Bitter

CROWN (N)

Ample portions of globally influenced dishes

Much to the delight of St Margarets residents, this fine-looking Georgian pub has been revived and revitalised. Setting the scene are an old lantern hanging above the entrance and a mosaic floor inlaid with the pub's name, while inside it feels relaxed and stylish, with parquet floors, feature fireplaces and bright colours; sit in the airy, elegant rear restaurant, with its high vaulted ceiling and garden view. There's something for everyone on the global menus, from sharing boards and classic pub dishes to Mediterranean-influenced fish stew or Asian-inspired Tom Yum Thai prawns and squid. Portions are ample and cooking fresh, tasty and reliable. Service is enthusiastic and the pretty beer garden is popular with drinkers and diners alike.

RICHMOND UPON THAMES
174 Richmond Rd,
ST MARGARETS, Twickenham, TW1 2NH
Tel.: (020)88925896
Website: www.crowntwickenham.co.uk

⊖ **St Margarets (Rail).** - Parking.

PRICES
Meals: a la carte £ 23/36

MAP: 37

CLOSING TIMES
Closed 26 December

Surrey Hills Shere Drop, Sharp's Cornish Coaster, Harveys Sussex Best Bitter and guest ales

KING'S HEAD

Familiar brasserie-style classics

Britain has its pubs and France its brasseries; The King's Head does its bit for the entente cordiale by combining both. Raymond Blanc's team has given this Victorian pub a tidy makeover and, although there might not be much character left, they have created a suitably warm environment. The brasserie at the back is run by a pleasant, enthusiastic team and the menus offer all comers plenty of choice. Classic brasserie dishes such as Toulouse sausages and beef stroganoff come with a satisfyingly rustic edge, while the dual-nationality element is maintained through the inclusion of a ploughman's board alongside the charcuterie. Steaks from on the charcoal grill are popular and families are lured in by the decent kiddies menu.

RICHMOND UPON THAMES
123 High St,
TEDDINGTON, TW11 8HG
Tel.: (020)31662900
Website: www.whitebrasserie.com

⊖ **Teddington (Rail).** - On-street parking.

PRICES
Meals: £ 12/14 and a la carte £ 19/34

MAP: 38

CLOSING TIMES
Closed 25 December

Fuller's London Pride, Sharp's Doom Bar and Truman's Swift

VICTORIA

Lies at the heart of the local community

Many pubs claim to be genuine locals - The Victoria is the real deal: it sponsors local clubs and the chef is patron of the local food festival; he also holds cookery workshops at the school next door. This is a beautifully decorated pub, with a restored bar, a wood burning stove and plenty of nooks and crannies; a few steps down and you're in the more formal conservatory overlooking the terrace. The cooking is modern British with the odd international note. Warm homemade bread could be followed by scotch egg with roast beetroot, cod with a white bean stew and, to finish, blood oranges with rhubarb sorbet. Produce is local where possible: veg is from Surrey and honey from Richmond. Service is engaging and there are bedrooms available.

RICHMOND UPON THAMES
10 West Temple Sheen,
EAST SHEEN, SW14 7RT
Tel.: (020)88764238
Website: www.thevictoria.net

⊖ **Mortlake (Rail).** - Parking.

PRICES
Meals: £ 15 (lunch and early dinner) and a la carte £ 23/44

7 rooms:
£ 120/130

MAP: 39

CLOSING TIMES
Open daily

Fuller's London Pride and Timothy Taylor Landlord

ANCHOR & HOPE

Hearty, no-nonsense and confident cooking

The Anchor & Hope is still running at full steam and its popularity shows no sign of abating. It's not hard to see why: combine a menu that changes with each service and is a paragon of seasonality, with cooking that is gutsy, bold and wholesome, and you end up with immeasurably rewarding dishes like suckling kid chops with wild garlic, succulent roast pigeon with lentils or buttermilk pudding with poached rhubarb. The place has a contagiously congenial feel and the staff all pull in the same direction; you may spot a waiter trimming veg or a chef delivering dishes. The no-reservation policy remains, so either get here early or be prepared to wait – although you can now book for Sunday lunch, when everyone sits down at 2pm for a veritable feast.

SOUTHWARK
36 The Cut,
SOUTHWARK, SE1 8LP
Tel.: (020)79289898
Website: www.anchorandhopepub.co.uk

⊖ **Southwark.** - On-street parking meters.

PRICES
Meals: £ 15 (weekday lunch) and
a la carte £ 21/33

MAP: 40

CLOSING TIMES
Closed Christmas-New Year, Sunday dinner, Monday lunch and bank holidays
bookings not accepted

Young's Bitter, Wells Bombardier and guest ales

CAMBERWELL ARMS (N)

Punchy flavours from a short, simple menu

The people behind the Anchor & Hope and Canton Arms not only know how to open great pubs but also seem to have a knack for identifying areas that are 'up and coming', although it could be said that their pubs very presence is often a contributory factor in this process. The open-plan kitchen and much-coveted adjoining counter separates the front bar from the rear dining room and as the pub doesn't take bookings you may find yourself sharing your table with others. The daily menu is refreshingly short, simple and supplemented by blackboard specials in the evening - and the serving team know it inside out. Starters are quite light to prepare you for the punchy, earthy flavours of the main course, many of which come courtesy of the BBQ grill.

SOUTHWARK
65 Camberwell Church St,
CAMBERWELL, SE5 8TR
Tel.: (020)73584364
Website: www.thecamberwellarms.co.uk

⊖ **Denmark Hill (Rail).** - On-street parking

PRICES
Meals: a la carte £ 24/34

MAP: 41

CLOSING TIMES
Closed 27 Dec-2 Jan, Sunday dinner, Monday lunch, bank holiday Mondays and Tuesday lunch after bank hols
bookings not accepted

Ringwood Best Bitter and St Austell Tribute

CROOKED WELL

Run with passion by its young owners

Three friends scoured the south of England before finding this old boozer in Camberwell. They've done it up very cleverly because it manages to look both new and lived-in at the same time and also feels like a proper 'local'. There's a strong emphasis on beers, great cocktails and an interesting wine list with plenty available by the glass and pichet, but the pub's growing reputation is mostly down to its food. The kitchen mixes things up by offering stout, traditional classics like rabbit and bacon pie alongside more playful dishes such as a deconstructed peach Melba. There are lots of things 'on toast' at lunchtime, while dishes like scotch egg with Heinz tomato soup are designed to evoke memories of childhood.

SOUTHWARK
16 Grove Ln,
CAMBERWELL, SE5 8SY
Tel.: (020)72527798
Website: www.thecrookedwell.com

⊖ **Denmark Hill (Rail).** - Free on-street parking after 6.30pm.

PRICES
Meals: £ 10 (weekday lunch) and
a la carte £ 21/39

MAP: 42

CLOSING TIMES
Closed Monday lunch

Sharp's Doom Bar

GARRISON

You'll leave feeling good about life in general

You'd be hard pressed to find a more charming pub than The Garrison. With its appealing vintage look, warm atmosphere and delightful staff, it's the perfect antidote to those hard-edged boozers that we've all accidentally found ourselves in at some point. Open from 8am for smoothies and breakfast, it gets busier as the day goes on - and don't bother coming for dinner if you haven't booked. Booth numbers 4 and 5, opposite the open kitchen, are the most popular while number 2 at the back is the cosiest. Daily specials on the blackboard supplement the nicely balanced menu and the cooking is perky and bright, with a subtle Mediterranean slant. Salads are done well and there's a daily steak, while puds are of a more traditional bent.

SOUTHWARK
99-101 Bermondsey St,
BERMONDSEY, SE1 3XB
Tel.: (020)70899355
Website: www.thegarrison.co.uk

⊖ **London Bridge.** - On-street parking.

PRICES
Meals: £ 12/16 and a la carte £ 21/35

MAP: 43

CLOSING TIMES
Closed 25-26 December
booking essential at dinner

Adnams Ales

THE GUN

Nooks, crannies and a terrific Thameside terrace

The Gun's popularity far outweighs its size but don't let the hordes from Canary Wharf at the bar put you off - just head to the far end and you'll be ably looked after by the smart and enthusiastic staff, or grab a table on the heated terrace and watch the 'Sweet Thames run softly'. The best things on the menu are the broadly British dishes, which is appropriate for such a historic pub - its links with Admiral Lord Nelson and ties to the river are celebrated in its oil paintings and the assorted weaponry on display. The eyes of most customers stop at the 45-day aged rare breed steaks but game is also a highlight, as is the Herdwick lamb chop and the baked Dorset crab - and the dishes are suitably stout in size.

TOWER HAMLETS
27 Coldharbour,
CANARY WHARF, E14 9NS
Tel.: (020)75155222
Website: www.thegundocklands.com

⊖ **Blackwall (DLR).** - On-street parking.

PRICES
Meals: a la carte £ 28/54

MAP: 44

CLOSING TIMES
Closed 25-26 December
booking essential

Jugged Hare Pale Ale, Adnams Southwold Bitter and Moor Nor'Hop

NARROW

Busy riverside pub owned by Gordon Ramsay

There can't be many London pubs with better views than The Narrow and Gordon Ramsay's group has certainly made the most of the Thames-side location by wrapping a conservatory around this Grade II listed former dockmaster's house. The place has a real buzz, thanks largely to the many regulars drinking at the bar, the weekly quiz nights and the occasional live music, and the large number of diners which includes plenty of tourists who have made a special trek down here. The menu gives them an opportunity to discover Blighty's more traditional culinary offerings such as scotch egg, cottage pie, toad in the hole and the ubiquitous fish and chips. Dishes on the whole hit the mark, although the kitchen can be a little heavy-handed at times.

TOWER HAMLETS
44 Narrow St,
LIMEHOUSE, E14 8DP
Tel.: (020)75927950
Website: www.gordonramsay.com

⊖ **Limehouse (DLR).** - Parking.

PRICES
Meals: a la carte £ 31/42

MAP: 45

CLOSING TIMES
Open daily
booking essential

Meantime and Fuller's London Pride

EARL SPENCER (N)

Traditional food prepared with genuine care

The owner worked at this Edwardian pub over a decade ago and so jumped at the chance of actually buying it himself - he felt he had "unfinished business" here. It's a handsome pub, standing a baseline lob away from the All England Tennis Club and its small terrace overlooks a showroom of the finest 4-wheel thoroughbreds. Inside is bright and welcoming, with many of the original features and fittings restored, but it's the cooking that really sets it apart. The experienced brigade are strict apostles of seasonality - the menu can sometimes change twice a day - and everything is homemade. Flavours are assured and ingredients marry well. The one entry in the debit column is that you have to keep going up to the bar to order everything.

WANDSWORTH
260-262 Merton Rd,
SOUTHFIELDS, SW18 5JL
Tel.: (020)88709244
Website: www.theearlspencer.com

⊖ **Southfields.** - On-street parking.

PRICES
Meals: a la carte £ 23/30

MAP: 46

CLOSING TIMES
Closed 25-26 December

Otter Amber, Sambrook's Wandle Ale and Adnams Broadside

PRINCE OF WALES

Quirky decoration and a wide-ranging menu

Idiosyncratic decoration and good food make this substantial Victorian pub stand out. Its deep green walls are lined with tankards and its ceiling is covered in playing cards; head further in and you'll find the dining room in the old billiard room. Here lights are fashioned from antlers and its walls are decorated with vintage farming photos and a little taxidermy; mind you, it's so dimly lit you'll be pushed see anything. The kitchen is out to impress and its daily changing menu reads well, ranging from rabbit and pork terrine to Cornish sardines and even a plate of Spanish delicacies. Although the ingredients are top-notch, the plates are sometimes a little too busy which perhaps explains the popularity of the simpler bar menu.

WANDSWORTH
138 Upper Richmond Rd,
PUTNEY, SW15 2SP
Tel.: (020)87881552
Website: www.princeofwalesputney.co.uk

⊖ **East Putney.** - On-street parking.

PRICES
Meals: a la carte £ 25/39

MAP: 47

CLOSING TIMES
Closed 23 December-1 January and Monday lunch except bank holidays

Timothy Taylor Landlord, Harvey's Sussex Best and Purity Mad Goose

GRAZING GOAT

Sedate dining room and generous portions

The Portman Estate, owners of some serious real estate in these parts and keen to raise the profile of their investment, encouraged an experienced pub operator more at home in Chelsea and Belgravia to venture a little further north and take over the old Bricklayers Arms. Renamed in homage to a past Lady Portman (who grazed goats in a field where the pub now stands as she was allergic to cows' milk), it is now a smart city facsimile of a country pub. It's first-come-first-served in the bar but you can book in the upstairs dining room. Pub classics are the order of the day, such as pies or Castle of Mey steaks, and Suffolk chicken is cooked on the rotisserie. The eight bedrooms are nicely furnished, with their bathrooms resembling Nordic saunas.

WESTMINSTER
6 New Quebec St,
REGENT'S PARK AND MARYLEBONE, W1H 7RQ
Tel.: (020)77247243
Website: www.thegrazinggoat.co.uk

⊖ **Marble Arch.** - On-street parking.

PRICES
Meals: a la carte £ 31/41

8 rooms:
£ 205

MAP: 48

CLOSING TIMES
Open daily
booking essential at dinner

Florence Brewery Ales

NEWMAN STREET TAVERN

Well run and a great atmosphere on both floors

Provided it isn't preceded by "ye" and "olde", there's something very comforting about the word "tavern". The experienced foursome behind Newman Street Tavern chose the word deliberately as they wanted to create a genuinely warm and welcoming place for customers to come and celebrate British food - and they got it spot on. The menu has been thoughtfully compiled and, with its soused Cornish anchovies, Blackface lamb, game tea, and Banbury cakes, is instantly appealing. There are no shortcuts in the kitchen: they do their own butchery, smoke their own fish, work closely with their suppliers and take issues of sustainability seriously. You can eat in the bustle of the bar or the charming and more sedate first floor dining room.

WESTMINSTER
48 Newman St,
REGENT'S PARK AND MARYLEBONE, W1T 1QQ
Tel.: (020)36671445
Website: www.newmanstreettavern.co.uk

⊖ **Goodge Street.** - On-street parking.

PRICES
Meals: £ 20 and a la carte £ 24/42

MAP: 49

CLOSING TIMES
Closed 24 December, 1 January,
Sunday dinner and bank holidays

Mighty Oak Oscar Wilde,
Meantime Ales and Shepherd
Neame Ales

ONLY RUNNING FOOTMAN

Stay on the busy ground floor for pub classics

Apparently the owners added 'only' to the title when they found out that theirs was the only pub in the land called 'The Running Footman'. Spread over several levels, it offers cookery demonstrations and private dinners along with its two floors of dining. Downstairs is where the action usually is, with its menu offering pub classics from steak sandwiches to fishcakes, but you can't book here and it's always packed. Upstairs is where you'll find a surprisingly formal dining room and here they do take reservations. Its menu is far more ambitious and European in its influence but the best dishes are still the simpler ones, with desserts a strength. You can't help feeling that you would be having a lot more fun below stairs, though.

WESTMINSTER
5 Charles St,
MAYFAIR, W1J 5DF
Tel.: (020)74992988
Website: www.therunningfootmanmayfair.com

⊖ **Green Park.** - On-street parking.

PRICES
Meals: £ 35 and a la carte £ 20/49

MAP: 50

CLOSING TIMES
Open daily

Wells Bombardier, Greene King IPA and Young's Bitter

THE ORANGE

As delightful as its façade suggests

The former home of the Orange Brewery is a handsome pub that's as charming as its stucco-fronted façade suggests. The locals will no doubt have filled the bar, where the wood-burning oven is quite a feature, but it's still worth trying your luck to get one of the tables here or in the adjacent room; if you book ahead you'll be upstairs which is just as pleasantly decorated but a little more sedate. There's a clear Mediterranean bias to the menu which also includes plenty of salads along with spelt or wheat based pizzas which come with some original toppings; there are also roasts on a Sunday and pies for the traditionalists. Unusually for a London pub, there are bedrooms upstairs: these are stylish and comfortable.

WESTMINSTER
37 Pimlico Rd,
VICTORIA, SW1W 8NE
Tel.: (020)78819844
Website: www.theorange.co.uk

⊖ **Sloane Square.** - On-street parking.

PRICES
Meals: a la carte £ 28/42

4 rooms:
£ 205/240

MAP: 51

CLOSING TIMES
Open daily

Meantime Ales and Adnams Ales

PANTECHNICON

Handsome Georgian pub with upstairs dining room

It may be the very antithesis of the spit 'n' sawdust pub, but The Pantechnicon is still a very welcoming and busy local. The brightly run ground floor is crammed with tables and works on a first-come-first-served basis; upstairs you'll find a far more formal, Georgian style dining room and there's even a top floor cocktail bar - this is Belgravia after all. Wisely, the same menu is served throughout - an appealing mix of the refined and the comforting. Castle of Mey 28-day aged steaks and salt and chilli squid are the two most popular choices; home-smoked salmon, burgers and fish pie are also done well. The name comes from the horse-drawn wagons that once transported the belongings of locals to and from a repository on Motcomb Street.

WESTMINSTER
10 Motcomb St,
BELGRAVIA, SW1X 8LA
Tel.: (020)77306074
Website: www.thepantechnicon.com

⊖ **Knightsbridge.** - On-street parking.

PRICES
Meals: a la carte £ 29/50

MAP: 52

CLOSING TIMES
Closed 25 December
booking advisable

Head in the Hat Brewery
Topee

PORTMAN

Head upstairs and order a sharing plate

When it went by the name of The Masons Arms this pub was widely known for its gruesome history. It was here that the condemned, on their way to Tyburn Tree gallows, would take their last drink, which purportedly led to the phrase "one for the road". Reincarnated as The Portman, the pub these days boasts a less disreputable clientele who are more attracted by the quality of the cooking. Food is served all day and you can choose to eat in the busy ground floor bar or in the unexpectedly formal upstairs dining room, all thick-pile carpet and starched tablecloths. Fortunately, the style of food remains thoroughly down-to-earth and satisfying and is accompanied by a well-organised wine list and an interesting selection of cocktails.

WESTMINSTER
51 Upper Berkeley St,
REGENT'S PARK AND MARYLEBONE, W1H 7QW
Tel.: (020)77238996
Website: www.theportmanmarylebone.com
⊖ **Marble Arch.** - On-street parking.

PRICES
Meals: £ 32/38 and a la carte £ 20/48

MAP: 53

CLOSING TIMES
Open daily

Rebellion Ales

PRINCE ALFRED & FORMOSA DINING ROOM

Rustic food in dining room; great pub attached

The Prince Alfred is a wonderful example of a classic Victorian pub and its period features include ornate tiles, plate glass, panels and snugs. Unfortunately, the eating is done in the Formosa Dining Room extension on the side but at least it's a lively room and the open kitchen adds to the general bonhomie. There's more than a rustic edge to the appealing menu which will please all traditionalists; the mature steaks, pork belly and sticky toffee pudding are perennials but there are also dishes geared to those whose tastes are a tad more continental, such as sea bream with couscous and peppers. The service team could perhaps try revealing a little more personality but prices are kept realistic and the place still feels like a local.

WESTMINSTER, 5A Formosa St,
BAYSWATER AND MAIDA VALE, W9 1EE
Tel.: (020)72863287
Website: www.theprincealfred.com

⊖ **Warwick Avenue.** - Parking by Warwick Avenue station (2min on foot).

PRICES
Meals: a la carte £ 24/41

MAP: 54

CLOSING TIMES
Open daily

Young's Bitter and Wells Bombardier

THOMAS CUBITT

There's certainly no spit 'n' sawdust here

The Thomas Cubitt is a pub of two halves: on the ground floor it's perennially busy and you can't book which means that if you haven't arrived by 7pm then you're too late to get a table. However, you can reserve a table upstairs, in a dining room that's a model of civility and tranquillity. Here, service comes courtesy of a young team where the girls are chatty and the men unafraid of corduroy. Downstairs you get fish and chips; here you get pan-fried fillet of brill with oyster beignet and truffled chips. The cooking is certainly skilled, quite elaborate in its construction and prettily presented. So, take your pick: upstairs can get a little pricey but is ideal for entertaining the in-laws; if out with friends then crowd in downstairs.

WESTMINSTER
44 Elizabeth St,
VICTORIA, SW1W 9PA
Tel.: (020)77306060
Website: www.thethomascubitt.co.uk

⊖ **Sloane Square.** - Parking meters in Elizabeth Street.

PRICES
Meals: a la carte £ 28/42

MAP: 55

CLOSING TIMES
Open daily
booking essential

Adnams Ales

TRUSCOTT ARMS N

Rejuvenated by a husband and wife team

A Victorian pub not so much revamped but resuscitated and restored. There's nothing quite like private ownership for putting the love back into a pub and the husband and wife team who took over this big old place invested considerable sums and are now deservedly reaping the benefits. There's a lovely pewter-topped bar where the locals gather and the pub is getting known too for the regularly changing local artwork it displays, particularly in the upstairs dining room which comes with a beautifully intricate corniced ceiling. The kitchen shows obvious ambition and uses fairly modern techniques to produce dishes featuring quite a number of ingredients and some interesting flavour combinations.

WESTMINSTER
55 Shirland Rd,
BAYSWATER, W9 2JD
Tel.: (020)72669198
Website: www.thetruscottarms.com

⊖ **Warwick Avenue.** - On-street parking.

PRICES
Meals: £ 32 (dinner) and a la carte £ 24/43

MAP: 56

CLOSING TIMES
Open daily

Redemption Big Chief, Truman's Blindside and Sambrook's Wandle Ale

9
ALDWYCH
627 DYE
19
Finsbury Park Station
N171 PYK

NORTH EAST

England

© J. Arnold / hemis.fr

This region cradles some of England's wildest and most dramatic scenery typified by Northumberland National Park, a landscape of rolling purple moorlands and roaring rivers bursting with salmon and trout. Kielder Forest's mighty wilderness has been called "the country's most tranquil spot" while Bill Bryson has waxed lyrical upon the glories of Durham Cathedral. Those who love the wind in their hair are equally effusive about the eleven-mile footpath that accompanies the pounding waves of Durham's Heritage Coast; further north are the long, dune-backed beaches of Northumberland. Rambling across the region is Hadrian's Wall, 73 miles of iconic Roman history, while a modern slant on architectural celebrity is proffered by the Millennium Bridge, BALTIC Centre and Angel of the North.

The famously bracing air whets hearty appetites for local Cheviot lamb, Coquetdale cheese or Holy Island oysters. And what could be more redolent of the North East than a breakfast of Craster kippers?

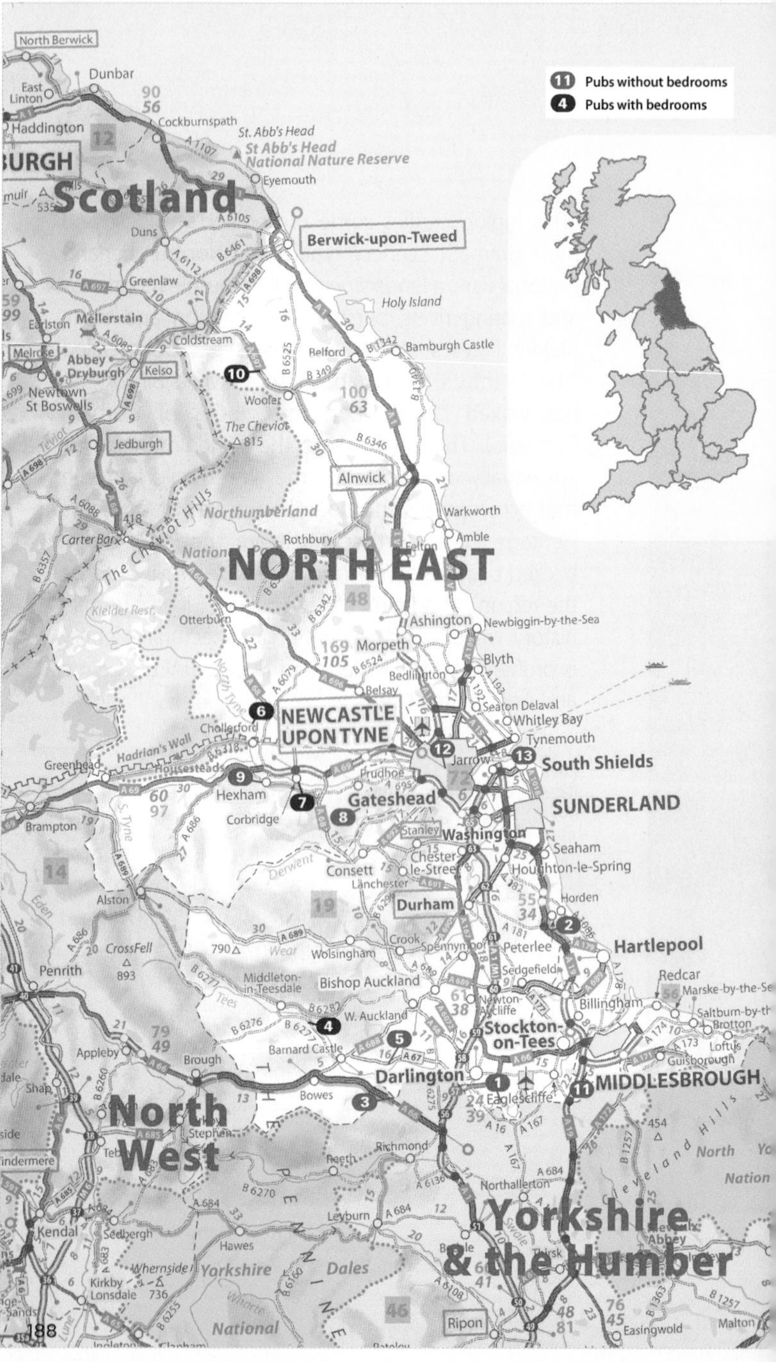
Pubs without bedrooms
Pubs with bedrooms
North Berwick
Dunbar
East Linton
Haddington
Cockburnspath
St. Abb's Head
St Abb's Head National Nature Reserve
Eyemouth
Scotland
Duns
Berwick-upon-Tweed
Greenlaw
Holy Island
Earlston
Mellerstain
Coldstream
Belford
Bamburgh Castle
Melrose
Abbey
Dryburgh
Kelso
Newtown St Boswells
Wooler
The Cheviot
Jedburgh
Alnwick
Warkworth
Amble
Northumberland
Carter Bar
The Cheviot Hills
Rothbury
Felton
NORTH EAST
Kielder Rest.
Otterburn
Ashington
Newbiggin-by-the-Sea
Morpeth
Blyth
Bedlington
Belsay
Seaton Delaval
Whitley Bay
NEWCASTLE UPON TYNE
Chollerford
Tynemouth
Hadrian's Wall
Greenhead
Housesteads
Jarrow
South Shields
Prudhoe
Hexham
Gateshead
SUNDERLAND
Corbridge
Brampton
Stanley
Washington
Seaham
Consett
Chester-le-Street
Houghton-le-Spring
Lanchester
Alston
Durham
Horden
Crook
Spennymoor
Peterlee
Hartlepool
Cross Fell
Wolsingham
Penrith
Middleton-in-Teesdale
Bishop Auckland
Sedgefield
Redcar
Marske-by-the-Sea
Newton Aycliffe
Billingham
Saltburn-by-the-Sea
W. Auckland
Brotton
Stockton-on-Tees
Loftus
Appleby
Barnard Castle
Guisborough
Brough
Darlington
MIDDLESBROUGH
Shap
Bowes
Eaglescliffe
North West
Stephen
Richmond
Reeth
Cleveland Hills
North York Moors National Park
Northallerton
Kendal
Sedbergh
Leyburn
Yorkshire & the Humber
Hawes
Bedale
Thirsk
Whernside
Yorkshire Dales National Park
Kirkby Lonsdale
Ripon
Easingwold
Malton

BAY HORSE

Everything from bread to ice cream is homemade

Set on a long grassy street in an attractive village, this early 18C creamwashed pub is framed by colourful planters and hanging baskets, and boasts a pleasant rear terrace and garden. Drinkers and diners mingle amongst antique chairs, low stools and leather banquettes in the open-fired bar area and the relaxed, informal atmosphere continues through into the dining room. For special occasions the private first floor room definitely adds some style, with its 20 foot Victorian table and adjoining lounge. Menus offer something for everyone, featuring classics such as moules marinière, daube of beef or omelette Arnold Bennett, as well as familiar pub favourites. Dishes range in their presentation from simple and rustic to modern and intricate.

45 The Green,
HURWORTH ON TEES, DL2 2AA
Tel.: (01325)720663
Website: www.thebayhorsehurworth.com

5.5 mi south of Darlington; signed off A 167;
in the middle of the village. Parking.

PRICES
Meals: £ 14 (lunch)/25 and
a la carte £ 28/50

MAP: 1

CLOSING TIMES
Closed 25-26 December and
Sunday dinner

Harviestoun Bitter & Twisted
and Roosters Yankee

CASTLE EDEN INN (N)

Experienced owners know their customers well

A former coaching inn of indeterminate age, on what was formerly the main road to London: local gossip says that Dick Turpin was once tied up outside while his captors enjoyed some refreshment – torture indeed! The experienced owners know their customers well and offer a wide choice of dishes, from classics like steak and ale pie to smoked cheese soufflé or pork belly with black pudding, and the 'monthly specials' menu offers great value. The central bar splits the place in two: on one side is the lounge where you can drink, eat or watch TV from the comfort of a sofa. On the other, is a rather smart restaurant with dressed tables; head to the far end – which used to be the stables – as it offers more character, especially in the evening.

Stockton Rd,
CASTLE EDEN, TS27 4SD
Tel.: (01429)835137
Website: www.castleedeninn.com

Just off A 19, 1 mi south of Peterlee. Parking.

PRICES
Meals: £ 18 (lunch) and a la carte £ 22/46

MAP: 2

CLOSING TIMES
Open daily

Timothy Taylor Landlord, Wylam Gold Tankard and Cameron's Castle Eden Ale

OAK TREE INN

Charming little place run by a husband & wife team

They say good things come in small packages and that's definitely the case with this charming whitewashed pub. Found on the main street of a small hamlet, it consists of a single room with a proper old-fashioned counter, six wooden tables flanked by green settles and a bench table for the locals. Claire - who both serves the drinks and delivers the food - provides a warm welcome at the bar, while behind the scenes in the kitchen, Alastair single-handedly holds the fort. The short menu takes on a fairly formal format, offering generous portions of hearty, flavoursome cooking with a rustic British style and some subtle modern twists: you might find confit belly pork, onion and thyme tart, turbot with orange or Best End of lamb with artichokes.

HUTTON MAGNA, DL11 7HH
Tel.: (01833)627371
Website: www.theoaktreehutton.co.uk

7 mi southeast of Barnard Castle off A 66. Parking.

PRICES
Meals: a la carte £ 30/43

MAP: 3

CLOSING TIMES
Closed 24-27 and 31 December, 1 January and Monday dinner only
booking essential

Wells Bombardier and Timothy Taylor Landlord

ROSE AND CROWN

Georgian inn overlooking three village greens

The Robinsons, who own the nearby Headlam Hall hotel, took over the running of this delightful Georgian inn when Chris and Alison Davy sold up after 23 years - but as the majority of the charming, chatty and helpful staff have remained, the transition was relatively smooth. The pub occupies a very pleasant spot overlooking three village greens and comes with a wonderfully characterful bar filled with horse brasses. On its other side is the somewhat misnamed 'brasserie', which offers a reassuringly familiar menu as well as afternoon tea, but most guests prefer the wood-panelled dining room with its list of classics. Bedrooms are individually decorated and well-equipped; those after more privacy and peace should ask for one in the annexe.

ROMALDKIRK, DL12 9EB
Tel.: (01833)650213
Website: www.rose-and-crown.co.uk

3.5 mi south of Middleton-on-Teesdale, on B 6177, next to church on village green. Parking.

PRICES
Meals: a la carte £ 22/40

14 rooms:
£ 95/200

MAP: 4

CLOSING TIMES
Open daily

Black Sheep Best Bitter and Thwaites Wainwrights

BRIDGEWATER ARMS (N)

Choose one of their fish dishes

A copperplate alphabet edging the ceiling and the cast list from a 1957 production of Jack and the Beanstalk are reminders that this traditional pub spent the first hundred years of its life as the village school. When chef Paul Grundy's lease on the brewery-owned pub ran out after several successful years, he was faced with a move. Spotting an opportunity, one of the pub's regulars decided to buy it himself, and to the locals' delight, reinstated Paul as chef. There's local beef and game on the menu along with the legendary cheddar cheese and spinach soufflé, but it's fish and seafood that the chef is known for, so let that lead your choice. Dishes are unashamedly classic, accurately executed and extremely satisfying.

WINSTON, DL2 3RN
Tel.: (01325)730302
Website: www.thebridgewaterarms.com

Between Barnard Castle and Darlington just off A 67. Parking.

PRICES
Meals: a la carte £ 25/50

MAP: 5

CLOSING TIMES
Closed 25-26 December, Sunday and Monday

Timothy Taylor Landlord and Greene King Ales

BARRASFORD ARMS

At the heart of the local community

In the heart of the Northumbrian countryside, close to Kielder Water and Hadrian's Wall, sits this family-run 19C stone inn, providing an ideal base for exploring the North Tyne Valley. Retaining its traditional character, the pub provides the perfect home from home. The cosy fire is a huge draw, as are the regular vegetable, darts and quoits competitions, but the star attraction is the food. Menus differ between lunch and dinner; the former being a touch less formal. Local rib-eye is a permanent feature, as is the twice-baked cheese soufflé, and many come for the local game, which is handled deftly. The owner works closely with his suppliers to ensure that the ingredients remain tip-top. Comfortable bedrooms are sensibly priced.

BARRASFORD, NE48 4AA
Tel.: (01434)681237
Website: www.barrasfordarms.co.uk

7 mi north of Hexham signed off A 6079. Parking.

PRICES
Meals: a la carte £ 23/36

7 rooms:
£ 50/87

MAP: 6

CLOSING TIMES
Closed 25-26 December, Sunday dinner, Monday lunch and bank holidays

Wylam Gold Tankard, Cumberland Corby Ale and High House Brewery Nels Best

DUKE OF WELLINGTON

Head to the terrace for Tyne Valley views

Dating from the 1823 - and named after the Duke, who was busy winning battles in France at this time - this pub is reputedly the oldest licensed premises in the county. Despite being tucked away in a tiny hamlet, it's clear that a good few people know about it, and when you're out on the terrace taking in the valley view, it'll soon become one of your favourite spots too. Within its stone walls is a smart, modern country style bar and a more formal dining room. Breakfast features brioche French toast and local eggs Benedict, and is followed by a good value set lunch and evening à la carte, where pub classics sit alongside more adventurous dishes such as saddle of roe deer. Bedrooms are stylish and luxurious and have characterful exposed beams.

Newton,
CORBRIDGE, NE43 7UL
Tel.: (01661)844446
Website: www.thedukeofwellingtoninn.co.uk

3.5 mi from Corbridge signposted off A 69. Parking.

PRICES
Meals: £ 18 (weekdays) and a la carte £ 22/36

7 rooms:
£ 70/120

MAP: 7

CLOSING TIMES
Open daily

Wylam Collingwood, Timothy Taylor Landlord and Hadrian Border Tyneside Blond

FEATHERS INN

The bookshelves are crammed with cookbooks

All three rooms in this characterful village centre pub have their bookshelves crammed with cookbooks and their walls filled with photos of those who supply their produce, both of which suggest that this is a place which takes its food seriously. The kitchen certainly does things properly, whether that's making its own black pudding or preparing the popular game dishes. The food is generous in both flavour and size and seasonality plays a large part - the menu changes on a daily basis and it's worth exploring the selection of local cheeses. The pub has a warm and welcoming feel thanks to its large central fireplace and stove, and feels genuinely part of the local community. It also offers really nice views of the surrounding countryside.

HEDLEY ON THE HILL, NE43 7SW
Tel.: (01661)843607
Website: www.thefeathers.net

6 mi north of Consett by A 694, B 6309 and minor road. Parking.

PRICES
Meals: a la carte £ 19/30

MAP: 8

CLOSING TIMES
Closed first 2 weeks January, Monday except bank holidays and Sunday dinner

Mordue Workie Ticket, Wylam Gold Tankard and Consett Ale Red Dust

RAT INN

Relax among the arbours in the multi-level garden

There are several suggestions as to how this 18C drovers' inn got its name - theories include rat catchers using it as a meeting place, a large rat once residing here and it being home to the local snitch during the Jacobite rebellion. Nobody actually knows the answer, so just sit back and enjoy the pleasant Tyne valley views. Situated in a small hillside hamlet, it's the perfect place to escape the rat race of the city, with its multi-levelled garden boasting arbours and picnic sets, and a traditional interior displaying wooden beams and an open range. The daily blackboard menu is concise but covers a good range of dishes, from pub classics like cottage pie to rib of beef for two to share. Produce is fresh, good quality and locally sourced.

Anick,
HEXHAM, NE46 4LN
Tel.: (01434)602814
Website: www.theratinn.com

1.75 mi northeast of Hexham signposted off A 6079. Parking.

PRICES
Meals: a la carte £ 19/38

MAP: 9

CLOSING TIMES
Closed 25 December, Monday except bank holidays and Sunday dinner

Wylam Gold Tankard, Hexhamshire Brewery Shire Bitter and Timothy Taylor Landlord

RED LION INN

Catch up with the locals and the latest sports

This classic stone pub started life as a mid-18C drovers' inn before becoming a stop-off point for the mail stagecoach between 1785 and 1835. It really is the heart of the village, so if you'd rather not catch up with the locals and the latest sporting events, head for the open-fired dining room instead of the bar. The menu has a traditional feel and offers plenty of choice, showcasing produce from both England and across the border. Dishes range from a prawn cocktail to scallops with black pudding; the Shetland mussels are not to be missed and the hearty homemade burger has now become a cult dish. Specials are chalked up the board and if you make it to pudding, you'll be rewarded with a tasty nursery selection. Bedrooms are fittingly homely.

Main Rd,
MILFIELD, NE71 6JD
Tel.: (01668)216224
Website: www.redlionmilfield.co.uk

7 mi southeast of Coldstream by A 697. In the village centre. Parking.

PRICES
Meals: a la carte £ 16/30

2 rooms:
£ 40/70

MAP: 10

CLOSING TIMES
Closed 1 January and 25 December
booking advisable

Black Sheep Best Bitter,
Wylam Collingwood and
Scottish Borders Foxy Blonde

CHADWICKS INN

The live acoustic sessions are a hit

Originally named The Pathfinder, this pub dates back over 200 years and was where the Spitfire pilots used to stop for a noggin before flying out on their missions. It's the only pub in the village, so you'll find regulars nursing their pints alongside those out for an evening meal. In warmer weather find a spot in the garden or on the sheltered patio area; in winter, head for the large open-fired bar or either of the two dining rooms with their smartly laid polished tables. The main à la carte features ambitious, intricate dishes, while a bistro menu of simpler offerings is available at lunch and in the early evening. The live acoustic sessions are becoming popular, as are the wine and tapas evenings. Service is friendly and fittingly formal.

High Ln,
MALTBY, TS8 0BG
Tel.: (01642)590300
Website: www.chadwicksinnmaltby.co.uk

7 mi south of Middlesborough by A 19 and A 1045. Parking at rear.

PRICES
Meals: a la carte £ 28/41

MAP: 11

CLOSING TIMES
Closed 26 December, 1 January and Monday except bank holidays
booking advisable

Wainstone Ales

BROAD CHARE

A choice of over 40 ales - some custom-made

Owned by Terry Laybourne and set next to its sister operation Caffé Vivo, Broad Chare really hit the ground running. It's located on the quayside, close to the Millennium Bridge and, with its 'Proper Beer, Proper Food' motto, is a hit with the locals. The snug ground floor with its low level stool seating offers a choice of over 40 ales - some custom-made for the pub - and a bar snack menu featuring the likes of scotch eggs, cauliflower with curried mayonnaise and deep-fried pig's ears. Dining also takes place upstairs, where, along with this affectionately named 'Geordie Tapas', you'll find everything from an appealing 'on toast' selection to hearty daily specials such as steak and kidney pudding - all followed by tasty nursery puddings.

25 Broad Chare,
NEWCASTLE UPON TYNE, NE1 3DQ
Tel.: (0191)2112144
Website: www.thebroadchare.co.uk

Close to Millennium Bridge in Quayside area of city centre.
On-street parking.

PRICES
Meals: a la carte £ 22/35

MAP: 12

CLOSING TIMES
Closed 25 December and Sunday dinner
booking advisable

Wylam Brewery Writer's Block, Timothy Taylor Landlord and Mordue Workie Ticket

STAITH HOUSE (N)

Cosy, quayside pub serving good value food

When you're dining on a fishing quay (or staith) with the smell of sea in the air, it makes sense to bypass pub fare like burger and chips - nice though it is - and plump for something brought in by the fishing fleets... perhaps some halibut, sea bass, cod or shellfish. Dishes change almost daily depending on the catch and cooking is robust, tasty and well-priced. The pub is cosy and simply furnished, with an open kitchen and décor that makes many a reference to the pub's location, with portholes, ship's lights and nautical charts. The music is loud and the service, although friendly, can be disorganised - but it just seems to add to the appeal. Check out the enormous whale's jaw bone outside the back door before you leave.

57 Low Lights,
NORTH SHIELDS, NE30 1JA
Tel.: (0191)2708441
Website: www.thestaithhouse.co.uk

On the fish quay. Pay and display parking adjacent.

PRICES
Meals: £ 10 (lunch and early dinner)
and a la carte £ 18/41

MAP: 13

CLOSING TIMES
Closed 25 December, 1 January and Sunday dinner
booking essential at dinner

Theakston Lightfoot and guest ales

NORTH WEST

England

© R. Harding / hemis.fr

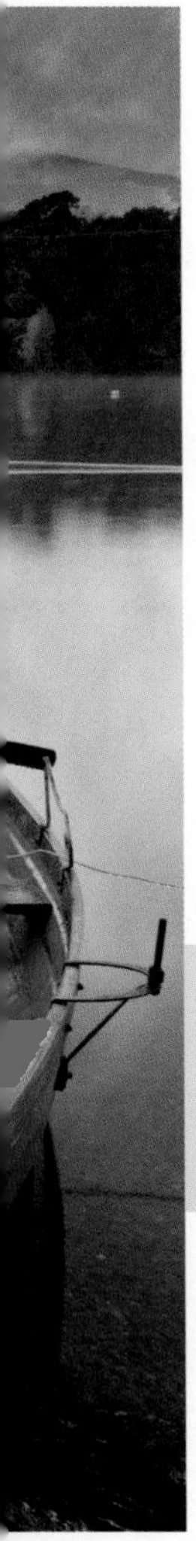

Energised by Liverpool's swagger as 2008's European City of Culture, the north west feels like a region reborn. Dovetailed by the confident sophistication of a reinvigorated Manchester, the country's oldest industrial heartland boasts an impressive cultural profile. And yet arty urban centres are a million miles away from the rural grandeur of the region: trails and paths criss-cross the area all the way from the Solway Firth to Cheshire. Cumbria is a walker's paradise: from Hadrian's Wall to the glories of the Lake District, and along the vast shoreline of Morecambe Bay with its rich gathering of waders and wildfowl, there's a vivid contrast in scenery. The architectural landscape of the region covers the ages, too. Lancaster Castle reverberates to the footsteps of ancient soldiers, while Chester's walled city of medieval buildings is a true gem.

Blackpool is now Europe's biggest seaside resort while the flavour of the north west is hotpot, black pudding and Morecambe Bay shrimps.

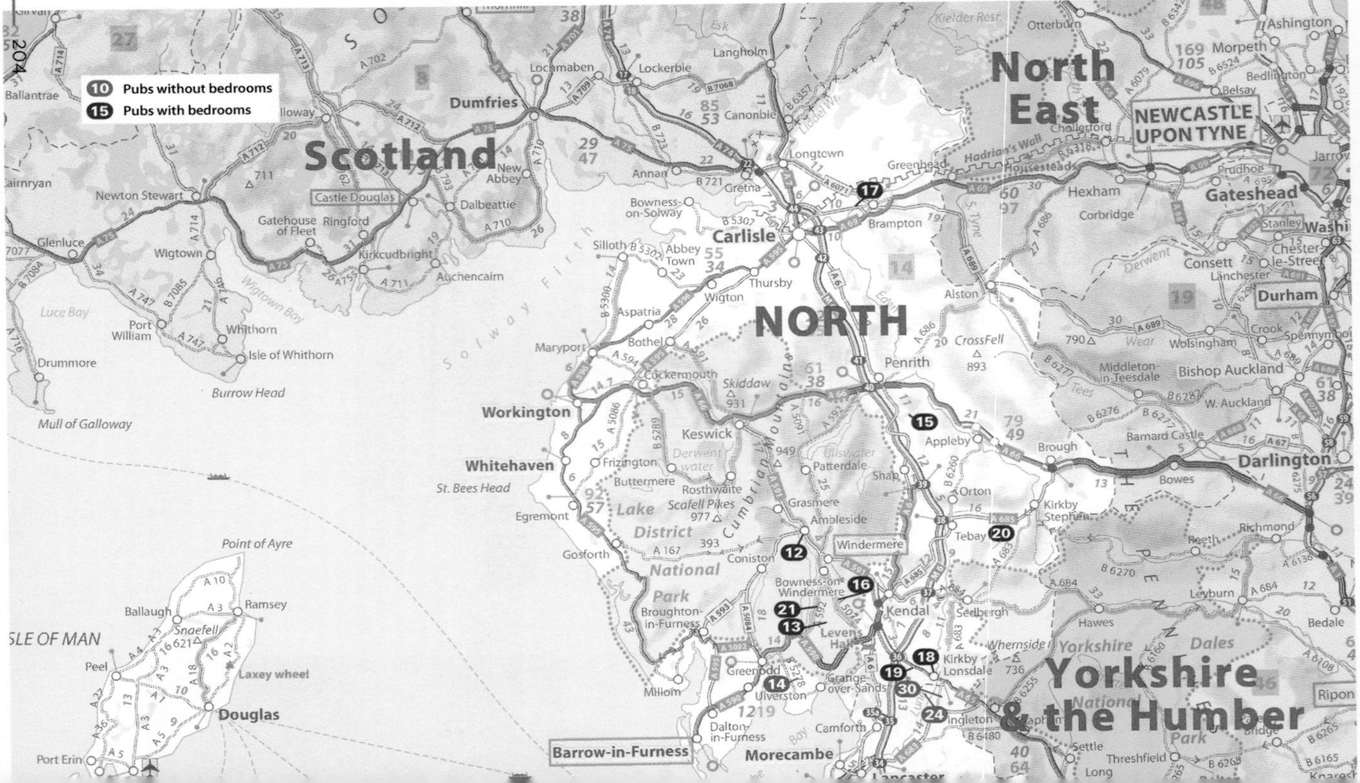
10 Pubs without bedrooms
15 Pubs with bedrooms
Scotland
North East
NORTH
Yorkshire & the Humber
NEWCASTLE UPON TYNE
Gateshead
Durham
Darlington
Carlisle
Workington
Whitehaven
Barrow-in-Furness
Morecambe
Douglas
Dumfries
Castle Douglas
Windermere
Ripon
Lake District National Park
Yorkshire Dales National Park
Cumbrian Mountains
Solway Firth
ISLE OF MAN
Ashington
Morpeth
Bedlington
Belsay
Otterburn
Chollerford
Hadrian's Wall
Housesteads
Hexham
Corbridge
Prudhoe
Jarrow
Stanley
Chester-le-Street
Consett
Lanchester
Crook
Spennymoor
Wolsingham
Bishop Auckland
W. Auckland
Middleton-in-Teesdale
Barnard Castle
Bowes
Richmond
Reeth
Leyburn
Bedale
Hawes
Settle
Threshfield
Long
Kielder Resr.
Greenhead
Brampton
Alston
CrossFell
Penrith
Appleby
Brough
Kirkby Stephen
Orton
Tebay
Shap
Kendal
Sedbergh
Kirkby Lonsdale
Whernside
Ingleton
Carnforth
Lancaster
Grange-over-Sands
Levens Hall
Bowness-on-Windermere
Ambleside
Grasmere
Patterdale
Coniston
Ulverston
Greenodd
Dalton-in-Furness
Broughton-in-Furness
Millom
Gosforth
Egremont
St. Bees Head
Rosthwaite
Scafell Pikes
Buttermere
Frizington
Keswick
Derwent water
Ullswater
Skiddaw
Cockermouth
Bothel
Maryport
Aspatria
Silloth
Abbey Town
Wigton
Thursby
Bowness-on-Solway
Gretna
Longtown
Canonbie
Langholm
Lockerbie
Lochmaben
Annan
New Abbey
Dalbeattie
Auchencairn
Kirkcudbright
Ringford
Gatehouse of Fleet
Newton Stewart
Wigtown
Wigtown Bay
Whithorn
Isle of Whithorn
Port William
Burrow Head
Glenluce
Luce Bay
Drummore
Mull of Galloway
Cairnryan
Ballantrae
Point of Ayre
Ramsey
Ballaugh
Snaefell
Laxey wheel
Peel
Port Erin

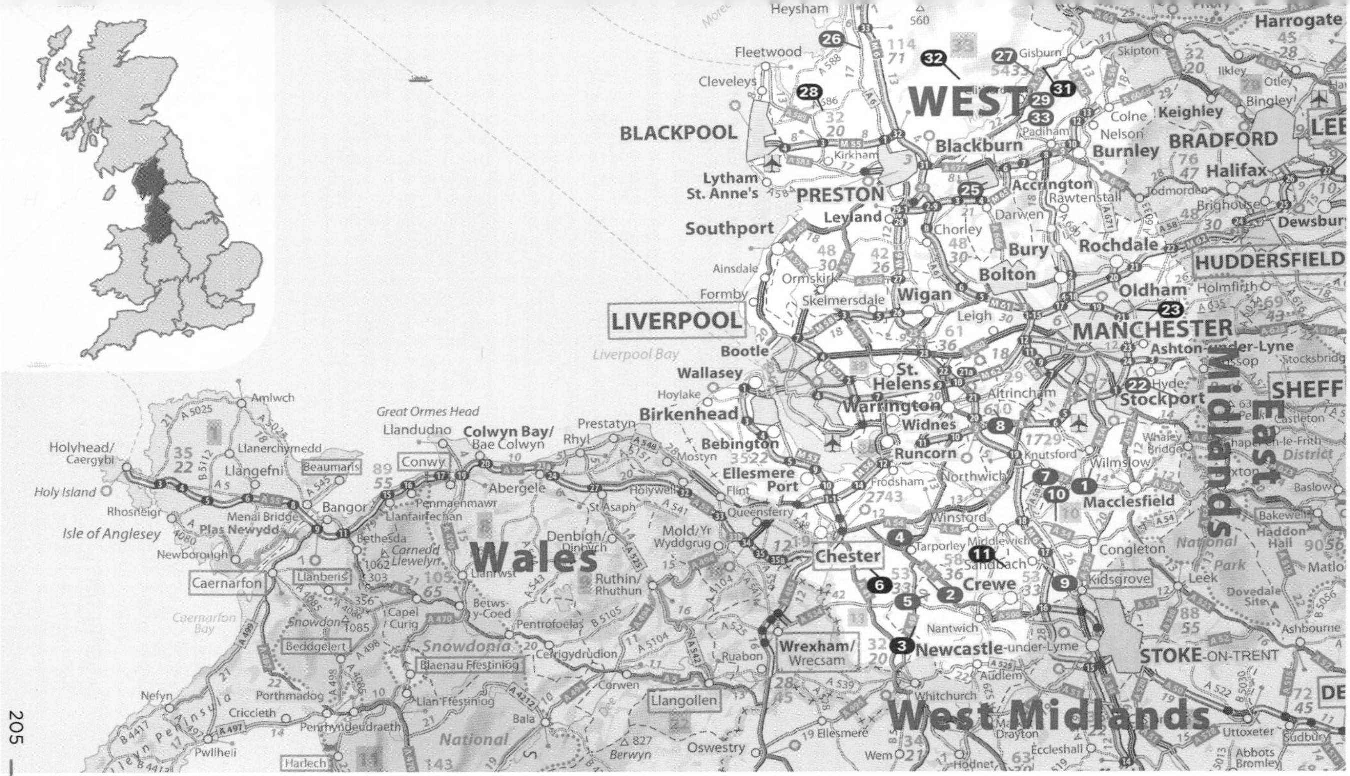
WEST
BLACKPOOL
PRESTON
LIVERPOOL
MANCHESTER
BRADFORD
HUDDERSFIELD
East Midlands
West Midlands
Wales
Harrogate
Heysham
Fleetwood
Cleveleys
Lytham St. Anne's
Southport
Ainsdale
Formby
Bootle
Wallasey
Hoylake
Birkenhead
Bebington
Ellesmere Port
Liverpool Bay
Skipton
Ilkley
Otley
Bingley
Keighley
Gisburn
Colne
Nelson
Burnley
Padiham
Blackburn
Kirkham
Accrington
Rawtenstall
Todmorden
Halifax
Brighouse
Dewsbury
Darwen
Chorley
Leyland
Bury
Rochdale
Bolton
Oldham
Holmfirth
Ormskirk
Skelmersdale
Wigan
Leigh
Ashton-under-Lyne
Stockport
Hyde
St. Helens
Warrington
Widnes
Runcorn
Altrincham
Knutsford
Wilmslow
Macclesfield
Northwich
Frodsham
Winsford
Middlewich
Tarporley
Sandbach
Chester
Crewe
Congleton
Kidsgrove
Nantwich
Newcastle-under-Lyme
STOKE-ON-TRENT
Leek
Wrexham/ Wrecsam
Audlem
Whitchurch
Ellesmere
Wem
Oswestry
Eccleshall
Uttoxeter
Ashbourne
Holyhead/ Caergybi
Holy Island
Isle of Anglesey
Amlwch
Llanerchymedd
Llangefni
Beaumaris
Menai Bridge
Plas Newydd
Rhosneigr
Newborough
Bangor
Caernarfon
Caernarfon Bay
Llanberis
Snowdon
Beddgelert
Great Ormes Head
Llandudno
Colwyn Bay/ Bae Colwyn
Conwy
Abergele
Rhyl
Prestatyn
Mostyn
Holywell
Flint
St Asaph
Denbigh/ Dinbych
Mold/Yr Wyddgrug
Queensferry
Ruthin/ Rhuthun
Llanrwst
Betws-y-Coed
Capel Curig
Snowdonia
Blaenau Ffestiniog
Llan Ffestiniog
Penmaenmawr
Llanfairfechan
Bethesda
Carnedd Llewelyn
Pentrefoelas
Cerrigydrudion
Corwen
Llangollen
Ruabon
Bala
Berwyn
National
Porthmadog
Penrhyndeudraeth
Criccieth
Pwllheli
Nefyn
Harlech
Lleyn Peninsula
Macclesfield
Whaley Bridge
Castleton
Bakewell
Haddon Hall
Baslow
Dovedale Site
Abbots Bromley
Sudbury
SHEFF
LEE
DE

WIZARD INN

200 years old and full of charm

With its flag floors, low wooden beams and open fires, this 200 year old pub is full of character and charm; its four rooms boasting a shabby-chic style and a homely, cosy feel. Being dog friendly and next to the famous Alderley Edge escarpment, it attracts its fair share of walkers, and its mix of drinkers and diners - and the resulting vibrant atmosphere - make it feel like a proper pub. The menu is wide-ranging, offering sandwiches or fish and meat platters and pub favourites like pies or burgers, as well as more substantial dishes such as slow-braised ox cheek with mash and the occasional retro dish like chicken Kiev. Specials include market fish of the day and the early bird menu is great value. Service is charmingly attentive.

Macclesfield Rd,
ALDERLEY EDGE, SK10 4UB
Tel.: (01625)584000
Website: www.ainscoughs.co.uk

1.25 mi southeast of Alderley Edge on B 5087. Parking.

PRICES
Meals: £ 20 (weekday dinner)/35
and a la carte £ 20/46

MAP: 1

CLOSING TIMES
Closed 25 December

Thwaites Wainwright and Triple C and Storm Silk of Amnesia

YEW TREE INN

Look out for the themed evenings

Once inside this handsome, part red brick, part black and white timbered pub, you'll find it isn't as big as you first thought - but there's room enough for one and all, whether that's locals with pints gathered to organise the latest village events or diners attending one of the regular themed evenings. Find a seat in the central bar or in one of the smaller rooms boasting wood and quarry tile flooring, mahogany panels and open fires. Extensive menus offer local and homemade produce, with dishes ranging from fish pie to braised ox cheeks; while the black pudding salad, chips in dripping and Cheshire brie for two are must-tries. Come on a Friday to sample some lesser-known guest ales, accompanied by a small selection of British tapas dishes.

Long Ln,
SPURSTOW, Bunbury, CW6 9RD
Tel.: (01829)260274
Website: www.theyewtreebunbury.com

7.5 mi northwest of Nantwich by A 51, A 534 and A 49. Parking.

PRICES
Meals: a la carte £ 20/40

MAP: 2

CLOSING TIMES
Open daily

Stonehouse Station Bitter and guest ales

CHOLMONDELEY ARMS

Choose from over 200 types of gin!

The Cholmondeley Arms started life in 1862 as the eponymous estate's schoolhouse and details like school blackboards, an 'old school favourites' section on the menu and an ale called 'teacher's tipple' are a reminder that it spent more than a century as a place of learning. High vaulted ceilings and large windows let in lots of light, while roaring fires give the place a cosy, welcoming feel. The menu offers tasty, modern pub favourites like devilled lamb's kidneys on toast, stalker's venison pie or homemade lamb faggots. Cask beers come from within a 30 mile radius and gin-lovers will be in clover with over 200 to choose from, plus five types of tonic. Head to the Old Headmaster's House to sleep it all off in one of the 6 comfy bedrooms.

Wrenbury Rd,
CHOLMONDELEY, SY14 8HN
Tel.: (01829)720300
Website: www.cholmondeleyarms.co.uk

11 mi west of Nantwich by A51 and A 534 on A 49. Parking.

PRICES
Meals: a la carte £ 19/33

6 rooms:
£ 60/100

MAP: 3

CLOSING TIMES
Open daily

Weetwood Ales, Salopian Shropshire Gold and Tatton Best

FOX AND BARREL

There's a great terrace at the back

With wood-panelled walls filled with framed pictures and shelves lined with books, you could be mistaken for thinking you're in a Brunning and Price pub, but then that's probably because the owners have both worked for the group in the past. The front bar with its open log fire is very much the drinkers' domain, while the smart terrace and large garden, complete with vintage tractor, attract one and all. Menus change virtually daily and offer plenty of originality and interest; you might find twice-baked cheese soufflé followed by loin of venison with spiced red cabbage, alongside old favourites like fish and chips. Dishes are generously proportioned, neatly presented and sensibly priced - and there's a good list of wines by the glass too.

Foxbank,
COTEBROOK, CW6 9DZ
Tel.: (01829)760529
Website: www.foxandbarrel.co.uk

On A 49 northeast of Tarporley. Parking.

PRICES
Meals: a la carte £ 16/36

MAP: 4

CLOSING TIMES
Closed dinner 25-26 December and 1 January

Weetwood Eastgate Ale, Wincle Waller and Deuchars IPA

NAG'S HEAD N

The delightful garden even has a bowling green

Arguably the prettiest of the Ribble Valley Inns, this attractive timbered property sits within a peaceful hamlet. The garden is a delightful spot and comes complete with a bowling green for those who fancy a game, while inside exposed beams, tiled floors and open fires provide plenty of character, helped along by saddle-shaped stools and tables made from shotguns. Photos of local Cheshire producers line the walls - giving a clue as to the importance regional ingredients play - and a charcoal grill takes pride of place in the kitchen, so it's no surprise to find plenty of steaks among the classic dishes. The nearby Weetwood Brewery provides most of the real ales but you'll also find Thwaites 1629 - named after the year that the pub was built.

Long Ln,
HAUGHTON MOSS, CW6 9RN
Tel.: (01829)260265
Website: www.nagsheadhaughton.co.uk

5.5 mi Northwest of Nantwich signposted off A 534. Parking.

PRICES
Meals: a la carte £ 22/40

MAP: 5

CLOSING TIMES
Open daily

Weetwood Ales, Tatton Best and Thwaites 1629

PHEASANT INN

Look out across the Cheshire plains

This well-run, modern pub is set atop a sandstone escarpment, with views across the Cheshire Plains to Wrexham and Liverpool. Outside space is plentiful, with various terraces and a garden, while the interior feels fresh and clean with its reclaimed beams and open fires. The snug is quite cosy, the dining room more formal – and the window tables are the first to be nabbed in either. The seasonal menu focuses on simple pub classics like ale, steak and mushroom pie, with some interesting specials, nibbles and deli boards to complement. The no-nonsense cooking has clear, gutsy flavours and the smartly dressed staff are keen to please. Spacious, beamed bedrooms are set in the main building; more modern rooms with views are located in the barn.

HIGHER BURWARDSLEY, CH3 9PF
Tel.: (01829)770434
Website: www.thepheasantinn.co.uk

2.5 mi southeast of Tattenhall. Parking.

PRICES
Meals: a la carte £ 20/42

12 rooms:
£ 100/160

MAP: 6

CLOSING TIMES
Open daily

Weetwood Ales

BELLS OF PEOVER

Flavoursome food and knowledgeable service

So, why does this refurbished 16C former coaching inn have the Stars and Stripes flying over it? Because, apparently, Generals Eisenhower and Patton were stationed nearby and were regulars. And the Bells? No, not from the church tower but the name of a family who once owned it. These days the pub offers keenly priced, flavourful food, with the likes of salads, burgers or a crisp belly pork sandwich at lunch; the menu expands in the evening to include dishes like pan-fried scallops, salt-baked fish or rabbit tortellini. You'll have to be quick to nab one of the handful of tables in the cosy, fire-lit bar, but there's always plenty of space in the three, tastefully furnished, contemporary dining rooms. Service is formal and knowledgeable.

The Cobbles,
LOWER PEOVER, WA16 9PZ
Tel.: (01565)722269
Website: www.thebellsofpeover.com

Off the B 5081, which runs through the village. Parking.

PRICES
Meals: £ 17 (lunch) and a la carte £ 23/39

MAP: 7

CLOSING TIMES
Open daily

Robinsons Dizzy Blonde and Unicorn, Hartleys Cumbria Way

CHURCH GREEN

They take pride in their kitchen garden

This double gable-fronted Victorian pub stands on the green next to St Mary's Church. Its experienced chef-owner, Aiden Byrne (who appeared on the Great British Menu) is supported by a well-structured team, who take pride in the pub's kitchen garden, which supplies everything from beetroot to soft fruits. The open-plan bar and restaurant are decorated in modern hues and there's a pleasant conservatory and attractive decked terrace to the rear. The appealing menu includes pub classics and a steakhouse section, where you choose a cut, then add sauce, garnish and any extras you want. There's a set tasting selection of more elaborate dishes on Saturday evenings and breakfast at the weekend, which includes a full English for children.

Higher Ln,
LYMM, WA13 0AP
Tel.: (01925)752068
Website: www.thechurchgreen.co.uk

7 mi west of Altrincham by A 56. Parking.

PRICES
Meals: a la carte £ 21/59

MAP: 8

CLOSING TIMES
Closed 25 December
booking essential

Caledonian Golden XPA, Bank's Best Bitter, Black Sheep Ale and Theakston Lightfoot

OLD HALL

Smartly refurbished, heavily timbered manor house

Testament to the strength of local feeling towards this black and white 17C former manor house is the fact that, having lain empty for several years, campaigning villagers managed to get it listed on the English Heritage 'buildings at risk' register. Eventually rescued from further decay by the current owners, total restoration has created a smart new look for the Old Hall's many rooms, whilst retaining the character that comes from original features like oak panelling and heavy timber beams. This is a proper pub with real ales aplenty and a daily menu which focuses on keenly priced pub classics; the no-frills style of cooking meaning that dishes like braised shoulder of lamb and steak and kidney pudding arrive exactly as they should.

High St,
SANDBACH, CW11 1AL
Tel.: (01270)758170
Website: www.oldhall-sandbach.co.uk

1.5 mi southwest of M 6 junction 17, off A 534. Parking.

PRICES
Meals: a la carte £ 20/40

MAP: 9

CLOSING TIMES
Open daily

Brunning & Price Original Bitter, Redwillow Feckless and Three Tuns XXX

SWETTENHAM ARMS

Take time to wander around the lavender meadow

If you rely on your sat nav you may well end up in the middle of the local ford, but don't give up just yet, as this pub's well worth the search. Formerly a nunnery, it's been in the capable hands of the Cunninghams for many years now; although there's still the occasional ghostly sighting of a nun. Its beaten copper bar, welcoming open fireplaces and shiny horse brasses mean that tradition reigns, which is a surefire hit with both drinkers and diners. The seasonally changing menu provides plenty of choice, from sharing platters and satisfying pub classics to carefully prepared, well-presented restaurant-style dishes, such as rack of local lamb with basil mousse. Be sure to find time to stroll around the lavender meadow or the RHS arboretum.

SWETTENHAM, CW12 2LF
Tel.: (01477)571284
Website: www.swettenhamarms.co.uk

Between Holmes Chapel and Congleton, signposted off the A 54.
Parking.

PRICES
Meals: a la carte £ 18/42

MAP: 10

CLOSING TIMES
Closed dinner 25 December

Timothy Taylor Landlord, Beartown Best, Tatton White Witch and Butchered Brown Ale

BEAR'S PAW

Sizeable pub with an equally large menu

Sister to the Pheasant at Tattenhall is this handsome 19C inn; probably best described as very big and very, very busy. There's a spacious, semi wood panelled bar with two vast fireplaces and a huge array of local ales. The menu is also sizeable, with enough choice to please all appetites; from nibbles like flavoured chipolatas or olives to deli boards including charcuterie and cheese selections - all served with rustic bread and house chutney. Main dishes look to Europe for their inspiration, but it's the good old British favourites like fish and chips or steak and ale pie that win the day. You can cook your own steak on a hot stone - and make sure you try the Bear's Paw Sundae for dessert. Bedrooms are stylish and well worth the money.

School Ln,
WARMINGHAM, CW11 3QN
Tel.: (01270)526317
Website: www.thebearspaw.co.uk

3.5mi west of Sandbach by A 533. Parking.

PRICES
Meals: a la carte £ 19/43

17 rooms:
£ 100/160

MAP: 11

CLOSING TIMES
Open daily

Weetwood Ales, Tatton Ale and Beartown Bear Ass

DRUNKEN DUCK INN

Easy to see why it's always so busy

Situated in the heart of the beautiful Lakeland countryside, this attractive inn takes its name from an old legend about a landlady, some ducks and a leaky beer barrel. The popular fire-lit bar is the cosiest place to sit, among hop bines, pictures of the hunt and old brewery advertisements; but there are also two more formal dining rooms. The same menu is served throughout, offering simple lunches and much more elaborate dinners, with prices to match; cooking is generous and service, attentive. Ales come from the on-site micro-brewery and are made with water from their own tarn. Boutique, country house bedrooms - some with patios - boast extremely comfy beds and country views. Afternoon tea can be taken in the lounge or residents' garden.

Barngates,
AMBLESIDE, LA22 0NG
Tel.: (01539)436347
Website: www.drunkenduckinn.co.uk

3 mi southwest of Ambleside by A 593 and B 5286 on Tarn Hows road. By the crossroads at the top of Duck Hill. Parking.

PRICES
Meals: a la carte £ 23/38

17 rooms:
£ 79/325

MAP: 12

CLOSING TIMES
Closed 25 December
booking essential

Barngates Brewery Cat Nap, Cracker, Brathay Gold and Red Bull Terrier

HARE AND HOUNDS

Cosy, characterful and charming

This charming 17C Lakeland pub is situated in the delightful village of Bowland Bridge, where Arthur Ransome wrote the book 'Swallows and Amazons'. There's a large terrace with chunky wooden tables to the front, leading through into a rustic, open-fired inner with stone walls, black and white village photos and exposed beams draped with hop bines. Menus offer typical, hearty, pub-style dishes - such as homemade pies or Lakeland hotpot with black pudding and home-pickled cabbage - and much of the produce is locally sourced. There's also a fine selection of ales to choose from, including 'Hare of the Dog', which is specially brewed for them by a Lakeland brewery. Bedrooms are well-equipped and elegant with smart bathrooms; some have roll-top baths.

BOWLAND BRIDGE, LA11 6NN
Tel.: (015395)68333
Website: www.hareandhoundsbowlandbridge.co.uk

7 mi south of Windermere signed off A 5074. In the village centre. Parking.

PRICES
Meals: £ 13 and a la carte £ 20/33

5 rooms:
£ 75/165

MAP: 13

CLOSING TIMES
Closed 25 December

Tirril Hare of the Dog, Coniston Bluebird and Kirkby Lonsdale Tiffin Gold

PIG & WHISTLE

Village local with space for just 28 people

This pub might be run by the same owners as esteemed nearby restaurant L'Enclume but regulars can rest safe in the knowledge that this will stay a comfy, cosy village local; a place to while away the evening with a pint but also a place to come for a good meal. Situated close to the main square in the delightful Lakeland village of Cartmel, it looks, from the outside, rather like a row of terraced cottages, and with its three tiny rooms - with space for just 28 people - it certainly has an intimate feel. Menus are rooted in the traditional pub vein and cooking is honest and careful with bold, defined flavours. Satisfyingly, prices remain reasonable. The simple wine list features just 6 bottles, with the real ales taking pride of place.

CARTMEL, LA11 6PL
Tel.: (01539)536482
Website: www.pigandwhistlecartmel.co.uk

3 mi northwest of Grange-over-Sands. On-street parking.

PRICES
Meals: a la carte £ 23/35

MAP: 14

CLOSING TIMES
Closed 25 December

Robinsons Trooper and Hartleys Cumbria Way

GEORGE AND DRAGON

Game from the moors and meat from estate farms

Consisting of 75,000 acres and covering much of Cumbria, the Lowther family estate includes properties ranging from a castellated mansion to this whitewashed coaching inn. Its characterful 18C bar features a flag floor, panelling and a wood burning stove, while the spacious restaurant takes on a more modern style, with its open kitchen and smart wood furnishings. When it comes to the food, it doesn't get more local than this, with vegetables from the kitchen garden, game from the surrounding moors and organic meats from the estate's farms. Appealing dishes might include twice-baked Cumbrian cheese soufflé, followed by Askham pork sausages or pan-fried wild sea bass. Modern bedrooms showcase furniture and paintings from the family's collection.

CLIFTON, CA10 2ER
Tel.: (01768)865381
Website: www.georgeanddragonclifton.co.uk

3 mi south of Penrith on A6. In centre of village. Parking.

PRICES
Meals: £ 13/40 and a la carte £ 26/38

11 rooms:
£ 79/155

MAP: 15

CLOSING TIMES
Closed 26 December

Cumberland Corby Blonde, Hawkshead Bitter and Eden Gold

PUNCH BOWL INN

Charming pub in a picturesque valley setting

Nestled among the hills in the heart of the picturesque Lyth Valley, this attractive 17C inn enjoys a truly delightful setting - and it's not just the views that are glorious, the pub itself is truly charming, with its antiques, cosy open fires and exposed wooden beams. Cooking has a classical base but displays some modern touches, and dishes display a degree of complexity that you wouldn't usually find in a pub. Dine in the rustic bar or, for more of an occasion, in the more formal restaurant. Smart, individually styled bedrooms boast good quality linen, roll-top baths and fluffy towels; 'Noble' features twin bath tubs and 'Danson' offers the best views. If you fancy sending a postcard, the reception also doubles as the village post office!

CROSTHWAITE, LA8 8HR
Tel.: (01539)568237
Website: www.the-punchbowl.co.uk

5.25 mi west of Kendal by All Hallows Lane; next to the church. Parking.

PRICES
Meals: a la carte £ 23/37

9 rooms:
£ 95/185

MAP: 16

CLOSING TIMES
Open daily

Barngates Cracker, Coniston Old Man and Winster Valley Old School

GOLDEN FLEECE N

Handy for Carlisle Airport and Hadrian's Wall

Yan, Tyan, Methera, Tethera, Pimp: words traditionally used by Cumbrian shepherds to count their sheep now guide you to the right bedroom when staying at this 18C coaching inn. But fear not, with beds as comfortable as those at the Fleece, you won't need to utter a word of shepherding dialect yourself. With such treats as twice-baked 3 cheese soufflé and pan-roasted Cumbrian lamb on offer, dining is a must. They've got tasty pub classics, juicy mature steaks and proper pub puddings, as well as seventies throwback chicken-in-a-basket and local ales. It's got interesting maps of ancient Cumbria and a cosy-making wood-burning stove, and is well located just off the A689 – handy for Carlisle Airport, Hadrian's Wall and Gretna Green.

Ruleholme,
IRTHINGTON, CA6 4NF
Tel.: (01228)573686
Website: www.thegoldenfleececumbria.co.uk

6.5 mi northeast of Carlisle by B 6264 and on A 689. Parking.

PRICES
Meals: a la carte £ 22/54

8 rooms:
£ 65/100

MAP: 17

CLOSING TIMES
Closed 1-7 January

Dent Golden Fleece, Allendale Wolf and Cumberland Corby Fox

SUN INN

Meat is from the butcher's two doors down

This 17C inn's hands-on owners don't have to go far to source quality seasonal produce as, with a butcher's two doors down, it's literally on their doorstep. Lunch offers a concise selection of classics like saddleback sausage and mash, along with some tapas-style bar snacks such as honey and mustard glazed chipolatas or salt and pepper squid. Dinner, on the other hand, is a more serious affair, with various different menus offering the likes of red leg partridge pithivier or slow-roasted shoulder of Lune Valley lamb. Well-lit modern bedrooms come with quality linen and thoughtful extras like homemade flapjack and fresh milk, and breakfast is well worth getting up for, with delicious offerings including poached fruits and homemade granola.

6 Market St,
KIRKBY LONSDALE, LA6 2AU
Tel.: (015242)71965
Website: www.sun-inn.info

In the centre of town. Long stay car park in Booth Rd.

PRICES
Meals: £ 30 (dinner) and a la carte £ 26/38

11 rooms:
£ 78/178

MAP: 18

CLOSING TIMES
Closed Monday lunch

Hawkshead Bitter, Thwaites Wainwright and Kirkby Lonsdale Singletrack

PLOUGH

A mix of pub classics and tasty small plates

This former coaching inn is set on the busy main road that links the Lake District to North Yorkshire and has a good reputation in the local area. There's a cosy, homely feel to the place, its two rooms featuring exposed beams, an assortment of antique tables, local art for sale and comfy sofas set around a wood burning stove. The cheery, knowledgeable team serve up a pleasing mix of dishes: you'll find a selection of classics, alongside a list of tasty small plates - such as crispy whitebait or courgette fritters - that can be mixed and matched as you please with an enticing array of side dishes. The bar is stocked with local ales including some artisan beers and bedrooms are smart, spacious and individually styled, with roll-top baths.

Cow Brow,
LUPTON, LA6 1PJ
Tel.: (015395)67700
Website: www.theploughatlupton.co.uk

4.75 mi northwest of Kirkby Lonsdale on A 65. Parking.

PRICES
Meals: a la carte £ 22/35

6 rooms:
£ 85/195

MAP: 19

CLOSING TIMES
Open daily

Kirkby Lonsdale Monumental Blonde, Jennings Cumberland Ale and Coniston Brewery Ales

KING'S HEAD

Owned by the same family since 1892

This whitewashed inn consists of four 17C cottages that were turned into a pub in late Victorian times - and have been owned by the same family since 1892. The pub's smartly refurbished interior features polished timbers, a flagged floor and a wood-burning stove; come summer, the garden fits the bill nicely, with a view out over the babbling beck and a wood inhabited by red squirrels. With a bounty of produce available on the pub's doorstep, the cooking here is, as you would expect, seriously seasonal; dishes like slow-roasted belly of pork, ale-battered cod, and venison and cranberry pie are well-prepared, appealingly presented and, most importantly of all, wonderfully tasty. Bedrooms are comfortable and elegant, with smart bathrooms.

RAVENSTONEDALE, CA17 4NH
Tel.: (01539)623050
Website: www.kings-head.com

5 mi southwest of Kirkby Stephen signed off A 685. On edge of village. Small car park and parking opposite.

PRICES
Meals: a la carte £ 20/37

6 rooms:
£ 70/98

MAP: 20

CLOSING TIMES
Closed 25 December

Jennings Cumberland Ale, Eden Dark Knight and Tirril Old Faithful

BROWN HORSE INN

Comes with smart bedrooms and even a brewery

This simple coaching inn has always been popular with the locals; but even more so since the creation of its on-site brewery. It has a shabby-chic style, with flagged floors, antique dressers and a real mix of furniture. In one corner, a miniature model of the bar (made by one of the regulars) and a London Underground map of local pubs provide talking points; while the split-level terrace is a real draw. Seasonal menus feature produce from the fields out back and game comes from shoots they organise themselves. Dishes are designed with hungry walkers in mind; the blackboard specials are a little more adventurous and often include home-reared pork. Bedrooms are a mix of classical and boutique styles; the latter have French windows and terraces.

WINSTER, LA23 3NR
Tel.: (015394)43443
Website: www.thebrownhorseinn.co.uk

4 mi south of Windermere by A 5074. Parking.

PRICES
Meals: a la carte £ 18/52

9 rooms:
£ 55/120

MAP: 21

CLOSING TIMES
Open daily

Winster Valley Brewery Ales

ODDFELLOWS

The lamb comes from the owners' fields

A complete refurbishment by its new owners has given Oddies - as it is affectionately known by the locals - a light, uncluttered feel; while wood burning stoves and an eclectic assortment of furniture add an element of cosiness. Built into the side of a former stone quarry on a winding lane leading up into the hills, the Oddfellows proudly retains its identity as a pub, with its bar and its hand pump beers the focal point of the room. An appealing, daily changing menu offers what they call 'British food with a modern twist'; this includes anything from a burger, fishcakes or a cheese and onion pie to sausage and mash or steak. Local suppliers are acknowledged on the menu, lamb comes from the owners' fields and bread is homemade.

Moor End Rd,
MELLOR, SK6 5PT
Tel.: (0161)4497826
Website: www.oddfellowsmellor.com

2.5 mi northwest of Marple by Marple Bridge and minor road. Parking.

PRICES
Meals: a la carte £ 19/38

MAP: 22

CLOSING TIMES
Closed Monday except bank holidays

Marston's Pedigree, Marble Manchester Bitter and Howard Town Wren's Nest

WHITE HART INN

Sympathetically extended stone-built inn

Set overlooking Saddleworth Moor, this stone-built inn has undergone various sympathetic extensions over the years, which are now home to a private dining room, a formal restaurant, a function room known as 'The Oak Room' and 12 bedrooms, named after local men of note. The bar boasts exposed beams, open fires and photos of the owner's travels; ironically, he once got thrown out of this pub for underage drinking, before eventually buying it himself. Dishes such as potted rabbit or calves' liver sit alongside pub classics like sausage and mash on the 'brasserie' menu, while the 'restaurant' menu takes things to another level with choices such as galantine of guinea fowl with quails' eggs or cauliflower cappuccino with foie gras and chestnuts.

51 Stockport Rd,
LYDGATE, Oldham, OL4 4JJ
Tel.: (01457)872566
Website: www.thewhitehart.co.uk

3 mi east of Oldham by A 669 on A 6050. Parking.

PRICES
Meals: a la carte £ 23/37

12 rooms:
£ 95/128

MAP: 23

CLOSING TIMES
Open daily

Timothy Taylor Golden Best and Landlord, J.W. Lees Ales and Copper Dragon Best Bitter

RED WELL INN

Pub offering home-smoked products

This attractive 16C stone inn takes its name from the well at the rear of the pub, whose bricks gradually turned red over the years due to minerals leached from the water. It's one of those places that's a real family affair, with the son behind the scenes in the kitchen and his parents looking after the guests. The rustic bar boasts a few sofas, scrubbed tables and a wood burning stove, while the restaurant in the old coach house is a little more formal. The same menu is served throughout and offers something for everyone, from 'nibbles' such as a homemade black pudding scotch egg with HP sauce to a more adventurous lamb and lobster combo; alongside products from their own Lune Valley Smokehouse. Be sure to try Mrs Talbot's sticky toffee pud.

ARKHOLME, LA6 1BQ
Tel.: (015242)21240
Website: www.redwellinn.net

9 mi southwest of Kirkby Lonsdale (3 mi out of village centre) on B 6254. Parking.

PRICES
Meals: a la carte £ 23/47

MAP: 24

CLOSING TIMES
Open daily
booking advisable

Tirril Ales and Lancaster Blonde

CLOG & BILLYCOCK

Regional specialities are the draw

This popular sandstone pub was originally called the Bay Horse, before being renamed after a fashion trend often sported by the former landlord - who liked to wear the quirky combination of clog shoes and a billycock hat. The addition of a large extension means the pub is now modern and open-plan. The walls are filled with photos of their local suppliers and the extensive menus offer a strong Lancastrian slant; you might find Morecambe Bay shrimps, Port of Lancaster smoked fish or Ribble Valley beef, alongside tasty sharing platters. Most produce comes from within 25 miles and suppliers are plotted on a map on the back of the menu. Cooking is rustic and generous; prices are realistic; and the service is friendly and organised.

Billinge End Rd,
PLEASINGTON, Blackburn, BB2 6QB
Tel.: (01254)201163
Website: www.theclogandbillycock.com

2 mi west of Blackburn, signed off A 677. Parking.

PRICES
Meals: a la carte £ 19/40

MAP: 25

CLOSING TIMES
Closed 25 December

Thwaites Ales

BAY HORSE INN

Local offerings include a Lancashire cheeseboard

This pub is flanked by the A6 and M6, and just a stone's throw away from the main Euston to Glasgow railway line, so it's hard to believe how peaceful it is here. Burgundy walls, low beamed ceilings, a stone fireplace and a characterful corner bar provide a cosy, welcoming atmosphere, while the brighter rear dining room overlooks an attractive summer terrace and a pleasant wooded garden. Seasonal menus offer traditional, tried-and-tested dishes and, since they've been passionate about supporting regional producers here long before it became fashionable to do so, you'll always find local offerings such as Higginson's pork and leek sausages, Swainson House Farm duck liver pâté or Cumbrian beef - with the Lancashire cheeseboard a speciality.

Bay Horse Ln,
BAY HORSE, Ellel, LA2 0HR
Tel.: (01524)791204
Website: www.bayhorseinn.com

1.5 mi south by A 6 on Quernmore Rd. Parking.

PRICES
Meals: a la carte £ 22/39

MAP: 26

CLOSING TIMES
Closed Monday except bank holiday lunch

Moorhouse's Pendle Witch, Thwaites Wainwright and Bay Horse Best Bitter

DUKE OF YORK INN

Ivy-clad and in the heart of the Trough of Bowland

This ivy-clad pub sits on the main road running through this pleasant hamlet, in the heart of the Trough of Bowland. If its character you're after, dine in the rustic bar with its flag floors and wood burning stove; the more modern alternative is the smart, airy dining room, adorned with wine bottles and a large mirror. The seasonal à la carte offers plenty of regional choices, with a decent selection of fish, often including lobster; the daily set menu is a steal - and there's a 5 or 7 course tasting option too. Produce is commendably local, with herbs from the chef-owner's garden - dishes might include Lancashire cheese soufflé, assiette of game or pan-roasted fillet of sea bass. Regular events include popular wine evenings.

Brow Top,
GRINDLETON, BB7 4QR
Tel.: (01200)441266
Website: www.dukeofyorkgrindleton.com

3 mi northeast of Clitheroe signed off A 671. Parking.

PRICES
Meals: £ 17 (weekdays) and
a la carte £ 22/48

MAP: 27

CLOSING TIMES
Closed 25 December, Monday except bank holidays and Tuesday following bank holidays

Lancaster Blonde and Timothy Taylors Landlord

CARTFORD INN

The owner played a part in designing the bedrooms

This 17C coaching inn can be found next to a small toll bridge by the Pilling Marshes, and is a great base for those who wish to explore Blackpool but would rather stay somewhere a little more peaceful. The owner played a major part in designing the bedrooms, which range from quirky to French farmhouse in style, and feature colourful glass fittings by a renowned local glassblower. When it comes to drinking or dining, find a seat in one of the cosy little rooms or on the pleasant terrace overlooking the river. Cooking is in the tried-and-tested vein and offers proper pub classics, with signature dishes - such as the Fleetwood fish pie, Pilling Marsh lamb hotpot, and oxtail and beef suet pudding - under the heading of 'Cartford Favourites'.

Cartford Ln,
LITTLE ECCLESTON, PR3 0YP
Tel.: (01995)670166
Website: www.thecartfordinn.co.uk

7 mi east of Blackpool by A 585 and A 586. Parking.

PRICES
Meals: a la carte £ 21/38

14 rooms:
£ 70/200

MAP: 28

CLOSING TIMES
Closed 25 December and Monday lunch except bank holidays

Theakston Old Peculier, Moorhouse's Pride of Pendle and Bowland Ales

THREE FISHES

Local suppliers and regional specialities

'Regional' and 'local' are the buzzwords at this behemoth of a country pub, which seems to take catering for vast numbers of people in its stride. The original in Nigel Haworth's 'Ribble Valley Inns' group, it celebrated its tenth birthday in 2014, and now has a modern style, typified by light wood and contemporary art to go with rustic features like stone walls and open fires. Produce is sourced from within 25 miles and pictorial homage is paid to their suppliers, or 'local food heroes'. Expect shrimps from Morecambe Bay, Ribble Valley beef, Goosnargh duck and Fleetwood fish, with specialities like the hotpot and the twice-baked cheese soufflé firmly rooted in the region. Sundays mean roast beef with all the trimmings; on Mondays it's BYO.

Mitton Rd,
MITTON, BB7 9PQ
Tel.: (01254)826888
Website: www.thethreefishes.com

2.5 mi northwest of Whalley on B 6246. Parking.

PRICES
Meals: a la carte £ 19/40

MAP: 29

CLOSING TIMES
Closed 25 December

Thwaites Wainwright, Bowland Hen Harrier and Lancaster Amber

HIGHWAYMAN

Showcases produce from surrounding counties

It's rumoured that this sizeable 18C coaching inn with its lovely terrace was once the midnight haunt of the local highwaymen. Set on the border of three counties - Cumbria, Lancashire and Yorkshire - it makes the most of its setting, with produce so local that a meal almost constitutes a regional geography lesson. The Lancashire hotpot is a signature dish; you'll find bacon from Sillfield Farm and shrimps from Morecambe Bay; seasonal classics like asparagus from Formby in spring and game in winter; as well as hearty puds like sticky toffee pudding. The rustic, no-nonsense approach to food means dishes are well-crafted and full of flavour. Mondays mean you can bring your own wine; enjoy a pint or two of Highwayman ale any day of the week.

NETHER BURROW, LA6 2RJ
Tel.: (01524)273338
Website: www.highwaymaninn.co.uk

2 mi south of Kirkby Lonsdale by A 65 and A 683. Parking.

PRICES
Meals: a la carte £ 19/40

MAP: 30

CLOSING TIMES
Closed 25 December

Thwaites Nutty Black, Coiled Spring and Wainwright

SPREAD EAGLE

Gutsy cooking is full of flavour

Very much a local pub, at the heart of the community, The Spread Eagle is stylish and full of character, with lovely river views. Eat by the fire in the cosy bar, or for a touch more comfort, head for the spacious restaurant. Cooking is gutsy and flavourful, with plenty of pub favourites like fish and chips, sausage and mash or steak, all available in two sizes. There are platters and tapas-style nibbles, perfect for sharing, and a specials list - with dishes such as roast duck breast or rich game casserole - aptly entitled 'The Weather Report' because, just like the weather, they change daily. Comfortable bedrooms have smart, modern bathrooms; room 6 is one of the largest and features a mezzanine level with 'his and hers' sofas.

SAWLEY, BB7 4NH
Tel.: (01200)441202
Website: www.spreadeaglesawley.co.uk

4 mi north of Clitheroe by A 59. Parking.

PRICES
Meals: £ 15 (lunch and early dinner) and a la carte £ 25/32

7 rooms:
£ 70/140

MAP: 31

CLOSING TIMES
Open daily

Thwaites Wainwright

INN AT WHITEWELL

14C inn set in prime shooting and fishing country

This 14C creeper-clad inn sits high on the banks of the River Hodder, in prime shooting and fishing country, in the heart of the Trough of Bowland. Antique furniture and a stunning view of the valley make the spacious bar the most atmospheric place to sit. Other similarly styled rooms boast the character but not the view; for a more formal meal, head for a linen-laid table in the raised-level, valley-facing restaurant. Classic menus offer wholesome, regionally inspired dishes like Lancashire hotpot or fillet of local beef. Spacious bedrooms are split between the inn and nearby coach house - some are traditional in style with four-posters and antique baths; others are more contemporary. The well-stocked vintners sells cookbooks and guides.

Forest of Bowland,
WHITEWELL, BB7 3AT
Tel.: (01200)448222
Website: www.innatwhitewell.com

6 mi northwest of Clitheroe by B 6243. Parking.

PRICES
Meals: a la carte £ 28/42

23 rooms:
£ 90/248

MAP: 32

CLOSING TIMES
Open daily

Bowland Ales, Copper Dragon Ales, Moorhouse's Pendle Witches Brew and Timothy Taylor Landlord

FREEMASONS

Refined dishes and an elegant dining room

Until the 1950s, this building was used by the Freemasons of the borough; thankfully, you no longer need a secret handshake to get in and the friendly staff welcome all-comers to enjoy the skilful, confident cooking of chef-owner Steven Smith. Fiercely seasonal dishes are traditional with a modern, sometimes playful edge; choices might include scorched langoustines with pork belly, Yorkshire rhubarb and dashi tea or 'Anna's happy trotters': roast loin with salt-baked pineapple, black pudding and pork pie sauce. Featuring a series of nooks and crannies, the pub has a charm all of its own; the antique-furnished upstairs has an elegant feel, while downstairs, with its flagged floors, low beams and open fires is more rustic.

8 Vicarage Fold,
WISWELL, BB7 9DF
Tel.: (01254)822218
Website: www.freemasonsatwiswell.com

Signposted off A 671 east of Whalley. Some parking in the village.

PRICES

Meals: £ 24 (lunch and early dinner)
and a la carte £ 37/67

MAP: 33

CLOSING TIMES

Closed 2-14 January and Monday-Tuesday except bank holidays

Lancaster Blonde, Reedly Hallows Pendleside and Bank Top Wiswell Brew

SOUTH EAST

England

© J. Arnold / hemis.fr

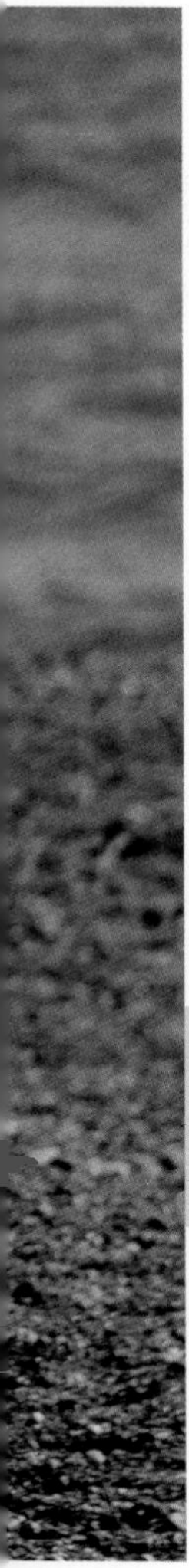

The south east abounds in handsome historic houses once lived in by the likes of Disraeli and the Rothschilds, and it's no surprise that during the Plague it was to leafy Chalfont St Giles that John Milton fled. It is characterised by rolling hills such as the Chilterns with their ancient beechwoods, and the lilting North and South Downs, which cut a rural swathe across busy commuter belts. The film and television worlds sit easily here: Hambleden and Turville, in the Chilterns, are as used to the sound of the autocue as to the crunch of ramblers' boots. Meanwhile, James Bond's Aston Martin glistens in Beaulieu's Motor Museum, in the heart of the New Forest. Spinnaker Tower rivals HMS Victory for dominance of the Portsmouth skyline, while in Winchester, the Great Hall, home for 600 years to the Arthurian round table, nods acquaintance with the eleventh century Cathedral.

Good food and drink is integral to the region, from Whitstable oysters and Dover sole to established vineyards.

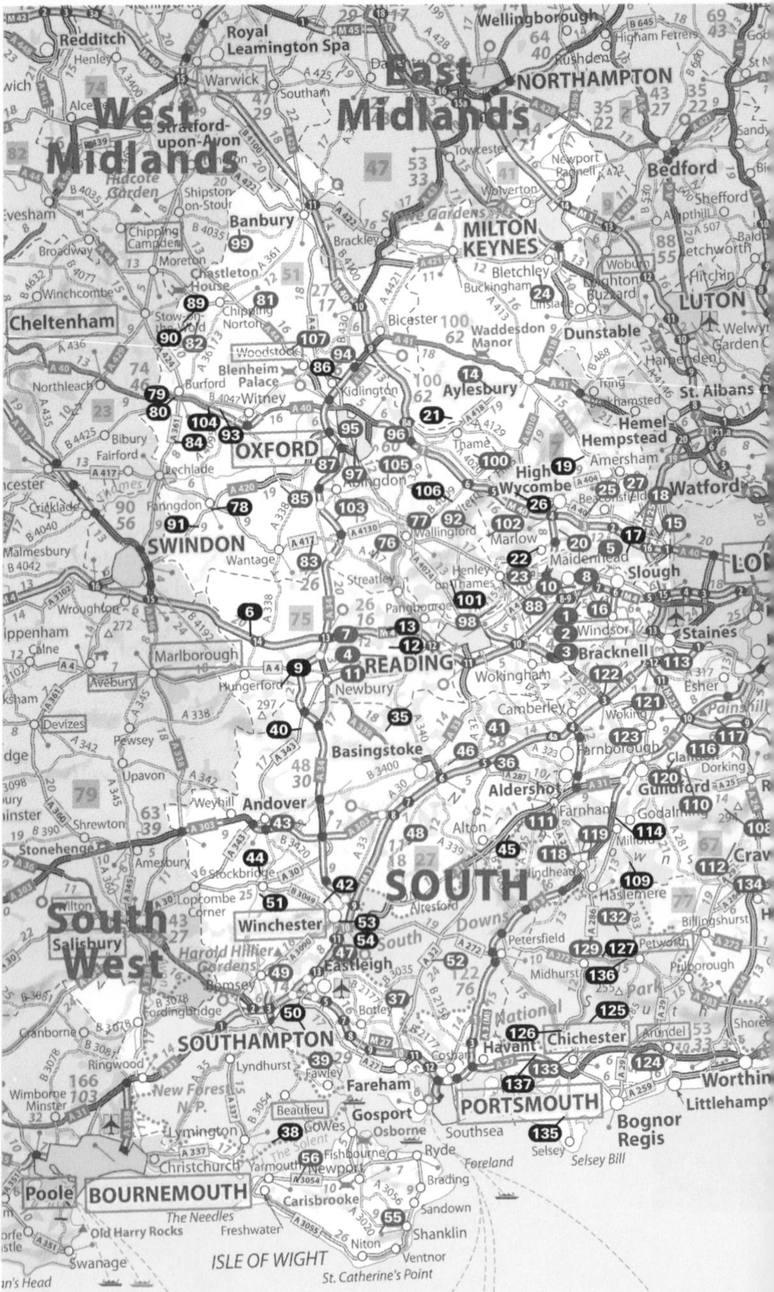

West Midlands
East Midlands
South
South West
Redditch
Royal Leamington Spa
Warwick
Stratford-upon-Avon
Wellingborough
NORTHAMPTON
Bedford
Banbury
MILTON KEYNES
Bletchley
Cheltenham
Chastleton House
Chipping Norton
Woodstock
Blenheim Palace
Bicester
Waddesdon Manor
Aylesbury
Dunstable
LUTON
St. Albans
Hemel Hempstead
OXFORD
Witney
Burford
Abingdon
High Wycombe
Watford
SWINDON
Wantage
Marlow
Maidenhead
Slough
Henley on Thames
Windsor
Staines
Bracknell
READING
Marlborough
Newbury
Hungerford
Wokingham
Basingstoke
Andover
Aldershot
Farnham
Guildford
Winchester
Eastleigh
Salisbury
SOUTHAMPTON
Fareham
Gosport
PORTSMOUTH
Havant
Chichester
Bognor Regis
Worthing
Poole
BOURNEMOUTH
Christchurch
Lymington
Cowes
Newport
Ryde
Sandown
Shanklin
Ventnor
ISLE OF WIGHT
Swanage
Old Harry Rocks
The Needles
St. Catherine's Point
Selsey Bill

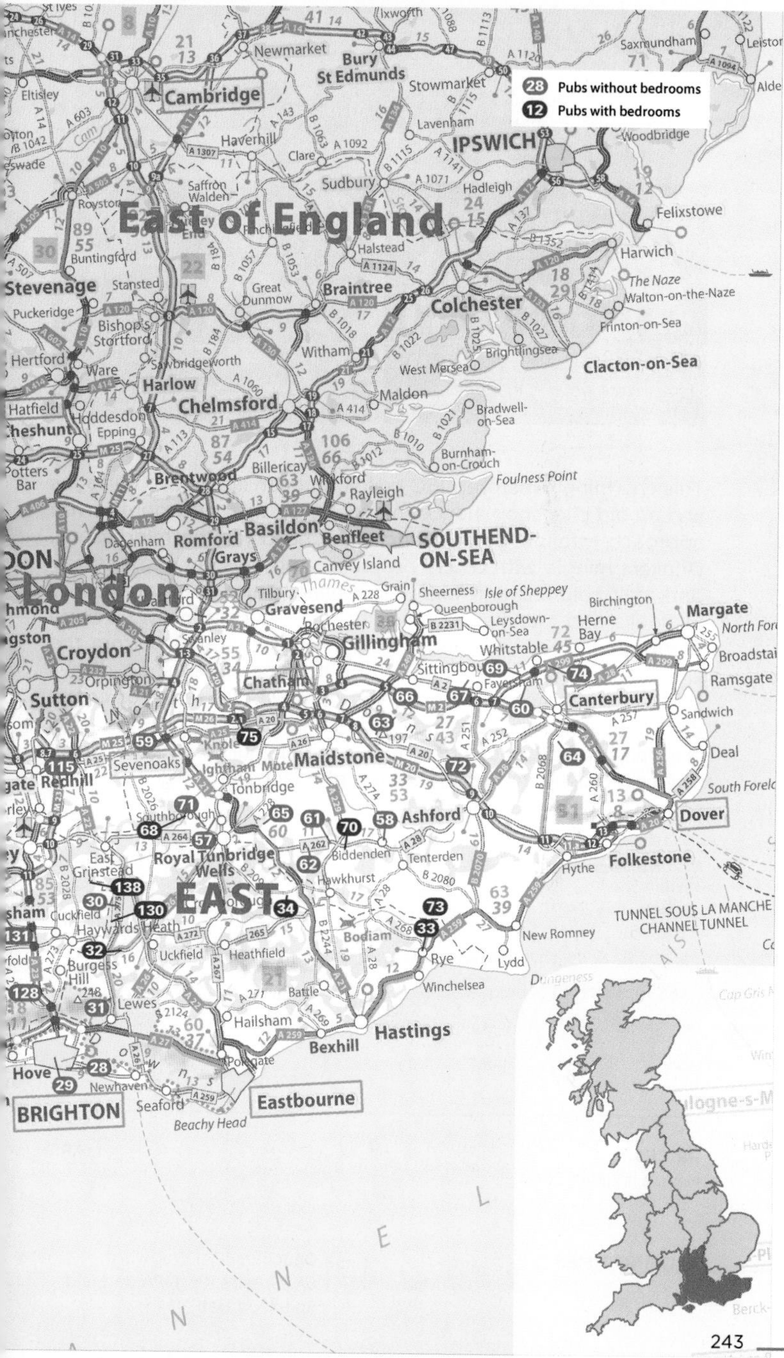
28 Pubs without bedrooms
12 Pubs with bedrooms
East of England
EAST
London
Cambridge
Newmarket
Bury St Edmunds
Stowmarket
Saxmundham
Leiston
Lavenham
IPSWICH
Woodbridge
Haverhill
Clare
Sudbury
Hadleigh
Felixstowe
Saffron Walden
Royston
Halstead
Harwich
Buntingford
Stevenage
Stansted
Great Dunmow
Braintree
The Naze
Walton-on-the-Naze
Colchester
Frinton-on-Sea
Puckeridge
Bishop's Stortford
Witham
Brightlingsea
Clacton-on-Sea
Hertford
Ware
Sawbridgeworth
West Mersea
Harlow
Chelmsford
Maldon
Hatfield
Hoddesdon
Bradwell-on-Sea
Cheshunt
Epping
Burnham-on-Crouch
Potters Bar
Brentwood
Billericay
Wickford
Foulness Point
Rayleigh
Basildon
Benfleet
SOUTHEND-ON-SEA
Dagenham
Romford
Grays
Canvey Island
Thames
Tilbury
Grain
Sheerness
Isle of Sheppey
Queenborough
Birchington
Margate
Gravesend
Rochester
Leysdown-on-Sea
Herne Bay
North Foreland
Croydon
Gillingham
Whitstable
Broadstairs
Sittingbourne
Ramsgate
Orpington
Chatham
Faversham
Sutton
Canterbury
Sandwich
Deal
Sevenoaks
Knole
Redhill
Ightham Mote
Maidstone
Tonbridge
South Foreland
Southborough
Ashford
Dover
Royal Tunbridge Wells
Biddenden
Tenterden
Folkestone
East Grinstead
Hawkhurst
Hythe
Cuckfield
Bodiam
TUNNEL SOUS LA MANCHE
CHANNEL TUNNEL
Haywards Heath
New Romney
Uckfield
Heathfield
Rye
Lydd
Burgess Hill
Battle
Winchelsea
Dungeness
Lewes
Hailsham
Hastings
Bexhill
Polegate
Hove
Newhaven
Eastbourne
BRIGHTON
Seaford
Beachy Head

CROWN

Robust, flavoursome cooking

This charmingly restored 16C building began life as two cottages and an old bike shop, hence the confusion with the doors as you approach - follow your instincts and head for the middle one. Drinkers mingle with diners beside roaring fires; amongst sturdy dark oak columns and below low beams, and there are plenty of nooks and crannies in which to tuck yourself away. Cooking is robust, flavoursome and British in essence, ranging from the likes of a burger or fish and chips to more interesting dishes such as Black Angus bavette with marrowbone sauce or crispy cauliflower with cheese sauce and Henderson's relish. Ingredients are well-sourced, cooking is careful and flavours are pronounced. The covered, heated courtyard is a pleasant spot.

High St,
BRAY, SL6 2AH
Tel.: (01628)621936
Website: www.thecrownatbray.com

1.75 mi south of Maidenhead by A 308. Parking.

PRICES
Meals: a la carte £ 26/44

MAP: 1

CLOSING TIMES
Closed 25 December and Sunday dinner

Deuchars IPA, Wadworth 6X, Greene King IPA and Old Speckled Hen

HINDS HEAD

Historic British dishes, wonderfully reinvented

Set in the heart of the pretty village of Bray, this charming 15C pub is full of character, with dark wood panelling, oak beams and log fires. Although situated not far from its alma mater, The Fat Duck, its menu is light years away. Down-to-earth, Historic British dishes might include oxtail and kidney pudding, pea and ham soup or strawberry trifle, and although they might sound simple, these dishes have been carefully researched and redesigned to deliver the perfect balance of texture and flavour, as well as being beautifully presented. This is a proper pub and, as such, is often busy with drinkers; the bar is the most atmospheric place to sit, although they don't take bookings here. Staff are a real asset: friendly, engaging and efficient.

High St,
BRAY, SL6 2AB
Tel.: (01628)626151
Website: www.hindsheadbray.com

1.75 mi south of Maidenhead by A 308. Parking in 2 village car parks and opposite the pub.

PRICES
Meals: £ 18 (weekday lunch) and
a la carte £ 34/54

MAP: 2

CLOSING TIMES
Closed 25 December and Sunday dinner
booking essential

Rebellion and Wadworth Ales

ROYAL OAK

Immensely satisfying seasonal food

Nick Parkinson is your host and his ability to put guests at ease is clearly one family trait he's inherited from his father, Sir Michael. The Royal Oak's characterful front bar is a great spot for a drink, while the rest of the beamed room and extension are given over to dining. The menu champions all things seasonal, with top quality ingredients used to create impeccably presented, flavourful dishes like wild Berkshire rabbit hache with confit egg yolk and grain mustard sauce or navarin of Cornish spring lamb with carrots, turnips and peas. Discreet, formal service provides a sense of occasion and the garden, with its elegantly manicured herb maze and water feature, is a tranquil spot in which to enjoy a pre or post-dinner drink.

Paley Street,
BRAY, SL6 3JN
Tel.: (01628)620541
Website: www.theroyaloakpaleystreet.com

3.5 mi southwest of Bray by A 308, A 330 and B 3024. Parking.

PRICES
Meals: £ 20 (weekday lunch) and
a la carte £ 25/52

MAP: 3

CLOSING TIMES
Closed Sunday dinner

Fuller's London Pride

BLADEBONE INN

Ambitious food from a young-chef owner

The mysterious name apparently originates from prehistoric times, when an aggressive mammoth which roamed the surrounding plains was killed and buried. Many years later its bladebone was found on the banks of the River Kennet, dragged back to the inn and hoisted above the door; a gleaming gold version now hangs in its place. Thankfully, the inside of the pub is homelier than the name suggests, with a snug, open-fired bar and dining room, and a terrace overlooking a rough garden where they grow more than 50 different herbs. The appealing menu offers everything from 'posh' fish finger sandwiches at lunch to duck with cherry beer and almonds, or meaty local rump steaks with triple-cooked chips - along with some interesting wines by the glass.

CHAPEL ROW, RG7 6PD
Tel.: (01189)712326
Website: www.thebladeboneinn.com

4 mi northeast of Thatcham by A4. Parking.

PRICES
Meals: £ 15 (weekday lunch) and
a la carte £ 25/39

MAP: 4

CLOSING TIMES
Open daily

West Berkshire Good Old Boy, Loose Cannon Abingdon Bridge and Rebellion Smuggler

WHITE OAK

Great value 'Menu Auberge'

Trifle – now there's a pud you want to see in a pub. Okay, so it's had a little makeover here because it comes with lavender custard and crushed meringue, but it shows that this is a pub with an inherent understanding of what its customers want. There are Aubrey Allen's finest steaks, plenty of Cornish fish, classics like shepherd's pie and other choices with more European credentials such as duck confit – all prepared with care and understanding. Look out too for the 'Menu Auberge' – a great value daily menu. One could argue about whether this is a contemporary pub or a pubby restaurant, as it's set up quite formally, but what is in no doubt is the warmth of the welcome and the affection in which the place is held by its many regulars.

Pound Ln,
COOKHAM, SL6 9QE
Tel.: (01628)523043
Website: www.thewhiteoak.co.uk

Across the common. Parking.

PRICES
Meals: £ 14/25 and a la carte £ 25/45

MAP: 5

CLOSING TIMES
Closed dinner Sunday and bank holidays

Greene King Ales

QUEEN'S ARMS

Rub shoulders with horse trainers and breeders

Nestled in the heart of racehorse country, this 18C inn encompasses all that is British. Framed prints and oils cover the walls, country pursuits can be arranged and don't be surprised to find yourself rubbing shoulders with a famous trainer or breeder. The bar has a satisfyingly rustic feel, with its open fire and mismatched seating, while the wood-panelled dining room with its gleaming glassware is a more formal affair. In keeping with the good old British surroundings, dishes are meaty and satisfying; you might find a hearty steak and ale pie, warming braised oxtail or some juicy local sausages – the tasty game is shot just over the road. Modern bedrooms are kitted out by leading clothing and countrywear companies such as Hunter and Orvis.

Newbury St,
EAST GARSTON, RG17 7ET
Tel.: (01488)648757
Website: www.queensarmshotel.co.uk

3 mi southeast of Lambourn via Eastbury on Newbury Rd. Parking.

PRICES
Meals: a la carte £ 24/33

8 rooms:
£ 75/130

MAP: 6

CLOSING TIMES
Open daily

Sharp's Doom Bar, Loose Cannon Abingdon Bridge and Gunners Gold

POT KILN

Gusty portions in prime game country

Part of the old brickworks, The Pot Kiln originally provided refreshment for the workers digging clay from the surrounding fields. Head for the cosy bar and order a pint of Mr Chubb's or Brick Kiln beer - from the West Berkshire Brewery, just down the road - then follow the deliciously tempting aromas through to the dining area, where flavoursome British dishes arrive in unashamedly gutsy portions. Chef-owner Mike Robinson takes advantage of the pub's situation in the middle of prime hunting territory and shoots much of the game himself; so you might find pigeon salad followed by pavé of Lockinge fallow deer on the menu. There's plenty of fish too, including local pike, trout and River Kennet crayfish, and service is pleasingly clued-up.

FRILSHAM, RG18 0XX
Tel.: (01635)201366
Website: www.potkiln.org

6 mi northeast of Newbury by B 4009 to Hermitage and minor road. Parking.

PRICES
Meals: £ 14 (weekday lunch) and
a la carte £ 28/35

MAP: 7

CLOSING TIMES
Closed 25 December and Tuesday

West Berkshire Brick Kiln Bitter and Mr Chubb's Lunchtime Bitter

BELGIAN ARMS

Pretty 17C inn by the village pond

This pretty 17C wisteria-clad inn is tucked away by a pond fringed with weeping willows, just off the village green, and there can be few settings more appealing than this. On warmer days, head for the terrace but if it's raining, fear not, as there's always the conservatory instead. The owners, one of whom is Nick Parkinson, have opened up the old interior and decorated it with photos of cricket and football, as well as Nick's father - Sir Michael - with his celebrated interviewees. There's no standing on ceremony here though, as this proud local has gutsy pub dishes on its menu and always plenty of events going on, from cribbage and cricket matches to barbeques, hog roasts and summer parties, complete with face painting and live bands.

Holyport St,
HOLYPORT, SL6 2JR
Tel.: (01628)634468
Website: www.thebelgianarms.com

2.5 mi south of Maidenhead by A 308, just off the village green behind the telephone box. Parking.

PRICES
Meals: a la carte £ 23/30

MAP: 8

CLOSING TIMES
Closed Sunday dinner in winter and Monday dinner in summer

Brakspear Bitter & Special and Marston's Pedigree

DUNDAS ARMS (N)

Sit in the garden and watch the boats go by

This 18C inn sits in a wonderful location between the Kennet River and the Kennet and Avon Canal, making its garden a go-to destination on a sunny summer's day. Enjoy tasty pub classics and a pint of real ale to the soundtrack of flowing water and chirruping birds as trains trundle past and barges float serenely by. Inside, a portrait of Charles Dundas, the man who built the canal, overlooks the library with its open fire; there's a pleasant contemporary dining room in which to enjoy a meal from the more adventurous evening menu, and a more rustic Penny Bar, so-called because a former landlord lined it with new pennies. Stylish, comfortable bedrooms are fittingly named after birds or fish; the latter category have their own riverside terraces.

53 Station Rd,
KINTBURY, RG17 9UT
Tel.: (01488)658263
Website: www.dundasarms.co.uk

Between Hungerford and Newbury signposted off A 4. On the north side of the village. Parking.

PRICES
Meals: £ 18 (lunch) and
a la carte £ 24/41

8 rooms:
£ 80/140

MAP: 9

CLOSING TIMES
Open daily

Ramsbury Gold, West Berkshire Good Old Boy and Mr Chubb's Lunchtime Bitter

CROWN (N)

The chef-owner visits his suppliers personally

The Crown sits in a pretty village, opposite a 300 year old oak tree which has stood for a century longer than the pub itself. Local drinkers fill the small bar, which leads through to two intimate, open-fired dining rooms with thick walls and mix and match chairs. The experienced chef-owner takes his cooking very seriously - so much so that he closes the pub on a Monday in order to go to the market and visit his suppliers. The warm rolls are delicious and the five starters, main courses and desserts are chalked on the board daily - the options are diverse and all are equally appealing and flavoursome. You could find anything from honey-smoked trout with beetroot and horseradish from the garden, to spiced pot-roasted pig cheek.

Burchett's Green,
MAIDENHEAD, SL6 6QZ
Tel.: (01628)824079
Website: www.thecrownatburchettsgreen.com

4 mi west of Maidenhead by A 4, A 404 and Burchett's Green Rd.
Parking.

PRICES
Meals: a la carte £ 22/30

MAP: 10

CLOSING TIMES
Closed last 2 weeks of August,
Christmas and Monday
dinner only and Sunday lunch

Guest ales

THE NEWBURY Ⓝ

Relaxed and trendy behind its traditional façade

Behind this high street pub's traditional façade lies a relaxed and trendy space. Beams, exposed brick and flagged floors provide the requisite character for a pub of its age, while the eclectic range of art on the walls gives the place a funky, up-to-date feel. The sofas by the wood burner in the bar are a popular spot, although most people head to the adjoining dining area; if you sit on the small terrace out the back, you will share it with smokers as well as the pub's smokery. The menu offers everything from fish and chips or a burger to more interesting dishes like beetroot ravioli and goat's cheese or roasted turbot with lentils and salsa verde. There's brunch at weekends, an experienced team in charge and a lively buzz when it's busy.

137 Bartholomew St,
NEWBURY, RG14 5HB
Tel.: (01635)49000
Website: www.thenewburypub.co.uk

On the western side of the Kennett Shopping Centre. Parking at shopping centre car park.

PRICES
Meals: a la carte £ 22/45

MAP: 11

CLOSING TIMES
Open daily

Timothy Taylor Landlord, Two Cocks Ales, West Berkshire Good Old Boy

BULL INN

Enjoy the local 'beer-tapas' under 15C beams

Locals and their dogs gather beside the fire in the rustic, quarry-tiled bar of this beamed 15C inn, while those wishing to eat head for the dining rooms, with their dramatic red and silver stag antler wallpaper and trio of twinkling chandeliers. The experienced chef-owner knows what people want, so while the blackboard bar menu focuses on pub-style dishes like burger or fish and chips, the main menu offers choices such as calves' liver, steamed hake or braised pork cheeks. There's a good range of wines, and the 'beer tapas' - which allows you to sample three of the local ales in small glasses - is a nice touch. The spacious garden plays host to alfresco diners, chickens and the annual village dog show, while bedrooms are cosy and great value.

Cock Ln,
STANFORD DINGLEY, RG7 6LS
Tel.: (01189)744582
Website: www.thebullinnstanforddingley.co.uk

Midway between Newbury and Theale by A 4 and Chapel Row Rd. Parking.

PRICES
Meals: a la carte £ 17/43

5 rooms:
£ 60/69

MAP: 12

CLOSING TIMES
Open daily

West Berkshire Good Old Boy, Two Cocks Cavalier and Sharp's Doom Bar

ROYAL OAK

Bursting with country charm

Bursting with country charm, The Royal Oak manages to pull off the tricky feat of being both a true locals pub and a popular destination for foodies. While the picture perfect village and its proximity to the M4 could account in part for the pub's attraction to visitors, it's the cooking which really gets them travelling here from a distance. Honest British dishes might include chicken livers on toast, salmon en croute or lamb and rosemary pie, with traditional puddings like cheesecake or fruit crumble to follow. The heavily beamed bar with its blazing log fires is the oldest and most characterful part of the pub, and where the action tends to happen. Country house style bedrooms are named after guns; Heym is the most comfortable.

The Square,
YATTENDON, RG18 OUF
Tel.: (01635)201325
Website: www.royaloakyattendon.com

6 mi northeast of Newbury by B 4009 and minor road; in the village centre. Parking opposite and in village car park.

PRICES
Meals: £ 13 (weekday lunch) and a la carte £ 25/42

10 rooms:
£ 90/130

MAP: 13

CLOSING TIMES
Open daily
booking advisable

West Berkshire Good Old Boy and Mr Chubb's Lunchtime Bitter

CROWN

Ask for tables 4 or 5 by the fireplace

Set in the charming village of Cuddington, this Grade II listed 16C building is the very essence of a proper English pub. Whitewashed walls and an attractive thatched roof hide a traditionally styled interior with welcoming open fires, dancing candlelight and a multitude of bygone artefacts; while a loyal band of locals keep up the drinking trade and a friendly team set the tone. There's a blackboard of daily specials and an à la carte that changes with the seasons: so you'll find hearty comfort food in winter and lighter sandwiches and salads in the summer (the smoked haddock with Welsh rarebit is a hit); arrive early if you fancy one of these in a spot in the sun. Tuesday to Friday 'food nights' include steak, curry, pies and fish 'n' chips.

Aylesbury Rd,
CUDDINGTON, HP18 0BB
Tel.: (01844)292222
Website: www.thecrowncuddington.co.uk

West of Aylesbury by A 418. Parking.

PRICES
Meals: a la carte £ 21/33

MAP: 14

CLOSING TIMES
Closed Sunday dinner

Fuller's London Pride and Adnams Soutwold Bitter

SWAN INN

The jewel here is the secluded garden

If you want to escape the hustle of London, this pub may well be the tranquil haven you're after. Close to the A40, M40 and M25 but in a secluded little world of its own, The Swan takes up prime position in this delightful village. Number three in the owner's collection, the Georgian red-brick building is fronted by beautiful cascades of wisteria and framed by manicured trees, with a secluded terrace and gardens to the rear. Menus change with the seasons but their signature bubble & squeak and rib-eye steak are mainstays. This is more than just typical pub food, so you might find confit duck with nutmeg boxty potato and sides such as such as leek, pancetta and parsley crumble. Satisfyingly, they open early for pre-Ascot or Wimbledon champagne.

Village Rd,
DENHAM, UB9 5BH
Tel.: (01895)832085
Website: www.swaninndenham.co.uk

6 mi northeast of Slough by A 412; in the centre of the village. Small car park.

PRICES
Meals: a la carte £ 21/36

MAP: 15

CLOSING TIMES
Closed 25-26 December
booking essential

Marlow Rebellion IPA and Caledonian Flying Scotsman

PALMER ARMS

The young owners have put the focus on the food

Despite its proximity to Windsor and the M4, this 15C pub feels like it's in a decidedly rural spot. It's run by a keen young couple and the pub's huge popularity bears testament to the fact that they're doing things right: it's the food - not the furnishings - that's the focus here. Menus display a well-balanced mix of pub favourites and more adventurous dishes, with the likes of venison and black pudding sausage roll or macaroni with smoked Applewood cheese; while desserts feature heart-warming crumbles alongside more modern creations such as peanut butter mousse. There's also a large garden with a children's play area and some resident chickens - and a private upstairs dining room with a lovely terrace and far-reaching views.

Village Rd,
DORNEY, SL4 6QW
Tel.: (01628)666612
Website: www.thepalmerarms.com

2.5 mi west of Eton on B 3026. Parking.

PRICES
Meals: a la carte £ 21/41

MAP: 16

CLOSING TIMES
Open daily
booking advisable

Greene King IPA, Abbot Ale and guest ales

BLACK HORSE

Hide in a cosy alcove or head for the terrace

Originally a lodging house for the builders of the next door church - which dates from 1610 - this whitewashed village pub is the perfect place for a pint and a meal. It's got thick walls and cosy alcoves, a wood-burning stove, a large front terrace and a gem of a garden for sunny days. The main dining area may feel quite formal and stylish, with its banquette seats and delightful portraits, but the down-to-earth staff are only too eager to help guide you through the menu. Sharing boards are a popular choice, starters might include sticky pork ribs or a hot smoked salmon fishcake, while mains could mean a steak, pork belly or a nice plump Dover sole. Uniquely styled bedrooms have spacious, modern bathrooms and Nespresso coffee machines.

Windmill Rd,
FULMER, SL3 6HD
Tel.: (01753)663183
Website: www.theblackhorsefulmer.co.uk

2 mi south of Gerrards Cross in centre of village beside St James church. Parking.

PRICES
Meals: £ 16 (weekday lunch) and a la carte £ 21/42

2 rooms:
£ 100/210

MAP: 17

CLOSING TIMES
Closed 25 December

Greene King IPA and London Glory

THREE OAKS

Great value set lunch and dinner menus

Turning into the car park and seeing all those smart cars makes you immediately aware that this isn't going to be your typical village local. Sharing the same owner as The White Oak in Cookham, this revamped pub attracts the local 'chic' set. There's a choice of six rooms – go for the brighter one at the back as it looks out over the colourful garden. Bright, enthusiastic service comes courtesy of local boys and girls, all dressed in black. The menu changes often but keeps things British and relatively safe, as the customers clearly don't take to anything too unfamiliar. Expect the likes of home-cured salmon, ham hock terrine, suckling pig and sticky toffee pudding. The set lunch and dinner 'Auberge' menus offer particularly good value.

Austenwood Ln,
GERRARDS CROSS, SL9 8NL
Tel.: (01753)899016
Website: www.thethreeoaksgx.co.uk

0.75 mi northwest of the town by A 413 following signs for Gold Hill. Parking.

PRICES
Meals: £ 15/19 and a la carte £ 22/42

MAP: 18

CLOSING TIMES
Open daily

Fuller's London Pride and Rebellion Ales

NAGS HEAD

An original mix of French and British dishes

This traditional 15C inn is run by the same team behind the Bricklayers Arms in Flaunden and is proving just as popular, so be sure to book ahead, especially at weekends. It has been made over, yet retains a wealth of original features: the two main dining areas have thick brick walls and exposed oak beams, while an extra helping of rusticity comes courtesy of the inglenook fireplace. Original menus mix Gallic charm with British classics, so you'll find things like foie gras or mushroom feuillette alongside eggs Benedict or sausage and mash; food is flavourful and service, cheerful and keen. Stylish modern bedrooms provide a comfortable night's sleep - number one is the best - and the tasty breakfasts ensure you leave satiated in the morning.

London Rd,
GREAT MISSENDEN, HP16 0DG
Tel.: (01494)862200
Website: www.nagsheadbucks.com

1 mi southeast by A 413 turning at Chiltern Hospital. Parking.

PRICES
Meals: £ 17 (weekdays) and
a la carte £ 25/48

5 rooms:
£ 95/115

MAP: 19

CLOSING TIMES
Closed 25 December

Sharp's Cornish Coaster, Rebellion IPA and Tring Side Pocket for a Toad

QUEENS HEAD

Keen young owners and a friendly team

Head towards Little Marlow's 12C church and, tucked away down a lane opposite the village's restored cattle pound, you'll find The Queens Head; a popular pub, with keen young partners at its helm and staff who provide poised, friendly service. It was once a spit and sawdust sort of place; its snug bar used to be a salting room and its priest hole makes it a popular place for filming. The garden gets into full swing during the summer months when hungry walkers gather to refuel. Lunch offers a quick fix with sandwiches, ploughman's and pub classics, as well as more refined dishes on the main à la carte - maybe scallops with black pudding, followed by Baileys brûlée. Menus change every 6-8 weeks and produce is from local farms, forages and shoots.

Pound Ln,
LITTLE MARLOW, SL7 3SR
Tel.: (01628)482927
Website: www.marlowslittlesecret.co.uk

3 mi east of Marlow on A 4155 by Church Rd. Parking.

PRICES
Meals: £ 30 and a la carte £ 24/36

MAP: 20

CLOSING TIMES
Closed 25-26 December

Fuller's London Pride and Rebellion Ales

MOLE & CHICKEN

Global menu influenced by the chef's travels

If you're struggling to get your bearings, look to the rooftops for the weather vane depicting a mole and a chicken. This remote pub was built in 1831 as part of the local farm workers' estate and later took on the role of village store. The interior is charming, with wonky low ceilings, open fires, elegant prints and two squashy sofas, but the biggest draw is the large garden, which offers commanding views over the surrounding counties. The menu is a slightly curious affair, featuring classics such as rump of local lamb alongside more unusual offerings like Cornish sprats with aioli or pork belly laksa - with influences from the chef's travels in Asia and The Lebanon clear to see. The delightful modern bedrooms are in an adjoining house.

Easington,
LONG CRENDON, HP18 8EY
Tel.: (01844)208387
Website: www.themoleandchicken.co.uk

3 mi north of Thame by B 4011. Parking.

PRICES
Meals: £ 16 (weekdays) and
a la carte £ 27/46

5 rooms:
£ 85/110

MAP: 21

CLOSING TIMES
Closed 25 December

Vale Brewery Easington Best

HAND AND FLOWERS ✿✿

High calibre classic cooking from a dedicated chef

Many must have driven past this pretty little pub on the edge of Marlow unaware of the dedication and passion of its tenants and the calibre of the cooking coming out of its kitchen. It's very much a pub, with low beams, flagged floors and a characterful lounge bar for pre and post-dinner drinks, and in keeping with this appealingly informal environment, the classic dishes are far from pretentious. There's plenty of choice, from a glazed omelette of smoked haddock and parmesan to the popular duck breast with duck fat chips and gravy; quality ingredients marrying perfectly to turn the simple into the sublime. A few lucky souls get to eat without booking at the metal-topped bar counter – and beautifully furnished bedrooms are a stone's throw away.

126 West St,
MARLOW, SL7 2BP
Tel.: (01628)482277
Website: www.thehandandflowers.co.uk

On the western side of the town on A 4155. Parking.

PRICES
Meals: £ 16 (weekday lunch) and
a la carte £ 43/64

8 rooms:
£ 140/190

MAP: 22

CLOSING TIMES
Closed 24-
26 December, 1 January and Sunday dinner
booking essential

Greene King Ales, Hardy &
Hansons H and F Ale

ROYAL OAK

A popular pub with a peaceful garden

Set less than 15 minutes from the M40 and M4, this part-17C pub is the ideal escape from the busy streets of London. As you approach, pleasant scents drift up from the herb garden, gentle 'chinks' emanate from the petanque pitch and the world feels at once more peaceful. While away the warmer days on the terrace or snuggle into pretty cushions beside the wood burning stove in winter, where rich fabrics and heritage colours provide a country-chic feel, and freshly cut flowers decorate the room. Not surprisingly, it's extremely popular and the eager team are often stretched to their limit. Cooking is British-led; you might find a slow-cooked ox cheek pasty or pork chops with salt and pepper squid. Wash these down with a pint of local Rebellion ale.

Frieth Rd,
BOVINGDON GREEN, Marlow, SL7 2JF
Tel.: (01628)488611
Website: www.royaloakmarlow.co.uk

1.25 mi west of Marlow by A 4155 and Bovingdon Green rd. Parking.

PRICES
Meals: a la carte £ 21/37

MAP: 23

CLOSING TIMES
Closed 25-26 December

Rebellion Ales

CROOKED BILLET

A charming 17C former farmhouse

This charming 17C thatched pub is the last place you expect to come across as you drive around the outskirts of Milton Keynes. Built using wood from an old sailing ship, it started life as a farmhouse in the 1600s. It later provided refreshment for farmers on their way to and from work and eventually evolved into the village pub. In the 20C, during the village festival, stalls and games were set up in the large garden; the same kind of community spirit remains today, and you will more often than not find a cheery bunch of locals propping up the bar. As we go to print, a new team are about to take over - we hope that they will continue to uphold the pub's high standards, as it has built up quite a reputation over the years.

2 Westbrook End,
NEWTON LONGVILLE, MK17 0DF
Tel.: (01908)373936
Website: www.thebillet.co.uk

6 mi southwest of Milton Keynes by A 421. Parking.

PRICES
Meals: a la carte £ 21/39

MAP: 24

CLOSING TIMES
Closed 25-26 December, Sunday dinner and Monday
booking advisable

Greene King Abbot Ale, Wadworth 6X and St Austell Proper Job

OLD QUEENS HEAD

Turn left to sit in the characterful former barn

This pub may not be quite as old as the ancient beech woodlands that surround it but it does have a part to play in the area's history. Legend has it that Lord Penn inherited the pub when he won a game of cards against Charles II. Whether this is true or not, no one knows, but it can be proved from the 1666 deeds that it was purchased by one of the King's physicians. Find a spot on the paved terrace or take in the view from the former barn - now the dining room; the surrounding rooms may be slightly newer but they continue the rustic theme. Big, hearty dishes are the order of the day - the bubble and squeak with oak-smoked bacon, free range poached egg and hollandaise sauce is a perennial favourite. Come on a Saturday for a laid-back brunch.

Hammersley Ln,
PENN, HP10 8EY
Tel.: (01494)813371
Website: www.oldqueensheadpenn.co.uk

4 mi northwest of junction 2 of M 40, via Beaconsfield and B 474.
Parking.

PRICES
Meals: a la carte £ 21/37

MAP: 25

CLOSING TIMES
Closed 25-26 December

Greene King IPA and Ruddles County

THREE HORSESHOES INN

Have tapas in the garden overlooking the pond

This 18C red-brick pub is set in a fantastic hillside location, deep in the countryside. The cosy bar with its attractive flag floor and inglenook fireplace is the place to be - although with space being limited, you might want to head to the restaurant, with its stunning beams and smart, minimalist feel. In warmer weather, make for the terrace, which boasts pleasant views over the duck pond to the hills beyond. Menus reflect the chef's background, so you'll find classically prepared dishes with the odd French touch. Lunch consists mainly of soups, salads and pâtés, while dinner offers a more formal à la carte and some lighter tapas dishes; the latter served in the bar and garden. Bedrooms are contemporary and lavish; Molières is the best.

Bennett End,
RADNAGE, HP14 4EB
Tel.: (01494)483273
Website: www.thethreehorseshoes.net

5 mi west of High Wycombe by A 40 and minor road north. Parking.

PRICES
Meals: £ 16 (weekdays) and a la carte £ 29/40

6 rooms:
£ 80/150

MAP: 26

CLOSING TIMES
Closed Sunday dinner and Monday lunch except bank holidays

Brakspear Oxford Gold, Rebellion IPA and Rebellion Mutiny

JOLLY CRICKETERS

Plenty of memorabilia for cricket fans

Somehow it's hard to imagine a pub called The Jolly Footballers. Indeed, no sport does nostalgia or evokes a spirit of bonhomie quite like cricket and this charming Victorian pub certainly does its bit for the gentleman's game: there's memorabilia aplenty, including signed cricket bats and Test Match programmes, and even the menu comes divided into 'Openers, Main Play and Lower Order'. But this is also a pub where people come to eat. The kitchen nicely balances classic dishes with more modern choices, so seasonal asparagus could be followed by monkfish with Moroccan spices and, for dessert, a generously sized and satisfyingly filling fruit crumble. In winter, sit by the fireplace and count down the months until summer comes around again.

24 Chalfont Rd,
SEER GREEN, HP9 2YG
Tel.: (01494)676308
Website: www.thejollycricketers.co.uk

2.5 mi northeast of Beaconsfield off A 355. Parking.

PRICES
Meals: a la carte £ 22/40

MAP: 27

CLOSING TIMES
Open daily
booking advisable

Fuller's London Pride, Rebellion IPA and Vale VPA

GINGER DOG

Check out the four-legged friend theme

This charming Victorian pub has a pleasing shabby-chic, canine theme, a welcoming atmosphere and a relaxed feel. Many of the original architectural features - such as the ornate woodwork - are juxtaposed with contemporary design touches; note the bowler hats unusually used as lampshades. Tables are smartly laid up behind the bar but you can eat anywhere. Fresh produce is to the fore on the menu, which is mostly British but with the odd nod to the Med, and could include rabbit and ham hock terrine, breast of pheasant with prunes, or marmalade steamed sponge. Water and some delicious slices of bread are not only brought to the table without hesitation but aren't charged for either; and a ginger 'dog' biscuit is served with the coffee.

12 College Pl,
BRIGHTON, BN2 1HN
Tel.: (01273)620990
Website: www.gingermanrestaurants.com

In heart of Kemp Town, just off Marine Parade (A 259) towards Lewes. Metered parking nearby.

PRICES
Meals: £ 13 (lunch) and a la carte £ 25/37

MAP: 28

CLOSING TIMES
Closed 25 December

Underdog Best Bitter

GINGER PIG

British dishes by the sea

Set just off the seafront, this smart building displays a mortar relief of a ship above the entrance and a beautifully restored revolving door, harking back to its former days as the Ship Inn. Its Victorian vintage is also evident in its appealing dining room and its long, wood-floored bar: the perfect setting for a cocktail or two. The extensive à la carte offers precisely prepared, flavoursome British dishes - including plenty of vegetarian options - and there's a great value set lunch menu, along with some good wine deals; order a coffee and it'll arrive with a quirky pig-shaped shortbread. They're used to being busy and service copes reasonably well under pressure, the only drawback being that it can lack a more personal touch.

3 Hove St,
HOVE, Brighton, BN3 2TR
Tel.: (01273)736123
Website: www.gingermanrestaurants.com

Off north side of shore road, Kingsway, A 259. NCP car park (2min walk) & parking meters (2hr maximum during day).

PRICES
Meals: £ 14 (weekday lunch) and
a la carte £ 24/35

MAP: 29

CLOSING TIMES
Closed 25 December

Harveys Sussex Best Bitter and Arundel Sussex Gold

RED LION

On the edge of Ashdown Forest

When Harold Macmillan was Prime Minster, the Red Lion was his local; it also played host to John F. Kennedy when he was invited here by the PM at the height of the Cold War. Its visitors these days may be a little less illustrious, but it's almost certain that the welcome is as warm as the one received by those famous men more than half a century ago. The concise menu offers a mix of pub classics and French influenced dishes, so expect fishcakes or steak and ale pie as well as goose rillettes with cornichons or a warming winter cassoulet, and crème brûlée on offer alongside sticky toffee pudding or apple crumble and custard. The bright conservatory is the best place to dine, and opens out onto a paved terrace and a lovely lawned garden.

Lewes Rd,
CHELWOOD GATE, RH17 7DE
Tel.: (01825)740265
Website: www.redlionchelwoodgate.co.uk

On A 275 between Forest Row and Danehill. Parking.

PRICES
Meals: a la carte £ 16/30

MAP: 30

CLOSING TIMES
Closed Sunday dinner

Harveys Sussex Best Bitter and Shepherd Neame Ales

JOLLY SPORTSMAN

Interesting bar bites & an evolving specials board

Down a myriad of country lanes, in a small hamlet, this olive green pub attracts locals in their droves. You're greeted by smoky aromas from an open fire and by a bubbly team; often even by the owner himself. Choose a spot in the cosy bar, in the warmly decorated red room or in the garden room with its concertina doors opening onto the large garden and terrace - and prepare for just as much choice when it comes to the food. There are interesting bar bites such as Cabezada and Guindillas, good value set menus, a rustic, British-based à la carte and blackboard specials, which quickly come and go; many of the herbs and fruits come from the polytunnel outside. A very good wine list and plenty of cask ales, ciders and perries are on offer too.

Chapel Ln,
EAST CHILTINGTON, BN7 3BA
Tel.: (01273)890400
Website: www.thejollysportsman.com

5.5 mi northwest of Lewes by A 275 and B 2116 off Novington Lane. Parking.

PRICES
Meals: £ 15 (lunch) and a la carte £ 26/41

MAP: 31

CLOSING TIMES
Closed 25 December
booking essential

Dark Star Hophead and Harveys Sussex Best Bitter

GRIFFIN INN

Wood-burning oven for summer barbecues

Under the same ownership for over 30 years, this hugely characterful red and white brick coaching inn is the kind of place that every village wishes it had. It boasts a linen-laid dining room, a traditional wood-panelled bar and a 'Club Room' adorned with cricketing memorabilia, as well as a sizeable garden and terrace - with a wood burning oven for sophisticated summer Sunday barbecues. A large freestanding blackboard in the bar offers a range of British classics with some Mediterranean influences, and there's a more structured à la carte available in the dining room. If you live locally, work it off by joining one of the pub's cricket teams; if not, follow narrow, sloping corridors to one of the individually decorated bedrooms.

FLETCHING, TN22 3SS
Tel.: (01825)722890
Website: www.thegriffininn.co.uk

In centre of village. Parking.

PRICES
Meals: £ 25 (weekday lunch) and a la carte £ 26/46

13 rooms: £ 70/145

MAP: 32

CLOSING TIMES
Closed 25 December

Harveys Sussex Best Bitter

SHIP INN

Laid-back vibe and modern pub favourites

Fittingly located at the bottom of Mermaid Street, The Ship Inn dates back to 1592, when it was used as a warehouse for impounding smuggled goods. This is a place that proves that smart surroundings aren't a prerequisite for good food. Modern pop art and boars' heads are dotted about the rooms, fairy lights are draped everywhere and if you sit on one of the battered sofas, don't be alarmed if you end up at a quirky angle or even falling through. The quality of the food then, comes as a surprise. Ingredients are well-sourced and preparation is careful. The result: flavoursome pub favourites with a modern twist - maybe prawn croquettes with a chilli dip or soy-braised pork belly. Compact bedrooms have eye-catching feature walls and bold styling.

The Strand,
RYE, TN31 7DB
Tel.: (01797)222233
Website: www.theshipinnrye.co.uk

Close to the Quayside. Local car park close by.

PRICES
Meals: a la carte £ 23/35

10 rooms:
£ 75/125

MAP: 33

CLOSING TIMES
Open daily

Long Man Best Bitter, Old Dairy Gold Top and Whitstable Brewery East India Pale Ale

BELL

Generous portions in a quirky 16C coaching inn

The lampshades are top hats, there are tubas in the loos and a pile of books appear to be holding up the beams: welcome to The Bell, a late 16C coaching inn which has been transformed into a quirky, shabby-chic pub with the emphasis firmly on the chic. There's a delightful snug, a bar with a vast inglenook fireplace, and a dining room called 'the stable with a table' and the seven rustic, individually styled bedrooms - each with their own silver birch tree - share the pub's idiosyncratic charm. Simple bar snacks might include Sussex smokies or scotch egg, while the seasonal menus offer generous portions of proper pub food like the Bell burger alongside more adventurous dishes such as Dorset crab or pork belly with black pudding.

High St,
TICEHURST, TN5 7AS
Tel.: (01580)200234
Website: www.thebellinticehurst.com

In the centre of the village. Parking.

PRICES
Meals: a la carte £ 27/40

7 rooms:
£ 85/190

MAP: 34

CLOSING TIMES
Open daily
booking advisable

Harveys Sussex Best Bitter and Old Dairy Gold Top

WELLINGTON ARMS

They keep sheep, pigs, chickens and bees!

If success is dependent on the effort put into sourcing local produce and making, growing and rearing everything possible, then The Wellington is a sure-fire winner. They have herb and vegetable beds, they keep their own sheep, pigs, chickens and bees, and the rest of their meats are sourced from within 20 miles. Inside the cosy quarry-tiled, low-beamed bar you'll also find their eggs, honey and preserves for sale. Menus feature 6 dishes per course - supplemented by a selection of blackboard specials - and cooking is generous and satisfying. Dishes might include twice-baked Westcombe cheddar soufflé, venison pie or steak from the farm just over the fields. Smart, rustic bedrooms come with sheepskin rugs and big, comfy beds.

Baughurst Rd,
BAUGHURST, RG26 5LP
Tel.: (0118)9820110
Website: www.thewellingtonarms.com

8 mi north of Basingstoke by A 339 and minor road through Ramsdell and Pound Green, on the Kingsclere / Newbury rd. Parking.

PRICES
Meals: £ 19 (weekday lunch) and
a la carte £ 21/43

3 rooms:
£ 95/200

MAP: 35

CLOSING TIMES
Closed Sunday dinner
booking essential

West Berkshire Good Old Boy and Old Father Thames and Two Cocks Cavalier

EXCHEQUER

Monday night is steak and grill night!

This pub has gone by many different monikers and its fortunes have changed as often as its name, but its current owners seem to have hit on a winning formula. It has undergone a slick, modern facelift: as you enter there's an inviting drinkers' area, complete with a log burning stove; while further on it's divided into three, with two semi-private areas and a smart, conservatory-style room. The menu offers gutsy British staples, with the likes of steak pie and crumble with custard, but there's also a nod to the East, courtesy of dishes such as prawn tempura. The blackboard best displays the kitchen's abilities – the well-crafted, boldly flavoured specials could include roast pheasant or grouse. Service is keen and completes the experience.

Crondall Rd,
CROOKHAM VILLAGE, GU51 5SU
Tel.: (01252)615336
Website: www.exchequercrookham.co.uk

1 mi north off A 287 in centre of village. Parking

PRICES
Meals: a la carte £ 20/39

MAP: 36

CLOSING TIMES
Closed 25 December

Hogs Back TEA, Andwell Red Mist and Ringwood Fortyniner

BAKERS ARMS

Veg is home-grown and bread baked twice daily

The owners met whilst working abroad on private yachts, eventually returning to their roots to run this roadside inn - which also doubles as the local post office. Their experience, effort and enthusiasm have stood them in good stead: cooking is unfussy and filling, they bake their own bread twice a day and they also grow some of the vegetables. Main dishes might include venison steak or slow-cooked Hampshire beef, while pudding could be a pear crumble or treacle tart - and, pleasingly, you can order two courses and a drink for a mere "Baker's Dozen"! The pub itself is charming, with leather sofas, a roaring log fire and walls hung with interesting oddments including beer adverts and stag heads. Beers are from the local Droxford-based brewery.

High St,
DROXFORD, SO32 3PA
Tel.: (01489)877533
Website: www.thebakersarmsdroxford.com

6 mi north of Fareham by A 32. Parking.

PRICES
Meals: £ 13 (weekdays) and
a la carte £ 23/32

MAP: 37

CLOSING TIMES
Closed Sunday dinner

Bowman Ales

EAST END ARMS

Owned by John Illsley from Dire Straits

Owned by John Illsley, bass guitarist of Dire Straits, this traditional country pub boasts a great display of black and white photos of legendary singers, musicians and celebrities from his personal collection. When he bought the place in the late '90s, the locals petitioned for him to keep it the same, so you'll find a slightly shabby bar with cushioned pews, open fire and dartboard, and a smarter pine-furnished dining room behind. Menus are fairly concise, and feature local produce in satisfying, British-based dishes listed in order of price. You might find whitebait or scallops followed by pigeon breast, venison or rump of lamb. Modern, cottage-style bedrooms provide a smart contrast and staff are friendly and attentive.

Lymington Rd,
EAST END, SO41 5SY
Tel.: (01590)626223
Website: www.eastendarms.co.uk

3 mi east of Lymington by B 3054. Parking.

PRICES
Meals: a la carte £ 23/41

5 rooms:
£ 71/120

MAP: 38

CLOSING TIMES
Closed dinner Sunday and Monday

Ringwood Fortyniner
and Best Bitter

BUGLE

Rustic and cosy, with views over the marina

Set in a charming spot in a quaint little village, this grade II listed building is popular with the sailing community - and owned by a keen seafarer - and its terrace has pleasant views over Southampton Water. With its exposed brick and well-worn stone floors, it has a rustic, cosy feel; there's an abundance of maritime character and a private dining room with a lovely Dickensian feel. Food ranges from simple soups, salads and sandwiches to dishes like pork belly or lamb rump. There are small plates such as Scotch egg, devilled whitebait or salt and pepper squid to mix and match, as well as pub classics like ale-battered fish and chips or home-cooked honey roast ham. Sporting events, quiz nights and themed food evenings bring in the crowds.

High St,
HAMBLE-LE-RICE, SO31 4HA
Tel.: (023)80453000
Website: www.buglehamble.co.uk

7 mi southeast of Southampton by A 3024 or A 3025 and B 3397. Pay and display parking nearby.

PRICES
Meals: a la carte £ 22/37

MAP: 39

CLOSING TIMES
Open daily
booking advisable

Bowman Ales, Itchen Valley and Flowerpots

YEW TREE

Classic dishes with the occasional twist

Just down the road from Highclere Castle - the setting for Downton Abbey - is this pretty 17C inn, where you have to stoop to enter into the rustic interior, with its low beamed ceilings and original flagstone floors. The bar, with is leather sofas and roaring log fires, is a great spot for a drink and a snack, while the three dining rooms with their flickering candles provide a more intimate atmosphere. The menu is divided into 'small', 'medium' and 'large' dishes - for both main courses and desserts - and classically based recipes are given modern twists; there are some interesting vegetarian options too. In summer, relax on the pretty rear terrace. If you fancy staying overnight, bedrooms are cosy, with good mod cons and smart wet rooms.

Hollington Cross,
ANDOVER RD, Highclere, RG20 9SE
Tel.: (01635)253360
Website: www.theyewtree.co.uk

5 mi south of Newbury on A 343. Parking.

PRICES
Meals: a la carte £ 23/41

8 rooms:
£ 95/120

MAP: 40

CLOSING TIMES
Open daily

Flack Manor Flack Catcher,
Upham Punter and Two Cocks
1643 Cavalier

HOGGET

Wholesome cooking respects the ingredients

This brightly painted pub with its busy bar, book-filled lounge and popular heated terrace is found in an unprepossessing spot at the junction of the A30 and the A287. Accessible menus offer wholesome, honest cooking which shows respect for locally sourced ingredients; dishes are sensibly priced and will include the likes of Hampshire sausages and mash, beer-battered hake and slow-cooked lamb shank, alongside salads, snacks and grazing boards to share. Puddings are hearty and filling, the gourmet burgers and Sunday roasts are popular, and service is efficient and cheery. Look out for members of the local football and cricket teams, who play on the field next door and pop over to either celebrate or commiserate after their matches.

London Rd,
HOOK, RG27 9JJ
Tel.: (01256)763009
Website: www.TheHogget.co.uk

At the junction of A 30 and A 287. Parking.

PRICES
Meals: a la carte £ 18/33

MAP: 41

CLOSING TIMES
Closed 25-26 December

Ringwood Best Bitter, Marston's Pedigree and Wychwood Hobgoblin

RUNNING HORSE (N)

Book the cosy cabana!

You won't miss this smart, grey-painted pub: just look out for the horse running along the side and the straw-roofed cabana at the front (heated, very cosy and it can be booked!) Sit near the log burner in the front of the shabby-chic, wood panelled bar or, for a more intimate meal, head to the rear dining area with its shelves of antique books. The menu is concise and constantly evolving and dishes are well-priced, fuss-free and big on flavour. Sharing platters include vegetarian, charcuterie and seafood options; other dishes might include home cured gravadlax, duck liver parfait or omelette Arnold Bennett. Service is pleasingly unpretentious and the simply furnished bedrooms are arranged around the garden, motel-style.

88 Main Rd,
LITTLETON, SO22 6QS
Tel.: (01962)880218
Website: www.runninghorseinn.co.uk

2.5 mi northwest of Winchester, signed off B 3049. Parking.

PRICES
Meals: a la carte £ 22/36

9 rooms:
£ 65/105

MAP: 42

CLOSING TIMES
Closed dinner 25 December

Upham Brewery Ales

PLOUGH INN

The chef will happily cook your day's catch

Set in a lovely location in the Test Valley, this red brick and tile pub takes pride of place at the hub of this characterful village. It's owned by an experienced chef, who left the bright lights of London for a place of his own. Inside, it's pleasingly rustic, with a laid-back feel: there's a small bar to one side, a wine cave under the stairs and a cheese trolley in the corner – which is wheeled over for you if you're having a ploughman's. Menus feature a likeable selection of pub classics with some more ambitious choices on the à la carte; dishes show a good respect for ingredients and are prepared in a modern way. This being prime fishing country, you are also more than welcome to bring your day's catch for the chef to prepare.

LONGPARISH, SP11 6PB
Tel.: (01264)720358
Website: www.theploughinn.info

7 mi east of Andover by A 303 and B 3048. Parking.

PRICES
Meals: a la carte £ 30/47

MAP: 43

CLOSING TIMES
Closed Sunday dinner and Monday

Ringwood Best Bitter, Meantime Brewery London Pale Ale, Longdog Golden Poacher

PEAT SPADE INN

In a pretty village in the heart of the valley

In the heart of the Test Valley is this charming and cosy 19C inn, where sporting memorabilia, period furnishings and warming open fires are accompanied by flickering candlelight. Country pursuits are the name of the game, so you'll find plenty of shooters and fishermen inside, alongside local farm workers and those leisurely passing through. Menus offer classic dishes with bold flavours; perhaps pork pâté with piccalilli, followed by Hampshire lamb three ways or whole lemon sole with capers and golden raisins. Stylish bedrooms are split between the main building and the annexe, and there's a residents' lounge which overlooks the courtyard garden and its sunken fire-pit. Staff are friendly and obliging; ask them to show you the gin menu.

Village St,
LONGSTOCK, SO20 6DR
Tel.: (01264)810612
Website: www.peatspadeinn.co.uk

1.5 mi north of Stockbridge on A 3507. Parking.

PRICES
Meals: a la carte £ 22/33

8 rooms:
£ 80/145

MAP: 44

CLOSING TIMES
Closed 25 December
booking advisable

Flowerpots Ales and Flack's Flack Catcher

THE ANCHOR INN

Friendly, welcoming and full of 14C charm

With its origins firmly in the 14C, this part-whitewashed, part-tile hung pub boasts much more in the way of history than sister establishment, The Peat Spade Inn. Pretty countryside and a little pond set the scene and the interior doesn't disappoint, boasting characterful low-beamed olive green rooms and a pleasing mix of cushioned pews, benches and old chairs. Good-sized menus offer classic pub dishes with a refined edge and cooking is hearty and flavoursome; you might find Portland crab salad, followed by venison pie or braised ox cheek. Service is fittingly keen and friendly, and there's a concise but well-chosen wine list. Bedrooms are characterful but if you retire before closing, you may be able to hear a gentle hum from the bar.

LOWER FROYLE, GU34 4NA
Tel.: (01420)23261
Website: www.anchorinnatlowerfroyle.co.uk

5 mi northeast of Alton by A 31. Parking.

PRICES
Meals: a la carte £ 25/46

5 rooms:
£ 120/150

MAP: 45

CLOSING TIMES
Closed 25 December

Triple fff Alton's Pride and Moondance, Andwell King John

CROWN

Everything from bread to fudge is homemade

Away from the sprawl of Basingstoke lies lesser known Old Basing, home to the Tudor ruins of Basing House. Within the village you'll also find The Crown, which is in the hands of two local chefs who gave it a lick of paint and set to the stoves. They may have started with a limited budget but their enthusiasm is palpable and they sensibly pay as much attention to the needs of the villagers just popping in for a drink as those coming for a meal. The menus come with a likeable simplicity and the classic, flavoursome food reveals a confident kitchen. Everything is homemade, from the bread to the fudge served with coffee; a good value lunch draws customers from the nearby business park and the concise dinner menu appeals to locals.

The Street,
OLD BASING, RG24 7BW
Tel.: (01256)321424
Website: www.thecrownoldbasing.com

2.5 mi east of Basingstoke by A 3010 following signs for Basing House. Parking.

PRICES
Meals: a la carte £ 25/38

MAP: 46

CLOSING TIMES
Closed 1 January and Sunday dinner

Fuller's London Pride, Andwell Gold Muddler and Sharp's Doom Bar

WHITE HORSE

Smart community pub with a flexible menu

This is a large pub which can get very busy, especially at weekends, so arrive early to bag a table. It's smart, with designer décor, arty photos, vintage adverts and leather sofas; one side is for drinkers, while the other side is set up for diners. When it comes to the menu, flexibility is key: have a bar snack like a pickled egg or some black pudding fritters; perhaps a lunchtime sandwich with some triple-cooked chips; a dish like chicken and leek pie or braised beef shin - or the full three courses. There are lovely local cheeses, bread from a nearby artisan baker, Sunday roasts and even afternoon teas. Add in a couple of terraces and a young, friendly team, and it's not hard to see why the White Horse is once again the hub of the village.

Main Rd,
OTTERBOURNE, SO21 2EQ
Tel.: (01962)712830
Website: www.whitehorseotterbourne.co.uk

8.5 mi south of Winchester by B 3335 and minor roads. Parking.

PRICES
Meals: a la carte £ 19/39

MAP: 47

CLOSING TIMES
Open daily

Ringwood Best Bitter, Flowerpots Bitter and Timothy Taylor Landlord

PUREFOY ARMS

Daily changing menus with Spanish influences

Don't be fooled by the somewhat austere façade; a charming young couple have totally restored this once crumbling pub, which was last rebuilt in the 1860s. It now comes with an attractive contemporary feel, although many of the original features have been retained. The daily changing menu, with its hints of Spain - especially in the bar nibbles - is very appealing. Some luxury ingredients may appear at weekends but the philosophy is tasty food at competitive prices and everything's homemade, including the bread. There are also dishes to share, such as the suckling pig, which requires pre-ordering. And the chocolates in the bar are courtesy of the owner's father, a retired chocolatier who has set up a studio in one of the barns.

Alresford Rd,
PRESTON CANDOVER, RG25 2EJ
Tel.: (01256)389777
Website: www.thepurefoyarms.co.uk

6.5 mi north of New Alresford on B 3046 in centre of village. Parking.

PRICES
Meals: £ 18 (weekday lunch) and
a la carte £ 23/33

MAP: 48

CLOSING TIMES
Closed 26 December, 1 January,
Sunday dinner and Monday

Palmers Copper Ale, Irving Frigate and Flack's Double Drop

THREE TUNS

Choice of small plates or classic pub dishes

Having been through a number of mismanagements in the past, this charming pub - which dates from the 1720s - finally has the tenants it deserves. Tucked down a quiet road, it oozes charm from the moment you walk in. The low beamed bar with its crackling fires is usually full of locals enjoying a drink and a 'small plate' such as devilled whitebait. Beyond is a panelled room where you'll find guests dining on well-priced and reassuringly 'proper' pub food, like a steak and kidney pie or home-baked honey-glazed ham and eggs; while dishes like belly of pork with black pudding or Hampshire rhubarb crumble show that this is a kitchen with a deft touch. Service is pitched just right and is provided by a young and very hospitable team.

58 Middlebridge St,
ROMSEY, SO51 8HL
Tel.: (01794)512639
Website: www.the3tunsromsey.co.uk

Towards the western end of the town, off the bypass. Parking.

PRICES
Meals: a la carte £ 20/33

MAP: 49

CLOSING TIMES
Closed 25-26 December

Ringwood Fortyniner, Flack's Double Drop, Wadworth St George & The Dragon and Upham Ales

WHITE STAR TAVERN, DINING AND ROOMS

All-day dining in the lively maritime district

You can't miss this striking black pub with its oversized windows and smart pavement terrace. Set in the lively maritime district, it's provided nourishment and shelter for seafarers since the 19C, although you'll find a much more diverse mix of visitors nowadays. It's a spacious place, made up of several different areas organised around a central bar, and displays an eclectic combination of furniture. The à la carte offers a good choice of modern British main courses - finished off with proper old-fashioned puddings - but there's also a selection of small plates on offer throughout the day; and they even open early for breakfast. Stylish, very comfortable bedrooms offer excellent facilities and are named after legendary White Star Liners.

28 Oxford St,
SOUTHAMPTON, SO14 3DJ
Tel.: (023)80821990
Website: www.whitestartavern.co.uk

Southeast of West Quay shopping centre, off Bernard Street. Parking meters directly outside and College St car park (2min walk).

PRICES
Meals: a la carte £ 19/40

14 rooms:
£ 105/145

MAP: 50

CLOSING TIMES
Closed 25-26 December

Itchen Valley Brewery White Star Ale and Timothy Taylor Golden Best

GREYHOUND ON THE TEST

Characterful pub with a mile of fishing rights

If ever there were a place close to J.R.Hartley's heart, it would have been Stockbridge: the River Test flows under the High Street and the oldest fishing club in England was founded here in 1882. This mustard-coloured pub plays its part too – head for the garden and you'll find over a mile of River Test fishing rights. At over 600 years old, it has plenty of character: low beams and wood burning stoves abound, and the elegant décor gives it a French bistro feel. When it comes to the food, there's a selection of well-presented, refined British classics. The good value set lunch keeps the regulars happy, local game and seafood are a feature, and the chef will happily cook your catch. Homely bedrooms have large showers and quality bedding.

31 High St,
STOCKBRIDGE, SO20 6EY
Tel.: (01264)810833
Website: www.thegreyhoundonthetest.co.uk

15 mi east of Salisbury by A 30. In centre of town. Parking.

PRICES
Meals: £ 19 (weekday lunch) and
a la carte £ 23/40

10 rooms:
£ 70/180

MAP: 51

CLOSING TIMES
Closed 25 December
booking advisable

Ringwood Best Bitter, Andwell and Flack's Double Drop

THOMAS LORD

Named after the founder of Lord's Cricket Ground

This smartly refurbished, early 19C pub is named after the founder of Lord's Cricket Ground, who retired to and is buried in the village - which explains the bats, county caps and other cricketing memorabilia filling the walls. Roaring fires and friendly faces keep the atmosphere warm and welcoming and there's a lovely garden - part of which is used to grow their own herbs and vegetables. The menu perfectly balances classic doorstop sandwiches, ploughman's lunches and risottos with dishes such as fried ham hock and black pudding, pork belly with boulangère potatoes, and treacle tart with bay leaf ice cream. They host music evenings twice a month and you might find the odd local having an impromptu tinkle on the piano in the bar.

High St,
WEST MEON, GU32 1LN
Tel.: (01730)829444
Website: www.thomaslord.co.uk

9 mi west of Petersfield by A 272 and A 32 south. Parking.

PRICES
Meals: £ 16 and a la carte £ 23/40

MAP: 52

CLOSING TIMES
Closed 25 December

Upham Ales and Ringwood Best Bitter

NO.5 BRIDGE STREET

Cooking displays Mediterranean influences

Enter the town from the south and you can't miss this roadside pub by the busy main roundabout. A top-to-toe makeover has given the place a fashionable, modern feel and, come summer, the internal courtyard is a real boon. The front bar with its metal-topped tables is the best place for a drink - the humorous wine and cocktail list makes for a good read - or head to the dining room at the back for table service and a view of the chefs at work in the open kitchen. The menu is divided into various sections, including 'small plates', 'market plates', 'soups and salads' and 'British charcuterie and cheese', and dishes veer towards the Mediterranean in their influences. Simply styled, comfortable bedrooms - those at the front hear the road noise.

5 Bridge St,
WINCHESTER, SO23 0HN
Tel.: (01962)863838
Website: www.no5bridgestreet.co.uk

In town centre. Pay and display parking nearby.

PRICES
Meals: a la carte £ 18/43

6 rooms:
£ 99/124

MAP: 53

CLOSING TIMES
Closed 25 December

Flack's Double Drop and Itchen Valley Ales

WYKEHAM ARMS

Celebrates all things British

This red-brick pub is the epitome of Britishness: it's named after the first bishop of Winchester who founded the boys' college and is decorated with all manner of British bric-a-brac, including school desks, hats, cartoons, a bishop's mitre and over a thousand tankards. Even its individually styled bedrooms - some above the pub, and some in an annexe over the road - are named after British individuals like Hamilton and Nelson (who reputedly stayed here when he travelled down to Portsmouth). Dishes are elaborate and adventurous, showcasing modern cooking techniques; for something a bit simpler, choose a dish from the 'home comforts' section of the menu: perhaps the rib-eye steak, belly of pork or beer battered haddock and chips.

75 Kingsgate St,
WINCHESTER, SO23 9PE
Tel.: (01962)853834
Website: www.wykehamarmswinchester.co.uk

Near Winchester College (St Mary's). Access to car park (for residents only) via Canon Street. Limited restricted on-street parking.

PRICES
Meals: £ 18/22 and a la carte £ 23/42

14 rooms:
£ 89/190

MAP: 54

CLOSING TIMES
Closed dinner 25 December
booking essential

Fuller's London Pride and Seafarers, George Gale HSB, Flowerpots Goodens Gold

TAVERNERS

Homemade seasonal dishes and an on-site deli

In a pretty – and often busy – little village, stands this passionately run, roadside pub. It's the kind of place that's all about the latest island ingredients and handmade, homemade everything. A blackboard asks for any surplus home-grown produce (in return for a local Taverners beer or two); the large garden is home to chickens, herbs and veg; and inside, various boards display food miles and tables of what's in season when. The pub even has its own on-site deli selling homemade produce including bread, sauces and pies. Cooking is fresh and tasty, mixing traditional pub classics such as lamb burgers with more ambitious daily specials like sea bass fillets. The hand-raised pork pie is a speciality, as is "my nan's" lemon meringue pie.

High St,
GODSHILL, PO38 3HZ
Tel.: (01983)840707
Website: www.thetavernersgodshill.co.uk

4 mi west of Shanklin by A 3020. Parking.

PRICES
Meals: a la carte £ 19/26

MAP: 55

CLOSING TIMES
Closed first 3 weeks January

Sharp's Doom Bar, Yates Golden Ale and Goddards Fuggle-Dee-Dum

NEW INN

Pub favourites, proudly made with island produce

This pub is tucked away on the main Newport to Yarmouth road and its name is somewhat of a misnomer, as there's been an inn here since 1743. It's full of character, with inglenook fireplaces, slate floors and simple, scrubbed wood tables. Things are also kept simple on the menu, where you'll find proper pub dishes like beef and ale pie, steak and chips, belly pork or ploughman's; all proudly made with island produce. Locally landed fish and seafood feature in the summer months – when the decked terrace also comes into its own – and there are more adventurous specials chalked up on boards daily. Testimony to the pub's popularity is the fact that it's not unusual to see guests who've sailed over from the mainland especially for lunch!

Mill Rd,
SHALFLEET, PO30 4NS
Tel.: (01983)531314
Website: www.thenew-inn.co.uk

7 mi west of Newport on A 3054. Parking.

PRICES
Meals: a la carte £ 17/39

MAP: 56

CLOSING TIMES
Open daily

Sharp's Doom Bar, Goddards Fuggle-Dee-Dum and Ringwood Best Bitter

KENTISH HARE (N)

It's all about the steaks from the Kamado Grill

What was the Hare and Hounds has become the Kentish Hare, after it was saved from redevelopment into flats by local residents Lord and Lady Mills, of Olympic Committee, Air Miles and Nectar Card fame. A top-to-toe refurbishment followed, the talented Tanner brothers were installed to run the place, and the villagers once more have a local they can be proud of. Smart and modern, with a hare motif running through it, some quirky wallpaper and furniture and an open kitchen, the Hare provides a great value set midweek menu, pub classics on the bar menu and dishes like roast rack of Romney lamb on the à la carte, while the speciality Kamado Grill section allows you to 'create your own' steak, with a choice of cut, sauce and accompaniment.

95 Bidborough Ridge,
BIDBOROUGH, TN3 0XB
Tel.: (01892)525709
Website: www.thekentishhare.com

2.5 mi southwest of Tonbridge by A26 on B2176. Parking

PRICES
Meals: £ 22 and a la carte £ 23/44

MAP: 57

CLOSING TIMES
Closed Sunday dinner and Monday except bank holidays

Harveys Sussex Best Bitter, Tonbridge Coppernob and Kentish Hare

THE THREE CHIMNEYS

Bags of character and British dishes

This delightful pub dates back to 1420 and has all the character you would expect of a building its age. The low-beamed, dimly lit rooms have a truly old world feel and for sunnier days there's a conservatory, a garden and a charming terrace. Menus feature mainly British dishes, such as smoked haddock, finished off with nursery puddings like apple crumble; there are some tempting local wines, ciders and ales on offer too. The story surrounding the pub's name goes that French prisoners held at Sissinghurst Castle during the Seven Years' War were allowed to wander as far as the three lanes but were forbidden to pass the junction where the pub was sited. 'Les trois chemins' (the three roads) was then later mistranslated into 'The Three Chimneys'.

Hareplain Rd,
BIDDENDEN, TN27 8LW
Tel.: (01580)291472
Website: www.thethreechimneys.co.uk

1.5 mi west by A 262. Parking.

PRICES
Meals: a la carte £ 24/37

MAP: 58

CLOSING TIMES
Closed 25 and dinner 31 December
booking essential

Adnams Best, Old Dairy Red Top and Hop Fuzz Ales

GEORGE & DRAGON

Local farm produce the order of the day

If it's character you're after, then this 450 year old inn on the edge of the village is the place to come. Outside there's a delightful mature garden with a large terrace, a children's play area and raised herb and salad beds. Inside, there's a lovely beamed bar where they serve a huge array of cocktails, and a charming first floor dining room with a sloping ceiling and wonky floor. Looking at the menu, there's no doubting you're in England: seasonal, regional ingredients feature in dishes such as bacon, kale and chestnut soup; celeriac and celery salad with English mustard dressing; and pork belly with apple sauce. The mature, 28-day hung steaks with triple-cooked chips are a perennial favourite, along with the steak sandwiches at lunch.

39 High St,
CHIPSTEAD, TN13 2RW
Tel.: (01732)779019
Website: www.georgeanddragonchipstead.com

Located in the centre of the village. Parking.

PRICES
Meals: a la carte £ 18/36

MAP: 59

CLOSING TIMES
Open daily

Westerham Grasshopper and George's Marvellous Medicine

THE DOVE

Family-run pub on aptly named Plum Pudding Lane

It's a family affair at this red-brick Victorian pub, with Chris and Dorota running the place and Chris's son, Ben, in the kitchen. Rather than sticking to traditional pub offerings, menus concentrate on dishes that would be equally at home in a restaurant such as wild sea bass, rump of lamb with pea and mint or wild mushroom risotto, although the occasional pubby dish, like a ploughman's board to share, does make an appearance. The Dove sits in the heart of a sleepy hamlet on the aptly named Plum Pudding Lane and, with its open fire, wood floors and old black and white photos, has a cosy, rustic feel. The pub's popularity, particularly with locals, means it does get busy; service can be a little haphazard but the welcome is always a jolly one.

Plum Pudding Ln,
DARGATE, ME13 9HB
Tel.: (01227)751360
Website: www.thedovedargate.co.uk

Between Faversham and Whitstable, south of A 299. Parking.

PRICES
Meals: a la carte £ 23/46

MAP: 60

CLOSING TIMES
Closed first week January, Sunday dinner, Tuesday lunch and Monday
booking advisable

Shepherd Neame Ales

GOUDHURST INN

An appealingly old-fashioned style

Anyone currently lamenting the state of their local should take heart from what happened to this pub. It was a down-at-heel place with something of a chequered past until a local chap bought it and did it up from top-to-toe, inside and out; and now it has resumed its place at the heart of village life. Vases of fresh flowers line the bar, the atmosphere is warm and friendly, the look remains suitably rustic and there's a lovely terrace at the back. The food is equally heartening and the kitchen goes local when it can – the wild boar sausages are from a local butcher, the scallops come from Rye and the lamb is from a nearby farm. Be sure to leave room for the gloriously 'proper' puds, like rhubarb crumble or sticky toffee pudding.

Cranbrook Rd,
GOUDHURST, TN17 1DX
Tel.: (01580)212605
Website: www.thegoudhurstinn.com

On A 262 towards Cranbrook. Parking.

PRICES
Meals: a la carte £ 22/43

MAP: 61

CLOSING TIMES
Open daily

Harveys Sussex Best, Timothy Taylor Landlord and Sharp's Doom Bar

THE VINE (N)

Provenance is at the top of the agenda

When childhood friends Tobyn and Ben acquired this part-17C pub, it was almost derelict and had squatters - what a long way it has come since then! Three cosy ground floor rooms have a rustic, shabby-chic feel, while the two upstairs dining rooms are more formal. Bar snacks like deer sausage rolls take the edge off your appetite, while traditional British dishes might include ham hock terrine with pickled pear, or brill with pressed potatoes and shrimps. Provenance is at the top of the agenda here and, since The Vine is situated in the 'Garden of England', there is plenty of quality produce right on their doorstep. This desire to keep things local also extends to the drinks, so enjoy a cider from Biddenham or a beer from Tenterden or Tonbridge.

High St,
GOUDHURST, TN17 1AG
Tel.: (01580)211753
Website: www.thevinegoudhurst.com

In village centre. Free parking in car-park behind the duck pond

PRICES
Meals: £ 20 (weekday lunch) and
a la carte £ 26/40

MAP: 62

CLOSING TIMES
Open daily

Dark Star Hophead, Old Dairy Red Top and Chapel Down Ales

THE WINDMILL (N)

Beams so low you have to duck

The pub is a great British institution and this one is as characterful as they come, with a giant inglenook and beams so low you have to watch your head. Hearty British dishes like a warming cock-a-leekie soup or a comforting plate of liver and onions fittingly form the core of the menu, with bar snacks like scotch egg with piccalilli or pork scratchings with apple compote; comforting puddings like those of the rice or sticky toffee variety, and sharing roasts on Sundays. Drinks are by no means ignored: if you fancy a G&T, there are at least four gins from which to choose, and beer drinkers can enjoy Kentish ales from the local Musket Brewery. Polite young staff ensure you get what you want when you want it, and deliver it with a smile.

32 Eyhorne St,
HOLLINGBOURNE, ME17 1TR
Tel.: (01622)889000
Website: www.thewindmillbyrichardphillips.co.uk

5.5mi east of Maidstone by A 20 and through village. Parking.

PRICES
Meals: £ 15 (lunch) and a la carte £ 26/45

MAP: 63

CLOSING TIMES
Open daily

Sharp's Doom Bar, Musket Ales Flintlock and Trigger

GRANVILLE

A popular pub; you won't leave hungry

Set on a small village T-junction, this pub may not look as impressive as the Tudor warship it's named after but it definitely has the size; and, like sister pub 'The Sportsman', you can guarantee it'll be busy. With a high ceiling, exposed rafters and an open-plan layout, the interior is a touch Scandinavian; the sofas making a great spot for a quick snack, while the hotchpotch of tables beyond are better for a proper meal. A constantly evolving blackboard menu offers unfussy dishes which arrive in generous, flavoursome portions; mostly on chunky wooden platters. Pumpkin seeds come with the tasty bread and the veg originates from their allotment. While you're waiting for your meal to arrive, grab one of the board games and get playing!

Street End,
LOWER HARDRES, CT4 7AL
Tel.: (01227)700402
Website: www.thegranvillecanterbury.com

3 mi south of Canterbury on B 2068. Parking.

PRICES
Meals: £ 18 (weekday lunch) and
a la carte £ 27/39

MAP: 64

CLOSING TIMES
Closed 25 December, Sunday dinner
and Monday

Shepherd Neame Ales and
seasonal guest ales

WHEELWRIGHTS ARMS N

Self-taught Zimbabwean chef

What do you get if you cross a self-taught Zimbabwean chef with an early 17C former Kentish farmhouse? Very tasty food for one thing; and a genuinely warm welcome for another. Outside it's all clapperboard and colourful flower baskets; inside it's rustic with a fireplace at each end, low beamed ceilings crammed with hanging hops and photos on the wall that tell the story of the pub's past. These days, local bands perform regularly; Morris dancers wave their hankies from time to time and the first Thursday of each month is quiz night, when they don't serve dinner. At any other time, you can expect an abundance of local, seasonal produce in classic dishes like rump of lamb and shoulder or braised beef rib with pan roast blade and cottage pie.

The Green,
MATFIELD, TN12 7JX
Tel.: (01892)722129
Website: www.thewheelwrightsarmsmatfield.co.uk

6 mi east of Royal Tunbridge Wells by A 264, in village centre. Parking.

PRICES
Meals: a la carte £ 20/34

MAP: 65

CLOSING TIMES
Closed Sunday dinner and Monday

Shepherd Neame Spitfire and Bishops Finger

RED LION

Honest, richly flavoured Gallic and English dishes

A 'Red Lion' pub has stood on this spot since Victorian times; the current one belonging to a very capable and experienced couple, who have run numerous pubs in the area over the years. They like to get involved, so you'll find him hard at work in the kitchen and her leading the friendly, engaging service. It's a simple place, featuring a cosy, open-fired bar where the locals tend to gather and a dining room with rich red walls, benches and Lloyd Loom chairs. The menu offers a mix of English and Gallic dishes; you might find a classic bouillabaisse or a venison casserole with truffled mash; game in season is a speciality and desserts might be a lemon torte or mulled pear. In true country style, dishes are honest, wholesome and richly flavoured.

Rawling St,
MILSTEAD, ME9 0RT
Tel.: (01795)830279
Website: www.theredlionmilstead.co.uk

South of Sittingbourne signposted off the A 2. Parking.

PRICES
Meals: a la carte £ 22/40

MAP: 66

CLOSING TIMES
Closed Sunday and Monday
booking advisable

Adnams Southwold Bitter, Old Dairy Copper Top and Musket Flintlock Kentish Best Bitter

THREE MARINERS

A great spot for walkers to refuel

If you've been negotiating the Saxon Shore Way, this 500 year old pub is a great place to refuel: it's set in a sleepy hamlet offering pleasant views over the marshes to the estuary beyond, and there's a warmth and quirkiness about it, from the roaring fires to the bright, friendly team. Constantly evolving menus offer an extensive range of British and Mediterranean-influenced dishes like garlic scallops or herb-crusted lamb rump, and the set menus represent good value: the Walkers' Lunch might include potted duck, chicken pie and homemade ice cream, and the Business Lunch, Parma ham, sea bass and artisan cheeses. Sharing dishes like 7 hour slow-roast shoulder of lamb or seafood paella can be ordered 24 hours in advance.

2 Church Rd,
OARE, ME13 0QA
Tel.: (01795)533633
Website: www.thethreemarinersoare.co.uk

2.5 mi northwest of Faversham by A 2 and B 2045. Parking.

PRICES
Meals: £ 13/22 and a la carte £ 25/39

MAP: 67

CLOSING TIMES
Closed dinner 24-25 December

Shepherd Neame Ales

LEICESTER ARMS (N)

Sit in the garden room for a rural view

Some menus have a way with words that get your taste buds tingling in anticipation: hake here is 'pan-roasted', with 'asparagus, bacon, garden peas and baby gem'; gnocchi is 'handmade', with 'courgette, ricotta, chilli and mint' and the rabbit and cider terrine comes with 'Indian Military chutney and toasted sourdough'. Despite the rhetoric, they are essentially offering rustic and satisfying pub classics – which is as it should be, seeing as this is indeed a pub. It dates from the 16C and has been sympathetically refurbished: avoid the small front room and sit instead in the garden room: a large bright space with a lovely rural view. Bedrooms are furnished in a contemporary style: ask for Room 8, which is the biggest, with the best outlook.

PENSHURST, TN11 8BT
Tel.: (01892)871617
Website: www.theleicesterarmshotel.com

5.5 mi. Southwest of Tonbridge on B 2176. Parking

PRICES
Meals: a la carte £ 20/39

13 rooms:
£ 99/169

MAP: 68

CLOSING TIMES
Open daily

Larkins Traditional and Harveys Bitter

THE SPORTSMAN ✿

Well-judged flavours in top quality dishes

Set on the edge of town, by the sea wall, the unassuming-looking Sportsman proves you should never judge a book by its cover, for while both its façade and its interior may appear rather modest, its food is top-class. The constantly evolving blackboard menu is guided by what's seasonal and local, with meat from nearby Monkshill Farm and fish from the local day boats. Dishes feature just four or five top quality, complementary ingredients and are prepared with precision; flavours are extremely well-judged and presentation is original. The bread, butter and even salt are homemade and the roasted pork belly is a favourite. If you want the full tasting menu, you must order in advance; the 5 course option can be ordered on arrival.

Faversham Rd,
SEASALTER, CT5 4BP
Tel.: (01227)273370
Website: www.thesportsmanseasalter.co.uk

2 mi southwest of Whitstable by B 2205 following the coast road.
Parking.

PRICES
Meals: £ 45/65 and a la carte £ 35/45

MAP: 69

CLOSING TIMES
Closed 25-26 December, Sunday dinner and Monday
booking advisable

Shepherd Neame Ales

THE MILK HOUSE (N)

Labour of love for local couple

The village of Sissinghurst was without its only pub for two years, so it's no wonder it's been buzzing since it reopened! Its renovation has been a labour of love for local couple, Dane and Sarah Allchorne, and changes have included that of the pub's name, from the Bull to the Milk House, after the original name of the road on which the pub stands (Milk Street). Turn right into the bar with its soft sofas and huge fire; sit here to eat from the Grazing Menu of appetising nibbles like salt and pepper squid. Turn left into the dining room for a seasonal menu of modern British dishes such as seared quail breast or whole grilled Dover sole. Pub Classics and Children's menus are available in either area. Bedrooms are smart and contemporary.

The Street,
SISSINGHURST, TN17 2JG
Tel.: (01580)720200
Website: www.themilkhouse.co.uk

In centre of village, 2 miles northeast of Cranbrook. Parking

PRICES
Meals: a la carte £ 17/41

4 rooms:
£ 95/120

MAP: 70

CLOSING TIMES
Closed 25 December

Adnams Southwold Bitter, Harveys Sussex Best Bitter and Old Dairy Red Top

GEORGE & DRAGON

Hugely characterful 13C pub serving gutsy dishes

Dating back to 1212, this black and white timbered Wealden Hall house boasts an impressive beamed ceiling and displays an unusual Queen's post in the upstairs dining room. It's thought to be the second oldest pub in the country and, in the past, provided refreshment for the soldiers returning from Agincourt. It's a hugely appealing place, with several characterful flag-floored rooms, vast inglenook fireplaces and a contrastingly modern, landscaped terrace. Cooking is generous and satisfying, and strives to keep things local and organic, with extensive menus offering a selection of pub classics alongside more elaborate British dishes such as bacon-wrapped pheasant. The Groombridge belly pork and Ashdown Forest venison are best sellers.

Speldhurst Hill,
SPELDHURST, TN3 0NN
Tel.: (01892)863125
Website: www.speldhurst.com

3.5 mi north of Royal Tunbridge Wells by A 26. Parking.

PRICES
Meals: a la carte £ 21/45

MAP: 71

CLOSING TIMES
Open daily

Harveys Sussex Best Bitter, Larkins Traditional and Brakspear Oxford Gold

PLOUGH

Impressive range of Kentish real ales

The term 'rustic' could have been invented for this 15C, rurally set pub, with its thick walls, farming implements, exposed beams and hop bines. Sit at table 6 or 7 on either side of the open fire, or go for table 10 - set almost in an inglenook - where you will be able to read a verse from the farmer's poem 'God Speed the Plough' on the wall in front of you. You'll find the usual suspects on the bar snack menu: ploughman's, fishcakes, burgers and the like, with dishes like chicken liver parfait, confit belly pork or halibut with chorizo on the à la carte. Nursery puddings such as apple crumble or sticky toffee pudding make for a pleasing end to your meal, and there are an impressive range of Kentish real ales with which to wash it down.

STALISFIELD, ME13 0HY
Tel.: (01795)890256
Website: www.theploughinnstalisfield.co.uk

7 mi southwest of Faversham by A 251. Parking.

PRICES
Meals: £ 14/20 and a la carte £ 26/33

MAP: 72

CLOSING TIMES
Closed Monday except bank holidays

Musket Flintlock, Tonbridge Coppernob, Whitstable Brewery IPA and Old Dairy Red Top

CROWN INN N

Comfort food at its best

Escoffier, Le Cordon Bleu, Martha Stewart, Take 6 Cooks... stacked on a table in the centre of the room, these well-thumbed books give a clue as to the focus at this rural village pub. Indeed, they and many others like them have provided inspiration over the years for self-taught chef-owner, Nicki: she and her assistant now make everything on-site bar the bread, with chutneys and preserves on sale in the bar and pizzas from the oven on summer weekends. Dishes like the rich twice-baked cheese soufflé, a generous serving of piping hot lasagne or the popular lamb burger are comfort food at its best and puddings are not to be missed, with homemade ice cream top of the list. Smart bedrooms come with modern shower rooms and a continental breakfast.

STONE IN OXNEY, TN30 7JN
Tel.: (01233)758302
Website: www.thecrowninnstoneinoxney.co.uk

6.5 mi. northeast of Rye by B 2082, in village centre. Parking

PRICES
Meals: a la carte £ 20/33

2 rooms:
£ 105

MAP: 73

CLOSING TIMES
Closed January, Sunday dinner and Monday except bank holidays

No real ales offered

PEARSON'S ARMS

Live music every Tuesday and Sunday

With the Thames Estuary stretching out in front of it, this characterful clapperboard pub is in a great spot. Inside, it's a hotchpotch of rooms full of worn but comfy seats, and exposed beams and wood floors provide a pleasant, rustic-chic style. Enter into the bar for a pint from the next door brewery and snacks such as whitebait, jellied eels and crispy pigs' ears. Alternatively, head upstairs to the dining room for superb water views and a more extensive selection of classic British dishes with a modern twist; perhaps potted shrimps, pan-fried scallops, liver with onions or steamed lemon sole; all made with Kentish produce. Service is friendly and copes well, and there's a great atmosphere, enhanced by live music every Tuesday and Sunday.

The Horsebridge,
SEA WALL, Whitstable, CT5 1BT
Tel.: (01227)773133
Website: www.pearsonsarmsbyrichardphillips.co.uk

In centre of town on seafront. On-street parking nearby.

PRICES
Meals: £ 13 (weekday lunch) and
a la carte £ 19/37

MAP: 74

CLOSING TIMES
Closed dinner Sunday, Monday and
Tuesday

Gadds' Seasider, Harveys Sussex Best Bitter, Whitstable Brewery IPA and Sharp's Doom Bar

THE BULL (N)

Classic British dishes in a 14C inn

This 14C inn is the public house equivalent of a wet fish handshake: it just doesn't give a great impression. Venture inside and it will grow on you, although you'll perhaps still think it a little plain. Dine here, however, and you'll realise that you actually have loads in common and before long you're getting on like a house on fire. Tasty traditional British dishes like ham hock terrine with homemade piccalilli or Kentish pheasant breast come courtesy of the enthusiastic, self-taught chef-owner. Spanish pork steak and USA hanger steaks are popular choices, while those with smaller appetites might prefer sausage and mash or a burger off the bar menu. Cement the relationship by spending the night in one of the smart, up-to-date bedrooms.

Bull Ln,
WROTHAM, TN15 7RF
Tel.: (01732)789800
Website: www.thebullhotel.com

In centre of village, 8 mi. northeast of Sevenoaks by A 25. Parking

PRICES
Meals: a la carte £ 28/42

11 rooms:
£ 69/159

MAP: 75

CLOSING TIMES
Open daily

Dark Star Hophead and Old Dairy Red Top

SWEET OLIVE AT THE CHEQUERS INN

Cosy inn with a French accent

A red-brick Victorian pub at the heart of an English village; cosy, welcoming and frequented by locals. What sets it apart is its decidedly Gallic feel, attributable in no small part to its French owners. One of the owners also happens to be the chef, so expect to see dishes like Mediterranean fish soup and onglet of beef on the menu; other staples include the more globally influenced tiger prawns in tempura or crispy duck salad, and the thoroughly British ox cheeks and mash or treacle sponge and custard. The old French wine boxes which bedeck the bar offer a clue as to wine list: most are from France, with many from the Alsace region, like one of the owners. Oenophiles will find plenty to get excited about on the separate fine wine list.

Baker St,
ASTON TIRROLD, OX11 9DD
Tel.: (01235)851272
Website: www.sweet-olive.com

4 mi southwest of Wallingford by minor road through South Moreton. Parking.

PRICES
Meals: a la carte £ 30/48

MAP: 76

CLOSING TIMES
Closed 3 weeks July, 2 weeks February, Sunday dinner and Wednesday booking essential

West Berkshire Good Old Boy and Brakspear Bitter

RED LION

The pork comes from the farm next door

It may have had a few ups and downs over the years but the Red Lion is now back in capable hands and has once again established itself as a 'proper' village pub. It's next to the local cricket pitch and, fittingly, is decorated in deep red, with stags' heads and art by the owners on the walls. When it comes to the food, dishes are well-executed and interesting. There are lots of tasty nibbles - the homemade black pudding scotch egg is a must-try - and a daily deal offering the 'pie of the day' along with a pint of Mr Chubb's Bitter. There's always plenty of pork too, as whole beasts are delivered from the farm next door, and game is often a feature. The freshly churned ice creams are not to be missed and service is warm and friendly.

BRITWELL SALOME, OX49 5LG
Tel.: (01491)613140
Website: www.theredlionbritwellsalome.co.uk

Midway between Watlington and Ewelme on B 4009. Parking.

PRICES
Meals: a la carte £ 23/38

MAP: 77

CLOSING TIMES
Closed Sunday dinner, Monday and lunch Tuesday
booking essential

West Berkshire Mr. Chubb's and Loose Cannon Gunners Gold

TROUT AT TADPOLE BRIDGE

Lawned gardens run down to the Thames

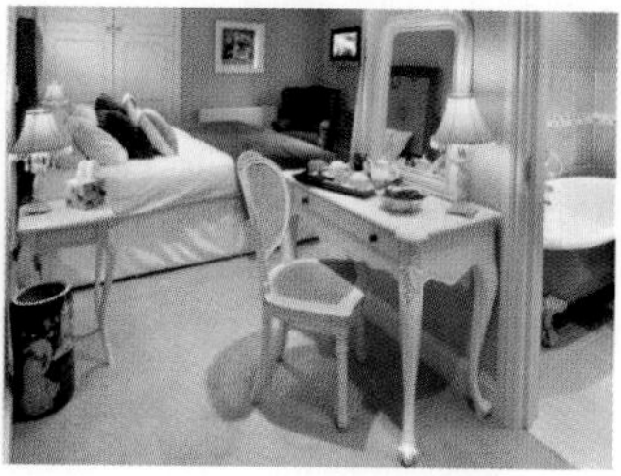

Sometimes when a pub starts serving food they take things too far and forget their other audience: their drinkers. Experienced owners have ensured it's not so at the Tadpole, and its many regulars congregate over their pints of Trout bitter in the characterful beamed bar. Those here to dine will find an appealing mix of British pub classics and Gallic influenced dishes, courtesy of the French chef; there's plenty of fish, of course, and game in season. You can eat anywhere but in summer what better place than the lawned gardens which run down to the River Thames? The pub has its own private moorings and you can hire their electric punt for a lazy trip down river, or stay the night in one of the spacious, traditionally decorated bedrooms.

BUCKLAND MARSH, SN7 8RF
Tel.: (01367)870382
Website: www.troutinn.co.uk

4.5 mi northeast of Faringdon by A 417 and A 420 on Brampton road. Parking.

PRICES
Meals: a la carte £ 17/43

6 rooms:
£ 85/160

MAP: 78

CLOSING TIMES
Closed 25-26 December

White Horse Wayland Smithy, Ramsbury Trout Best Bitter and Loose Cannon Abingdon Bridge

HIGHWAY INN

The courtyard bedrooms are ideal for dogs

If you're visiting the Cotswolds, Burford makes a great stop off point, courtesy of its lovely winding river and bustling atmosphere. The Highway Inn sits at its centre - a 15C pub filled with character, where you'll find sloping floors, exposed wooden beams and antiques aplenty; try to bag a table in one of the bay windows or close to the roaring fire. Cooking keeps things fittingly classical and everything is homemade. You'll always find a pie and a beer-battered fish 'of the day', accompanied by hand-cut chips, along with the likes of braised pork belly, duo of lamb or duck confit. Individually designed bedrooms have a cosy, classical style and good modern facilities; the courtyard rooms are ideal for those travelling with dogs.

117 High St,
BURFORD, OX18 4RG
Tel.: (01993)823661
Website: www.thehighwayinn.co.uk

In town centre. Parking unrestricted on the eastern side of the High St.

PRICES
Meals: £ 15 and a la carte £ 21/38

10 rooms:
£ 60/140

MAP: 79

CLOSING TIMES
Closed 4-20 January and 24-26 December

Hook Norton Old Hooky and Wye Valley Pale Ale

LAMB INN

A delightful spot in the Cotswolds

Cosiness is a quality for which British pubs are renowned and this delightful pub - a collection of 15C weavers' cottages - certainly has 'snug' and 'warm' down pat. A pair of sitting rooms exude charm, with comfy armchairs, oil paintings and antiques; here and in the bar, the 'Garden and Fireside Menu' offers anything from prawn cocktail or ploughman's to pork chops and mash. In the elegant, candlelit dining room, things get more ambitious, with a tasting menu and an à la carte displaying classic dishes like ham hock and pea soup or rack of lamb; if meat from Ruby and White butchers is listed, be sure a cut ends up on your plate. The terrace and gardens make summer extra special and comfortable bedrooms have a loveliness all of their own.

Sheep St,
BURFORD, OX18 4LR
Tel.: (01993)823155
Website: www.cotswold-inns-hotels.co.uk/lamb

Parking at Bay Tree Hotel.

PRICES
Meals: £ 20/25 and a la carte £ 25/46

17 rooms:
£ 155/275

MAP: 80

CLOSING TIMES
Open daily

Wickwar Cotswold Way and Hook Norton Old Hooky

CROWN INN

Try the steak and Hooky ale pie

This 17C inn is found in among pretty stone houses in a picturesque village on the edge of the Cotswolds. It boasts a welcoming slate-floored conservatory, a beamed dining room and a rustic stone-walled bar - as well as a front terrace and a secluded garden for sunnier days. The chef-owner has built up quite a reputation for his seafood in these parts, so you'll find that some dishes - such as the fishcakes and the king scallop and bacon salad - are permanent fixtures, along with the locally renowned steak and Hooky ale pie. At lunch, the daily blackboard reads like a top ten of old pub favourites, with the likes of beer-battered cod and chips or pork sausages and mash; all of the meats, fruit and vegetables are sourced from the local farms.

Mill Ln,
CHURCH ENSTONE, OX7 4NN
Tel.: (01608)677262
Website: www.crowninnenstone.co.uk

3.5 mi southeast of Chipping Norton by A 44. Parking.

PRICES
Meals: a la carte £ 19/33

MAP: 81

CLOSING TIMES
Closed 25-26 December,
1 January and Sunday dinner

Hook Norton Hooky Bitter, Timothy Taylor Landlord and Wells Bombardier

CHEQUERS

Welcoming and traditional

It may have an 'OX' postcode but this mellow sandstone pub, sitting proudly at the heart of the village, is clearly in Cotswold country. It's a vital part of the local community and the owners appear to have got the formula just right; it's filled with locals playing darts and the keen serving team exude as much warmth as the roaring fire in the inglenook. The bar is well-stocked with local ales, while the counter behind is filled with enticing hams and olives, just waiting to be nibbled on. Menus are firmly rooted in tradition, with hearty dishes such as ham hock and pease pudding, calves' liver and bacon or steaks cooked on the Josper grill. It's a popular place but there are always 6 tables left unreserved, for those without a booking.

Church Rd,
CHURCHILL, OX7 6NJ
Tel.: (01608)659393
Website: www.thechequerschurchill.com

3 mi southwest of Chipping Norton on B 4450. Parking.

PRICES
Meals: £ 13 (lunch) and a la carte £ 18/35

MAP: 82

CLOSING TIMES
Closed 25 December and
dinner 26 December and 1 January

Hook Norton Old Hooky, Bath Ales and Box Steam Ales

EYSTON ARMS

Warm service and an international menu

A pub has stood on this site for many years – although it was once much smaller and adjoined by estate workers' cottages, as this characterful village was, and still is, largely owned by the local estate. Inside, original tiled floors and exposed brickwork remain but it's been given a typical modern dining pub makeover with scrubbed tables and plenty of candles, along with caricatures of the locals and a great array of photos taken by the owner's daughter on her travels. Staff are warm and welcoming and as a result, they have gained a loyal local following. The menu offers a diverse range of dishes with influences from across the globe; maybe salad of wood pigeon with beetroot and goat's cheese, alongside lemongrass and chilli-cured salmon.

High St,
EAST HENDRED, OX12 8JY
Tel.: (01235)833320
Website: www.eystonarms.co.uk

4.5 mi east of Wantage by A 417. Parking.

PRICES
Meals: a la carte £ 25/39

MAP: 83

CLOSING TIMES
Closed 25 December and Sunday dinner

Hook Norton Hooky Bitter and Wadworth 6X

FIVE ALLS

Classical cooking and cosy, modern bedrooms

The pub's curious logo refers to the fulfilment of the 5 human needs - the lawyer pleads for all, the parson prays for all, the soldier fights for all and the farmer pays for all, while at the centre, the devil governs all. When it comes to fulfilment, they certainly seem to have it covered here: there's an open-fired bar stocked with fine ales, where they serve snacks and takeaway burgers, and three large dining rooms furnished with antiques. There's also a terrace and a garden with an Aunt Sally area and, completing the picture, some cosy, modern bedrooms; and that's before even mentioning the food! Cooking is satisfyingly traditional, offering everything from potted shrimps with melba toast to a cured meat platter and hearty steaks.

FILKINS, GL7 3JQ
Tel.: (01367)860875
Website: www.thefiveallsfilkins.co.uk

Midway between Burford and Lechlade-on-Thames. Parking.

PRICES
Meals: £ 17/21 and a la carte £ 27/41

4 rooms:
£ 90/150

MAP: 84

CLOSING TIMES
Closed 25 December and Sunday dinner

Brakspear Ales

WHITE HART

15C chantry house with a secret tunnel

This intriguing 15C chantry house displays many original features, including a two-storey, flag-floored hall with a vaulted ceiling (now the dining room), a minstrels' gallery and a secret tunnel; as well as a pleasant terrace and a cosy beamed bar with an inglenook fireplace. They make good use of the wealth of produce on their doorstep, so you'll find meat from nearby farms or estates; flour - for the homemade bread - from the local mill; and fruit and veg from the pub's own plot or the locals' gardens. Menus offer a diverse range of dishes - from sharing boards to slow-roast pork or tempura courgette flowers - and excellent desserts. Service is slick and friendly, and the annual beer festival and hog roast always makes for a great day out.

Main Rd,
FYFIELD, OX13 5LW
Tel.: (01865)390585
Website: www.whitehart-fyfield.com

10 mi southwest of Oxford by A 420. Parking.

PRICES

Meals: £ 20 (weekday lunch) and
a la carte £ 28/41

MAP: 85

CLOSING TIMES

Closed Monday except bank holidays

Abingdon's Loose Cannon, Sharp's Doom Bar and Box Steam Tunnel Vision

BELL AT HAMPTON POYLE

Choose something from the wood-burning oven

Tiled flooring and a bright, fresh look make the Bell seem almost Mediterranean, which is not a style one usually associates with a pub in rural Oxfordshire, but it seems to work. The owners have made the kitchen a very visual element of the operation, with its wood-burning oven and large open-plan pass – and they've created a very accessible menu which covers all tastes: there's meze, homemade pizza, and seafood and charcuterie boards, as well as staples such as calves' liver and some decent steaks. They tweak it a little with the seasons and also strive to keep prices in check. If you've had too much to drive, there are smart bedrooms above the bar and in a small cottage.

11 Oxford Rd,
HAMPTON POYLE, OX5 2QD
Tel.: (01865)376242
Website: www.thebellathamptonpoyle.co.uk

9 mi north of Oxford by A 34. Parking.

PRICES
Meals: £ 10 (lunch and early dinner) and a la carte £ 26/68

9 rooms:
£ 95/155

MAP: 86

CLOSING TIMES
Open daily

Hook Norton Hooky Bitter and Wye Valley Butty Bach

BLACK BOY

Classic pub dishes with a Gallic edge

Big, bold and busy - it's The Black Boy. As well as having French roots, the chef did a long stint with Raymond Blanc, so it comes as no surprise that there's a Gallic edge to the essentially classic menu, but don't get the wrong idea; this is proper pub food, no messing, with unadorned mains, like braised pork belly or sausage and mash, for under a tenner. Bring some bling to your Black Boy burger by eating it in the small side restaurant; the low-lit bar is the less popular, but by no means less pleasant, alternative. There are homemade breads, mix and match tapas dishes and the roasts go down a storm on a Sunday. Tuesday is quiz night, Thursday is for jazz-lovers and Sunday mornings are when the kids can get creative in the kitchen.

91 Old High St,
HEADINGTON, Oxford, OX3 9HT
Tel.: (01865)741137
Website: www.theblackboy.uk.com

East of Oxford off London Rd. On-street parking around the pub.

PRICES
Meals: a la carte £ 21/42

MAP: 87

CLOSING TIMES
Closed 26 December and 1 January

Hook Norton Old Hooky and St Austell Proper Job

THREE TUNS

Look out for the old coffin drop above the bar!

This pretty, red-brick, town centre pub was originally three houses, one of which used to be a mortuary and, if you take a look above the central bar, you can still see the coffin drop. The atmosphere is far from deathly in this bijoux inn, however; the best place to sit being among the drinkers in its lively, open-fired front bar (ask for table 10). The formal dining room has just four tables and is the place for a quieter, more intimate meal. There's something to please all palates on the seasonal menu, and traditional dishes like ham hock terrine or seafood pot au feu are well-presented, satisfying and full of flavour. Breads are homemade, meat comes from the butchers next door and there's an excellent value 2 course lunch menu Tues-Sat.

5 Market Pl,
HENLEY-ON-THAMES, RG9 2AA
Tel.: (01491)410138
Website: www.threetunshenley.co.uk

In the centre of town. Local pay and display parking.

PRICES
Meals: £ 10/15 and a la carte £ 25/40

MAP: 88

CLOSING TIMES
Closed 25 December, Monday except bank holidays and Sunday dinner

Ringwood Fortyniner, Brakspear Bitter and Oxford Gold

KINGHAM PLOUGH

Well prepared, constantly evolving modern dishes

Set on the green of a beautifully unspoilt village in the Evenlode Valley, this pub boasts a rustic lounge-bar, a laid-back restaurant and an easy-going team. It's owned by Emily Watkins, former sous-chef at The Fat Duck, so you'll find the odd dish such as snails on toast that harks back to her Heston days; although the majority of dishes are rooted in a gutsy pub vein - albeit a very modern one. The bar menu offers tasty snacks such as scotched quails' eggs or Welsh rarebit, while the concise restaurant menu features the latest seasonal produce from foraging expeditions and nearby farms. Preparation is careful, slow cooking reigns and dishes evolve throughout the evening as new ingredients arrive. For the weary, 7 comfy bedrooms await.

The Green,
KINGHAM, OX7 6YD
Tel.: (01608)658327
Website: www.thekinghamplough.co.uk

In village centre. Parking.

PRICES
Meals: a la carte £ 28/47

7 rooms:
£ 80/145

MAP: 89

CLOSING TIMES
Closed 25 December

Hook Norton Hooky Bitter, Wye Valley HPA and Butcombe Bitter

THE WILD RABBIT N

Michelin Pub of the Year 2015

Our 2015 Pub of the Year is this charming sandstone inn owned by the Bamford family, of Daylesford fame. Renamed from the Tollgate Inn, it's been given an understated Cotswold makeover, meaning flag floors, log fires, leather sofas and expanses of wood and stone. The Daylesford influence is obvious, and nowhere more so than when it comes to the food: there are displays of bread, cheese and dried ham, an open kitchen, and rustic cooking which is British at heart and full of flavour. Dishes might include hare ravioli, roast partridge or Gloucester Old Spot for two – with steaks cooked on the Josper oven a popular choice. Bedrooms are named after woodland animals and feature a preponderance of natural products. Rabbit is naturally the best.

Church St,
KINGHAM, OX7 6YA
Tel.: (01608)658389
Website: www.thewildrabbit.co.uk

9 miles east of Stow-on-the-Wold, sign-posted off A 436. Parking.

PRICES
Meals: a la carte £ 33/51

12 rooms:
£ 95/225

MAP: 90

CLOSING TIMES
Closed Monday
booking advisable

Timothy Taylor Landlord, Prescott Hill Climb and Sharp's Doom Bar

ENGLAND • South East • Oxfordshire

EAGLE TAVERN

Welcoming local, run by a self-taught chef

There's many a rural pub where a stranger walks through the door and the room falls silent; not so at the Eagle Tavern, where the locals welcome you with open arms. It was built in 1901 for the farmers of this sleepy hamlet and, although it might look slightly different nowadays, a convivial atmosphere still reigns. It's a spacious place with a homely bar and a dining room furnished in wood and wicker, and is run by a self-taught Slovakian chef, who cooks food he himself likes to eat. Dishes range from the simple to the ambitious - maybe a juicy burger with all the extras or home-salted beef brisket with piccalilli and rye bread crumble - and the local suppliers, like 'Paul's Poultry', are all named. Bedrooms are cosy and worth the money.

LITTLE COXWELL, SN7 7LW
Tel.: (01367)241879
Website: www.eagletavern.co.uk

2.5 mi south of Faringdon by A 417. Parking in the village.

PRICES
Meals: £ 12 (weekday lunch) and a la carte £ 18/33

6 rooms: £ 60/90

MAP: 91

CLOSING TIMES
Closed Sunday dinner and Monday

White Horse Village Idiot and Wickwar Coopers and BOB

FIVE HORSESHOES

Take in delightful country views from the terrace

This charming 17C inn with delightful country views is set in the heart of walking country. When the weather's warm, head for the large garden and terrace where, on Fridays and Saturdays, they fire up the wood oven and bespoke pizzas are the name of the game. Inside, the two intimate rooms and large conservatory are warm and welcoming and also share the view; order a homemade ginger beer then seek out the small blackboard which lists the specials. The daily changing set menu represents the best value and cooking is wholesome and hearty, featuring plenty of meaty dishes, game in season and proper puddings like steamed treacle sponge. They like to keep things as local as possible here, so even the wines come from a vineyard just down the road.

MAIDENSGROVE, RG9 6EX
Tel.: (01491)641282
Website: www.thefivehorseshoes.co.uk

6.25 mi northwest of Henley-on-Thames by A 4130, B 480 and Maidensgrove rd. Parking.

PRICES
Meals: £ 13 (weekday lunch) and
a la carte £ 22/41

MAP: 92

CLOSING TIMES
Closed Monday except bank holidays

Brakspear Bitter

OLD SWAN

Stylish bedrooms up a winding staircase

They may be a few hundred miles apart but the Old Swan and its sister, the Cary Arms, share a few things in common, including stylish accommodation and a passion for fresh, simply cooked food. The Old Swan is just the sort of place you expect to come across in Oxfordshire, with its smart parquet floor, roaring open fires and collection of horse brasses and Toby jugs. For summer there's boules and a giant chess set in the garden - set next to large herb plots which supply the pub all year round and contribute to unfussy pub classics and tasty daily specials from the Brixham day boats. Chic bedrooms are accessed via a winding staircase and display period furnishings, quality linens and the latest mod cons - some even boast feature bathrooms.

MINSTER LOVELL, OX29 ORN
Tel.: (01993)774441
Website: www.oldswanandminstermill.com

3.5 mi west of Witney by B 4047. Parking.

PRICES
Meals: a la carte £ 28/40

16 rooms:
£ 145/375

MAP: 93

CLOSING TIMES
Open daily
booking essential

Marston's Ales

NUT TREE

✿

Superb dishes of organic or wild produce

You want a tasty, top quality meal in good old pub surroundings: enter the Nut Tree. It's owned by a local and his wife, who have managed to retain a satisfyingly pubby feel in the cosy beamed bar, while also providing a more formal atmosphere in the smart restaurant. Appealing menus change constantly as the latest seasonal ingredients arrive and produce is organic, free range or wild wherever possible; there's always plenty of choice too, from baguettes and bar snacks to ambitious tasting selections. Breads and ice creams are homemade, salmon is smoked on-site and sausages and pork pies are for sale. Combinations are classical and satisfying, and to ensure only the freshest meats are used, they rear their own rare breed pigs out the back.

Main St,
MURCOTT, OX5 2RE
Tel.: (01865)331253
Website: www.nuttreeinn.co.uk

7 mi from Bicester by A 41 east and a minor road south; at T-junction beyond the motorway turn right. Parking.

PRICES
Meals: £ 18 (weekdays)/55 and a la carte £ 32/53

MAP: 94

CLOSING TIMES
Closed 27 December-2 January, Sunday dinner and Monday except bank holidays

Vale Best Bitter, Oxfordshire Pride and Sharp's Doom Bar

THE ANCHOR N

Sleek styling in the heart of Jericho

With its subtle art deco styling, tea towel napkins and black and white dining room floor tiles, The Anchor is not your typical pub. Indeed, it opens at 9am on weekdays for coffee and cakes and 10am at weekends for a leisurely brunch, while its children's menu offers choices like crudités and dip or fish pie alongside the ubiquitous burger. There is a bar, of course: popular with locals out for a drink, although this is as likely to be a cocktail as a pint of beer, and the accompanying bar snack will be rabbit rillettes or a haggis scotch egg rather than pork scratchings or a packet of crisps. The main menu changes regularly and dishes range from the dry-aged steak cooked on a Josper Grill to steamed mussels or quinoa with radicchio and fennel.

2 Hayfield Rd,
OXFORD, OX2 6TT
Tel.: (01865)510282
Website: www.theanchoroxford.com

Just north of city centre off Woodstock Rd. Limited parking.

PRICES
Meals: a la carte £ 19/43

MAP: 95

CLOSING TIMES
Open daily

Wadworth Ales

MAGDALEN ARMS

Menus change twice a day, depending on deliveries

This battleship-grey pub is a relative newcomer to the established Oxford scene but it's already a hit with the locals. The place buzzes - even on a weeknight - and there's always something to keep you entertained, be it a board game or a turn on the bar billiards table. The spacious, open-plan interior boasts deep red walls, quirky old standard lamps and an eclectic collection of 1920s posters, while huge blackboards display nibbles and the twice daily changing menu. Order at the bar for a casual lunch or head through to the curtained-off dining room for table service. The experienced chef uses local ingredients to create tasty, good value dishes; perhaps pork and rabbit rillettes, braised ox cheek or seven hour lamb for five to share.

243 Iffley Rd,
OXFORD, OX4 1SJ
Tel.: (01865)243159
Southeast of city centre on A 4158. On-street parking.

PRICES
Meals: a la carte £ 23/34

MAP: 96

CLOSING TIMES
Closed 24-26 December, 1 January, Monday lunch and bank holidays

Theakston Best Bitter, Caledonian Deuchars IPA, XPA and Flying Scotsman

RICKETY PRESS

Top seasonal ingredients provide vibrant flavours

Run by three old school friends, the Rickety Press is found in a highly residential area; its name a reference to the Oxford University Press, whose HQ was once close by. It's a friendly, shabby-chic kind of a place run by a professional team and has a conservatory, a large room filled with wooden pews and a cosy bar with a chessboard, a vast array of books and characterful reclaimed tables; stop here for a pint of Arkell's ale and a scotch egg, or a sandwich filled with Sandy Lane lamb or Cerne Abbas cheddar and chutney. The main menu changes every month and features vibrant, seasonal ingredients that provide plenty of flavour; you might find roast pumpkin and sage soup to start, followed by corn-fed chicken with rösti and wild mushrooms.

67 Cranham St,
OXFORD, OX2 6DE
Tel.: (01865)424581
Website: www.thericketypress.com

Off Walton Street in Jericho. On-street parking.

MAP: 97

PRICES
Meals: a la carte £ 17/38

CLOSING TIMES
Closed 25-27 December

Arkell's Ales

PLOWDEN ARMS

Interesting dishes and some Eliza Acton influences

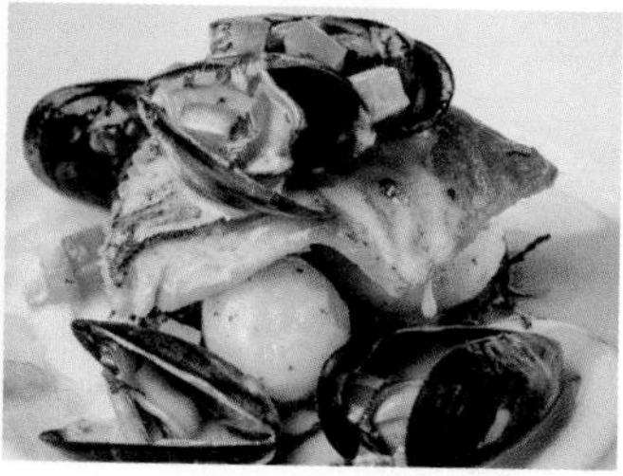

This appealing pub sits close to Shiplake College and started life in the mid-18C as the Plough Hotel, but it was later renamed after an eminent local lawyer. It has a delightful garden and three different rooms where open fires, flickering candles and hop bines set the scene. 1920s jazz music plays in the background and the air is one of relaxation. The experienced chef offers some interesting dishes: on the large blackboard you'll find snacks such as chicken scotch eggs or local chipolatas, alongside specials like red mullet with anchovy cream. The main menu, meanwhile, features a number of Eliza Acton influenced creations - maybe herrings in oatmeal or potted livers with pear chutney - with the inspiration for each dish listed beside it.

Reading Rd,
SHIPLAKE, RG9 4BX
Tel.: (01189)402794
Website: www.plowdenarmsshiplake.co.uk

2 mi south of Henley-on-Thames on A 4155. Parking.

PRICES
Meals: a la carte £ 21/39

MAP: 98

CLOSING TIMES
Closed Mondays except bank holidays

Brakspear Bitter, Ringwood Boondoggle and Wychwood Hobgoblin

WYKHAM ARMS

A true village pub set down narrow lanes

If you're after a true village pub, the 17C Wykham Arms may well be it. Set down narrow lanes in the middle of the countryside, this thatched pub certainly plays its role in the community. It boasts attractive sand-coloured stone walls adorned with pretty climbing plants and a pleasant terrace with cast iron furniture. So as not to price out the locals, menus offer a range of dishes right through from light bites and bar snacks to the full three courses; so you might find Salcombe crab and mango salad or Warwickshire pork belly. Suppliers are proudly noted on the blackboard and the chef is only too happy to answer any questions. There's a good choice of wines and what better way to celebrate than with lobster and champagne on the terrace?

Temple Mill Rd,
SIBFORD GOWER, OX15 5RX
Tel.: (01295)788808
Website: www.wykhamarms.co.uk

8 mi west of Banbury by B 4035. Parking.

PRICES
Meals: a la carte £ 25/34

MAP: 99

CLOSING TIMES
Closed Monday except bank holidays

Purity Pure UBU, St Austell Trelawny and Wye Valley Ales

SIR CHARLES NAPIER ✿

A skilled kitchen delivers dishes full of flavour

Set in a small hamlet on the hillside, this attractive 18C flint pub might just have it all. The delightful terrace and gardens buzz with conversation in the warmer months, while sculptures of beasts and figures peer out from behind bushes or lie on the lawn. Inside yet more creatures hide about the place – and all are for sale. It's worth heading to the cosy bar with its open fires and comfy sofas, although the beamed dining room adorned with flowers and art is equally charming. Cooking is refined and has a strong French accent, offering the likes of eel and foie gras terrine followed by noisette of venison or boeuf Bourguignon. Dishes are skilfully prepared and capture flavours to their full. A well-chosen wine list completes the picture.

Sprigs Holly,
SPRIGG'S ALLEY, OX39 4BX
Tel.: (01494)483011
Website: www.sircharlesnapier.co.uk

2.5 mi southeast of Chinnor by Bledlow Ridge rd. Parking.

PRICES
Meals: £ 18 (weekdays) and a la carte
£ 38/58

MAP: 100

CLOSING TIMES
Closed 24-26 December, Sunday dinner and Monday except bank holidays
booking advisable

Wadworth 6X

CHERRY TREE INN

Take time to wander around the ornamental garden

An attractive-looking pub with an attractive-sounding name: the trees in question no longer bear fruit but make sure you go for a wander to see the cherry orchard (now an ornamental garden) and the gilded 370ft well which were a gift from the Maharajah of Benares to this rural village 150 years ago. The wisteria-clad, 400 year old pub has a cosy, relaxing feel; its four intimate dining areas each with their own charm and character. Four stylish bedrooms beckon to the overnight guest but first enjoy a meal from the monthly changing à la carte or the seasonal, fish-based blackboard menu. Classic pub dishes like the popular handmade burgers sit alongside more modern creations; food is full of flavour and served by an attentive team.

STOKE ROW, RG9 5QA
Tel.: (01491)680430
Website: www.thecherrytreeinn.co.uk

Between Henley-on-Thames and Wallingford off A 1430. Parking.

PRICES
Meals: a la carte £ 19/34

4 rooms:
£ 65/110

MAP: 101

CLOSING TIMES
Closed 2 January

Brakspear Ales and
Wychwood Hobgoblin

QUINCE TREE

Take something home from their adjoining deli

This early 19C inn with its impressive brick façade can be found in a delightful setting next to a country estate in a fold of the Chiltern Hills. Smart gardens lead to a sunny terrace, while inside it has a pleasant country-chic style, with leather banquettes and modern artwork featuring alongside exposed brick and oak timbers. There are a few leather bucket seats opposite the bar for drinkers but the focus here is on dining – either in the main room or the more formal restaurant. Menus offer an appealing range of dishes, from several varieties of sharing platters and pub classics with a twist to much more original, modern dishes such as spiced tagine of skate – and if you fancy taking something home, there's also a deli to the rear.

STONOR, RG9 6HE
Tel.: (01491)639039
Website: www.thequincetree.com

4 mi north of Henley-on-Thames by A 4130 on B 480. Parking.

PRICES
Meals: a la carte £ 24/40

MAP: 102

CLOSING TIMES
Closed 25 December, 1 January and Sunday dinner
booking advisable

Marston's EPA and Oyster Stout

FISH

A real taste of France in Oxfordshire

Its owners have brought a taste of France to Oxfordshire, so expect French pictures, French music and a largely French wine list, as well as French food and charming Gallic service. Feast on meaty terrines, escargots or moules marinière; such dishes mingle merrily with British classics like steak and kidney pie, Gressingham duck breast or fillet of lamb. L'entente cordiale continues on the dessert menu, with crème brûlée clamouring for your attention alongside treacle sponge. This is robust country cooking in its most classic form, with pretty much everything homemade using seasonal ingredients. Head to the rear of the pub for the lovely garden and conservatory, and be sure to ask Sebastian (one of the owners) for his wine recommendations.

4 Appleford Rd,
SUTTON COURTENAY, OX14 4NQ
Tel.: (01235)848242
Website: www.thefishatsuttoncourtenay.co.uk

Between Abingdon and Didcot on B 4016. Parking.

MAP: 103

PRICES
Meals: £ 14 (weekdays) and a la carte
£ 25/47

CLOSING TIMES
Closed January, Monday except bank holidays and Sunday dinner

Greene King Ales

SWAN INN

Charming in every respect!

Set on the banks of a meandering river, The Swan Inn is a delightful place - so booking is a must. Outside, you'll find honey-coloured walls covered in wisteria and a lovely garden filled with fruit trees; while the interior boasts an open oak frame and exposed stone walls covered with old lithographs and handmade walking sticks. A well-versed team serve tasty dishes from the daily menu, which features the latest seasonal produce from nearby farms and estates. Cooking is fairly modern in style, with some dishes a contemporary take on older recipes; you might find roe deer carpaccio with truffled mayonnaise, fillet of bream with tandoori potatoes or baked ginger pudding with hot spiced treacle. Well-appointed bedrooms have a luxurious feel.

SWINBROOK, OX18 4DY
Tel.: (01993)823339
Website: www.theswanswinbrook.co.uk

3 mi northeast of Burford by A 40 and minor road north. Parking.

PRICES
Meals: a la carte £ 19/38

11 rooms:
£ 85/180

MAP: 104

CLOSING TIMES
Open daily

Hook Norton Hooky Bitter, Butcombe Bitter and Wye Valley Dorothy Goodbody

MOLE INN

Attractive interior and lovely landscaped terrace

The Mole has made quite a name for itself in the area and deservedly so. Beautiful landscaped gardens and a pleasant terrace front the building, while inside, attractive beamed ceilings and exposed brick walls create a warm and welcoming atmosphere. The menu is equally appealing, catering for all tastes and appetites; you might find sautéed squid with linguine and chorizo, followed by twice-cooked belly of pork with gratin dauphinoise. Sourcing is a serious business and it's a case of 'first come, first served' if you want the full choice. The Tuesday grill and Wednesday fish night menus are decided the day before, so if there's something you've set your heart on, it's worth calling to reserve your dish. Service remains smooth under pressure.

TOOT BALDON, OX44 9NG
Tel.: (01865)340001
Website: www.themoleinn.com

6 mi southeast of Oxford off A 4074. Parking.

PRICES
Meals: £ 20 and a la carte £ 28/34

MAP: 105

CLOSING TIMES
Closed 25 December
booking advisable

Hook Norton Old Hooky and White Horse Wayland Smithy

FAT FOX INN

Run with integrity by experienced owners

This pub was originally called the Fox and Hounds but there were so many other pubs of the same name in the surrounding villages that it became a little confusing; so the owners decided to hold a renaming competition and the Fat Fox was born. It's in the heart of a busy market village and dates from the 1800s and, although it's nothing fancy, is run with honesty and integrity by its experienced owners. The menu reflects what they themselves like to eat in a pub and covers all bases from potted mackerel or local rabbit broth to filling pheasant pie. Fight the cats for a spot on the sofas by the wood burning range in the buzzy bar or make for the slightly more formal dining room; afterwards, settle in for the night in one of the cosy bedrooms.

13 Shireburn St,
WATLINGTON, OX49 5BU
Tel.: (01491)613040
Website: www.thefatfoxinn.co.uk

9 mi southwest of Thame by B 4012, A 40 and B 4009. Parking.

PRICES
Meals: a la carte £ 16/36

9 rooms:
£ 60/119

MAP: 106

CLOSING TIMES
Closed dinner 25 December and 1 January

Ringwood Boondoggle and Marston's Ales

KILLINGWORTH CASTLE

Interesting dishes follow the seasons

This pub's name is slightly odd... first of all, it's nowhere near Killingworth, and secondly, there's no castle nearby! It's a large building dating from the 1500s and, after a year standing derelict, is now under the ownership of the Alexanders, who have set about returning it to its 'proper' pub status. Open fires, thick stone walls and old mix and match furniture provide a rustic feel, and black and white photos depicting its past adorn the walls. The chatty staff clearly know what they're doing and the food is great value, especially the dish of the day. The main menu follows the seasons and provides plenty of interest, offering the likes of sticky pork belly or lamb with truffle mash. You will leave feeling suitably fortified.

Glympton Rd,
WOOTTON, OX20 1EJ
Tel.: (01993)811401
Website: www.thekillingworthcastle.com

3.5 mi northwest of Woodstock by Hensington Rd and Banbury Rd on B 4027. Parking.

PRICES
Meals: a la carte £ 21/34

MAP: 107

CLOSING TIMES
Open daily

Yubberton Ales and Loose Cannon Abingdon Bridge

ABINGER HATCH

An outside bar and kitchen for summer BBQs

This attractive 18C pub is found in a charming spot at the centre of a small hamlet on the Wotton Estate, deep in walking country, and with its low beams, cosy corners and roaring log fires it oozes country gentility. It's open throughout the day, offering snacks and drinks, sharing boards and comforting dishes such as anchovies with a soft boiled hen's egg, Mrs Kirkham's macaroni cheese and a 'pie of the day'. In the winter you'll often see the local hunt in for lunch, while on summer Saturdays the outside bar and kitchen really comes into its own and dishes from the barbecue are the order of the day. After lunch grab a picnic mat and a board game or head for the boules pitch at the end of the garden for a spot of friendly competition.

Abinger Ln,
ABINGER COMMON, RH5 6HZ
Tel.: (01306)730737
Website: www.theabingerhatch.com

Between Guildford and Dorking off A 25 in village centre. Parking.

PRICES
Meals: a la carte £ 20/27

MAP: 108

CLOSING TIMES
Open daily

Ringwood Best Bitter and Sambrook's Wandle Ale

SWAN INN

A contemporary look and smart bedrooms

The elegant tile-hung façade of the Swan Inn hints at its 200 year old heritage, although following a fire in 2003, its interior is now of a more contemporary vintage. The pub's latest owners moved here from Knightsbridge, swapping the bustling city streets for a more sedate pace of life. Lunchtime sees the Surrey set popping in for maybe Maryland crab cakes or the 'terrine of the day', while the à la carte changes daily depending on the latest local produce available. The experienced owners keep a keen eye over proceedings and cool, contemporary bedrooms complete the picture. Wandering round the green it's hard to believe that eleven glass works once stood here, supplying many of the country's finest buildings, including St Stephen's Chapel.

Petworth Rd,
CHIDDINGFOLD, GU8 4TY
Tel.: (01428)684688
Website: www.theswaninnchiddingfold.com

On A 283 on the eastern side of the village. Parking.

PRICES
Meals: a la carte £ 22/39

10 rooms:
£ 100/180

MAP: 109

CLOSING TIMES
Open daily

Surrey Hills Shere Drop and Adnams Southwold Bitter

QUEEN'S HEAD

Create a different experience each time you come

Part of a group of properties run by three lifelong friends, this charming 17C pub is one of those places where you can create a different experience each time you come. It's divided into four rooms and each has its own unique style, with furnishings ranging from the traditional to the modern: one room has an inglenook fireplace; another, a stove guarded by an old musket; some have bovine-themed pictures and others, faux beams; there's also a lovely terrace to consider, along with a large garden where village celebrations are held. The simple menu offers something for everyone, from sharing boards or potted ham hock to steak and ale pie or a roast – there's also a large blackboard of daily specials. The tasty salad and veggies are home-grown.

The Street,
EAST CLANDON, GU4 7RY
Tel.: (01483)222332
Website: www.queensheadeastclandon.co.uk

Between Guildford and East Horsley off A 246. Parking.

PRICES
Meals: £ 18 (weekday lunch) and
a la carte £ 22/36

MAP: 110

CLOSING TIMES
Closed 25 December

Hogs Back Ales, Surrey Hills Ales and Ringwood Best Bitter

WHEATSHEAF N

Meat is the speciality here

If you missed the sign above the door which says 'Pub and Grill', the wooden pig, sheep and cow on the wall illustrating the different cuts of meat are a further clue as to the speciality here. The homemade burgers are a popular choice and these and the steaks use 21 day matured grassland beef from the local Surrey Farm; other highlights include the fish specials and the cheese selection. Despite its smart, red-brick exterior, the feel here is far removed from that of a traditional pub: there's a bar with sofas at the front, an open-plan kitchen and a smart, narrow dining room which seems to stretch back for miles, its walls adorned with an array of mirrors and old black and white photos of the town. Keen young staff know their stuff.

19 West St,
FARNHAM, GU9 7DR
Tel.: (01252)717135
Website: www.thewheatsheafatfarnham.co.uk

In the centre of town. Pay and display parking nearby.

PRICES
Meals: a la carte £ 19/39

MAP: 111

CLOSING TIMES
Closed 25 December

Hogs Back TEA and Ringwood Fortyniner

PARROT INN

Fresh home-grown and homemade produce

When a pub sells its own home-grown and homemade produce - bread, cheese, cakes and preserves, as well as eggs and meat from its own farm - you can be pretty much guaranteed that their cooking is going to be fresh and full of flavour. With well-priced, generously proportioned dishes such as vegetable and stilton pie or pork belly with chorizo and baked butter bean, the Parrot certainly doesn't disappoint. This is a pub where they make their own black pudding and aren't afraid to serve less well-known offerings such as oyster sausages or mutton. The 300 year old pub's interior is traditional, with plenty of character in the form of exposed brick, flag floors and low wooden beams. Sup real ale as you watch a cricket match on the green.

FOREST GREEN, RH5 5RZ
Tel.: (01306)621339
Website: www.theparrot.co.uk

8 mi south of Dorking by A 24, A 29 and B 2126 west. Parking.

PRICES
Meals: a la carte £ 22/36

MAP: 112

CLOSING TIMES
Closed 25 December and Sunday dinner

Ringwood Best Bitter, Hogs Back TEA and Tillingbourne Falls Gold

THREE HORSESHOES

17C origins but 21C sensibilities

There's not much left of this pub's 17C origins - but who cares when they've done such a good job of modernising it? Prop up the long bar with the locals or sit in the cosy, poster-lined snug, the rear dining room or the Garden room; each is furnished with leather chairs and chunky wood tables, its walls filled with interesting photos and pictures. If the sun is out, then you should be too: grab a watering can (to identify your order) and head for the pretty walled garden. The menu's also got something for everyone - perhaps you're after a light offering like a sandwich or a salad, or maybe a meaty main course such as calves' liver and bacon. They've got pub classics covered, sharing plates for those 'à deux' and specials on the blackboard too.

25 Shepperton Rd,
LALEHAM, TW18 1SE
Tel.: (01784)455014
Website: www.3horseshoeslaleham.co.uk

2.5 mi southeast of junction 13 of M 25 by A 30, A 308 and B 376. Parking.

PRICES
Meals: a la carte £ 23/48

MAP: 113

CLOSING TIMES
Closed 26 December

Fuller's Seafarers Ale and London Pride

STAG ON THE RIVER

Sit on the terrace, overlooking the old millstream

Perched on the banks of the River Wey, this pretty little 16C pub was once a mill and its smartly furnished terrace overlooks the old millstream. This isn't the kind of spot you just happen to stumble upon, so you can guarantee a large number of those around you are from the local area. You'll need to arrive early if you want a choice of table, be it on the terrace or beside the roaring fire in the smart, modern interior. The menu ranges from sandwiches and pub classics to more interesting dishes such as a fish platter or chateaubriand for two; the 8hr roasted pork belly and the haddock and bacon rarebit fishcakes are also worth a try. Attractively appointed, contemporary bedrooms come with a complimentary bottle of locally brewed beer.

Lower Eashing Rd,
LOWER EASHING, GU7 2QG
Tel.: (01483)421568
Website: www.stagontherivereashing.co.uk

1.75 mi west of Godalming by A 3100 and Eashing Lane. Parking.

PRICES
Meals: a la carte £ 22/39

7 rooms:
£ 65/130

MAP: 114

CLOSING TIMES
Closed 25 December

Hogs Back TEA, Ringwood Fortyniner and Banks's Bitter

THE PENDLETON IN ST JOHNS (N)

Gallic classics in a buzzing atmosphere

It's got a new name to go with its smart new look and, what with the Redhill residents, happy their local's still a pub rather than private housing, and the hordes of loyal customers who have followed owners Jon and Cynthia Coomb from their previous establishments, this place is very popular so make sure you book. Although the seasonal dishes tend to be French classics, there's also a smattering of Mediterranean and South American influences, so don't be surprised to see words such as 'ceviche' or 'charcuterie' on the menu. Portions are generous and flavours, well-pronounced, with no unnecessary over-elaboration. Cocktails are proving popular and the wines have been well chosen. Service is special and the atmosphere, buzzing.

26 Pendleton Rd, St Johns,
REDHILL, RH1 6QF
Tel.: (01737)760212
Website: www.thependleton.co.uk

1 mi south of Redhill by A23 and Pendleton Rd. Parking.

PRICES
Meals: a la carte £ 25/39

MAP: 115

CLOSING TIMES
Closed 25 December-2 January,
Sunday dinner, Monday and Tuesday
bookings advisable at dinner

Camden Town Gentleman's Wit, Camden Ink and Pale Ale

ANCHOR (N)

Classic dishes bursting with flavour

It's not an unusual name for a pub, but it begins to seem so when you find out that the pub in question is actually nowhere near any water. However, it is near a cycle route which was known in the 19C as 'The Mecca of all good cyclists', and this explains the number of bicycle-themed objects therein. Originally constructed as almshouses for the poor, the inn is reputed to be over four hundred years old; today it has a smart yet rustic feel with polished slate floors and on-trend grey walls. One of the owners is Steve Drake of Drake's restaurant and the head chef is also a Drake's alumni, so it's no surprise to find that classic dishes like wild rabbit terrine and slow-cooked leg of guinea fowl are carefully executed and bursting with flavour.

High St,
RIPLEY, GU23 6AE
Tel.: (01483)211866
Website: www.ripleyanchor.co.uk

In the centre of the village. Parking.

PRICES
Meals: a la carte £ 24/41

MAP: 116

CLOSING TIMES
Closed Sunday dinner and Monday

Timothy Taylor Landlord, Tillingbourne Falls Gold and Andwell Resolute Bitter

OLD PLOUGH

A welcoming sight for those travelling by train

The fourth venture for this small pub group, the Old Plough has been smartly done up, once again becoming a welcoming sight for those journeying home from the station. It's managed to retain a satisfyingly pubby feel, thanks to an open-fired bar filled with comfy chairs, and chunky wood furnishings in the restaurant. The menu is the same wherever you sit and offers starters such as wild mushroom and spinach tart or duck liver terrine with spiced plum chutney, followed by main courses of thyme rotisserie chicken, French fish stew or tagliatelli with tomato and black olive sauce. At lunchtime you'll find the likes of bubble and squeak, devilled lamb's kidneys on toast or a crab & mayo sandwich, and sharing dishes are on offer throughout the day.

2 Station Rd,
STOKE D'ABERNON, KT11 3BN
Tel.: (01932)862244
Website: www.oldploughcobham.co.uk

Between Cobham and Leatherhead on A 245. Parking.

PRICES
Meals: a la carte £ 22/42

MAP: 117

CLOSING TIMES
Closed 26th December

Fuller's London Pride, Surrey Hills Shere Drop and George Gale Seafarers

THREE HORSESHOES (N)

Owned by the locals, with a homely, lived-in feel

This is the sort of pub where a line of locals turn away from their drink to look at you as you come through the door – but we can forgive them this, as not only are they very welcoming, the fact of the matter is that without them, there would be no pub: following a five year period of closure, they clubbed together to save it – and it has been at the heart of the community ever since. This local success story is as much about the food as the beer, with hearty, traditional meals served daily – high on flavour yet low on price – and everything, including bread and ice cream, homemade. Real fires, fresh flowers, books and village info give the place a homely, lived-in feel. Head for 'Brian's Corner': the cosy snug at the back.

Dye House Rd,
THURSLEY, GU8 6QD
Tel.: (01252)703268
Website: www.threehorseshoesthursley.com

Between Farnham and Godalming, signed off B 3001. Parking.

PRICES
Meals: a la carte £ 21/43

MAP: 118

CLOSING TIMES
Closed Sunday dinner

Hogs Back TEA, Surrey Hills Shere Drop, Langham Hip Hop and Dark Star Hophead

DUKE OF CAMBRIDGE

Hidden away in the heart of the forest

This 18C pub may be well-known to local dog walkers but isn't somewhere you're likely to just stumble upon by chance, as it's hidden away in the heart of the forest. Despite a refurbishment, it retains a pleasantly rustic feel, with a small, flag-floored bar, a cosy snug and neatly laid wooden tables filling the rest of the room; there's also an appealing heated terrace covered by an impressive oak-beamed roof – a great vantage point if you have children who want to visit the large play area. Menus offer everything from deli boards to share and old pub classics like steak and ale pie, to a few more adventurous dishes such as sea bass with chorizo, red onion and tomato fricassee; there are some interesting dishes for children too.

Tilford Rd,
TILFORD, GU10 2DD
Tel.: (01252)792236
Website: www.dukeofcambridgetilford.co.uk

Between Farnham and Godalming, signed off B 3001. Parking.

PRICES
Meals: a la carte £ 21/36

MAP: 119

CLOSING TIMES
Closed 25 December

Hogs Back TEA, Ringwood Fortyniner and Banks's Bitter

ONSLOW ARMS

Smartly refurbished village pub

Following in the footsteps of the group's first two pubs, the Onslow Arms has been taken back to its roots and re-established as a proper village pub. It has undergone a smart refurbishment but wooden beams, open fires and copper artefacts still give a glimpse as to its true age - although nobody seems to know exactly when it was built. Locals prop up the bar or sit at the high tables opposite, while diners head for the restaurant, but wherever you sit, the menu's the same. It's a popular spot with the local workers and ladies who lunch, so you'll find sharing platters and light bites in the middle of the day and more sophisticated dishes in the evening; maybe lemon and thyme rotisserie chicken or braised Gressingham duck with parsnip mash.

The Street,
WEST CLANDON, GU4 7TE
Tel.: (01483)222447
Website: www.onslowarmsclandon.co.uk

4.75 mi northeast of Guildford by A 25 on A 247. Parking.

PRICES
Meals: a la carte £ 23/41

MAP: 120

CLOSING TIMES
Open daily

Sharp's Cornish Coaster, Surrey Hills Shere Drop and Tillingbourne Hop Troll

THE INN @ WEST END

A lively atmosphere and genuine hospitality

It's not the best-looking pub in the world – but what it lacks in rustic charm, it more than makes up for in personality; its lively atmosphere and genuine hospitality being two of the reasons it's always so busy. Another big draw is the food: there's something for everyone on the menu, from sandwiches and pub classics like sausage and mash to dishes like lobster Caesar salad and deep-fried poached egg; with fish specials and plenty of game in season. Portions are generous and flavours robust, with global influences, good quality ingredients and some original touches. The owners also have a wine shop in the car park, so it comes as no surprise to find an interesting list of well-chosen wines, strong on pinot noir and claret.

42 Guildford Rd,
WEST END, GU24 9PW
Tel.: (01276)858652
Website: www.the-inn.co.uk

2.5 mi southeast of junction 3 of M 3 on A 322. Parking.

MAP: 121

PRICES
Meals: £ 13/28 and a la carte £ 26/50

CLOSING TIMES
Open daily

Fuller's London Pride, Dark Star Hophead and Butcombe Adam Henson's Rare Breed

BRICKMAKERS

Head for the garden with its gazebo and heaters

The name of this 400 year old pub comes from its popularity with workers from the nearby former brickmaking works who would pop in for a pint on their way home. Beamed ceilings, flag floors and open fires provide a rustic edge, and a makeover has given it a bang-up-to-date look. Come summer, the garden is the place to be, with its smart tables, gazebo and heaters. They serve breakfast; a range of sandwiches, salads, small plates and aptly named 'comfort plates' at lunch, and traditional British dishes at dinner, such as mini toad in the hole, twice-cooked pork belly or English duck breast. Desserts might include Cambridge Burnt Cream and the tongue-in-cheek Eton tidy with its evenly distributed layers of strawberries, cream and meringue.

Chertsey Rd,
WINDLESHAM, GU20 6HT
Tel.: (01276)472267
Website: www.thebrickmakerswindlesham.co.uk

1 mi east on B 386. Parking.

PRICES
Meals: a la carte £ 20/37

MAP: 122

CLOSING TIMES
Open daily

Fuller's London Pride, Courage Best Bitter and Sharp's Doom Bar

RED LION

Take a seat in the colourful courtyard garden

Set in a residential area but just five minutes from the centre of Woking, the Red Lion ticks all the boxes for the locals - and for visitors too. When the weather's right, make for the pleasant rear terrace or landscaped garden, which has won them 'Best Floral Pub' prize in Woking In Bloom; if you're hungry, head for a sofa beside the open fire in the bar or take a seat in the rustic beamed dining room amongst the Brooklands racing memorabilia. The menu offers something for everyone, from sandwiches and pub classics to more interesting dishes such as piri piri chicken breast with pomegranate and coriander couscous. With tasty food and cheery staff too, it's a deservedly popular place, so book a table or make sure you arrive early.

High St,
HORSELL, Woking, GU21 4SS
Tel.: (01483)768497
Website: www.redlionhorsell.co.uk

1.5 mi northwest of Woking by Brewery Rd and Church Hill. Parking.

PRICES
Meals: a la carte £ 22/41

MAP: 123

CLOSING TIMES
Closed 26 December
booking advisable

Fuller's London Pride, St Austell Tribute and Caledonian Flying Scotsman

THE GEORGE AT BURPHAM

Beams, fires and a smugglers' wheel

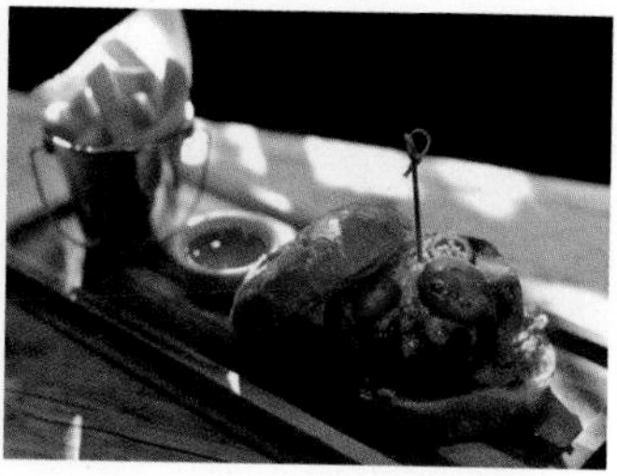

This pub was on the brink of closure when a local consortium headed by three local businessmen stepped in and saved it. It has been given a smart new look, a new name and a new tagline which sums up the spirit of its reincarnation: 'By the locals, for the locals, of the locals... and a very warm welcome to everyone'. Dogs are patently included within the 'everyone', with dog biscuits provided on the bar, and whether you're a hungry walker back from the South Downs or a thirsty cricketer fresh from the adjacent pitch, you'll be given cheery treatment from the friendly, long-standing staff. The seasonal menu is full of tasty, popular classics; and beams, fires and a smugglers' wheel on the ceiling add character to the modern interior.

Main St,
BURPHAM, BN18 9RR
Tel.: (01903)883131
Website: www.georgeatburpham.co.uk

3 mi northeast of Arundel by A 27.

PRICES
Meals: £ 21 and a la carte £ 20/42

MAP: 124

CLOSING TIMES
Open daily

Arundel Sussex Gold and By George, Harveys Wild Hop and Greene King IPA

FOX GOES FREE

Oozes traditional English charm

Set in the beautiful South Downs countryside, close to Goodwood, this charming 17C flint pub was once the haunt of William III and his Royal Hunting Party. It boasts a superb garden and terrace with lovely outlooks and retains most of its original features, including exposed stone walls, low beamed ceilings, brick floors, inglenook fires and even an old bread oven. There are three dining areas, two with table service and one where you order at the bar; behind which you'll find a good selection of hand-pulled ales. Dishes range from simple pub classics on the bar menu to an à la carte featuring local pork chops, braised venison shank or steak and kidney pie for two. Bedrooms are clean and unfussy; those above the pub have low ceilings.

CHARLTON, PO18 0HU
Tel.: (01243)811461
Website: www.thefoxgoesfree.com

Midway between Chichester and Midhurst off the A 286. Parking.

PRICES
Meals: a la carte £ 21/31

5 rooms:
£ 65/175

MAP: 125

CLOSING TIMES
Open daily

Ballard's Best Bitter, Chivertons Otter Ale and Arundel The Fox Goes Free

ROYAL OAK INN

Arrive early to get a seat by the fire

Set in the heart of the village, among some stunning properties, this 18C inn boasts a small outside seating area with immaculately kept planters and a welcoming interior filled with exposed stone, brick and wood. There's a really relaxing feel to the place but you'll have to make like the locals and arrive early if you want to bag a sofa or a spot by the fire. Although combinations may be classical, the seasonal cooking is fairly refined. There are always some interesting vegetarian options, steaks play an important role and there's a good selection of cheese. Spacious, well-equipped bedrooms are split between the main house and a small stable conversion, while the three cottages each have two bedrooms, making them perfect for families.

Pook Ln,
EAST LAVANT, PO18 0AX
Tel.: (01243)527434
Website: www.royaloakeastlavant.co.uk

Off A 286 after the hump back bridge. Parking.

PRICES
Meals: a la carte £ 20/45

8 rooms:
£ 95/320

MAP: 126

CLOSING TIMES
Open daily

Long Man Ales and Morland Old Speckled Hen

HALFWAY BRIDGE

Dishes might come from Morocco or the Med

Dating from the 17C and set on the edge of the Cowdray Park polo grounds, the Halfway Bridge looks like the quintessential Sussex pub with its brick and flint exterior. Its owners, who also have the Crab & Lobster in Sidlesham, have given it a sympathetic overhaul so that the cosy interior comes with oodles of charm. The bar, with its open fireplace and old pictures of the inn, is a great place to sit, and overnight guests just need to stroll up the road for a couple of minutes to get to the converted stables which house the country-chic bedrooms. The menu offers a good range of classically based dishes presented in quite a modern style; influences could come from Morocco, France or Italy and puds are nursery-style with a twist.

HALFWAY BRIDGE, GU28 9BP
Tel.: (01798)861281
Website: www.halfwaybridge.co.uk

Between Petworth and Midhurst on A 272. Parking.

PRICES
Meals: a la carte £ 26/53

7 rooms:
£ 85/230

MAP: 127

CLOSING TIMES
Open daily

Langham Hip Hop and Halfway to Heaven, Sharp's Doom Bar

GINGER FOX

The desserts are a highlight at this charming pub

The first thing you notice is the pub's charming thatch - spot the fox running across it and you know you've come to the right place. The play area in the garden is a reassuring sight for parents; base yourself in 'the den' and you can keep an eye on your children as you eat. A monthly changing menu offers good value, flavoursome dishes; there's the occasional pub classic like beef and ale pie, but dishes are generally more akin to those served in a restaurant; perhaps crispy lamb sweetbreads, scallops with onion purée, roast partridge or wild halibut with sprouting broccoli. The vegetarian tasting plate will please any herbivores in your party and desserts are a highlight, so save space for some doughnuts or a slice of Bakewell tart.

Muddleswood Rd,
ALBOURNE, Henfield, BN6 9EA
Tel.: (01273)857888
Website: www.gingermanrestaurants.com

3 mi southwest of Henfield on A 281. Parking.

PRICES
Meals: £ 15 (weekdays) and
a la carte £ 25/36

MAP: 128

CLOSING TIMES
Closed 25 December

Harveys IPA and Dark Star Partridge Best Bitter

DUKE OF CUMBERLAND ARMS

Sit by the stream in the pretty tiered gardens

A hidden gem affectionately known as The Duke, this 16C hillside pub nestles in pretty tiered gardens with trickling streams, trout ponds and a splendid view over the South Downs. The pub's interior is as enchanting as the garden, with a cosy beamed, fire-lit front bar and an open plan, flag-floored dining area - and the charming staff provide efficient service. An appealing menu offers carefully prepared, seasonal dishes; lunch is a two course affair, with choices like fish and chips or braised ox cheeks, a selection of organic baguettes and homely puddings like hot chocolate fondant. Dinner shifts up a gear with the full three courses; dishes might include potted pheasant with cranberry compote or pork belly with apple and Calvados glaze.

HENLEY, GU27 3HQ
Tel.: (01428)652280
Website: www.dukeofcumberland.com

2.75 mi north of Midhurst off A 286. Parking.

PRICES

Meals: a la carte £ 33/41

MAP: 129

CLOSING TIMES

Closed 25-26 December and dinner Sunday-Monday

Harveys Sussex Best Bitter and Langham Ales

CROWN INN (N)

Renowned local chef cooks classic dishes

Having survived untouched since the 16C, this pub was nearly destroyed in a fire caused by lightning in 2003 and remained closed for over five years. Finally restored to its former glory in 2009, it entered a new era in early 2013 with the arrival of renowned local chef Mark Raffan, who not only brought with him his many years of experience, but also his army of loyal followers. With its exposed brick, wooden beams and feature inglenook, the front bar is full of character, while the smart dining room houses a grand piano, played on Friday nights. Classical dishes form the core of the menu, while the more ambitious blackboard specials embrace the seasons. Simple bedrooms have views of the village green; room one has a four-poster.

The Green,
HORSTED KEYNES, RH17 7AW
Tel.: (01825)791609
Website: www.thecrown-horstedkeynes.co.uk

West of Danehill, signposted off A 275. Parking.

PRICES
Meals: a la carte £ 25/45

4 rooms:
£ 80/110

MAP: 130

CLOSING TIMES
Closed Sunday dinner

Sharp's Doom Bar, Dark Star Hophead and Firebird Paleface APA

CRABTREE (N)

A family-run affair with a cosy, lived-in feel

Having had new life breathed into it, this pub is back once more at the heart of community, serving everything from bar snacks to feasts of several courses. A family-run affair, it has a cosy, lived-in feel, helped along by warming fires and cheery, helpful staff. Various rooms provide a characterful backdrop to your meal: there's the Garden Room which is light and airy; the Pass Room which allows you to see into the kitchen, and the tiny Smithy Room, which was once - you guessed it - the village smithy. Traditional English dishes like rump of Sussex lamb come with a touch of refinement and plenty of flavour, and the wine list is well-priced and full of helpful information, including which wines are suitable for vegetarians and vegans.

Brighton Rd,
LOWER BEEDING, RH13 6PT
Tel.: (01403)892666
Website: www.crabtreesussex.com

5 mi south of Horsham on A 281. Parking.

PRICES
Meals: £ 15 (weekday lunch) and
a la carte £ 25/36

MAP: 131

CLOSING TIMES
Closed Sunday dinner

Hall and Woodhouse Ales

NOAH'S ARK INN

Watch the local cricket team from the garden

This quintessentially English pub is found in a picturesque location on the village green, next to the church – its large garden overlooking the cricket pitch. Rumour has it that the pub was once accessed by a narrow path over a moat, where visitors had to go in two-by-two, hence its unusual name. The gloriously rustic interior features a bar, which offers a good selection of real ales; a large, baronial-style room with cosy sofas, a tiled floor, exposed beams and a wood-burning stove; and 'the restaurant' with its scrubbed tables and large inglenook fireplace. Generously sized dishes are mainly traditional, with the occasional modern touch; perhaps tempura battered haddock and chips or cockle 'popcorn' with a plum and chilli dip.

The Green,
LURGASHALL, GU28 9ET
Tel.: (01428)707346
Website: www.noahsarkinn.co.uk

Between Petworth and Chiddingfold off the A 283. Parking.

PRICES
Meals: a la carte £ 22/37

MAP: 132

CLOSING TIMES
Open daily

Greene King Ales and guest ales

EARL OF MARCH

Classic British dishes overlooking the South Downs

This 18C inn offers the perfect blend of country character and contemporary styling, boasting a wood burning stove and cosy sofas in the bar, a smart restaurant, and a relaxed feel throughout. Its terrace affords amazing views of the South Downs, with the main stand at Goodwood racecourse in the distance, and its private dining room changes use seasonally; home to shooting parties in winter and serving champagne and seafood in summer. The owner spent time as executive head chef at The Ritz, so expect good quality, seasonal produce; dishes are British and mainly classical in style, and might include vegetable soup, lamb chops, pan-fried fillet of Sussex beef or Gressingham duck breast. Desserts are old favourites like sticky toffee pudding.

MID LAVANT, PO18 0BQ
Tel.: (01243)533993
Website: www.theearlofmarch.com

3 mi north of Chichester on A 286. Parking.

PRICES
Meals: £ 20 (lunch and early dinner)
and a la carte £ 28/42

MAP: 133

CLOSING TIMES
Open daily

Harveys Sussex Best Bitter, Timothy Taylor Golden Best and Landlord

CHEQUERS INN

The chef-owner likes to forage and track game

As you step inside this pub, you're instantly surrounded by the oaky aroma of an open fire and the murmur of the day's tales being recounted by cheery locals. The origins of the inn can be traced back to the 15C, which comes as no surprise when you look around the charming stone-floored bar, but there's also a slightly unusual corrugated dining room extension (formerly the village hall), a large paved terrace and a spacious garden. The experienced chef-owner loves the hands-on approach, so he's often out in the woods foraging for wild mushrooms and tracking down game, or out in the garden gathering the latest yield; maybe artichoke, pears or greengages. Classically based menus display a good understanding of how best to prepare ingredients.

ROWHOOK, RH12 3PY
Tel.: (01403)790480
Website: www.thechequersrowhook.com

3 mi west of Horsham by A 281. Parking.

PRICES
Meals: a la carte £ 27/38

MAP: 134

CLOSING TIMES
Closed 25 December and Sunday dinner

Harveys Sussex Best Bitter, Shepherd Neame Spitfire and Long Man Best Bitter

CRAB & LOBSTER

Located within the Pagham Harbour Nature Reserve

This historic inn, with its pretty gardens, is superbly located within the striking landscape of Pagham Harbour Nature Reserve; a marshy haven for wildlife, particularly birds. Sympathetically modernised, it retains a flagged floor, open fires and the odd beam; there are a few tables for drinkers but, being a dining pub, most tables are laid up for eating. The well-presented dishes are very much at the restaurant end of the scale; perhaps saffron-scented seafood risotto with seared scallops and crab mascarpone or poached fillet of halibut on a sweetcorn and spring onion chowder - although lunch also sees lighter options like sandwiches and salads. Comfortable bedrooms have a modern, minimalist style; one has a garden and an open-fired stove.

Mill Ln,
SIDLESHAM, PO20 7NB
Tel.: (01243)641233
Website: www.crab-lobster.co.uk

5 mi south of Chichester by B 2145, then turn right into Rookery Lane. Parking.

PRICES
Meals: £ 22 (weekday lunch) and a la carte £ 29/63

5 rooms: £ 90/275

MAP: 135

CLOSING TIMES
Open daily
booking advisable

Langham Best Bitter and Hip Hop

HORSE GUARDS INN

Chatty young staff add to the charm

In an elevated spot in the heart of a quiet village sits this pretty mid-17C inn, with views over Rother valley and the South Downs from its lovely lavender-filled garden. Happily, it's equally charming inside, with its low beams, fireplaces, period features and fresh flowers. Specialities and the names of suppliers are chalked up on the blackboard and there's a good mix of the rustic, like wild mushrooms on toast, and the more elaborate, like stone bass with roast fennel. Local seafood is handled with skill and some of the vegetables and salads come from their own patch. The staff are young, chatty and willing, and contribute considerably to the charm. There are three simple bedrooms available; families can book the cottage next door.

Upperton Rd,
TILLINGTON, GU28 9AF
Tel.: (01798)342332
Website: www.thehorseguardsinn.co.uk

Just off A 272 in heart of the village. Unrestricted on-street parking.

PRICES
Meals: a la carte £ 21/37

3 rooms:
£ 85/140

MAP: 136

CLOSING TIMES
Closed 25 December

Harveys Sussex Best, Hammerpot Shooting Star and Langham Hip Hop

RICHMOND ARMS

Luxurious bedrooms at the foot of the South Downs

This appealing, laid-back country pub is found in a lovely little village at the foot of the South Downs, opposite the duck pond; keep an eye out for the colourful decoy ducks. In warmer weather, try for one of the handful of tables outside amongst the colourful hanging baskets; otherwise, head inside, where you'll find fresh flowers and a blackboard listing enticing nibbles such as halloumi chips or ham cut on an antique slicing machine. The menu offers plenty of appeal; game comes from the family estate in Anglesey, and there's a delightful rotisserie and a Japanese robata grill used to cook local mature steaks. Two luxurious bedrooms are above – and on Friday and Saturday there's a vintage Citroën van selling pizzas in the car park.

Mill Rd,
WEST ASHLING, PO18 8EA
Tel.: (01243)572046
Website: www.therichmondarms.co.uk

4.5 mi northwest of Chichester, located on far side of village pond. Parking.

PRICES
Meals: a la carte £ 28/45

2 rooms:
£ 95/125

MAP: 137

CLOSING TIMES
Closed Christmas-New Year, last week July, first week November, Sunday dinner, Monday and Tuesday

Harveys Sussex Best Bitter

CAT INN

Very much a village pub and a hit with the locals

Set in an idyllic village and only four centuries younger than the 11C church it overlooks, The Cat is very much a village pub, where you'll find locals relaxing by the inglenook with a pint. There are beamed ceilings, pewter tankards, open fires and plenty of corners in which to get cosy; one of these even contains a surprisingly deep well. Run by an experienced owner who cut his teeth at Gravetye Manor just down the road, it can get very busy; but, full or not, the friendly service doesn't falter. Cooking focuses on tasty pub classics and is carefully executed and good value; dishes might include roast belly of pork, Rye Bay lemon sole or steak, mushroom and ale pie. Four tastefully decorated bedrooms complete the picture.

Queen's Sq,
WEST HOATHLY, RH19 4PP
Tel.: (01342)810369
Website: www.catinn.co.uk

Between East Grinstead and Haywards Heath off B 2028; follow signs for the church. Parking.

PRICES
Meals: a la carte £ 22/36

4 rooms:
£ 85/160

MAP: 138

CLOSING TIMES
Closed 25 December and Sunday dinner

Harveys Ales, Larkins Traditional and Black Cat Original

SOUTH WEST

England

© R. Harding / hemis.fr

Six hundred miles of relentlessly breathtaking coastline pound the majestic South West, assuring it of a dramatic backdrop whatever the season. Its prestige is bolstered by four UNESCO World Heritage sites: one of them is Dorset's spectacular Jurassic Coast, which includes the 180 billion pebbles of Chesil Beach. Further north, Dartmoor and Exmoor embody the region's untamed beauty. The built environment may be of a more recent time line, but examples are still impressive, ranging from thirteenth century Lacock, home of many a filmed costume drama, to Elizabethan Longleat with its Capability Brown designed parkland, and late Victorian Lanhydrock, "the great house of Cornwall". The same county boasts its very own "theatre under the stars", The Minack, where the drama of nature collides with the drama of the written word.

Days out in this unforgettable region come complete with pasties and a pint of local ale, or freshly caught lobster, scallops or mussels enjoyed along the quay.

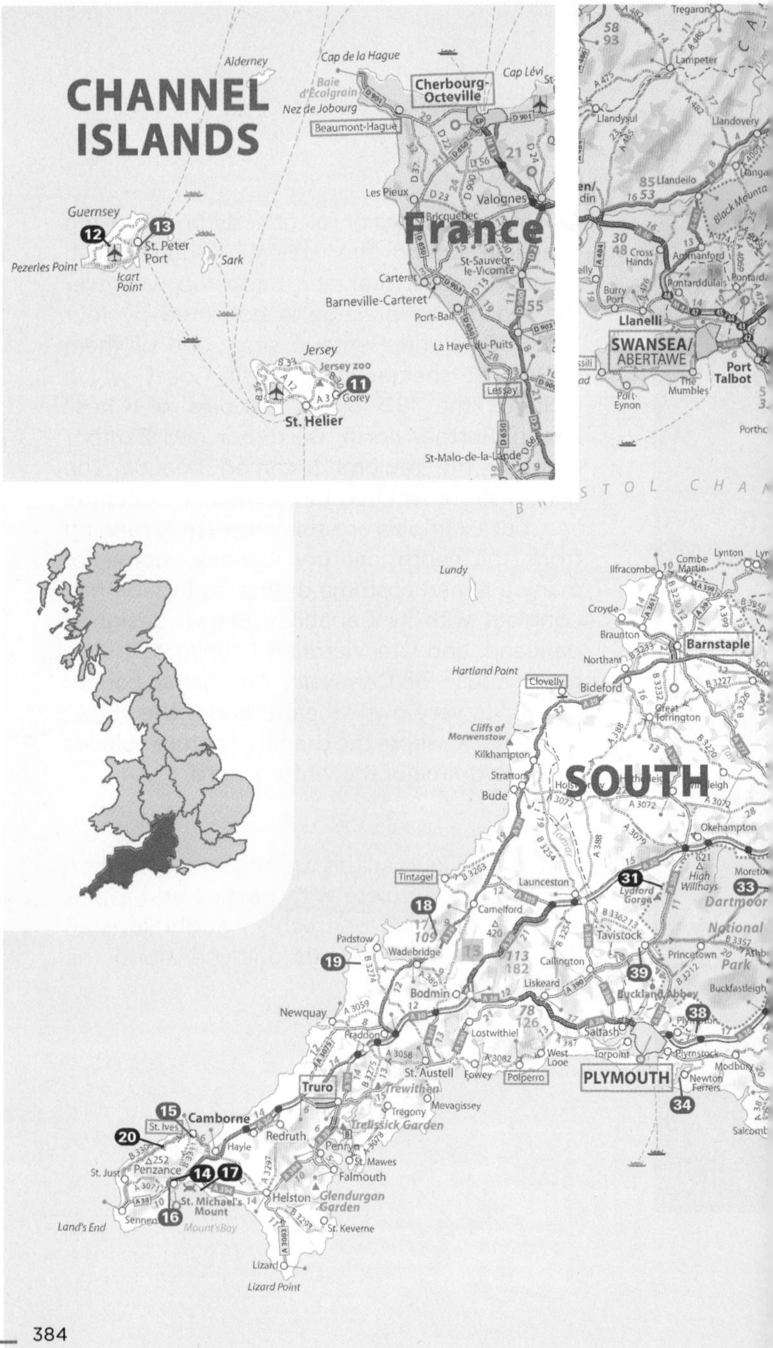
CHANNEL ISLANDS
Alderney
Cap de la Hague
Cherbourg-Octeville
Cap Lévi
Baie d'Écalgrain
Nez de Jobourg
Beaumont-Hague
Les Pieux
Valognes
Bricquebec
France
Guernsey
12
13
St. Peter Port
Sark
Pezeries Point
Icart Point
St-Sauveur-le-Vicomte
Carteret
Barneville-Carteret
Port-Bail
La Haye-du-Puits
Jersey
Jersey zoo
11
Gorey
St. Helier
Lessay
St-Malo-de-la-Lande
Tregaron
Lampeter
Llandysul
Llandovery
Llandeilo
Black Mountain
Cross Hands
Ammanford
Pontarddulais
Burry Port
Llanelli
SWANSEA/ ABERTAWE
Port Talbot
The Mumbles
Port-Eynon
BRISTOL CHANNEL
Lundy
Ilfracombe
Combe Martin
Lynton
Croyde
Braunton
Barnstaple
Northam
Hartland Point
Clovelly
Bideford
Great Torrington
Cliffs of Morwenstow
Kilkhampton
Stratton
Bude
SOUTH
Holsworthy
Okehampton
Tintagel
Launceston
31
Lydford Gorge
High Willhays
Dartmoor National Park
33
18
Camelford
Padstow
19
Wadebridge
Tavistock
Callington
Liskeard
Princetown
39
Buckland Abbey
Buckfastleigh
Bodmin
Newquay
38
Plympton
Fraddon
Lostwithiel
Saltash
Torpoint
Plymstock
West Looe
St. Austell
Fowey
Polperro
PLYMOUTH
Newton Ferrers
34
Modbury
Truro
Trewithen
Mevagissey
Tregony
15
Camborne
St. Ives
20
Redruth
Trelissick Garden
Hayle
Penryn
St. Mawes
St. Just
Penzance
14
17
Falmouth
St. Michael's Mount
Helston
Glendurgan Garden
Land's End
Sennen
16
Mount's Bay
St. Keverne
Lizard
Lizard Point
Salcombe

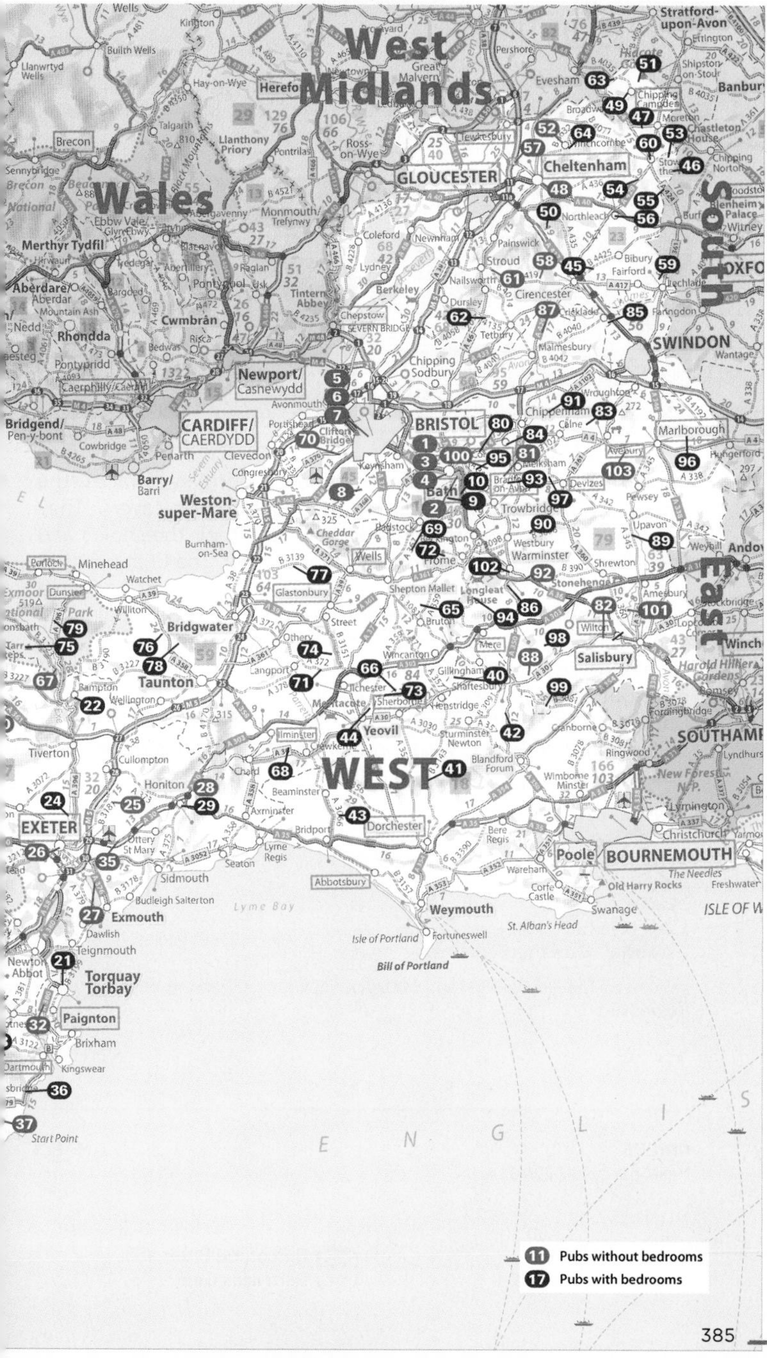
West Midlands
Wales
South
East
WEST
Stratford-upon-Avon
Ettington
Shipston-on-Stour
Banbury
Chipping Campden
Broadway
Moreton
Chastleton House
Chipping Norton
Stow-on-the-Wold
Evesham
Pershore
Great Malvern
Ledbury
Hereford
Kington
Builth Wells
Llanwrtyd Wells
Hay-on-Wye
Talgarth
Llanthony Priory
Black Mountains
Brecon
Sennybridge
Brecon Beacons National Park
Ross-on-Wye
Pontrilas
Monmouth/Trefynwy
Abergavenny
Ebbw Vale/Glynebwy
Merthyr Tydfil
Hirwaun
Tredegar
Blaenavon
Abertillery
Raglan
Pontypool
Usk
Aberdare/Aberdar
Mountain Ash
Rhondda
Pontypridd
Caerphilly/Caerffili
Cwmbrân
Risca
Bedwas
Tintern Abbey
Chepstow
Severn Bridge
Newport/Casnewydd
Avonmouth
Portishead
Clifton Bridge
CARDIFF/CAERDYDD
Bridgend/Pen-y-bont
Cowbridge
Penarth
Barry/Barri
Clevedon
Congresbury
Weston-super-Mare
Severn Estuary
Tewkesbury
GLOUCESTER
Cheltenham
Winchcombe
Coleford
Lydney
Newnham
Berkeley
Painswick
Stroud
Nailsworth
Dursley
Cirencester
Tetbury
Northleach
Bibury
Fairford
Lechlade
Burford
Woodstock
Blenheim Palace
Witney
OXFORD
Cricklade
Faringdon
SWINDON
Wantage
Malmesbury
Chipping Sodbury
Wroughton
Chippenham
Calne
Marlborough
Avebury
Hungerford
BRISTOL
Keynsham
Bath
Melksham
Bradford-on-Avon
Devizes
Trowbridge
Pewsey
Upavon
Cheddar Gorge
Radstock
Wells
Frome
Westbury
Warminster
Shrewton
Weyhill
Andover
Burnham-on-Sea
Glastonbury
Shepton Mallet
Longleat House
Stonehenge
Amesbury
Stockbridge
Porlock
Minehead
Watchet
Dunster
Exmoor National Park
Williton
Bridgwater
Street
Bruton
Wilton
Salisbury
Winchester
Taunton
Langport
Othery
Wincanton
Gillingham
Mere
Shaftesbury
Harold Hillier Gardens
Romsey
Bampton
Wellington
Ilchester
Montacute
Sherborne
Henstridge
Yeovil
Sturminster Newton
Fordingbridge
Cranborne
Ringwood
SOUTHAMPTON
Lyndhurst
New Forest N.P.
Tiverton
Cullompton
Chard
Ilminster
Crewkerne
Beaminster
Blandford Forum
Wimborne Minster
Honiton
Axminster
EXETER
Ottery St Mary
Lyme Regis
Seaton
Bridport
Dorchester
Bere Regis
Poole
BOURNEMOUTH
Christchurch
Lymington
Sidmouth
Budleigh Salterton
Exmouth
Dawlish
Teignmouth
Lyme Bay
Abbotsbury
Weymouth
Wareham
Corfe Castle
Swanage
Old Harry Rocks
The Needles
Freshwater
ISLE OF WIGHT
St. Alban's Head
Isle of Portland
Fortuneswell
Bill of Portland
Newton Abbot
Torquay
Torbay
Paignton
Brixham
Dartmouth
Kingswear
Start Point
E N G L I S
11 Pubs without bedrooms
17 Pubs with bedrooms

CHEQUERS

Sophisticated cooking and elaborate presentation

Set in a residential street amid elegant Georgian terraces, the Chequers isn't far from its sister, the Marlborough Tavern. They may look similar from the outside but cross their thresholds and you'll see each has something different to offer. The Chequers has some pubby character with its simple tables, parquet floor and central bar but it's also been smartened up with a bright paint job. The cooking is fairly sophisticated and presentation, elaborate, so alongside robust pub favourites you might find starters of beetroot and caraway cured salmon or salt cod fishcake with Bath pig chorizo, followed by red wine braised beef cheek or stuffed chicken breast with fondant potato. Lunch is good value and desserts offer something a little different.

50 Rivers St,
BATH, BA1 2QA
Tel.: (01225)360017
Website: www.thechequersbath.com

Close to The Royal Crescent, off Upper Church St. Parking bays opposite.

PRICES
Meals: a la carte £ 29/43

MAP: 1

CLOSING TIMES
Closed 25 December

Butcombe Bitter and Bath Ales Gem

HARE & HOUNDS (N)

Modern versions of classic dishes, and great views

This is a huge place, attracting large numbers of people – so not the best choice for a quiet, romantic evening – but for a birthday celebration or a night out with friends, it's ideal. There has been a property here since the 16C, when a hunting lodge was built; over the years it's variously been an inn and a hotel but is now very much a local pub. Its hillside location near the racecourse affords superb views over the Bath countryside, and its gardens and large terrace come into their own in the warmer months. Inside it's light and airy: take a seat with a view in the conservatory, cosy up by the fire or watch the chefs hard at work in the kitchen pass. Menus are appealingly pithy and offer modern versions of classic dishes.

Lansdown Rd,
BATH, BA1 5TJ
Tel.: (01225)482682
Website: www.hareandhoundsbath.com

1.5 mi north of the city centre on Lansdown Rd. Parking.

PRICES
Meals: a la carte £ 22/32

MAP: 2

CLOSING TIMES
Open daily

St Austell Tribute

MARLBOROUGH TAVERN

Cosy, smart pub near the Royal Crescent

On the eastern edge of Victoria Park, only a stone's throw from the Royal Crescent, sits this 18C pub, surrounded by grand terraced properties. Despite its traditional outer appearance, it's surprisingly chic and fashionable inside, boasting a modern, open-plan interior, boldly patterned wallpaper and contemporary art; not forgetting a rather pleasant walled terrace to the rear. At lunch they offer sandwiches, pub classics and a good value set menu, while dinner steps things up a gear with some interesting specials; there might be potted Wiltshire game, followed by south coast plaice with Cornish samphire, and finished off with iced coffee and honeycomb parfait with hot apple spring roll and blackberry and apple fool.

35 Marlborough Buildings,
BATH, BA1 2LY
Tel.: (01225)423731
Website: www.marlborough-tavern.com

East side of Royal Victoria Park. Parking bays opposite.

PRICES
Meals: £ 15 (lunch) and a la carte £ 24/39

MAP: 3

CLOSING TIMES
Closed 25 December

Butcombe Ales and Box Steam Ales

WHITE HART

Shows the value of good sourcing

Situated close to the railway, just over the river, The White Hart has a real neighbourhood feel. It attracts a loyal local following, so get here early or book ahead as it fills up quickly. Food-wise, the mantra here is 'keep it simple', with the sourcing of ingredients afforded paramount importance. Portions are large and cooking, hearty, with dishes like baked fillet of pork wrapped in bacon, breast of chicken with lentils or whole baked sea bass with lime, ginger and chilli butter. Most people have a main dish and share a side and a dessert, but the smaller tapas plates are also very popular. The pub has a rustic feel, with scrubbed wooden floors and worn wooden tables and the rear terrace is a great spot in warmer weather.

Widcombe Hill,
BATH, BA2 6AA
Tel.: (01225)338053
Website: www.whitehartbath.co.uk

On southern side of the city just off A 36. On-street parking.

PRICES
Meals: £ 13 (weekday lunch) and
a la carte £ 24/34

MAP: 4

CLOSING TIMES
Closed 25-26 December, Sunday dinner
and bank holidays
booking essential at dinner

Butcombe Bitter and Rare Breed, Otter Amber and Sharp's Doom Bar

ALBION PUBLIC HOUSE AND DINING ROOMS

Fun and friendly

Tucked away down a cobbled street in a fashionable neighbourhood quarter, the trendy 17C Albion is exactly as a pub should be - fun, friendly and casual - with an equal split of drinkers and those out for a relaxed meal. Lunchtime sees sandwiches alongside 'brunch' dishes like eggs Benedict and traditional mains like sausage and mash, while the evening à la carte offers straightforward and satisfying seasonal dishes like slow-roasted pork belly or haunch of local roe deer, with everything made in-house, including the ice creams and the rustic bread. Booking is imperative, as drinkers multiply throughout the evening; if the weather's fine then the benches on the terrace make a pleasant spot to take in the comings and goings of the area.

Boyces Ave,
CLIFTON VILLAGE, Bristol, BS8 4AA
Tel.: (0117)9733522
Website: www.thealbionclifton.co.uk

In Clifton Village. Parking in Victoria Square or surrounding roads.

PRICES
Meals: a la carte £ 23/32

MAP: 5

CLOSING TIMES
Closed 25-26 December and dinner Sunday-Monday
booking essential

St Austell Ales and Otter Bitter

KENSINGTON ARMS

You almost think you're on the King's Road

The crest of the Royal Borough of Kensington and Chelsea swings on the board outside, proclaiming the motto 'quam bonum in unum habitare': what a good thing it is to dwell together in unity - and with this pub at the heart of the neighbourhood, what a good thing indeed. With its charming Victorian style, large wood-floored bar and impressive high-ceilinged dining room, you could be mistaken for thinking someone had simply picked up a London pub and dropped it down here. Menus change daily and have a strong British base, featuring maybe buttered asparagus or calves' liver and bacon. Seasons play an important role, so you'll find hearty, nourishing dishes and proper homemade puddings in the colder months. Service is particularly warm.

35-37 Stanley Rd,
BRISTOL, BS6 6NP
Tel.: (0117)9446444
Website: www.thekensingtonarms.co.uk

In city centre. Unrestricted parking outside pub and in nearby streets.

PRICES
Meals: a la carte £ 19/42

MAP: 6

CLOSING TIMES
Closed 25-26 December and Sunday dinner

Greene King Ales

PUMP HOUSE

Victorian former pumping station by the docks

Standing proudly on the quayside, this cavernous Victorian building was once a pumping station for the adjacent docks; evidence of which can be seen in the form of exposed stone walls, quarry tiled floors and original pipework. When the sun's out, sit on the terrace and watch the boats; on colder days head for the large bar or one of the many tables or sofas dotted about over the various different levels. Dishes change with the seasons and focus on a selection of modern classics, including the likes of braised lambs' hearts and coddled egg with marmite soldiers. From Weds-Sat they offer a tasting menu of more refined dishes; you can have any menu anywhere, but the latter is perhaps best suited to the linen-laid mezzanine restaurant.

Merchants Rd,
BRISTOL, BS8 4PZ
Tel.: (0117)9272229
Website: www.the-pumphouse.com

On the eastern side of the docks. Parking.

PRICES
Meals: a la carte £ 23/35

MAP: 7

CLOSING TIMES
Closed 25 December

Butcombe Ales, Bath Ales and Box Steam Ales

PONY & TRAP

Skilfully crafted classical dishes and rural views

This pub's name conjures images of a rural idyll and that's exactly what you'll find here - ask for a table in the rustic rear room or on the terrace, where you can enjoy the wonderful countryside views; at the front is a cosy, characterful bar with stone walls, church pews and an old range laden with pans. Brother and sister team Josh and Holly Eggleton took on this pub almost a decade ago when they were barely out of their teens and have made a real success of it. She runs the service with aplomb while he's hard at work in the kitchen, creating tasty, classical British dishes, with pub favourites at lunch and the occasional innovative touch at dinner. It takes skill to make something as simple as, say, a faggot look and taste quite so good.

Knowle Hill,
New Town, **Chew Magna**, BS40 8TQ
Tel.: (01275)332627
Website: www.theponyandtrap.co.uk

1.5 mi south of the village; follow signs for Bishop Sutton. Parking.

PRICES
Meals: £ 50 and a la carte £ 24/38

MAP: 8

CLOSING TIMES
Closed Monday except December and bank holidays
booking essential

Butcombe Ales and Sharp's Doom Bar

WHEATSHEAF

Former farmhouse now has a chic, modern look

The Wheatsheaf began life as a farmhouse in 1576. Centuries and several seamless additions later, it boasts chic, über-modern styling typified by delightful pink flocked wallpaper and vivid artwork, and a relaxed atmosphere helped on its way by open fires, comfy low sofas and an abundance of books and magazines - not forgetting the pub's friendly resident spaniels. The flavourful, seasonal food is presented in a contemporary style - often on slate plates - and dishes might include homemade fish pie, game broth or slow-roasted belly pork with black pudding; with desserts such as chocolate fondant or almond and prune cake. Bedrooms follow the pub's lead, with a spacious, modern feel and an emphasis firmly on quality; Buttercup is the largest.

COMBE HAY, BA2 7EG
Tel.: (01225)833504
Website: www.wheatsheafcombehay.com

Signposted off A 367, 5 mi south of Bath. Parking.

PRICES
Meals: £ 14 (weekday lunch) and a la carte £ 23/40

3 rooms: £ 120/150

MAP: 9

CLOSING TIMES
Closed 1 week January, 24-25 December, Sunday dinner and Monday except bank holidays

Butcombe Ales

WHEELWRIGHTS ARMS

A very peaceful former carpenter's workshop

If you're after a spot of peace and quiet, make a beeline for the sleepy village of Monkton Combe, where you can relax to the sound of birdsong at this charming inn. It's made up of two open-fired, stone-walled buildings: one of which was originally a private residence and the other, a carpenter's workshop where they used to make waggon wheels (hence the pub's name). Concise menus offer a couple of sharing plates and a selection of traditional dishes, along with some slightly more creative specials. If there's four of you, order 48 hours in advance for the Sunday special - and a prime rib of beef will be delivered to your table for you to carve yourself. As with the rest of the pub, the individually designed bedrooms are warm and welcoming.

Church Ln,
MONKTON COMBE, BA2 7HB
Tel.: (01225)722287
Website: www.wheelwrightsarms.co.uk

2 mi southeast of Bath city centre by A 3062. Parking.

PRICES
Meals: £ 13 (weekday lunch) and a la carte £ 23/34

7 rooms: £ 85/150

MAP: 10

CLOSING TIMES
Closed dinner 25-26 December and 1 January

Butcombe Bitter and Otter Bitter

BASS AND LOBSTER

Oysters and seafood after a walk on the beach

This bright, modern pub, set close to the sandy beach, has smartly laid wooden tables, a mock wooden floor, some banquette seating and a small decked terrace. Having lived and worked on the island for many years, the experienced owner has built up a network of local suppliers and uses these whenever possible. Fresh seafood and shellfish dominate the seasonal menu and dishes are simply cooked and immensely flavourful: try the roast fillet of sea bass, the Chancre crab linguine with prawns or some fantastic steely oysters. Wonderfully earthy Jersey Royals make a great side dish and the prices also bring a smile to one's face, with the lunch menu representing particularly good value. Smooth service comes from a friendly European team.

Gorey Coast Rd,
GOREY (JERSEY), JE3 6EU
Tel.: (01534)859590
Website: www.bassandlobster.com

On the coast road. Parking.

PRICES
Meals: £ 13/21 and a la carte £ 27/40

MAP: 11

CLOSING TIMES
Closed Sunday dinner and Monday

John Smith's Bitter

FLEUR DU JARDIN

Island seafood and summer BBQs

Set in a small hamlet, not far from the sea, this attractive inn started life as several stone cottages. The first thing you'll notice is the stylish terrace and lovely landscaped garden, and it will come as no surprise that they host regular summer BBQs. Pleasingly, the interior lives up to every expectation too, with its series of charming, adjoining rooms, rustic beams, exposed stone walls and open fires. When it comes to dining, the regularly changing menu ranges from homemade burgers to sea bass with pesto potatoes; specials feature tasty island seafood and every dish is prepared with care and a lightness of touch. Completing the picture are stylish New England themed bedrooms with luxury bathrooms - there's even a heated outdoor pool.

Grand Moulins,
KINGS MILLS (GUERNSEY), GY5 7JT
Tel.: (01481)257996
Website: www.fleurdujardin.com

In the centre of the village. Parking.

PRICES
Meals: £ 13/16 and a la carte £ 23/35

13 rooms:
£ 55/120

MAP: 12

CLOSING TIMES
Closed dinner 25 December and 1 January

Liberation Ales, White Rock Wonky Donkey and Lost Tourist

SWAN INN

An enthusiastic Frenchman at the helm

With its smart, bottle-green façade, this pub wouldn't look out of place in London, although its tightly packed, shabby-chic interior might not go down so well. It's very passionately and personally run by a gregarious French owner, and his enthusiasm can be felt throughout the place. On the ground floor there's a traditional bar complete with a coal fire, some booths and walls filled with sporting paraphernalia; above, there's a more sedate dining room with polished wood tables and leather chairs. Both the choice of dishes and the portions themselves are large, and tempting as it may be, you're unlikely to make it through all three courses. Dishes stick mainly to tried-and-tested pub classics but you'll find a few Asian influences too.

St Julian's Ave,
ST PETER PORT (GUERNSEY), GY1 1WA
Tel.: (01481)728969
St Julian's Ave is opposite South Quay. Parking on South Quay (50yds).

PRICES
Meals: a la carte £ 19/32

MAP: 13

CLOSING TIMES
Closed 25 December, Sunday in winter and bank holiday Mondays

Randalls Ales

COLDSTREAMER

Striking pub with a bright, spacious interior

Dating from 1895, this striking pub sits in the heart of Gulval and, like much of the village, was built by the Bolitho family. Following the death in service of Harry Bolitho it was given to the Coldstream Association, before being taken over by two local brothers. It's a spacious place, with a bright dining room and a large bar adorned with Coldstream Guards memorabilia. The seasonal menu features fish from Newlyn, meat from Penzance and products from the village's now retired Smoker. Cooking is generous and modern; maybe salt cod fritters at lunch and more elaborate dishes like lamb rump with caramelised shallots at dinner. May sees an asparagus menu and the regular wine dinners prove popular. Bedrooms are fresh and well-appointed.

GULVAL, TR18 3BB
Tel.: (01736)362072
Website: www.coldstreamer-penzance.co.uk

1.25 mi northeast of Penzance off A 30 in centre of village. Plenty of parking in the square.

PRICES
Meals: a la carte £ 21/32

3 rooms:
£ 65/85

MAP: 14

CLOSING TIMES
Closed 25-26 December

Skinner's Cornish Trawler and Cornish Crown Porter, Rebel Brewing Company 80 Shilling

HALSETOWN INN

Asian flavours and regular theme nights

'Proper pub, thoughtful food' is their strapline and it sums up this endearingly quirky place pretty well. It's a bit scruffy from the outside and fairly modest inside, but it's got character and more importantly, it's got soul. There are various little areas where you can eat - find a spot in front of the bar or on the back terrace, which is a real suntrap. The kitchen tends to eschew the usual pub classics and instead offers an interesting selection of dishes enlivened with some global flavours, with a particular nod towards Asia - and the prices are good too. Wednesday theme nights include Chinese and Thai and they plough their own furrow on Sundays when, in lieu of a traditional lunch, they operate their own burger van in the car park.

HALSETOWN, TR26 3NA
Tel.: (01736)795583
Website: www.hasletowninn.co.uk

1.5 mi southwest of St Ives on B 3311. Parking.

PRICES
Meals: £ 12 (weekday lunch) and
a la carte £ 20/33

MAP: 15

CLOSING TIMES
Closed January and Sunday dinner

Sharp's Doom Bar and
Skinner's Betty Stogs

TOLCARNE INN

Fish and shellfish are the stars of the show

Having been flooded a number of times over the years, this unremarkable looking but refreshingly unaffected 18C pub is now protected by a tall sea wall - it's a shame it hides the view of Mount's Bay, but at least it keeps the wind off the terrace. Inside the family-run inn, things are cosy and traditional with a wood-burner at one end keeping the drinkers warm, and the rest of the place laid out for eating. The owner-chef is an experienced chap who cooks with intelligence and care. Being in Newlyn and within a literal stone's throw from the boats, it's no surprise that fish and shellfish are the stars of the show. The blackboard changes daily and you can always expect wonderfully fresh and uncomplicated dishes that deliver plenty of flavour.

Tolcarne Pl,
NEWLYN, TR18 5PR
Tel.: (01736)363074
Website: www.tolcarneinn.co.uk

By the sea wall in the centre of town. Parking.

PRICES
Meals: a la carte £ 21/35

MAP: 16

CLOSING TIMES
Open daily

Skinner's Betty Stogs and St Austell Tribute

VICTORIA INN

Cosy and characterful with a suntrap terrace

Simple but characterful, with a cosy, homely feel, this pink-washed inn sits in the heart of the village and appeals to drinkers and diners alike. Its owners are keen for it to remain a proper pub, so you'll see locals here for a beer alongside families who've hot-footed it in from the beach for lunch, sand between their toes. The menu offers sandwiches and soups as well as pub classics - like ham, free range eggs and real chips - and choices such as honey-roasted Cornish duck breast or whole lemon sole with asparagus and new potatoes. Dishes are tasty and the chef-owner - a local boy returned home - is proud to showcase local produce. There's some great local art on the walls, the terrace is a suntrap and two modest bedrooms are upstairs.

PERRANUTHNOE, TR20 9NP
Tel.: (01736)710309
Website: www.victoriainn-penzance.co.uk

3 mi east of Marazion, south of A 394. Parking.

PRICES
Meals: a la carte £ 23/37

2 rooms:
£ 50/75

MAP: 17

CLOSING TIMES
Closed 25-26 December, 1 January, Monday in winter and Sunday dinner

Sharp's Doom Bar

ST KEW INN

Attractive front garden with patio heaters

St Kew Inn was built in the 15C to serve the masons who constructed the magnificent next door church and boasts flag floors, stone walls and wooden beams. It sits in a quintessentially English location and its attractive front garden is as much of a draw as the pub itself come the warmer weather. A massive electric umbrella means that sudden summer showers are not a problem, and there are heaters too should it turn nippy. Cooking is fresh and tasty, with a wide range of appealing, good value dishes from which to choose; lunch means choices like Fowey mussels, Welsh rarebit, corned beef hash and a range of sandwiches, while dinner offers similar (minus the sandwiches), plus perhaps some grilled lemon sole or pan-fried lamb's liver.

ST KEW, PL30 3HB
Tel.: (01208)841259
Website: www.stkewinn.co.uk

3 mi northeast of Wadebridge by A 39 and minor road north. Parking.

PRICES
Meals: a la carte £ 23/37

MAP: 18

CLOSING TIMES
Open daily

St Austell Proper Job and Tribute

CORNISH ARMS

Classics and seafood specials from Rick Stein

Rick Stein liked his local so much that he bought the lease on it! Instead of then heading down the 'gastropub' route, he has sensibly kept things simple, with a nicely priced menu of pub classics like a ploughman's, scampi or sausage and mash. Summer means an influx of tourists, who enjoy the local seafood specials, Sunday roasts and nursery puddings and there are plenty of events like pub quizzes, curry nights and live music to keep the regulars happy in winter. Service is chirpy and cheerful, the bar, beamed and cosy, and the dining area, light and airy. The wine list offers a well-priced selection, with plenty to choose from by the glass or carafe - and keep a look out for the man himself, who pops in for a pint from time to time.

Churchtown,
ST MERRYN, PL28 8ND
Tel.: (01841)532700
Website: www.rickstein.com

2.5 mi west of Padstow on B 3276. Parking.

PRICES
Meals: a la carte £ 20/32

MAP: 19

CLOSING TIMES
Open daily
bookings not accepted

St Austell Ales

GURNARD'S HEAD

Remote, shabby-chic and dog friendly

Set in a remote location, surrounded by nothing but fields and livestock, the Gurnard's Head provides a warm welcome that sets you immediately at your ease. It's dog-friendly, with stone floors and shabby-chic décor, and blazing fires and brightly coloured walls help create a relaxed, cosy feel. Menus include a good value set lunch and rely on regional produce, including some locally foraged ingredients. Dishes might include pressed terrine of ham hock, pigeon with celeriac purée and mushroom jus or gurnard with braised fennel and scallop velouté. The wine list includes a very interesting selection by the glass and service is friendly, remaining calm even when it's busy. Compact bedrooms feature good quality linen and colourful throws.

Treen,
ZENNOR, TR26 3DE
Tel.: (01736)796928
Website: www.gurnardshead.co.uk

7.5 mi west of St Ives on B 3306. Parking.

PRICES
Meals: £ 19 (weekday lunch) and a la carte £ 25/33

7 rooms:
£ 85/170

MAP: 20

CLOSING TIMES
Closed 25 December and 4 days early December
booking advisable

St Austell Tribute, Meantime Pale Ale and Bays Springtime

CARY ARMS

Luxurious bedrooms and coastal views

Set in an idyllic spot on the English Riviera, The Cary Arms is built into the rocks, with terraces down to the shore and far-reaching views. Its boutique-chic, New England style bedrooms come with stunning bathrooms complete with roll-top baths; the stylish, ultra-comfy residents lounge continues the nautical theme, and there's even a spa room for treatments. If the rooms are all about luxury, the food, by contrast, is straightforward in style; we're talking reasonably priced pub dishes of simply cooked fish and meats. At the hub of the operation is its atmospheric stone and slate floored bar where you're served by chatty staff; in summer, there's also a wood burning pizza oven on the terrace, to make the most of the wonderful location.

Babbacombe Beach,
BABBACOMBE, TQ1 3LX
Tel.: (01803)327110
Website: www.caryarms.co.uk

2.75 mi northeast of Torquay by A 379. Chargeable parking at adjacent beach car park.

PRICES
Meals: a la carte £ 25/34

8 rooms:
£ 125/275

MAP: 21

CLOSING TIMES
Open daily

Otter Ale, Bays Topsail and Hunter's Pheasant Plucker

SWAN

Dates from 1450 but has a modernised interior

The Swan's history can be traced back to 1450, when it provided accommodation for craftsmen working on the local church. The original inglenook fireplace and bread oven remain in situ but, aside from that, it has a modern, open-plan layout and a fresh, new feel; if you fancy a more intimate experience, head for the upstairs dining room. When it comes to the food, it sticks to unfussy pub classics, with the likes of homemade soup or whitebait, followed by pies, steaks or liver and bacon - and finished off with comforting old school desserts like treacle pudding. Dishes arrive neatly presented on wooden boards, with fish originating from Devon and Cornwall, and meats from nearby Waterhouse Farm. Smart, modern bedrooms are found on the 2nd floor.

Station Rd,
BAMPTON, EX16 9NG
Tel.: (01398)332248
Website: www.theswan.co

6 mi north of Tiverton by A 396 and B 3190. Public car park opposite.

PRICES
Meals: a la carte £ 20/33

3 rooms:
£ 65/85

MAP: 22

CLOSING TIMES
Closed 25 December and Monday

Red Rock Devon Storm, Otter Bright and Exmoor Gold

NORMANDY ARMS

American GIs were billeted here in the war

This pretty pub takes its name from the American occupation of this part of Devon prior to the Normandy landings - and is now under the command of a keen young couple with lots of experience. You'll find local drinkers on the sofas by the wood burning stove and those eating, in the bar or the small dining room with its colourful artwork. Reka looks after things out front, while Andrew does the cooking. Lunch sticks mainly to familiar pub dishes, such as a homemade scotch egg or a ploughman's, while dinner could see loin of lamb en croute or roasted plaice on the bone. Cooking is carefully done, ingredients are local and flavours are distinct. Come for the International Festival of Wormcharming and stay in one of the pleasant bedrooms.

Chapel St,
BLACKAWTON, TQ9 7BN
Tel.: (01803)712884
Website: www.thenormandyarms.co.uk

5.5 mi west of Dartmouth signposted off A 3122. Limited parking.

PRICES
Meals: £ 30 (weekday dinner)
and a la carte £ 27/39

3 rooms:
£ 95/105

MAP: 23

CLOSING TIMES
Closed January
and Sunday-Monday in winter
dinner only and lunch in August

Otter Ale and Hunter's Devon Dreamer

LAZY TOAD INN

Lamb from their farm and home-grown veg

This sweet, Grade II listed pub comes with lovely oak-beamed ceilings and slate floors, and is set in an equally attractive village near the river. In summer, head for the beautiful walled garden or charming cobbled courtyard - once used by the local farrier and wheelwright. If it's a flying visit, opt for glass of Mo's homemade cordial and some tasty pork scratchings; if you've got longer, choose from the wide-ranging, constantly evolving main menu. Much of the produce comes from their polytunnel, vegetable plot and orchard opposite; visit in the spring and you can also sample Black Welsh Mountain lamb raised on their smallholding. Fresh flowers and homemade biscuits welcome you in the comfy bedrooms - Room 1 can be noisy before closing.

BRAMPFORD SPEKE, EX5 5DP
Tel.: (01392)841591
Website: www.thelazytoadinn.co.uk

5 mi north of Exeter by A 377. Parking.

PRICES
Meals: a la carte £ 23/34

5 rooms:
£ 58/105

MAP: 24

CLOSING TIMES
Closed 3 weeks January, Sunday dinner, Monday and bank holidays

Hanlons Yellow Hammer & Firefly, St Austell Tribute and guest ales

FIVE BELLS INN (N)

Pretty, 16C thatched pub and great value food

Narrowly saved from conversion into houses by the present owners, this pretty thatched 16C pub deep in the Devon countryside had the locals tirelessly campaigning for its survival during its closure. In appreciation of their efforts, the table opposite the front door has been named a 'Stammtisch' or 'locals' table' - so whatever you do, don't sit there! The experienced chef uses the finest local ingredients to create well-balanced dishes with real clarity of flavour. There's a blackboard of pub favourites and a small à la carte offering more creative dishes - though the chef's classical roots are clearly evident. The set lunch menu offers excellent value for money and, on Sunday, roasts take centre stage. Service is smooth and friendly.

CLYST HYDON, EX15 2NT
Tel.: (01884)277288
Website: www.fivebells.uk.com

4.5 mi south of Cullompton by B 3181 and minor road east, turning right just before village sign. Parking.

PRICES
Meals: £ 15 (weekday lunch) and
a la carte £ 25/39

MAP: 25

CLOSING TIMES
Open daily
bookings advisable at dinner

Otter Ales and St Austell Tribute

RUSTY BIKE

Nose-to-tail dining in a bohemian atmosphere

This small backstreet boozer was closed for 7 years before larger-than-life owner Hamish skilfully transformed it into a bohemian-style dining pub. It's made up of three rustic rooms filled with reclaimed furniture and an eclectic mix of art, and to pass the time there are magazines, board games and a vintage table football game. When it comes to the cooking, it's hearty, satisfying and follows a traditional British nose-to-tail approach: produce is sourced from within 20 miles; rare breed pigs are butchered on-site; they make their own bread and pasta; and they smoke their own bacon and cure their own bresaola and hams. Alongside your potted Ruby Red beef or Dexter beef shank hash, try a home-brewed cider or specially commissioned beer.

67 Howell Rd,
EXETER, EX4 4LZ
Tel.: (01392)214440
Website: www.rustybike-exeter.co.uk

On northern edge of city centre. On-street parking.

PRICES
Meals: a la carte £ 26/39

MAP: 26

CLOSING TIMES
Open daily
dinner only and Sunday lunch

Fat Pig Ale

PUFFING BILLY

Bright country dining pub overlooking the railway

You'd think this was a typical old railway inn: set right on the street, with a whitewashed exterior and the name of a train. Venture inside and you're in for a shock, for the reality is a bright, modern and open-plan country dining pub, with high vaulted ceilings, a semi-circular bar and a friendly, welcoming atmosphere. An eclectic menu offers tasty, globally influenced dishes such as squid, prawn and chorizo chowder, alongside local specialities like pan-roasted Devon beef rump or rack of West Country lamb. If you like to be where the atmosphere is, sit close to the bar; if it's a quiet meal you're after, head for the far end instead. Trainspotters should take a seat by the window to watch the engines chug along the scenic coastline.

Station Rd,
EXTON, EX3 0PR
Tel.: (01392)877888
Website: www.thepuffingbilly.co.uk

Brown tourist sign off A 376 to Exmouth, 3 mi from junction 30 of M 5. Parking.

PRICES
Meals: £ 17 (weekdays) and
a la carte £ 20/33

MAP: 27

CLOSING TIMES
Open daily

Otter Bitter and Hanlons Yellow Hammer

HOLT

Very passionately run and family-owned

This is a family owned and run pub, where the passion for food and drink is almost palpable. Angus McCaig oversees goings-on in the Holt's kitchen, while brother Joe works out front; their parents meanwhile run the well-known Otter Brewery down the road. Sustainable, regional produce is the central tenet of their ethos with everything cooked in-house and meats and fish cured and smoked on-site. Oft-changing, eco-friendly menus are printed on paper made from recycled hops and list rustic dishes like slow-roasted pork belly or seared lamb rump, with tapas and sandwiches also available at lunch. The pint of smoked prawns is a real winner - and try the tasting rack: a third of a pint of three Otter Brewery ales, matched with recommended dishes.

178 High St,
HONITON, EX14 1LA
Tel.: (01404)47707
Website: www.theholt-honiton.com

At lower end of High Street. Dowell Street car park (2min walk).

PRICES
Meals: £ 11 (weekdays) and a la carte
£ 20/29

MAP: 28

CLOSING TIMES
Closed 25-26 December,
1 January, Sunday and Monday

Otter Ales

RAILWAY

Authentic, affordable Mediterranean cooking

This smart, modern pub offers authentic Mediterranean cooking at affordable prices; a combination patently pleasing the people in this East Devon market town. Touches like the Bibendum statues and various cookery books dotted around suggest a serious approach, underlined by the open kitchen and the pub's strap-line, 'Every plate a picture of freshness and flavour'. Nibble on olive oil dipped bread while you read the menu, where classics like fritto misto sit alongside homemade pastas, brick-fired pizzas and steaks; the warm Sicilian tart is a house favourite and specials might include seared scallops or wild boar terrine. An eclectic wine list and an olive oil top-up service add to the fun and comfortable bedrooms complete the picture.

Queen St,
HONITON, EX14 1HE
Tel.: (01404)47976
Website: www.therailwayhoniton.co.uk

2 min off the High Street, via New Street. Parking.

PRICES
Meals: a la carte £ 18/38

5 rooms:
£ 85/115

MAP: 29

CLOSING TIMES
Closed 25-26 December,
Sunday and Monday

Branscombe Vale Branoc,
St Austell Tribute and Palmers
200

MASONS ARMS

Charming service sophisticated dishes

This pretty thatched inn is set in a secluded village in the beautiful foothills of Exmoor. Built in the 13C by the masons who also constructed the village church, it exudes rural charm, featuring a cosy, beamed bar with an inglenook fireplace, that plays host to the locals. Cooking is more sophisticated than you'd expect to find in most pubs, with canapés and petit fours served alongside attractively presented British and French classics such as Devon beef fillet or monkfish loin, which have the pronounced, assured flavours that come from using the finest of local produce. Dine beneath a celestial ceiling mural in the bright rear dining room, with delightful views out over the rolling hills towards Exmoor. Charming service complements the food.

KNOWSTONE, EX36 4RY
Tel.: (01398)341231
Website: www.masonsarmsdevon.co.uk

7 mi southeast of South Molton by A 361; opposite the village church. Parking.

PRICES
Meals: £ 25/36 and a la carte £ 36/48

MAP: 30

CLOSING TIMES
Closed first week January, 1 week mid February, 10 days August-September, Sunday dinner and Monday

Cotleigh Tawny Owl

DARTMOOR INN

Specialities cooked on the charcoal grill

A pub might have a snazzy new look or a barrel-load of special offers on but it's the feel of a place which dictates whether you'll want to spend time there - this rustic pub being a case in point. The exterior is rather non-descript but the owners offer a genuinely warm welcome, the local staff are friendly and there's a buzzing air of satisfaction. The numerous rooms are decorated in a shabby-chic style; low ceilings add a cosy feel, while artwork provides a modern touch. Classic dishes like liver and onions or slow-cooked belly pork are satisfying and full of flavour; there is an emphasis on local produce and Devon Ruby Red beef and dishes from the charcoal grill are the specialities. Spacious, elegant bedrooms have a French feel.

Moorside,
LYDFORD, EX20 4AY
Tel.: (01822)820221
Website: www.dartmoorinn.com

8.5 mi northeast of Tavistock on A 386. Parking.

PRICES
Meals: £ 17 (weekdays) and
a la carte £ 20/45

4 rooms:
£ 75/135

MAP: 31

CLOSING TIMES
Closed Sunday dinner and Monday lunch except bank holidays

Otter Ale and St Austell Tribute

CHURCH HOUSE INN

Seasonal dishes inspired by the Mediterranean

The Church House Inn was originally built in the 14C to provide accommodation for stone masons constructing the nearby church; it was rebuilt in the 18C and still displays some of its eye-catching, original Strawberry Gothic windows. Inside, it's fresh and simple, with a formally laid restaurant and a bar offering locally brewed beer; there are beams, open fires and plenty of nooks and crannies in which to settle, and local art hangs on the walls. The multitude of menus can be a little confusing, with different blackboards offering everything from tapas and sharing plates to vegetarian dishes and wines by the glass, but once you've decided what to go for, you'll find the cooking hearty and comforting and the service, friendly and helpful.

Village Rd,
MARLDON, TQ3 1SL
Tel.: (01803)558279
Website: www.churchhousemarldon.com

Between Torquay and Paignton off A 380. Parking.

PRICES
Meals: a la carte £ 23/36

MAP: 32

CLOSING TIMES
Closed dinner 25-26 December

St Austell Ales, Teignworthy Gun Dog and Otter Ale

THE HORSE

Tasty, unfussy cooking with Italian influences

It's hard to believe that this pub, in the heart of rural Dartmoor, was semi-derelict when its owners took it on. While locals gather in the bar to watch the sport, diners head for rustic, flag-floored rooms created from the converted stable and barn; or out to the sunny, Mediterranean-style courtyard. With an actor-turned-chef at the helm you might expect some melodrama in the kitchen; you won't get this, but you will get tasty, unfussy dishes with more than a hint of Italy. Frittata, panini, sandwiches and pizza are served at lunch, with dishes like crab linguine or gnocchi on the menu at dinner. Authentic, thin crust pizzas come from a custom-built oven, while desserts such as burnt toffee panna cotta finish your meal off with a flourish.

7 George St,
MORETONHAMPSTEAD, TQ13 8PG
Tel.: (01647)440242
Website: www.thehorsedartmoor.co.uk

In heart of village. Two car parks within 1min walk.

PRICES
Meals: a la carte £ 20/35

MAP: 33

CLOSING TIMES
Closed 25 December and Monday lunch

Dartmoor Legend and IPA, Otter Ale, Hanlons Yellow Hammer and Teignworthy Reel Ale

SHIP INN

Seafaring memorabilia and wonderful water views

Wonderful waterside views are one of the main attractions of this fine pub, set in a peaceful spot on the south side of the Yealm Estuary. It's well run, large and very busy, with friendly staff who cope admirably under pressure. Its oldest part dates from the 18C and its characterful interior features wooden floors and open fires, while its collection of maritime memorabilia, including numerous old photographs, gives a tangible sense of seafaring history. The menu offers pub classics such as rib-eye steak or sausage and mash, followed by tried-and-tested desserts like bread and butter pudding. The wine list is well-presented, with a good selection by the glass. Be careful where you park your car because time and tide wait for no man!

NOSS MAYO, PL8 1EW
Tel.: (01752)872387
Website: www.nossmayo.com

10.5 mi southeast of Plymouth; signed off A 379; turn right onto B 3186. Restricted parking, particularly at high tide.

PRICES
Meals: a la carte £ 22/32

MAP: 34

CLOSING TIMES
Open daily

St Austell Tribute, Dartmoor Jail Ale and Otter Amber

JACK IN THE GREEN

Warm and welcoming, with a vast choice of menus

This is a place that you could easily pass by - but if you did, you'd be missing out. Inside it's warm and welcoming, both in its décor and in the friendliness of its team, with the larger-than-life owner ensuring that the locals are kept 'in-the-know' by sending out newsletters and recipe cards. They take a very serious approach towards their cooking and have supported local producers since long before it became the fashion. There's a vast array of menus to mix and match between, so you can start with an old pub classic, move on to a more modern, restaurant-style dish and then return to a tasty, old-school favourite for dessert; the six highlighted dishes make up the 'Totally Devon' set menu, which focuses on the region's finest produce.

London Rd,
ROCKBEARE, EX5 2EE
Tel.: (01404)822240
Website: www.jackinthegreen.uk.com

7.25 mi east of Exeter by A 30 and B 3184 on B 3174. Parking.

PRICES
Meals: £ 25 and a la carte £ 30/38

MAP: 35

CLOSING TIMES
Closed 25 December-3 January

Otter Ale, Butcombe Bitter and Sharp's Doom Bar

TOWER INN

Traditional pub cooking with tasty twists

Leave your car in the car park as you enter the village and make the 10 minute walk up the hill: not only is it the easiest place to park but it's also a pleasant stroll. Built in 1347 as cottages for the workers building the next door chantry, the pub is now overlooked by the ruins of the former tower. It's a charming place, boasting dark red walls, polished tables and roaring fires, not forgetting fresh flowers and flickering candles. Menus differ from lunch to dinner and change every 3 months. It's pub food with an extra little twist; nothing gimmicky, just good cooking that adds something a little different - so your lunchtime fish and chips might come in vodka batter and your evening sea bass, with crab dumplings. Simple bedrooms await.

Church Rd,
SLAPTON, TQ7 2PN
Tel.: (01548)580216
Website: www.thetowerinn.com

6 mi southwest of Dartmouth by A 379. Parking with exceptionally narrow access.

PRICES
Meals: £ 20 (weekday dinner) and a la carte £ 21/33

3 rooms:
£ 60/85

MAP: 36

CLOSING TIMES
Closed first 2 weeks January and Sunday dinner in winter

Otter Bitter, St Austell Proper Job, Sharp's Doom Bar and Butcombe Bitter

MILLBROOK INN

The olive oil is from their farm in Andalucía

You'll find this characterful, shabby-chic pub squeezed in between the houses on a narrow village street. Low beamed ceilings and an open fire create a cosy atmosphere and two terraces provide a pleasant alternative come summer. It's very passionately run: they use olive oil from their farm in Andalucía and sell fresh, local produce 24hrs a day in the 'Veg Shed'. Cooking is traditional and hearty with some Mediterranean influences; you might find potted South Devon crab, bouillabaisse or Chateaubriand with pommes pont neuf and béarnaise sauce. The blackboard offers a good value set menu and if you're in a group, you can order 72 hours ahead for a whole roast suckling pig. They host regular live music nights and guest chefs feature in winter.

SOUTH POOL, TQ7 2RW
Tel.: (01548)531581
Website: www.millbrookinnsouthpool.co.uk

5.5 mi southeast of Kingsbridge off A 379. On-street parking in the village.

PRICES
Meals: £ 12 (weekday lunch) and a la carte
£ 24/49

MAP: 37

CLOSING TIMES
Open daily

Red Rock and Exeter Brewery Ales

TREBY ARMS

Visually appealing dishes with playful elements

A quotation chalked on the timbers warns that 'you can't please all of the people all of the time' but they seem to be doing a pretty good job of it here! Owner-chef Anton was winner of 'MasterChef: The Professionals, 2012', and Plympton residents were no doubt relieved when he returned to work afterwards at this whitewashed pub. Built by Isambard Kingdom Brunel to serve workers constructing the Devon-Cornwall train bridge, it's still a pub for drinkers as much as for diners, as evidenced by the locals' pint jugs hanging over the bar. The carefully prepared, visually appealing and clearly flavoured modern dishes often feature a playful twist to surprise and delight - and the 'taster' menus best demonstrate the chef's considerable talent.

SPARKWELL, PL7 5DD
Tel.: (01752)837363
Website: www.thetrebyarms.co.uk

10 mi east of Plymouth signposted off A 38. Parking.

PRICES
Meals: £ 20 (lunch) and a la carte £ 26/49

MAP: 38

CLOSING TIMES
Closed 25-26 December, 1 January and Monday
booking essential

Dartmoor Jail Ale and IPA, St Austell Tribute and Otter Seville Bitter

CORNISH ARMS

Sophisticated desserts are worth saving room for

It might have been refurbished but the Cornish Arms is still a pleasingly traditional pub. It's run in partnership by the St Austell brewery and local lad John Hooker, and has a warm, welcoming feel. The quarry-tiled bar is usually filled with regulars playing darts, watching the football or sitting at simple wooden tables snacking on homemade sausage rolls or fishcakes; a few steps up is the equally relaxed restaurant. The talented, ambitious chef prepares both carefully crafted classics - like braised ox cheek with horseradish, mash and beef gravy - and more elaborate offerings such as fillet of stone bass with potted shrimp, bisque and braised lettuce. Desserts are sophisticated and a treat for both the eyes and the stomach.

15 West St,
TAVISTOCK, PL19 8AN
Tel.: (01822)612145
Website: www.thecornisharmstavistock.co.uk

In the centre of town. Limited parking at the rear.

PRICES
Meals: a la carte £ 19/36

MAP: 39

CLOSING TIMES
Closed dinner 24 December

St Austell Ales

STAPLETON ARMS

Pub classics and plenty of local ales

A welcoming, well-run pub, with a homely, shabby-chic style, its rustic, wood-floored bar offering the obligatory comfy sofas and open fire, and its brightly painted dining room being the more formal option. Menus showcase pub classics like beer-battered haddock with triple-cooked chips or pork loin with mash and greens, with the occasional international influence also putting in an appearance. Snacks like pork pie, scotch egg and biltong can be wrapped up to take home; they hold monthly themed dinners and even craft and cookery mornings for kids. Bedrooms are spacious with Egyptian cotton linen, smart bathrooms and a mix of modern and antique furnishings - and you can keep your packing light as they also provide maps, wellies and picnics.

Church Hill,
BUCKHORN WESTON, SP8 5HS
Tel.: (01963)370396
Website: www.thestapletonarms.com

7 mi west of Shaftesbury by A 30 and minor road north. Parking.

PRICES
Meals: a la carte £ 24/37

4 rooms:
£ 70/120

MAP: 40

CLOSING TIMES
Closed 25 December

Butcombe Bitter, Keystone Bedrock and Moor Revival

NEW INN

Stylish bedrooms and large orchard garden

The picture postcard village of Cerne Abbas is overlooked by the famous Chalk Giant - and this 16C former coaching inn is another impressively sized and rather ancient village landmark. Its décor is traditional, with exposed beams and dark wood tables, but a little revamp has made it slightly less cluttered than it once was. Apart from a few midday sandwiches, the same menu is offered at lunch and dinner. Expect a mix of traditional and more modern dishes - good pub grub with no unnecessary fuss, just freshly prepared, ably cooked and using locally sourced ingredients. A pleasant landscaped courtyard leads out to the pub's vast back garden with its delightful apple trees. Bedrooms are stylish; some are in the converted stable block.

14 Long St,
CERNE ABBAS, DT2 7JF
Tel.: (01300)341274
Website: www.thenewinncerneabbas.co.uk

In the centre of the village. On-street parking.

PRICES
Meals: a la carte £ 28/43

12 rooms:
£ 80/180

MAP: 41

CLOSING TIMES
Closed 25-26 December

Palmers Ales

FONTMELL

Pleasingly different from the norm

This stylish, modern pub is set in a small hamlet and features a comfy bar - complete with an open fire and a piano - and a spacious dining room, which straddles the brook below. Sit in the latter of the two rooms, surrounded by shelves filled with books, knick-knacks and wine bottles, and keep an eye out for the visiting otters. The concise daily menu offers an eclectic mix of carefully executed dishes, ranging from homely pub classics to those that display Mediterranean and even some Thai influences. You might find Dorset lamb and black pudding suet pudding or Sicilian-style linguine alla Norma, and on Sundays, the likes of kedgeree and eggs Benedict on the simpler 'Supper' menu. Smart bedrooms are named after butterflies; one has a roll-top bath in the room.

FONTMELL MAGNA, SP7 0PA
Tel.: (01747)811441
Website: www.thefontmell.com

4.75 mi south of Shaftesbury on A 350 in centre of village. Parking.

PRICES
Meals: £ 16 (weekdays) and a la carte £ 23/39

6 rooms:
£ 75/155

MAP: 42

CLOSING TIMES
Closed 26 December

Keystone Ales, Butcombe Bitter and guest ales

THREE HORSESHOES INN

Be sure to try the tasty triple-cooked chips

It's all about the food here at The 'Shoes; a cosy, traditional pub set in a lovely spot on the edge of the Dorset Downs. A glance at the menu will explain the pub's reputation – it all sounds so appealing that it's a dilemma deciding what to choose. Great ingredients go into the dishes, which are packed with flavour and come with a proper pubby earthiness, whether that's wild boar scotch eggs, deep-fried rabbit with coleslaw or a veal and bone marrow burger. The day's fish specials are chalked up on the board and they make their own breads, ice creams, chutneys and pickles. Prices are sensible and the triple-cooked chips are worth the journey alone. Bedrooms are simple but spacious; the two in the annexe have super views across the valley.

POWERSTOCK, DT6 3TF
Tel.: (01308)485328
Website: www.threeshoesdorset.co.uk

5.5 mi northeast of Bridport by A 3066. Parking.

PRICES
Meals: a la carte £ 21/37

3 rooms:
£ 70/110

MAP: 43

CLOSING TIMES
Closed 25 December and Monday in winter

Palmers Ales

ROSE & CROWN

Menus showcase West Country produce

This pretty part-thatched pub dates back to the 14C, when it was built to house the workers constructing the spire of the adjacent church. With an open-fired lounge and a bar complete with a grandfather clock, it has plenty of rustic charm, but on a sunny day you can't beat a spot in the conservatory, which opens out onto the garden. Menus showcase seasonal West Country produce: start with something from the 'nibbles' section - such as whitebait - then move on to the likes of treacle-cured salmon with oriental salad followed by tomato and mozzarella crusted sea bream or Creedy Carver duck breast with bacon and shallot tarte Tatin. Bedrooms, located in the old cow shed, come with country-chic décor and private terraces with views.

TRENT, DT9 4SL
Tel.: (01935)850776
Website: www.roseandcrowntrent.co.uk

4 mi northwest of Sherborne signposted off B 3148. Parking.

PRICES
Meals: a la carte £ 20/36

3 rooms:
£ 75/110

MAP: 44

CLOSING TIMES
Open daily

Butcombe Bitter, Wadworth Henry's Original IPA and White Horse Village Idiot

VILLAGE PUB

Stylish, cosy country pub with a heated terrace

With an interior straight out of any country homes magazine, the Village Pub has that cosy, open-fired, village pub vibe down to a tee. Four small, intimate rooms are set around a dimly lit copper-topped bar and there's a carefully manicured terrace complete with patio heaters to the rear. The menu exudes modern appeal; nibbles like sea trout blinis are an irresistible teaser, there are starters like homemade country terrine, mains like shoulder of venison with braised red cabbage and comforting desserts such as treacle tart. Meat comes from within a 30 mile radius, with charcuterie often from Highgrove and vegetables from partner Barnsley House just up the road. Bedrooms have a similarly tasteful style; number Six has a four-poster bed.

BARNSLEY, GL7 5EF
Tel.: (01285)740421
Website: www.thevillagepub.co.uk

4 mi northeast of Cirencester on B 4425. Parking.

PRICES
Meals: a la carte £ 25/40

6 rooms:
£ 140/170

MAP: 45

CLOSING TIMES
Open daily
booking essential

Butcombe Bitter, Hook Norton Ales and Wye Valley Ales

KINGS HEAD INN

Dine next to the inglenook fireplace in the bar

Sitting on a picturesque village green, bisected by a stream filled with bobbing ducks, this charming 16C former cider house provides the perfect backdrop for a holiday snap. The interior doesn't disappoint either: the large, heavily beamed bar with its vast inglenook fireplace, the solid stone floors and the comfortable, laid-back feel create a wonderful atmosphere, and the cosy bedrooms - split between the pub and the courtyard - finish it all off perfectly. Appealing bar snacks might include spiced whitebait or pheasant in a basket, while the main menu offers pub classics like steak or fish and chips alongside some interesting modern dishes such as vodka and tonic soft shell crab or beef carpaccio with orange and juniper reduction.

The Green,
BLEDINGTON, OX7 6XQ
Tel.: (01608)658365
Website: www.kingsheadinn.net

4 mi southeast of Stow-on-the-Wold by A 436 and B 4450. Parking.

PRICES
Meals: a la carte £ 27/40

12 rooms:
£ 75/125

MAP: 46

CLOSING TIMES
Closed 25 December

Hook Norton Hooky Bitter, Wye Valley Dorothy Goodbody and Butts Barbus Barbus

HORSE & GROOM

Good selection of wines by the glass

Having grown up working in their parents' pub, brothers Will and Tom jumped at the chance to start their own venture when this listed Georgian building came on the market. Built from honey-coloured Cotswold stone, it's set on the main street of a pretty village high on the hillside, and features stone walls and open fires as well as five stylish, contemporary bedrooms. Study the daily blackboard menu and then order at the bar, but bear in mind that it's a popular place, so you'll need to have booked or be willing to wait. The food is good value, fresh and flavoursome; expect the likes of parmesan and rosemary crumbed sardine fillets, pan-roast skate wing or braised blade of Dexter beef, with classic puddings such as steamed lemon curd sponge.

BOURTON-ON-THE-HILL, GL56 9AQ
Tel.: (01386)700413
Website: www.horseandgroom.info

2 mi west of Moreton-in-Marsh on A 44. Parking.

PRICES
Meals: a la carte £ 21/36

5 rooms:
£ 80/170

MAP: 47

CLOSING TIMES
Closed 25, 31 December and Sunday dinner except bank holidays
booking essential

Goffs Jouster, Purity Mad Goose, Stroud Budding and Whale Ale Pale Whale

ROYAL OAK

Large garden with heaters and a skittle alley

The 'Pavilion' may sound like a strange name for their skittle alley and function room but it all becomes clearer once you learn that batting legend Tom Graveney was a previous landlord. Turn left and you'll discover a bar with a worn floor, a wood-burning stove and plenty of framed sporting prints; turn right and you'll find a dark wood furnished dining room with an open fire, red walls filled with an array of jugs and vessels, and several blackboards announcing the month's events. Lunch offers tasty, satisfying dishes such as kedgeree or duck hash with bubble and squeak, while dinner steps things up with the likes of goat's cheese and beetroot terrine or rump of lamb with baby onions. The large garden, with its patio heaters, is a hit.

The Burgage,
Prestbury, **CHELTENHAM**, GL52 3DL
Tel.: (01242)522344
Website: www.royal-oak-prestbury.co.uk

Follow signs from the city to the racecourse via Prestbury Rd and New Barn Ln. On-street parking.

PRICES
Meals: a la carte £ 22/39

MAP: 48

CLOSING TIMES
Closed 25 December

Purity Mad Goose, Wye Valley HPA and Timothy Taylor Landlord

EIGHT BELLS INN

Keep an eye out for the hidden tunnel

If you're following the Cotswold Way, stop at this 14C pub, close to the historic high street of this old wool merchant's town. It originally accommodated the stonemasons working on St James's church and later stored the eight bells from the church tower; keep an eye out for the hidden tunnel in the dining room. Rebuilt in the 17C using the original stone and timbers, it retains its good old community feel and welcomes drinkers and diners alike. The neighbouring counties are represented in their real ale selection and they even offer scrumpy on tap. Cooking is traditionally British - pies are the real thing, puddings are gloriously homemade and specials are just that, so arrive early. Bedrooms are traditional - mind your head on the beams!

Church St,
CHIPPING CAMPDEN, GL55 6JG
Tel.: (01386)840371
Website: www.eightbellsinn.co.uk

In centre of town. Unrestricted parking on road.

PRICES
Meals: a la carte £ 24/36

6 rooms:
£ 75/140

MAP: 49

CLOSING TIMES
Closed 25 December

Hook Norton Hooky Bitter, Wye Valley HPA and Goffs Jouster

THE GREEN DRAGON INN

Who doesn't love a roaring fire on a winter's day?

This characterful stone pub can be found nestled in a peaceful country lane that borders the grounds of the Cowley Manor hotel. The surrounding area is serious walking territory, so at lunchtime you'll find plenty of ramblers tucking into hearty burgers or sausages - alongside others sampling some of the more unusual dishes, such as deep-fried pheasant and chestnut samosas or sea bass baked in a banana leaf. Huge open fireplaces are a focal point in two of the rooms and what better way to start the day than breakfast by a roaring fire? Keep an eye out for the carved mice that hide among the woodwork - the hallmark of Robert 'Mouseman' Thompson. Bedrooms are simple and modern; the St George suite is the best and boasts a super king sized bed.

COCKLEFORD, GL53 9NW
Tel.: (01242)870271
Website: www.green-dragon-inn.co.uk

5 mi south of Cheltenham by A 435. Parking.

PRICES
Meals: a la carte £ 23/35

9 rooms:
£ 70/175

MAP: 50

CLOSING TIMES
Closed dinner 25-26 December and 1 January

Sharp's Doom Bar, Hook Norton Old Hooky and Otter Bitter

EBRINGTON ARMS

A proper village local

This 17C inn snuggles into a charming chocolate box village in the glorious Cotswold countryside; its beamed, flag-floored bar with blazing log fire providing the hub from which locals and visitors come and go, while owners Claire and Jim oversee proceedings with humour and grace. The characterful dining rooms provide an intimate atmosphere for a meal, while the delightful sloping garden is the place to be in good weather. Monthly menus offer hearty dishes like ham hock terrine, rump of lamb or roast breast of guinea fowl, with game to the fore in season and fresh fruit and veg supplied by village farms. Comfortable bedrooms come with countryside views and plenty of thoughtful extras; Room 3 has a four-poster and Room 4, a claw-foot bath.

EBRINGTON, GL55 6NH
Tel.: (01386)593223
Website: www.theebringtonarms.co.uk

2 mi east of Chipping Campden signposted off B 4035. Parking.

PRICES
Meals: a la carte £ 20/33

5 rooms:
£ 104/160

MAP: 51

CLOSING TIMES
Open daily

Prescott Hill Climb, North Cotswold Windrush and Yubberton Ales

ROYAL OAK

Watch the steam trains chug past from the garden

There's no doubt that the selling point of this pub is its large garden: aside from being a great place to sit and eat – especially in barbecue season – it offers plenty to keep you occupied. Children are kept busy watching the chickens or in the play area, while those of more mature years can sit back and appreciate the chug of the trains passing by on the Gloucestershire-Warwickshire Steam Railway; sporty individuals can even don their shorts and make for the tennis court! Inside, there's a nice bar and two snug dining rooms but head for the conservatory to be rewarded with the best views. The experienced owner has good local connections when it comes to sourcing his produce and the dishes are honest and traditionally based.

GRETTON, GL54 5EP
Tel.: (01242)604999
Website: www.royaloakgretton.co.uk

On the edge of the village, 2 mi northwest of Winchcombe. Parking.

PRICES
Meals: a la carte £ 19/32

MAP: 52

CLOSING TIMES
Open daily

Wye Valley HPA, Jennings Bitter and Prescott Grand Prix

FOX INN

Creeper-clad and quintessentially English

Lying at the heart of a peaceful Cotswold village is this creeper-clad, quintessentially English pub. Well-regarded locally and often busy, it's as characterful inside as its exterior suggests, with beamed ceilings, solid stone walls, flagged floors and plenty of cosy nooks and crannies. The lovely garden has plenty of seating for long, sunny summer afternoons, while the wood burning stoves make cold winter days desirable. Wherever you sit, Mr Fox is never too far away, be he a wall-mounted head, a cartoon or a cuddly toy, as featured in the individually furnished, comfortable bedrooms. The regularly changing menu keeps things fresh, with the focus on carefully prepared, tasty British classics like local steak, calves' liver or Dover sole.

LOWER ODDINGTON, GL56 0UR
Tel.: (01451)870555
Website: www.foxinn.net

3 mi east of Stow-on-the-Wold signposted off A 436. Parking.

PRICES
Meals: a la carte £ 25/38

3 rooms:
£ 75/110

MAP: 53

CLOSING TIMES
Open daily
booking essential

Hook Norton Ales

THE PUB AT SLAUGHTERS COUNTRY INN

A great place for afternoon tea

Its name might not conjure up the loveliest of thoughts but Lower Slaughter is actually one of the prettiest and most idyllic of the Cotswold villages. At its heart, beside the river, stands a fine light-stone hotel with cosy bedrooms - once a 'crammer' school for Eton College - and within it, you'll find a trio of rooms that make up the pub; chock-full of character, with wonky low ceilings and stone floors. To accompany the selection of juices and real ales, you'll find an appealing menu of wholesome dishes, offering everything from field mushrooms on toast to the pie of the day; while puddings stray from the norm with the likes of crème caramel with poached autumn fruits. Have afternoon tea on the beautiful terrace overlooking the gardens.

LOWER SLAUGHTER, GL54 2HS
Tel.: (01451)822143
Website: www.theslaughtersinn.co.uk

1.75 mi northwest of Bourton-on-the-Water by A 429. Parking.

PRICES
Meals: a la carte £ 24/44

30 rooms:
£ 85/360

MAP: 54

CLOSING TIMES
Open daily

Wychwood Hobgoblin and Brakspear Ales

FEATHERED NEST

Superb views and over 200 wines!

Set in a small hamlet, this pub has really come into its own under its latest owners, who spent several years in Portugal gaining experience in the hospitality industry. It's the type of place that offers something for everyone, with its laid-back bar, rustic snug, casual conservatory and formal dining room. Sit on quirky bar stools made from horse saddles and sample unfussy dishes from the daily blackboard menu or head through to elegant antique tables for more complex offerings such as grouse with celeriac pudding or halibut tempura with charred squid - not forgetting a list of over 200 wines. Once fully sated, make for one of the comfy bedrooms complete with antique furnishings, quality linens and a smart roll-top bath. The views are superb.

NETHER WESTCOTE, OX7 6SD
Tel.: (01993)833030
Website: www.thefeatherednestinn.co.uk

Signposted off A 424 southeast of Stow-on-the-Wold. Parking.

PRICES
Meals: a la carte £ 38/52

4 rooms:
£ 150/250

MAP: 55

CLOSING TIMES
Closed 25 December, Sunday dinner and Monday except bank holidays

Hook Norton Hooky Bitter, Purity Pure UBU, Ringwood Boondoggle and Prescott Hill Climb

WHEATSHEAF INN

Furnished with interesting French market finds

The owners of this smart, 17C coaching inn also own the old cottage next door, where you'll find stylish, contemporary bedrooms with some quirky touches; some have baths in the rooms and most are furnished with interesting finds from French flea markets. The pub has a stone-floored, open-fired bar in the centre and a traditional, clubby dining room on either side - look out for the semi-private 'Poker Table' in the alcove - and the pretty tiered terrace provides plenty of extra space when the weather's good. The same menu is available throughout, offering classical dishes and something to suit every taste: maybe pappardelle of braised beef or cheese soufflé to start and slow-cooked pork belly or confit duck leg with cassoulet to follow.

West End,
NORTHLEACH, GL50 3EZ
Tel.: (01451)860244
Website: www.cotswoldswheatsheaf.com

In centre of town. Parking.

PRICES
Meals: £ 15 (weekday lunch) and a la carte £ 23/40

14 rooms: £ 120/180

MAP: 56

CLOSING TIMES
Open daily

Hobsons Best, Otter Amber and Oxfordshire Churchill

GLOUCESTER OLD SPOT

No surprise that rare breed pork's the speciality

There's no denying that British pub names are a varied and interesting bunch. This little beauty used to be called the ubiquitous 'Swan' but now its moniker has more meaning, as its owners specialise in rare breed pork; enjoy such delights as crispy Old Spot pig's cheeks, rolled and boned belly pork, or pork T-bone steak. If you don't fancy pig, fret not: there are plenty of other tasty offerings on the seasonal menu, from a crusty lunchtime cob filled with roast lamb and mint & cucumber relish to pan-fried sea bass with seared squid and prawns. The atmosphere is cosy and relaxing and the staff, cheery and welcoming - although it was not ever thus: there used to be a hanging post in the garden where many miscreants met their demise.

Tewkesbury Rd,
PIFF'S ELM, GL51 9SY
Tel.: (01242)680321
Website: www.thegloucesteroldspot.co.uk

4 mi northwest on A 4019, midway between Cheltenham and Tewkesbury. Parking.

PRICES
Meals: £ 13 (lunch) and a la carte £ 21/41

MAP: 57

CLOSING TIMES
Closed 25-26 December

Purity Mad Goose, Wye Valley Butty Bach and Butcombe Adam Henson's Rare Breed

THE BELL

Bring your dog or tie up your horse!

A new team have brought considerable local experience with them to this charming Cotswold pub, but wisely decided not to change too much of the villagers' beloved local. Flagged floors, exposed stone and an abundance of beams lend character while the open fires add cosiness and warmth. Four rooms are served by the central bar and all-comers are equally welcome, whether here for a pint or a three course meal. Menus are the same at lunch and dinner, and offer the expected burger or fish and chips as well as dishes which allow a little more creativity from the chef, like curried day boat seafood stew or braised pork belly with cheek croquettes. Dogs are welcome and there's even a place to tie up horses, so leave the car and enjoy a cocktail.

SAPPERTON, GL7 6LE
Tel.: (01285)760298
Website: www.bellsapperton.co.uk

5 mi west of Cirencester by A 419. Parking.

PRICES
Meals: a la carte £ 20/39

MAP: 58

CLOSING TIMES
Open daily

Hook Norton Old Hooky, Butcombe Adam Henson's Rare Breed and Stroud Ales

SWAN

British cooking showcases produce from the garden

There are few more charming Cotswold villages than Southrop and it's here you'll find the equally delightful Swan. This 17C Virginia creeper covered inn comes with characterful beamed dining rooms, open fires and modern artwork. It also plays a key role in the community; you'll always find plenty of locals in the snug bar and there's even a skittle alley at the back. Cooking is firmly British based and features produce from the extensive gardens; you might find brawn with pickled artichokes or roast breast of guinea fowl with pea purée. Just down the road, they have three delightful cottages (minimum 2 night stay), and if you're feeling particularly inspired after your meal, you can always enrol at the owners' nearby cookery school.

SOUTHROP, GL7 3NU
Tel.: (01367)850205
Website: www.theswanatsouthrop.co.uk

3 mi northwest of Lechlade-on-Thames on Eastleach rd. On-street parking around the village.

PRICES
Meals: a la carte £ 26/45

MAP: 59

CLOSING TIMES
Open daily

Sharp's Doom Bar, Otter Ale and Hook Norton Ales

BELL

Plenty of choice and an ever-evolving fish board

If you're looking for a good base from which to explore the Cotswolds, then this smart inn could well fit the bill - although, as it offers pretty much everything under one roof, you may be reluctant to ever actually leave. It's been given a new lease of life by an experienced restaurateur and comes with the prerequisite open fires and stone floors. Staff are pleasant and welcoming and there's bags of choice on the menu - parfaits, terrines, pies, slow-cooked meats and mature steaks from the local butcher - along with a continually changing fish board. For dessert, the romantically inclined can share a chocolate fondue and get dipping with their strawberries, before retiring to one of the comfy bedrooms; ask for one with a country view.

Park St,
STOW-ON-THE-WOLD, GL54 1AJ
Tel.: (01451)870916
Website: www.thebellatstow.com

On the eastern edge of town on A 436. Parking.

PRICES
Meals: a la carte £ 22/33

5 rooms:
£ 70/120

MAP: 60

CLOSING TIMES
Closed 5-8 May

Hook Norton Lion, North Cotswold Windrush and Cotswold Cask

BISLEY HOUSE N

Stroud's oldest pub sports a bright, modern look

Stroud's oldest pub, the former brewery-owned Bisley House, is hidden away on a residential side street and has been given a new lease of life by Rorie Scott and family. It now sports a surprisingly bright and modern look, with tiled floors, white walls - and not a beam or a horse brass in sight! The menu changes almost daily and offers an interesting range of dishes, from moules marinière or chicken liver parfait, to braised ox cheek with horseradish mash, duck leg with mustard sauce or Moroccan spiced lamb stew. The cooking is simple, fresh and tasty - and the locals clearly love it. Service is friendly and attentive, the soundtrack's a good'un, and if you venture out the back, you'll find a suntrap of a terrace built into the hill.

Middle St,
STROUD, GL5 1DZ
Tel.: (01453)751328
Website: www.bisleyhousecafe.co.uk

Turn right onto Nelson St at the mini roundabout opposite Police Station on Cornhill. On-street parking adjacent.

PRICES
Meals: a la carte £ 21/30

MAP: 61

CLOSING TIMES
Closed Monday

Stroud Budding, Wye Valley Bitter and Butty Bach

GUMSTOOL INN

A flexible menu and some interesting specials

This converted farm outbuilding - now an attractive country pub - is set in the grounds of the stylish Calcot Manor Hotel, on a 700 year old estate. With wood-panelled walls, flag flooring and leather furnishings, it successfully combines classic country style with a more modern edge. It's warm and cosy in winter, bright and airy in the spring and the paved terrace is ideal in summer. The flexible menu format offers snacks and two sizes of starter, followed by a selection of seasonal, rustic, hearty main courses; the extensive daily specials also provide some interesting choices. Service is polite and friendly but make sure you are courteous in return as in days gone by, wrongdoers were placed on the local gumstool and ducked in the pond.

Calcot,
TETBURY, GL8 8YJ
Tel.: (01666)890391
Website: www.calcotmanor.co.uk

3.5 mi west of Tetbury on A 4135, in grounds of Calcot Manor Hotel. Parking.

PRICES
Meals: a la carte £ 22/36

35 rooms:
£ 262/315

MAP: 62

CLOSING TIMES
Open daily

Sharp's Doom Bar and Bath Ales Gem

SEAGRAVE ARMS

Modern dishes use produce from the local larder

A handsome, Grade II listed building of Cotswold stone, with an elegant Georgian façade, the Seagrave Arms was built as a coach house and converted into a pub in 1840. Smaller inside than the exterior leads you to believe, it has a cosy, fire-warmed bar and two traditional dining rooms, while the large terrace provides a good spot for an alfresco meal in the warmer months. Bedrooms are classic in style and are split between the inn and an annexe; one has a four-poster bed, though the suite, with its spacious bathroom and roll-top bath, is the best. Refined and attractively presented modern dishes use well-judged combinations of ingredients from the local larder. Expect Cotswold lamb, Gloucester Old Spot and vegetables from the Vale.

Friday St,
WESTON-SUB-EDGE, GL55 6QH
Tel.: (01386)840192
Website: www.seagravearms.co.uk

3 mi northwest of Chipping Campden. Parking.

PRICES
Meals: £ 23 (weekday lunch) and a la carte £ 26/34

8 rooms:
£ 75/165

MAP: 63

CLOSING TIMES
Open daily

Cotswold Brewing Co. Cotswold Cask and Cotswold Lion Golden Fleece

LION INN

15C inn set close to the castle in a historic town

You'll find this bijou Cotswold stone inn in the heart of a historic town close to Sudeley Castle. It dates from the 15C and has been transformed from 'spit and sawdust' to 'country chic'. Turn right for the flagstone-floored dining room, or left for the rustic bar and snug - relax in front of the fire with a pint and the papers or challenge your nearest and dearest to a game of Scrabble. Menus are guided by the latest seasonal produce available, but don't expect to find too many pub classics therein; more their style are dishes like partridge and pigeon terrine, quail stuffed with mushrooms or venison pie with English greens and smoked pancetta. The stylish, contemporary bedrooms come with homemade biscuits and board games instead of TVs.

North St,
WINCHCOMBE, GL54 5PS
Tel.: (01242)603300
Website: www.thelionwinchcombe.co.uk

In the town centre off the High Street. Public car park at the rear.

PRICES
Meals: a la carte £ 22/40

7 rooms:
£ 100/175

MAP: 64

CLOSING TIMES
Open daily
booking advisable

Ringwood Best Bitter,
Brakspear Oxford Gold and
guest ales

THREE HORSESHOES INN

Rustic former forge popular with locals

Despite being hidden away in a small hamlet off the beaten track, this is a pub that's well-known in the area. Its enthusiastic owners know the score when it comes to running successful pubs and have injected a new lease of life into the place. The characterful interior has exposed beams and in winter, a fire roars in the inglenook. The three horseshoes in the pub's name refer back to a time when the building was a smithy; the old forge would have been where the dining room now stands. The menu isn't large but covers all bases, from pork pies and pub classics to the likes of duck with orange sauce and pork belly with Savoy cabbage. Leave room for some of the excellent cheeses, then retire to one of the comfy, simply furnished bedrooms.

BATCOMBE, BA4 6HE
Tel.: (01749)850359
Website: www.thethreehorseshoesinn.com

Midway between Castle Cary and Frome, signed off A 359; tucked away behind the church. Parking.

PRICES
Meals: a la carte £ 18/35

3 rooms:
£ 60/85

MAP: 65

CLOSING TIMES
Closed 25 December

Butcombe Bitter, Plain Ales Innocence and guest ales

QUEENS ARMS

Enticing bar nibbles and a relaxed, bohemian feel

Aside from the enticing range of bar nibbles, The Queens Arms divides its food between two menus: on the first are pub classics like a ploughman's or sausage and mash; on the other you'll find a more interesting array of dishes - perhaps bream en papillote with chilli, basil, coriander and udon noodles. There's an appealing selection of apple juices and ciders and they also have a great range of whiskies and beers; dishes come with wine and beer pairings and the pub also hosts regular regional beer festivals. With open fires and a hotchpotch of tables including a glass-topped cartwheel, there's a relaxed, bohemian feel; keep an eye out for 'Bertie the Bull', who appeared in Carry On Cowboy! Bedrooms are modern, with good facilities.

CORTON DENHAM, DT9 4LR
Tel.: (01963)220317
Website: www.thequeensarms.com

3 mi north of Sherborne by B 3145 and minor road west. Parking.

PRICES
Meals: £ 15 (weekday lunch) and a la carte £ 26/44

8 rooms:
£ 80/130

MAP: 66

CLOSING TIMES
Open daily
booking advisable

Timothy Taylor Landlord, Moor Ales and Bath Ales

WOODS

Try the meat from the owner's farm

It doesn't look much like a pub – in fact, with its shop window still in situ, it looks more like the bakery it once was – but its cosy, hugely characterful interior soon allays any doubts: a fire blazes in the hearth, locals prop up the bar and wooden beams abound, while the walls are lined with rustic oddments ranging from agricultural implements to hunting paraphernalia and even a pair of antlers. Carefully prepared, tasty dishes offer more than the usual pub fare: you might find seared steak or pancetta and black pudding salad at lunch, and the likes of scallops with cauliflower purée or chicken ballotine with wild garlic mousse at dinner. Provenance is taken seriously here, with quality local produce including meat from the owner's farm.

4 Banks Sq,
DULVERTON, TA22 9BU
Tel.: (01398)324007
Website: www.woodsdulverton.co.uk

In the centre of the town. Pay and display parking close by.

PRICES
Meals: a la carte £ 24/33

MAP: 67

CLOSING TIMES
Closed 25 December, dinner 26 December and 1 January
bookings advisable at dinner

St Austell Dartmoor, Otter Ale and Red Rock Devon Coast

LORD POULETT ARMS

Lavender-framed terrace and delightful wild garden

The picture perfect, lavender-framed terrace of this 17C inn overlooks a boules pitch to an untamed secret garden; inside you'll find lovely old tables, squashy armchairs, glowing candles and beams fringed with hop bines. The menu offers a refreshing mix of modern and traditional dishes created using local produce: maybe rabbit terrine with piccalilli, roast parsnip soup, homemade fishcakes or a hearty ham hock macaroni. To finish, try the selection of West Country cheeses or a proper, old-fashioned pudding like the lusciously rich treacle tart. Cooking is skilful and flavoursome and they also offer a fine selection of real ales. Bedrooms are smart and stylish: two boast feature baths and they all have Roberts radios instead of TVs.

High St,
HINTON ST GEORGE, TA17 8SE
Tel.: (01460)73149
Website: www.lordpoulettarms.com

3 mi northwest of Crewkerne signposted off A 356. On-street parking.

PRICES
Meals: a la carte £ 22/38

5 rooms:
£ 65/150

MAP: 68

CLOSING TIMES
Closed 25-26 December and 1 January

Otter Ale, Branscombe Vale Branoc and Butcombe Bitter

HOLCOMBE INN

Cosy beamed inn with luxurious bedrooms

Set deep in the heart of the Somerset countryside, on the edge of a small village, the 17C Holcombe Inn provides all the charm you'd expect of a building its age, with exposed beams, flag floors and cosy open fires. Come summer, the large garden with its lovely southerly aspect makes a great place to sit and as you unwind, you feel as if you really have escaped to the middle of nowhere. Satisfyingly, this is a place that has a good reputation for its food too, with menus offering quite a range of dishes, from good old pub classics like homemade pie of the day to more sophisticated offerings like ballotine of local chicken or pork belly with black pudding. Bedrooms are luxuriously appointed and some boast views over Downside Abbey.

Stratton Rd,
HOLCOMBE, BA3 5EB
Tel.: (01761)232478
Website: www.holcombeinn.co.uk

On the western edge of the village on Stratton-on-the-Fosse rd. Parking.

PRICES
Meals: a la carte £ 26/49

8 rooms:
£ 75/120

MAP: 69

CLOSING TIMES
Open daily

Otter Ale and Bath Ales Gem

BIRD IN HAND

Tiny, quirky and very good value

When the owner of the Pump House pub found out his own local was going to close, he did what any panicking regular would like to do - he bought the place! This tiny country pub, with its three small but smartly decorated rooms, is a complete contrast to his first venture and boasts quirky touches like an antelope's head, cast iron advertising signs and walls covered with pages from Mrs Beeton's Book of Household Management. Lunchtime sees a simple, super value set price menu, while the evening à la carte offers dishes like onglet steak with oxtail and bone marrow or roast fillet, faggot and belly of suckling lamb. Cooking is tasty, carefully executed and keeps things simple, letting the British ingredients speak for themselves.

17 Weston Rd,
LONG ASHTON, BS41 9LA
Tel.: (01275)395222
Website: www.bird-in-hand.co.uk

2.5 mi southwest of Bristol city centre, well signposted off the A 370. Parking on the High Street.

PRICES
Meals: £ 14 and a la carte £ 21/32

MAP: 70

CLOSING TIMES
Closed 25 December and Sunday dinner
booking essential at dinner

St Austell Tribute, Box Steam Piston Broke and Bath Ales Gem

DEVONSHIRE ARMS

Diverse menu takes a tour around Europe

This spacious Grade II listed hunting lodge is set right on the village green and has a contemporary interior, with a snug locals bar, a relaxing, open-plan front bar and a more formally set dining room. The menu is appealingly eclectic, with plenty of fish and locally sourced meats, and includes influences from all over Europe, so expect to see words like bresaola, brûlée, pancetta and parmesan as you read through. Lunch might be grilled scallops or home-smoked chicken with tarragon mayonnaise; at dinner expect generously proportioned dishes such as polenta with blue cheese, local rib-eye and chips or a deliciously rich, meaty burger. Extremely comfortable, well-equipped bedrooms boast excellent quality linen and toiletries.

LONG SUTTON, TA10 9LP
Tel.: (01458)241271
Website: www.thedevonshirearms.com

4 mi east of Langport by A 372. Parking.

PRICES
Meals: a la carte £ 25/39

9 rooms:
£ 85/145

MAP: 71

CLOSING TIMES
Closed 25-26 December and 1 January

Moor Ales, Otter Ales, Hopback Crop Circle and Cheddar Potholer

TALBOT INN

Food is full of flavour; staff go the extra mile

This 15C coaching inn on the Mells Estate, sister to the Beckford Arms at Tisbury, has been given a shake-up style-wise but thankfully without losing any of its substantial charm. A cobbled courtyard leads through to a series of rustic rooms featuring stone floors and painted panelling; there's a cosy sitting room with an open fire, a snug bar offering real ales and the elegantly dressed Coach House Grill Room to keep carnivores happy at weekends. Food is seasonal, modern and full of flavour, with gutsy main courses like braised roe deer with creamed mash or roasted partridge with celeriac purée. Delightful, understated bedrooms are comfortable and well-priced - and the staff may be casually attired but their manner is anything but.

Selwood St,
MELLS, BA11 3PN
Tel.: (01373)812254
Website: www.talbotinn.com

3 mi northwest of Frome by A 362. On-street parking.

PRICES
Meals: a la carte £ 22/33

8 rooms:
£ 95/150

MAP: 72

CLOSING TIMES
Open daily

Butcombe Ales and Keystone Talbot

WHITE POST (N)

Stunning West Country views

This pub sits on the Dorset/Somerset border, with stunning views of the West Country. Back in the days when different counties had different licensing hours, the pub used to have two bars - one in each county - and when time was called in one room, the locals would simply move to the other room to continue drinking. These days the focus is more on dining than drinking: local chef Brett Sutton is known for his flamboyant cooking displays, but there are plenty of pub classics on the menu alongside his more imaginative creations and quirky touches like piggy nibbles - pulled pork, chorizo and glazed sausage - and the Sunday roast board: surely every carnivore's dream dish? Bedrooms are simply furnished: ask for Dorset, which has the best views.

RIMPTON, BA22 8AR
Tel.: (01935)851525
Website: www.thewhitepost.com

On B 3148 between Marston Magna and Sherbourne. Parking.

PRICES
Meals: a la carte £ 21/43

3 rooms:
£ 80/95

MAP: 73

CLOSING TIMES
Closed 1-14 January and Sunday dinner

Butcombe Bitter and Dorset Brewing Company Dorset Knob

WHITE HART Ⓝ

Seasonal cooking using the wood burning oven

This 16C inn hasn't just had a makeover; it's had a facelift, some Botox and some fillers too. Sister to the Swan at Wedmore, it sits on the main market square of this pretty Somerset village; a beautiful parquet-floored entrance leading to six characterful rooms, including 'the barn' where you can watch the chefs at work. Seasonal food centres around the wood burning oven, with simple, flavourful dishes like aromatic pulled pork bap or Dorset clams with home-smoked pork belly. Sharing platters are a crowd pleaser, as is the lovely rustic focaccia with chunky hummus, while homemade ice creams include flavours like salted caramel and hazelnut brittle. Modern, uniquely styled bedrooms have a cosy feel; Room 3, with a bath centre stage, is the best.

Market Pl,
SOMERTON, TA11 7LX
Tel.: (01458)272273
Website: www.whitehartsomerton.com

8 mi northwest of Yeovil by A 37, B 3151 on B 3153. On-street parking.

PRICES
Meals: a la carte £ 21/34

8 rooms:
£ 85/130

MAP: 74

CLOSING TIMES
Open daily

Cheddar Ales, Bath Ales and North Curry Brewery Red Heron

TARR FARM INN

Idyllically located by a sparkling river

Arrive on the wrong side of the river and you might get a shock - you'll be able to see the pub but, unless you have a 4x4, contending with the water isn't an option. That said, if you've travelled by foot then there's no better way to approach than by crossing the 17 spans of the charming 1000 BC, stone-slab clapper bridge. The setting is nothing short of idyllic: birds sing in the trees and cool, clear water gurgles under the bridge. If the sun's out, head for the garden for a spot of afternoon tea; if the rain's lashing down, make for the narrow, beamed bar or the cosy restaurant. Menus provide plenty of choice, from potted shrimps and sharing boards through to rack of Exmoor lamb or Devon Ruby steak. Bedrooms are comfy and well-equipped.

TARR STEPS, TA22 9PY
Tel.: (01643)851507
Website: www.tarrfarm.co.uk

Signed off B 3223 Dulverton to Exford road. Parking.

PRICES
Meals: a la carte £ 24/37

9 rooms:
£ 75/150

MAP: 75

CLOSING TIMES
Closed 1-13 February

Exmoor Ale, Milk Street Funky Monkey, St Austell Tribute and Proper Job

BLUE BALL INN

Lovely tiered gardens with a skittle alley

This characterful thatched former barn is located in the beautiful Quantock Hills; it dates from the 15C and boasts a cosy, rustic feel, with exposed rafters, open fires, tartan carpets and stags' heads. Lunchtime sandwiches, 'posh' ploughman's and classics like guinea fowl and mushroom pie or sausage and mash provide fuel for passing walkers; dinner sees well-presented, modern dishes with a touch of originality - perhaps linguine with hare bolognese or pork cutlet with braised cheek - and the bacon and black pudding scotch egg is a favourite at either sitting. Behind the pub, you'll find a lovely tiered garden and a skittle alley, while the pretty thatched cottage alongside contains comfy, stylish bedrooms named 'Pheasant', 'Hind' and 'Stag'.

TRISCOMBE, TA4 3HE
Tel.: (01984)618242
Website: www.blueballinn.info

Between Taunton and Williton off A 358. Parking.

PRICES
Meals: a la carte £ 26/38

3 rooms:
£ 55/110

MAP: 76

CLOSING TIMES
Closed 25-26 December, dinner 1 January, Sunday dinner and Monday

Quantock Rorke's Drift and Exmoor Stag

SWAN

Seasonal British ingredients and unfussy cooking

If good British ingredients that match the seasons and unfussy, flavoursome dishes are your thing, then this 18C coaching inn is the place for you. Portions are generous: expect the likes of stuffed Cornish sardines or ham, cheddar and parsley croquettes, followed by braised pheasant with juniper and thyme or orange-marinated Orchard Farm pork T-bone with fennel. Inside it's spacious and airy: there's a large bar with bare floorboards and simple wooden tables; a cosy little area with rugs and leather furniture; and, past the open kitchen and display of home-baked breads, a comfortable dining room - be sure to book, as it's a rightly popular place. Stylish bedrooms complete the picture; those at the top of the stairs can be noisy.

Cheddar Rd,
WEDMORE, BS28 4EQ
Tel.: (01934)710337
Website: www.theswanwedmore.com

In the centre of the town. Parking.

PRICES
Meals: a la carte £ 23/36

6 rooms:
£ 85/125

MAP: 77

CLOSING TIMES
Closed 25 December
booking essential

Bath Ales Gem, Otter Bitter and Cheddar Potholer

RISING SUN INN

Traditional, family-run and great for walkers

Sitting on the side of a hill in the Quantocks, the Rising Sun Inn looks like a traditional country pub. Inside, however, you'll discover that, although there's the odd beam and a pleasing mix of old tables and chairs, it's also pretty modern, with smart slate floors and bright artwork helping to keep the mood light. It's not a big place but there are several rooms in which to sit: the snug, which is hidden away at the back, the piano room, the first floor gallery, or, of course, the bar. Menus offer plenty of choice, and feature typical pub-style light bites as well as more hearty classics, from calves' liver and bacon to pork belly with cider sauce or rack of lamb with mint jus. Upstairs, two contemporary bedrooms offer great views.

WEST BAGBOROUGH, TA4 3EF
Tel.: (01823)432575
Website: www.risingsuninn.info

10.5 mi northwest of Taunton, off A 358. On-street parking.

PRICES
Meals: a la carte £ 22/37

2 rooms:
£ 65/95

MAP: 78

CLOSING TIMES
Closed 25 December

Exmoor Ales, Butcombe Ales and St Austell Proper Job

ROYAL OAK INN

Delightful 12C farmhouse down country lanes

Mind the pheasants as you navigate the winding lanes of Exmoor towards this charming little village. Beside the ford, you'll see this delightful 12C former farmhouse and dairy, which is one of the country's most photographed pubs. Turn left into the dining room or right into the rustic bar, where you'll find a small gathering of locals and their dogs and a wood-furnished dining area. The menu changes every 3 months and offers a mix of pub dishes and British classics; there's also a selection of daily specials chalked on a board above the fire. Dishes are tasty, satisfying and well-executed – the desserts, in particular, are very tempting. Spacious country bedrooms come with huge bathrooms and rain showers; most of them have four-poster beds.

Halse Ln,
WINSFORD, TA24 7JE
Tel.: (01643)851455
Website: www.royaloakexmoor.co.uk

5 mi north of Dulverton off B 3223. Parking.

PRICES
Meals: a la carte £ 20/33

8 rooms:
£ 55/140

MAP: 79

CLOSING TIMES
Open daily

Exmoor Ales and guest ales

THE NORTHEY

Family-run coaching inn

Having passed from one generation of Warburtons to the next, this traditional-looking coaching inn is a real family affair. It's a sizeable place, with an open-plan interior and fairly modern styling: the bar boasting low level seating and vivid artwork; the large rear dining room, heavy wooden furniture and a more formal feel. The chef has extensive experience countrywide, so you can rest assured that the appealing monthly menus are as good as they sound. Dishes are unfussy, seasonal and British, and everything is made on the premises, including the bread. There are tasty local steaks and, with seafood arriving fresh from Cornwall, the fish dishes - particularly the mussels - are a strength. Smart, contemporary bedrooms have bathrooms to match.

Bath Rd,
BOX, SN13 8AE
Tel.: (01225)742333
Website: www.ohhcompany.co.uk

4.75 mi northeast of Bath on A 4. Parking.

PRICES
Meals: a la carte £ 26/50

5 rooms:
£ 89/160

MAP: 80

CLOSING TIMES
Closed 25-26 December

Wadworth 6X, Ramsbury Best Bitter and Timothy Taylor Landlord

THE FOX

Cooking uses what's in the garden

Raising the profile of this pub, both locally and farther afield, has been a labour of love for its young owner, Alex, who has given it one of those clever refurbishments that cost a lot of money but make everything look largely unchanged. It is set in front of the village hall and lies very much at the heart of the community. There's always a great choice of beer on draught but the real surprise is out back: there are raised beds of salad leaves, rhubarb, herbs and fruits, and behind these, you'll find chickens and a pigsty. In a move towards self-sufficiency, the kitchen also makes its own sausages and dries its own meat for the excellent charcuterie dishes. And what does Alex do on his day off? He goes foraging for more local produce.

The Street,
BROUGHTON GIFFORD, SN12 8PN
Tel.: (01225)782949
Website: www.thefox-broughtongifford.co.uk

Between Bradford-on-Avon and Melksham off B 3107. Parking.

PRICES
Meals: £ 17 (weekday lunch) and
a la carte £ 27/47

MAP: 81

CLOSING TIMES
Closed 26-27 December, 1-2 January,
Sunday dinner and Monday

Bath Ales and Butcombe Ales

SHIP INN

Peacefully located by the river

If you find yourself anywhere near the delightful village of Burcombe on a sunny summer's day, be sure to make your way to this charming 17C pub. Its riverside garden is just the place to linger over a leisurely lunch, with only the wind in the trees and the quack of the local ducks to disturb the silence. If you've arrived too late to nab a table, then head inside; with its open fire, low oak beams and chunky wood furniture, the pub itself is an equally enchanting place to dine. The seasonal menu offers honest portions of traditional dishes; perhaps pan-fried pigeon breast, homemade fishcakes, pot-roasted lamb shank or smoked fish kedgeree. 'Lunchtime bites' offer a lighter alternative and the twice-daily changing specials board adds interest.

Burcombe Ln,
BURCOMBE, SP2 0EJ
Tel.: (01722)743182
Website: www.theshipburcombe.co.uk

5.25 mi west of Salisbury by A 36 off A 30. Parking.

PRICES
Meals: a la carte £ 23/44

MAP: 82

CLOSING TIMES
Closed 25 December

Wadworth 6X, Butcombe Bitter and Hopback Summer Lightning

WHITE HORSE INN

Genuine hospitality and a jolly atmosphere

The White Horse Inn dates back to 1780 and is named after the hillside carving at nearby Cherhill Down. The cosy bar with its wood burning stove and jolly atmosphere is where you'll find the regulars, while diners head for the rustic room next door. It's the kind of place that offers genuine hospitality, with Tara's bubbly personality and Danny's all-encompassing menu helping to draw customers from far and wide. You might find a croque monsieur or a homemade cheeseburger at lunchtime, with more ambitious dishes on the à la carte: maybe salmon gravadlax, Blue Vinny soufflé, roast monkfish or loin of venison from their own farm. Head outside, beyond the large garden and you'll find snug, simply furnished, well-priced bedrooms.

COMPTON BASSETT, SN11 8RG
Tel.: (01249)813118
Website: www.whitehorse-comptonbassett.co.uk

4 mi east of Calne signposted off A 4. Parking.

PRICES
Meals: a la carte £ 25/40

8 rooms:
£ 75/95

MAP: 83

CLOSING TIMES
Closed 2-9 January, Sunday dinner and Monday

Bath Ales Gem, Wadworth 6X and Sharp's Doom Bar

METHUEN ARMS

Top notch ingredients and flavoursome dishes

This 17C coaching inn stands in the heart of an attractive little town and is named after the family who own nearby Corsham Court. It's run by experienced owners Martin and Debbie, who place great emphasis on the quality of their food. You can eat anywhere: in the 'Little Room' by the bar; in the 'Nott Room' with its flagged floor and open fire; or in the characterful restaurant with its penny farthing and exposed stone walls. Lunch sees everything from a grilled aubergine and melted cheese sandwich to deep-fried squid with harissa mayonnaise, while dinner steps things up a gear with the likes of local venison with beetroot and spelt risotto or herb-crusted Cornish brill with leeks, chorizo and mussels. Comfy, boutique-style bedrooms await.

2 High St,
CORSHAM, SN13 0HB
Tel.: (01249)717060
Website: www.themethuenarms.com

In the centre of the town. Parking.

PRICES
Meals: £ 16/27 and a la carte £ 27/45

14 rooms:
£ 85/175

MAP: 84

CLOSING TIMES
Open daily

Otter Amber Ale, St Austell Proper Job and Moles Best

RED LION

Meats and fish smoked and ales brewed on-site

Just off the Thames path, you'll find this traditional 17C inn. With a cosy, low-beamed interior crammed full of bric-a-brac, it looks like a proper pub; and pleasingly, it adopts a good old English attitude too. The bar serves 10 different ales - some of which are brewed in-house - as well as 30 speciality bottled beers, which can be sampled while tucking into a pub classic, dog at your feet. Next door is a small but airy stone-walled dining room with a beautiful carved slab. Here you'll find slightly more refined classics such as oysters, venison stew and treacle tart. Produce is fresh and extremely local - and if you're down a pound or two, they'll accept some home-grown fruit or veg as payment. Comfy, modern bedrooms are in the old stables.

74 High St,
CRICKLADE, SN6 6DD
Tel.: (01793)750776
Website: www.theredlioncricklade.co.uk

At the eastern end of the High St. Unrestricted parking on the High St.

PRICES
Meals: a la carte £ 20/40

5 rooms:
£ 80/85

MAP: 85

CLOSING TIMES
Open daily

Hop Kettle Ales

BATH ARMS

Bags of country appeal and outdoor space

The Bath Arms offers a warm welcome, open fires, plenty of country appeal and a wealth of outdoor space. Once part of the Longleat Estate, it is run with a passion by local boy Dean Carr, who returned from his culinary experiences in the Big Smoke to put some love back into this community pub. The menus offer something for everyone, from filled baguettes or shepherd's pie to dishes such as fillet of red mullet with fennel salad or slow-braised rabbit with polenta and bacon; not forgetting favourites like the fishcakes or the now legendary sticky beef with braised red cabbage. Traditional desserts like tarte Tatin round things off nicely - and there are two ultra-spacious, contemporary bedrooms should you wish to stay the night.

Clay St,
CROCKERTON, BA12 8AJ
Tel.: (01985)212262
Website: www.batharmscrockerton.co.uk

2 mi south of Warminster just off A 350 on Shearwater rd. Parking.

PRICES
Meals: a la carte £ 22/33

2 rooms:
£ 80/110

MAP: 86

CLOSING TIMES
Closed dinner 25-26 December

Ringwood Ales and
Wessex Ales

POTTING SHED PUB

A relaxed feel and an unusual horticultural theme

Despite its contemporary name and décor, the Potting Shed is very much a proper pub, where locals gather for a pint and a chat. Situated opposite its sister establishment, the Rectory Hotel, it consists of five spacious, light-filled rooms, with open fires and a relaxing feel. The pub's large gardens provide it with an abundance of fresh, seasonal herbs and vegetables - and the horticultural theme continues inside, with trowel door knobs, wheelbarrow lights and fork and spade pump handles. Monthly changing menus offer fresh, satisfying dishes like local trout, wild rabbit fettuccine and apple and blackberry crumble. Lollipops on the bar ensure that the kids are kept happy, while dog biscuits do the same for your four-legged friends.

The Street,
CRUDWELL, SN16 9EW
Tel.: (01666)577833
Website: www.thepottingshedpub.com

4 mi north of Malmesbury by A 429. Parking.

PRICES
Meals: a la carte £ 23/36

MAP: 87

CLOSING TIMES
Open daily

Timothy Taylor Landlord, Malmesbury Four Candles and Butcombe The Original

THE FORESTER

Worth finding for its classic country cooking

Hidden down narrow lanes in a delightful Wiltshire village, this 13C thatched pub has a gloriously rustic feel. Exposed stone walls feature throughout and vast open fires ensure that it's always cosy. There's a lovely bar crammed with cookery books, and two main dining areas - one in a cleverly added extension that's perfectly in keeping. The experienced owners take a very hands-on approach and, along with the chef, are passionate about using good country ingredients, with meats coming from local farms and estates and fish from the Brixham day boats. Menus change with the seasons and there's always a daily 3 course set selection dedicated to seafood. Dishes are well-prepared and flavoursome, with a classical country base and a refined edge.

Lower St,
DONHEAD ST ANDREW, SP7 9EE
Tel.: (01747)828038
Website: www.theforesterdonheadstandrew.co.uk

5 mi east of Shaftesbury by A 30, taking Tisbury and Donhead rd. Parking.

PRICES
Meals: £ 19/23 and a la carte £ 24/38

MAP: 88

CLOSING TIMES
Closed Sunday dinner

Butcombe Bitter and Otter Bitter

RED LION FREEHOUSE

Dishes show a real understanding of flavour

Enthusiastically run, cosy, and proudly impervious to the trend for designer pubs, the Red Lion is a charming thatched property with a pretty little garden, in a tiny hamlet on the edge of Salisbury Plain. Seven simple wooden tables are set around the bar, a wood burner crouches in the inglenook and exposed beams lend a reassuringly solid air. The daily à la carte features down-to-earth dishes that are stunning in their simplicity, precisely composed and packed with flavour; this might include wild boar terrine, coq au vin or roast partridge. The resident Springer Spaniel often welcomes you with a wag of his tail and service is equally convivial. Set opposite, smart, well-equipped bedrooms come with private terraces; all have river views.

EAST CHISENBURY, SN9 6AQ
Tel.: (01980)671124
Website: www.redlionfreehouse.com

Between Pewsey and Amesbury off the A 345. Parking.

PRICES
Meals: £ 16 (weekday lunch) and a la carte £ 30/50

5 rooms: £ 130

MAP: 89

CLOSING TIMES
Open daily
booking advisable

Keystone, Ramsbury, Stonehenge and Plain Ales

THREE DAGGERS

Produce from the owner's farm down the road

Originally named after the local landowners, this pub has been refurbished and reborn as the 'Three Daggers' - a reference to the insignia on the Paulet family's coat of arms. It's an attractive place, with a large conservatory overlooking the garden, and the original beams and flagstones are still in place, so the character quotient remains high. When it comes to the food, there's something for everyone: a homemade soup, the 'pie of the day' or a local lamb burger; and the sharing plates - the Huntsman's and the Fisherman's - prove extremely popular. They have their own farm shop and brew their own beers too, so are pretty self-sufficient. Charming bedrooms feature bespoke oak furnishings and you're given free reign of the farmhouse kitchen.

47 Westbury Rd,
EDINGTON, BA13 4PG
Tel.: (01380)830940
Website: www.threedaggers.co.uk

4 mi east of Westbury on B 3098. Parking.

PRICES
Meals: a la carte £ 20/39

9 rooms:
£ 85/165

MAP: 90

CLOSING TIMES
Open daily

Three Daggers Ales

FOXHAM INN

The regular gourmet nights are a hit

Located in a sleepy Wiltshire village, the family-run Foxham Inn is a secret that the locals have clearly been trying to keep to themselves. For pleasant views over the fields and paddocks, bag a seat on the semi-covered terrace; on colder days, make for the cosy bar with its scrubbed pine tables, old church pews and wood burning stove, or if you fancy some live cooking action, head through to the airy extension, where you can look into the kitchen. The menu offers a good range of dishes at a uniform price for each course, along with sandwiches and panini at lunch. Everything from the condiments to the ice creams is homemade and flavours are clear and defined. The regular gourmet nights are a hit and two homely bedrooms complete the picture.

FOXHAM, SN15 4NQ
Tel.: (01249)740665
Website: www.thefoxhaminn.co.uk

7 mi northeast of Chippenham signposted off B 4069 in west end of village. Parking.

PRICES
Meals: a la carte £ 25/39

2 rooms:
£ 65/90

MAP: 91

CLOSING TIMES
Closed 2 weeks early January and Monday
booking advisable

Butcombe Bitter and Ramsbury Flint Knapper

ANGEL INN

Plenty of old-school favourites

This pretty looking, family-run former coaching inn has a typically English feel; its spacious bar is home to wood fires and comfy sofas and the beamed dining room is packed with locals discussing the shoot, dogs by their sides. Menus change as and when, depending on what produce is freshly available; maybe devilled lamb's kidneys on toast or smoked ox cheek to start, followed by braised and rolled shin of beef with madeira sauce or roasted haunch of venison with rabbit Wellington. The sharing boards are firm favourites and steaks are a feature - choose your cut, then add a sauce and an accompaniment. Some of the main courses do need side dishes, which can push up the price. Bedrooms are currently too modest to recommend.

High St,
HEYTESBURY, BA12 0ED
Tel.: (01985)840330
Website: www.theangelatheytesbury.co.uk

4 mi southeast of Warminster on A 36. Parking.

PRICES
Meals: a la carte £ 20/41

MAP: 92

CLOSING TIMES
Open daily

Greene King IPA and
Old Speckled Hen

TOLLGATE INN N

Cheery, attentive service sets it apart

If there was an award for the most welcoming pub then this village inn would surely be crowned the winner. With their wide smiles and easy rapport, the attentive staff pitch things just right; from the cheery hello as you enter, to the charming personal touches provided for those staying in one of the cosy bedrooms - no wonder the place is buzzing! The menu keeps things simple, as befits a pub; with hearty, flavoursome dishes like slow-braised pork belly or sausage and mash alongside steaks, fish of the day and a range of homemade pies. If starters are your thing, try four of them served together on a sharing plate; the daily quiche is a nice retro touch at lunch and there are coffee and homemade cakes for those just after a snack.

Ham Grn,
HOLT, BA14 6PX
Tel.: (01225)782326
Website: www.tollgateinn.co.uk

Midway between Bradford-on-Avon and Melksham on B 3107. Parking.

PRICES
Meals: a la carte £ 20/39

4 rooms:
£ 70/110

MAP: 93

CLOSING TIMES
Closed Sunday dinner and Monday

Sharp's Doom Bar, Box Steam Tollgate Gold and Tunnel Vision

BATH ARMS

A quirky and colourful dog-friendly inn

This pub is found within the Longleat Estate and boasts a rustic, dog-friendly bar with an open fireplace, a grand main dining room and a delightful terrace - witness to some impressive sunsets. Appealing menus offer everything from light dishes, salads and sandwiches through to main courses like stuffed saddle of rabbit or braised shoulder of lamb. The sharing plate is popular and the fishcakes are a veritable institution. Much of the produce comes from the estate (game, specialist cheeses and even flavoured organic vodkas) and they rear pigs and even have their own herb garden. Staff clearly enjoy their work and are willing to go the extra mile for their customers. Quirky, individually themed bedrooms offer good levels of comfort.

Longleat,
HORNINGSHAM, BA12 7LY
Tel.: (01985)844308
Website: www.batharms.co.uk

3 mi southwest of Warminster by A 362 and minor road, adjacent to the Longleat Safari Park. Parking.

PRICES
Meals: a la carte £ 21/39

16 rooms:
£ 65/145

MAP: 94

CLOSING TIMES
Open daily

Wessex Horningsham Pride and Golden Apostle, Sharp's Doom Bar

MUDDY DUCK (N)

Smart bedrooms and switched-on staff

A historic pub - and reputedly Wiltshire's most haunted - the former King's Arms dates from the 17C, although there has been a house here since the reign of Henry VIII. From the front it looks like a manor house; inside it's full of character, with a giant inglenook in the bar and a stylish rustic feel in the dining room. Appealing menus offer mostly classic British dishes, with the occasional Asian flavour; there are plenty of tasty nibbles and extras, and children get their own 'Ducklings' menu of mini meals. Bedrooms are smart; those in the converted barn are real get-away-from-it-all places, featuring their own separate snug with a wood burning stove. Switched-on staff are in tune with their guests' needs, and nothing is too much trouble.

42 Monkton Farleigh,
MONKTON FARLEIGH, BA15 2QN
Tel.: (01225)858705
Website: www.themuddyduckbath.co.uk

7 mi east of Bath signposted off A 363. Parking.

PRICES
Meals: a la carte £ 17/42

5 rooms:
£ 100/250

MAP: 95

CLOSING TIMES
Open daily

Fuller's London Pride, Otter Ales and Flack Manor Double Drop

BELL

Pub favourites and ambitious, accomplished dishes

Despite an extensive refurbishment, this charming 16C building has managed to retain plenty of its original pubby character, particularly in the open-fired bar, where you'll find hop-covered beams and a menu of old pub favourites. If you're looking for the bell the pub's named after, you'll find it hanging in the fireplace of the crisply laid dining room. Here you can sit on smart tartan banquettes and enjoy a more sophisticated atmosphere, dining on ambitious, accomplished dishes such as crispy fried duck egg with chorizo and tomato salsa, followed by local estate venison with carrot and celeriac purées. At the back, 'Café Bella' is a popular meeting place for the locals, while stylish, well-appointed bedrooms welcome those staying over.

The Square,
RAMSBURY, SN8 2PE
Tel.: (01672)520230
Website: www.thebellramsbury.com

4 mi northwest of Hungerford signposted off B 4192. Parking.

PRICES
Meals: a la carte £ 24/37

9 rooms:
£ 110/150

MAP: 96

CLOSING TIMES
Closed 25 December

Ramsbury Brewery Gold, Bitter and other guest ales

GEORGE & DRAGON

It's all about seafood from St Mawes

This 16C coaching inn has a rustic feel throughout; its cosy inner boasting solid stone floors, wooden beams and open fires. There's a strong emphasis on seafood, with fish delivered daily from Cornwall to ensure it arrives on your plate in tip-top condition. That the menu is written anew each day also speaks volumes about the pub's take on food; seafood dishes could be a plate of fishy hors d'oeuvres, pan-fried cod with bacon or a whole grilled lemon sole; more meaty choices might include rack of lamb or roast fillet of beef. Some dishes come in two sizes and can be taken as either a starter or a main course. There is also a good value set three course menu. Old-world charm meets modern facilities in the individually designed bedrooms.

High St,
ROWDE, SN10 2PN
Tel.: (01380)723053
Website: www.thegeorgeanddragonrowde.co.uk

2 mi northwest of Devizes on A 342. Parking.

PRICES
Meals: £ 17 (weekdays)/20 and a la carte £ 16/52

3 rooms: £ 85/125

MAP: 97

CLOSING TIMES
Closed Sunday dinner

Butcombe Bitter, Sharp's Doom Bar and Kennet & Avon Dundas

BECKFORD ARMS

Sunday is film night at this charming inn

Set next to the 10,000 acre Fonthill Estate, this charming 18C inn offers a delightful terrace and a large garden - complete with hammocks, a petanque pitch and a dog bath - as well as a beamed dining room, a rustic bar and a lovely country house sitting room, where films are screened on Sunday nights. Tasty, unfussy cooking relies on excellent ingredients, with the daily menu offering classics and country-style fare such as roast partridge or pork with Morteau sausage, while for a snack, the homemade pork scratchings are a hit. Tastefully furnished bedrooms offer thoughtful comforts, while two smart duplex suites are a few minutes' drive away. The charming young team will gladly provide hampers and arrange fishing and shooting trips.

Fonthill Gifford,
TISBURY, SP3 6PX
Tel.: (01747)870385
Website: www.beckfordarms.com

Between Shaftesbury and Warminster signposted off A 350. Parking.

PRICES
Meals: a la carte £ 20/37

10 rooms:
£ 95/175

MAP: 98

CLOSING TIMES
Closed 25 December
booking essential

Butcombe Bitter and Keystone Beckford Phoenix

KING JOHN INN

Be sure to try the locally shot game dishes

The beautiful black and white hunting photos that line the walls of this creeper-clad Victorian pub are a clue both to its clientele and to its menus. The sofas are a popular place to relax with a drink after a day's shooting, before enjoying locally stalked venison or whole roast grouse at one of the scrubbed wooden tables. Other dishes on the classically based menus might include homemade chicken Kiev, steak and chips or oxtail and pumpkin ravioli; fish is regularly brought up from the coast and the soufflés and home-baked bread are fast becoming trademarks. Like the open-plan, fire-lit interior, the service is relaxed and informal. There's also a wine shop and comfy, stylish bedrooms which blend antique furniture with modern facilities.

TOLLARD ROYAL, SP5 5PS
Tel.: (01725)516207
Website: www.kingjohninn.co.uk

5 mi southeast of Shaftesbury on B 3081. Parking.

PRICES
Meals: a la carte £ 30/55

11 rooms:
£ 135/195

MAP: 99

CLOSING TIMES
Closed 25 December

Butcombe Ales and Dorset Chesil

LONGS ARMS

Traditional British fare and home-smoked products

The appetite for British food shows no sign of abating, particularly in British pubs. How apt it is to see traditional dishes like goats' scrumpets or crispy tongue and pickles in a pub like this - named after local landowners, the Long family, in whose manor house Sir Walter Raleigh allegedly smoked the first tobacco in England. The only smoking that goes on nowadays is that of meat and fish in the pub's own smokehouse. Meat is hung and butchered on-site, there's a kitchen garden and everything is made in-house, including bread, ice cream, feta cheese, faggots, black pudding and haggis. Service is warm and friendly and the pub itself is bursting with character; think exposed Bath stone walls, bay windows, a woodburner and flagged floors.

UPPER SOUTH WRAXALL, BA15 2SB
Tel.: (01225)864450
Website: www.thelongsarms.com

3 mi north of Bradford-on-Avon by A 363, signed off B 3109. In centre of village opposite the church. Parking.

PRICES
Meals: a la carte £ 23/42

MAP: 100

CLOSING TIMES
Closed 3 weeks January-February, Sunday dinner and Monday
booking essential

Wadworth Henry's Original IPA and 6X

BRIDGE INN

Sit in the garden overlooking the River Avon

Situated in the Woodford Valley, a few miles south of Stonehenge, the aptly named Bridge Inn stands on the banks of the Avon, overlooking the river crossing; its garden, with picnic tables from which to watch the swans and ducks, is an alfresco diner's delight. The pub is modern, with a light, airy feel. Its relaxed atmosphere means that locals with dogs rub shoulders with diners, and you can peek through the glass windows to see the chefs at work in the kitchen. Lunch sees a light bites menu of interesting sandwiches, while the à la carte offers dishes such as fishcakes, pot-roasted lamb shank or the popular pork belly. This is the sister pub to the Ship Inn at Burcombe; get your hands on a loyalty card and you can reap the benefits at both.

UPPER WOODFORD, SP4 6NU
Tel.: (01722)782323
Website: www.thebridgewoodford.co.uk

North of Salisbury off A 360; follow signs for The Woodfords. Parking.

PRICES
Meals: a la carte £ 23/44

MAP: 101

CLOSING TIMES
Closed 25 December and Sunday dinner January-February

Hopback Summer Lightning, Wadworth 6X and Butcombe Best Bitter

WEYMOUTH ARMS

Immensely characterful with charming bedrooms

If you fancy a slice of history with your lunch, you won't be disappointed. This Grade II listed building started life as a private home (round the back, an archway is inscribed with '1771 D.C.', as the house once belonged to Daniel Capel, a well-known clothier); in the 19C it became a lodging house and, a century later, was turned into a public house. It's immensely characterful, displaying original wood panelling, antiques and lithographs, as well as two fireplaces originally intended for nearby Longleat House (Lord Weymouth of Longleat was once a frequent visitor). Cooking is fittingly traditional, with fresh ingredients featuring in dishes such as chicken liver pâté and apple and pear crumble. Cosy bedrooms have charming original fittings.

12 Emwell St,
WARMINSTER, BA12 8JA
Tel.: (01985)216995
Website: www.weymoutharms.co.uk

In centre of town just off George St. Pay and Display parking adjacent.

PRICES
Meals: a la carte £ 19/40

6 rooms:
£ 65/85

MAP: 102

CLOSING TIMES
Closed Monday-Wednesday lunch

Butcombe Gold and Bitter

BELL

Relax on the spacious south-facing terrace

One way to improve any walk, apart from having proper shoes and fair weather, is to end up at a decent pub. If you've been out on the Cherhill Downs, then pop into the Bell at West Overton. The pub was rescued by a local couple, who realised a dream by buying it, but who were also sensible enough to hire an experienced pair to run it. The same menu is served in the bar and restaurant, and the latter is far from stuffy as they don't want to scare anyone away; there's also a large, south-facing terrace out the back, perfect for alfresco lunches. The menu offers an appealing blend of pub classics and dishes of a Mediterranean bent, such as Cornish bream with chorizo and olives. Presentation is modern but not at the expense of flavour.

Bath Rd,
WEST OVERTON, SN8 1QD
Tel.: (01672)861099
Website: www.thebellwestoverton.co.uk

4 mi west of Marlborough on A 4. Parking.

PRICES
Meals: a la carte £ 25/44

MAP: 103

CLOSING TIMES
Closed Sunday dinner and Monday except bank holidays

Moles Best, Ramsbury Gold and Box Steam Chuffin' Ale

WEST MIDLANDS

England

© G. Munday / Design Pics / Photononstop

The names Gas Street Basin, Custard Factory and Mailbox may not win any awards for exoticism, but these are the cutting edge quarters fuelling the rise of modern day Birmingham, at the heart of a region evolving from its grimy factory gate image. Even the Ironbridge Gorge, the cradle of the Industrial Revolution, is better known these days as a fascinatingly picturesque tourist attraction. The old urban landscapes dot a region of delightful unspoilt countryside with extensive areas of open moorland and hills, where stands Middle Earth, in the shape of Shropshire's iconic Wrekin hill, true inspiration of Tolkien. Shakespeare Country abounds in pretty villages, such as Henley-in-Arden, Shipston-on-Stour and Alcester, where redbrick, half-timbered and Georgian buildings capture the eye.

Taste buds are catered for courtesy of a host of local specialities, not least fruits from the Vale of Evesham and mouth-watering meats from the hills near the renowned gastro town of Ludlow.

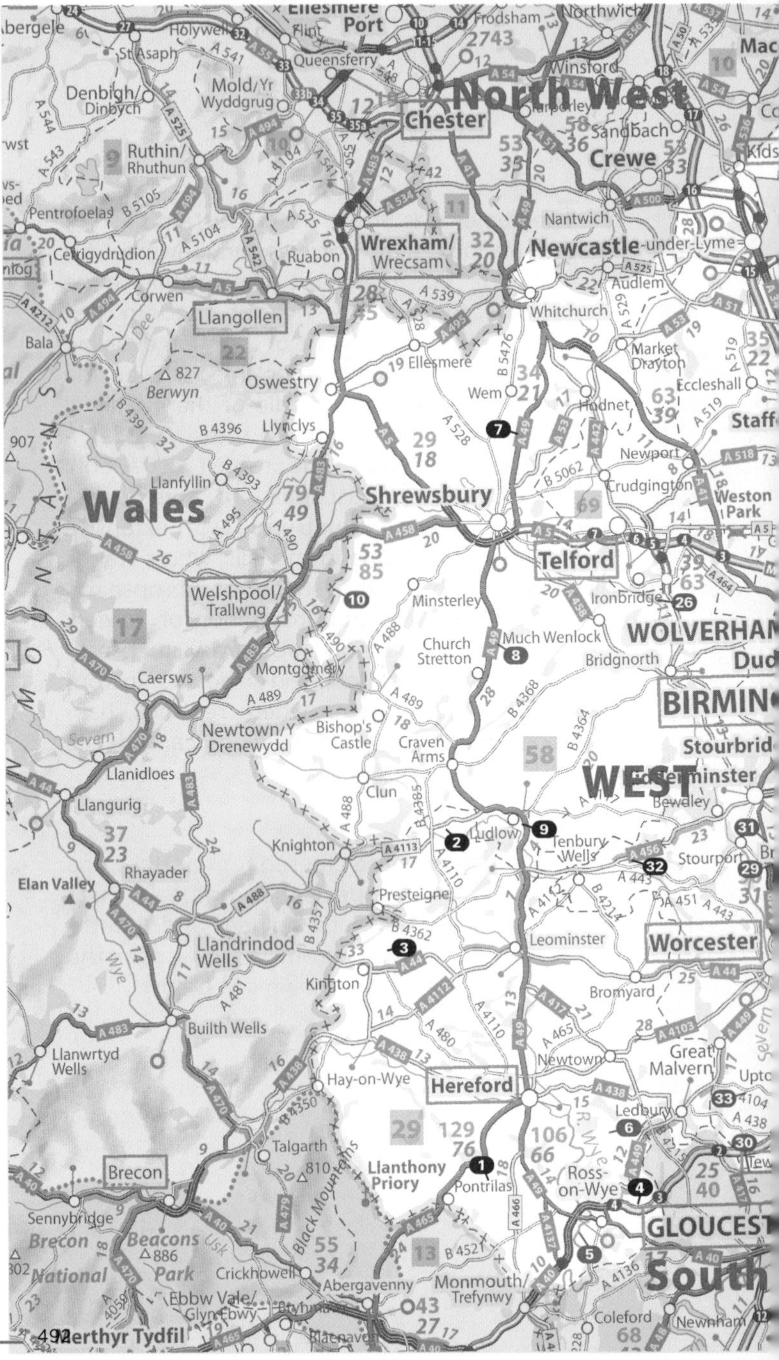
Ellesmere Port
Frodsham
Northwich
Abergele
Holywell
Flint
St Asaph
Queensferry
Winsford
Denbigh/
Dinbych
Mold/Yr
Wyddgrug
North West
Chester
Sandbach
Crewe
Ruthin/
Rhuthun
Pentrofoelas
Nantwich
Wrexham/
Wrecsam
Newcastle-under-Lyme
Cerrigydrudion
Ruabon
Audlem
Corwen
Llangollen
Whitchurch
Bala
Market
Drayton
Ellesmere
Berwyn
Oswestry
Wem
Eccleshall
Llynclys
Hodnet
Newport
Llanfyllin
Crudgington
Wales
Shrewsbury
Weston
Park
Telford
Welshpool/
Trallwng
Minsterley
Ironbridge
WOLVERHAM
Church
Stretton
Much Wenlock
Bridgnorth
Caersws
Montgomery
BIRMIN
Newtown/Y
Drenewydd
Bishop's
Castle
Craven
Arms
Stourbrid
Severn
Llanidloes
WEST
Kidderminster
Llangurig
Clun
Bewdley
Ludlow
Knighton
Tenbury
Wells
Stourport
Rhayader
Elan Valley
Presteigne
Llandrindod
Wells
Leominster
Worcester
Kington
Bromyard
Builth Wells
Llanwrtyd
Wells
Newtown
Great
Malvern
Hay-on-Wye
Hereford
Ledbury
Talgarth
Brecon
Llanthony
Priory
Pontrilas
Ross-
on-Wye
Black Mountains
Sennybridge
GLOUCEST
Brecon
Beacons
Park
National
Crickhowell
Abergavenny
Monmouth/
Trefynwy
South
Ebbw Vale/
Glyn Ebwy
Merthyr Tydfil
Coleford
Newnham

Buxton
Baslow
Chesterfield
Chatsworth House
Bakewell
Haddon Hall
Clay Cross
Hardwick Hall
Mansfield
National Park
Matlock
Alfreton
Sutton-in-Ashfield
Leek
Dovedale Site
Ripley
Belper
Heanor
Hucknall
Ashbourne
Ilkeston
STOKE-ON-TRENT
NOTTINGHAM
DERBY
West Bridgford
Stone
Uttoxeter
Sudbury
Long Eaton
Abbots Bromley
Burton-upon-Trent
Rempstone
Loughborough
Melton Mowbray
Rugeley
Swadlincote
Shepshed
Ashby de la Zouch
East Midlands
Cannock
Coalville
Lichfield
Oakham
Tamworth
Brownhills
Oadby
Walsall
LEICESTER
Uppingham
Sutton Coldfield
Atherstone
Hinckley
Welland
Market Harborough
Nuneaton
Bedworth
Lutterworth
Husbands Bosworth
Desborough
Halesowen
Rothwell
Solihull
COVENTRY
Rugby
Kenilworth
Wellingborough
Redditch
Royal Leamington Spa
Henley
Warwick
Daventry
Droitwich
Southam
Alcester
MIDLANDS
Stratford-upon-Avon
Ettington
Towcester
Pershore
Hidcote Garden
Shipston-on-Stour
Wolverton
Evesham
Banbury
Stowe Gardens
Chipping Campden
MILTON KEYNES
Brackley
Broadway
Moreton
Chastleton House
Bletchley
Winchcombe
Buckingham
South East
Stow-on-the-Wold
Chipping Norton
Bicester
Cheltenham
Waddesdon Manor
Woodstock
West
Blenheim Palace
Northleach
Burford
Witney
Kidlington
Aylesbury
Painswick
Pubs without bedrooms
Pubs with bedrooms

KILPECK INN (N)

Impressive green credentials

The former Red Lion narrowly escaped being turned into private housing thanks to the villagers' valiantly fought 'Save Our Pub' campaign. Refurbished and reborn as the Kilpeck Inn, it serves pub classics, locally sourced meats like braised beef or slow-roasted pork belly and old fashioned English puddings like those of the sticky toffee or rice varieties. Any carbon emissions generated on your journey are sure to be offset by the pub's green credentials: with measures such as solar panels and a rainwater recovery system, it must be one of the country's most environmentally friendly eateries. Ecological efficiency does not come at the expense of style, however, and the spacious interior and four bedrooms are smart, modern and characterful.

KILPECK, HR2 9DN
Tel.: (01981)570464
Website: www.kilpeckinn.com

The village is signposted off A 465, 10 mi southwest of Hereford. Parking.

PRICES
Meals: £ 13 (weekday lunch) and a la carte £ 18/30

4 rooms: £ 70/120

MAP: 1

CLOSING TIMES
Open daily

Wye Valley Butty Bach and Bitter

THE LION (N)

Relaxed and stylish, with river views

This 18C inn stands on the banks or the River Teme, next to an attractive medieval bridge, and is owned by local mineral water company Radnor Hills. An extensive refurbishment has created a relaxed, stylish environment: there's a proper bar with a wood-burning stove and a selection of real ales, and a slightly smarter dining room with river views. The same menu is served wherever you sit, offering everything from a beef and thyme burger to lemon-marinated chicken with Thai spiced greens, and from a gypsy tart to rhubarb parfait. Dishes are nicely presented and local produce plays a big part - you'll find a list of their suppliers on the back of the menu. Smart modern bedrooms have good facilities and some look out across the water.

LEINTWARDINE, SY7 0JZ
Tel.: (01547)540203
Website: www.thelionleintwardine.co.uk

10 mi west of Ludlow by A 49 on A 4113. Parking.

PRICES
Meals: a la carte £ 25/46

8 rooms:
£ 85/125

MAP: 2

CLOSING TIMES
Closed 25 December

Wye Valley Butty Bach and Ludlow Best

STAGG INN

Delightfully cosy, passionately run pub

Situated at the meeting point of two former drovers' roads, this characterful part-medieval, part-Victorian pub was once called 'The Balance', as it marked the point where farmers would stop to weigh their wool. Inside, it's delightfully cosy - one room was once a butcher's shop and another still displays an old bread oven. Cooking is fittingly straightforward, relying on classically based recipes, careful preparation and top quality produce; menus are short, simple and to the point; and the dishes themselves are truly satisfying. The owners are keen to promote the area and serve local beers, ciders and unusual vodkas - such as potato or marmalade flavour. Bedrooms in the pub are snug but can be noisy; opt for one in the former vicarage. Booking essential.

TITLEY, HR5 3RL
Tel.: (01544)230221
Website: www.thestagg.co.uk

3.5 mi northeast of Kington on B 4355. Parking.

PRICES
Meals: a la carte £ 31/42

6 rooms:
£ 70/140

MAP: 3

CLOSING TIMES
Closed 2 weeks January-February, first 2 weeks November, 25-26 December, Monday and Tuesday

Wye Valley Butty Bach and Ludlow Gold

MOODY COW (N)

More traditional than its name might suggest

Allegedly named by a previous landlord because of his less than amicable divorce, the Moody Cow is a more traditional pub than its moniker might suggest, with a hop-covered wooden bar, deep sofas and a warming wood burning stove. The food matches the surroundings with a range of classic dishes like chicken liver parfait, sausage and mash or slow-roasted pork belly and, what it may lack in originality, it makes up for with quality ingredients, careful cooking and distinct flavours. Just make sure you leave room for the crème brûlée! The friendly owners run this pub with real commitment and passion and grow some of the ingredients themselves in their kitchen garden. The cosy bedroom is accessed via an exterior spiral staircase.

UPTON BISHOP, HR9 7TT
Tel.: (01989)780470
Website: www.moodycowpub.co.uk

3 miles northeast of Ross-on-Wye signposted off the A 40. Parking.

PRICES
Meals: a la carte £ 24/41

1 room:
£ 65/88

MAP: 4

CLOSING TIMES
Closed 5-21 January, Sunday dinner and Monday

Wye Valley HPA and Otter Brewery Ales

MILL RACE

You can even order food and wine to take away!

This isn't the kind of place you'd expect to find in a small country village - but the locals aren't complaining. It doesn't really look like a pub, either outside or in, save for the bar counter; you enter via a Gothic-style door, pass a board pinpointing their suppliers and head towards the chefs hard at work in the semi open-plan kitchen. You'll find regulars standing around the bar, pint in hand, and local families out for the night in the darker, slate-floored areas. Cooking is fairly simple, showcasing plenty of produce from their estate and farm and letting the ingredients speak for themselves. The small team flit about, coping well when it's busy - which it usually is - and regular theme nights include the likes of 'game' and 'pudding'.

WALFORD, HR9 5QS
Tel.: (01989)562891
Website: www.millrace.info

3 mi south of Ross-on-Wye on B 4234. Parking.

PRICES
Meals: a la carte £ 26/38

MAP: 5

CLOSING TIMES
Open daily

Wye Valley Ales and Butcombe Ales

BUTCHERS ARMS

Traditional cooking, with décor to match

The flags must surely be flying at half-mast in this part of the world as Stephen Bull has finally hung up his apron. He remains the owner of this cosy, timbered pub, but it now falls to Phil Vincent to feed the hungry hordes of Herefordshire. He's an experienced chef, and his cooking is unfussy and traditional, relying on quality local produce to deliver bold flavours. Expect game in season and plenty of offal; there's tasty home-baked bread and hearty, reasonably priced dishes like wild rabbit, leek and cider pie, or roast duck with orange sauce. Like the cooking, the décor is traditional, with a welcoming log fire, wattle walls and beams slung so low you're forced to duck. Phil's daughters Leonie and Jemma run the show with aplomb.

WOOLHOPE, HR1 4RF
Tel.: (01432)860281
Website: www.butchersarmswoolhope.com

Midway between Hereford and Ledbury signposted off A 438. Parking.

PRICES
Meals: a la carte £ 23/35

MAP: 6

CLOSING TIMES
Closed Sunday dinner in winter and Monday except bank holidays

Wye Valley Butty Bach and Ledbury Gold

INN AT GRINSHILL

Cooking revolves around the seasons

Family-owned and very personally run, this inn stands in the middle of a pretty Shropshire village. Being a true country inn, the food offering revolves around the seasons, so expect catch of the day, shoot of the day or pie of the day, as well as a wide choice of dishes ranging from a simple sandwich or sharing board to pub classics like fish and chips – and more elaborate choices like rabbit loin with sage and juniper sauce or brill with wild mushrooms and fish cream. A cosy bar plays host to walkers and locals and there's a contemporary restaurant too, with purple chairs, clean white lines and a view to the kitchen. Six pretty bedrooms are individually decorated and comfortable. Can't find the television? Have a look behind the mirror.

The High St,
GRINSHILL, SY4 3BL
Tel.: (01939)220410
Website: www.theinnatgrinshill.co.uk

Between Shrewsbury and Whitchurch just off the A 49. Parking.

PRICES
Meals: a la carte £ 19/46

6 rooms:
£ 90/120

MAP: 7

CLOSING TIMES
Closed first week January, Sunday dinner, Monday and Tuesday

Greene King Ales, Hereford HLA and Hobsons Twisted Spire

THE POUND (N)

Some of the best fish and chips around

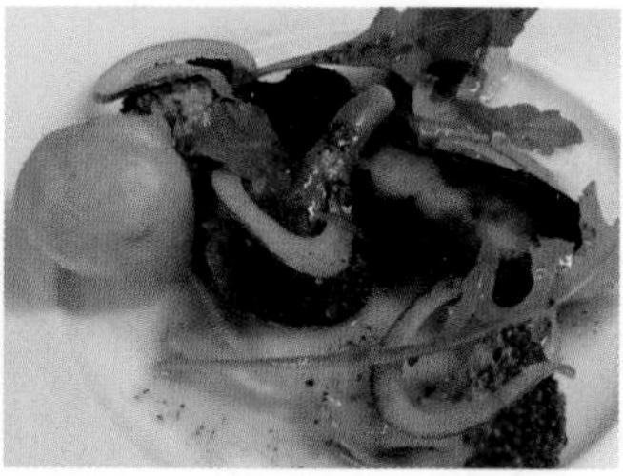

It's a strange name for a pub and, although it seems originally to have referred to a place to keep animals - the inn having been a stop off point for farmers and their livestock - the pub sign now shows a gold sovereign: the pound coin first minted by Henry VII in the decade the pub was built. Inside is not as characterful as the thatched exterior leads you to expect: there are beams, flagged floors and an inglenook, but the overall feel is one of modernity, with smartly laid tables and plenty of space. Service is efficient and the experienced chef's cooking, precise and accomplished. There's a popular light bites menu, and dishes on the à la carte range from a homemade burger to pan-fried sea bass - with some of the best fish and chips around!

LEEBOTWOOD, SY6 6ND
Tel.: (01694)751477
Website: www.thepound.org.uk

Between Church Stretton and Shrewsbury on A 49. Parking.

PRICES
Meals: a la carte £ 20/31

MAP: 8

CLOSING TIMES
Closed one week autumn, Sunday dinner and Monday

Wye Valley Butty Bach and Salopian Shropshire Gold

CHARLTON ARMS (N)

In a commanding position on the banks of the Teme

Claude Bosi is arguably the man who put Ludlow on the map, food-wise, with the original Hibiscus; the Charlton Arms is owned by his brother Cedric and his wife, Amy, who've given it a freshen up, bringing a modern touch to this traditional inn. It is situated in a commanding position next to the picturesque Ludford Bridge, on the banks of the River Teme, and remains all things to all people, with drinkers watching the sport in the snug and diners populating the airy lounge bar and the more comfortable restaurant with its superb river view. Menus also promise something for everyone and dishes are good value and full of flavour. Up-to-date bedrooms are named after famous plays and feature art from the Ludlow Festival; most look onto the water.

Ludford Bridge,
LUDLOW, SY8 1PJ
Tel.: (01584)872813
Website: www.thecharltonarms.co.uk

On the south side of the town where B 4361 crosses the River Teme.
Parking.

PRICES
Meals: a la carte £ 22/33

9 rooms:
£ 60/120

MAP: 9

CLOSING TIMES
Closed 25-26 December

Ludlow Gold, Wye Valley Butty Bach and Hobsons Best Bitter

SUN INN

A real family affair; opt for a tasty fish special

A welcoming, traditional country pub on the English-Welsh border, the Sun Inn is a family affair, with experienced chef Peter in the kitchen, his wife Jean and daughter-in-law Sally delivering good, old-fashioned hospitality to their customers - and even the grandchildren helping out on occasion. It's not a plush place but it's cosy enough, with a comfy bar on one side and a brightly painted dining room on the other. The regularly changing, concise menu offers tasty, satisfying and comforting home-cooked dishes, so expect rich, creamy homemade soups, steak and ale pie, delicious homemade faggots with mash and peas, and sticky toffee pudding - and make sure you try the excellent fish specials, which are written up on a glass board.

MARTON, SY21 8JP
Tel.: (01938)561211
Website: www.suninn.org.uk

5.5 mi northeast of Montgomery on B 4386. Parking.

PRICES
Meals: a la carte £ 23/35

MAP: 10

CLOSING TIMES
Closed Sunday dinner, Monday and lunch Tuesday

Hobsons Best Bitter and Twisted Spire

THE GEORGE

In the same family for three generations

The moment you walk in the George, feel the warmth from the roaring fires and start to soak up the cosy, relaxed atmosphere, you just know that it's going to be good. A traditional pub set on the village green, it's simply furnished, with stone floors, scrubbed wooden tables and pictures of locals on the walls. The bubbly manager - the third generation of her family to have owned the pub - brings a woman's touch to the place, with the latest fashion mags for flicking through and candles and fresh flowers on every table. Like the décor, the food is simple but well done. The menus change daily according to the produce available; the team use local suppliers where possible and also grow some of their own vegetables in the garden.

ALSTONEFIELD, DE6 2FX
Tel.: (01335)310205
Website: www.thegeorgeatalstonefield.com

7.5 mi north of Ashbourne by A 515. Parking.

PRICES
Meals: a la carte £ 22/49

MAP: 11

CLOSING TIMES
Closed 25 December

Marston's Pedigree and Burton Bitter, Ringwood Best Bitter, Banks's Sunbeam and Brakspear Oxford Gold

DUNCOMBE ARMS (N)

Owned by the scion of a famous brewery family

Residents of Ellastone must have been happy when this previously derelict pub reopened as, not only did they gain a stylish dining pub as their local, they also got the Hon. Johnny Greenall of the famous brewery family as the owner – a pretty good pedigree, it must be said, when it comes to running a pub. Add to this the fact that wife, Laura, is a descendant of the Duncombe family, after which the pub is named, and you've a recipe for success. Several rooms each have their own identity: Johnny's Bar features horse racing memorabilia, The Augustus is cosy and characterful, while The Parlour and Oak Room is airy, modern and decorated with cow prints. Food keeps to a core of classic pub dishes and there's a wonderful view from the terrace.

Main Road,
ELLASTONE, DE6 2GZ
Tel.: (01335)324275
Website: www.duncombearms.co.uk

Between Ashbourne and Uttoxeter on B 5032. Parking.

PRICES
Meals: a la carte £ 23/47

MAP: 12

CLOSING TIMES
Open daily

Timothy Taylor Landlord, Sharp's Doom Bar and Marston's Pedigree

THE TROOPER

Rare breed steaks and wood-fired pizzas

With the A5 starting life as the Roman military road to north Wales, and the hamlet of Wall host to what was once an important forces' staging post, it seems fitting that this pub should be named The Trooper. Feast like a Roman general after battle at the self-styled 'Staffordshire steakhouse': choose from a wonderful selection of mature steaks, from local rump to fantastically marbled Kobe beef; rare breed steaks go up to 20oz for the truly ravenous and a fine array of sides includes the somewhat unusual parsley root fries. Not in a meaty mood? A wood-fired pizza oven, which takes three hours to reach the correct temperature, cooks tasty pizzas to order from freshly made dough. Grab a seat on the terrace when the weather allows.

Watling St,
WALL, WS14 0AN
Tel.: (01543)480413
Website: www.thetrooperwall.co.uk

Just south of Lichfield off A 5127, adjacent to the A 5. Parking.

PRICES
Meals: a la carte £ 18/42

MAP: 13

CLOSING TIMES
Open daily

Marston's Pedigree, Greene King IPA, Holden's Golden Glow and guest ales

FUZZY DUCK (N)

Fashionably attired, with boutique bedrooms

The shower gel, shampoo and soap in the stylish boutique bedrooms of this delightful red brick country pub give a clue as to its owners: siblings Adrian and Tania also own Baylis and Harding, the toiletries company. Having made a success of the brand, and ready for a new challenge, they decided to take on their village local, transforming it from a boarded up boozer to a modern, fashionably attired dining pub. Seasonal British dishes might include roast duck with lentils and sprouting broccoli or braised ox cheek with French beans and celeriac mash; there's a 'pub classics' section with choices like the Aubrey Allen burger, and desserts like rice pudding are pleasingly old school, with the 'chocolate whatchamacallit' a must for chocoholics.

Ilmington Rd,
ARMSCOTE, CV37 8DD
Tel.: (01608)682635
Website: www.fuzzyduckarmscote.com

8.5 mi north of Moreton-in-Marsh off A 429 in village centre. Parking.

PRICES
Meals: a la carte £ 19/46

4 rooms:
£ 110/160

MAP: 14

CLOSING TIMES
Closed 1 week January and Monday
booking advisable

Wye Valley Ales, North Cotswold Ales and Purity Mad Goose

KING'S HEAD

Hosted Shakespeare's parents' wedding breakfast!

Set close to the Cotswolds, in the picturesque village of Aston Cantlow, is the 13C Norman church where Shakespeare's parents were married; and they are thought to have had their wedding breakfast at this attractive ivy-clad inn. The timbered bar is hugely characterful – the experienced owner has decorated it with contemporary black and white photos he took himself – and behind that, is a chic, country-style restaurant in pastel shades. Menus focus on the classics but there's the odd modern twist, so your pork might come with a cheek bon bon or your lamb, with Bombay potato and yoghurt dressing. Regular duck suppers celebrate the pub's past, when during wartime rationing the landlord was allowed to serve duck, as he reared his own.

21 Bearley Rd,
ASTON CANTLOW, B95 6HY
Tel.: (01789)488242
Website: www.thekh.co.uk

6 mi northwest of Stratford-upon-Avon, signposted off A 46. Parking.

PRICES
Meals: a la carte £ 18/44

MAP: 15

CLOSING TIMES
Open daily

Purity Pure Gold and Mad Goose, and Greene King Abbot Ale

CHEQUERS INN

Quirky pub with chandeliers and gilt mirrors

The signs outside scream country gastropub but to assume so would be off the mark; with its chandeliers, brushed velvet furniture and round-backed Regency chairs, this place is anything but formulaic. The open-fired bar is a popular spot with villagers, no doubt pleased with the large selection of beers as well as their local's transformation from run down boozer to smart, contemporary inn. When it comes to the cooking, menus display a broad international style. There are good old British classics like prawn cocktail, and cauliflower cheese and ham hock with bubble and squeak, alongside dishes of a more Mediterranean persuasion, like rabbit rigatoni or a salami platter. Tuesday evening is fish night, with fish and chips to eat in or take away.

91 Banbury Rd,
ETTINGTON, CV37 7SR
Tel.: (01789)740387
Website: www.the-chequers-ettington.co.uk

Southeast of Stratford-upon-Avon where the A 422 crosses the A 429. Parking.

PRICES
Meals: a la carte £ 21/35

MAP: 16

CLOSING TIMES
Closed Sunday dinner and Monday

Greene King IPA, Purity Mad Goose and Butcombe Bitter

BLUEBELL

Daring to be different with its plush furnishings

This part-timbered building on the high street is not your usual kind of pub. True, it comes with exposed beams, open fires and mix and match chairs - but some of those chairs have French-style gilding, and one of the rooms has grey padded walls and sumptuous curtains fringed with peacock feathers. This mix of rustic character and formal elegance seems to be a hit with the customers, as does the wide-ranging selection of wines, beers, cocktails and tasty British dishes. The experienced chef uses the best local suppliers and cooking is honest and seasonal, with dishes ranging from fish and chips to pot-roast pheasant; there's also a good value set menu to consider. Puddings are more modern and could include crème brûlée with blackcurrant sorbet.

93 High St,
HENLEY-IN-ARDEN, B95 5AT
Tel.: (01564)793049
Website: www.bluebellhenley.co.uk

8 mi northwest of Stratford-upon-Avon on A 3400. Parking.

PRICES
Meals: £ 15/25 and a la carte £ 25/41

MAP: 17

CLOSING TIMES
Open daily

Purity Mad Goose and Pure UBU, Wye Valley HPA and Hook Norton Hooky Bitter

CRABMILL

Made up of various beamed snugs and lounges

This characterful timbered pub is the ideal place to kick back and relax, whether you sit in the lawned garden, on the peaceful terrace or inside the pub itself. It's made up of various beamed snugs and lounges, which are fitted out with a mixture of traditional old wood furnishings and contemporary leather chairs set at black wood tables. You can eat anywhere but if you're tucked away in a corner and it's busy - which it usually is - you may need to flag down one of the team to place your order. The good-sized à la carte offers modern Mediterranean-influenced dishes; start with a tasty sharing plate and move on to one of the interesting main courses, maybe venison pavé, sweet potato and corned beef hash or ostrich fillet wrapped in Serrano ham.

Preston Bagot,
HENLEY-IN-ARDEN, B95 5EE
Tel.: (01926)843342
Website: www.thecrabmill.co.uk

1 mi east of Henley-in-Arden on A 4189. Parking.

PRICES
Meals: £ 15 (weekdays) and a la carte
£ 22/40

MAP: 18

CLOSING TIMES
Closed Sunday dinner
booking essential

Purity Pure UBU, Whale Ale Pale Whale and Sharp's Doom Bar

HOWARD ARMS

The very essence of an English country pub

This 400 year old Cotswold stone inn, set on a peaceful village green, is the very essence of an English country pub. Bright flower displays welcome you at the front, and round the back there's a small garden and terrace. Inside, you'll find the expected stone-faced walls, exposed beams, flagged floors and a huge inglenook fireplace, and a mix of chairs, pews and benches; there's also a raised-level dining room with a large dresser and fully laid dark wood tables. Blackboards are dotted about the place, displaying hearty dishes that are mainly British-based; you might find braised beef and ale pie or calves' liver and bacon. Featuring antique furniture, the original bedrooms are warm and cosy; those in the extension are more contemporary.

Lower Green,
ILMINGTON, CV36 4LT
Tel.: (01608)682226
Website: www.howardarms.com

Between Stratford-upon-Avon and Moreton-in-Marsh signposted off A 429. Parking.

PRICES
Meals: a la carte £ 23/43

8 rooms:
£ 60/150

MAP: 19

CLOSING TIMES
Open daily

Hook Norton Old Hooky, Timothy Taylor Landlord and Wye Valley Butty Bach

CROSS AT KENILWORTH

Dishes not only look impressive but taste good too

When you first catch sight of this pub's smart exterior, you'll just know that they take things seriously here and when an eager member of staff greets you, settles you in and explains the menu, this first impression is confirmed. Further proof comes on your plate: skilfully executed, classical cooking uses prime seasonal ingredients, and dishes not only look impressive but taste good too. If you're seated in the back room, which opens onto the terrace, you get to watch the kitchen in action. The bright and airy room next door used to be a classroom – a fact alluded to by the eye-catching wall lamps shaped like hand bells. The front bar, with its adjoining snug and wood burning stove, makes a cosy place for a beer and a homemade sausage roll.

16 New St,
KENILWORTH, CV8 2EZ
Tel.: (01926)853840
Website: www.thecrosskenilworth.co.uk

On northwestern side of town on A 429, Coventry Road. Parking.

PRICES
Meals: £ 25 (lunch) and a la carte £ 30/45

MAP: 20

CLOSING TIMES
Closed Sunday dinner, Monday and bank holidays

Wells Bombardier and Hook Norton Old Hooky

BOOT INN

From picnic boards to sophisticated specials

Whether you're hastening down the M40 or pottering along on a narrow boat, it's worth stopping off at this large, buzzy red-brick pub. Set close to the junction of the Grand Union and Stratford-upon-Avon canals, it draws in a mixed crowd - from the young to the old, businesspeople to pleasure seekers - and you may well wonder where they all come from. With its traditional quarry-floored bar, modern first floor restaurant and large terrace complete with a barbecue, it's deservedly popular, so booking is a must. Dishes vary greatly, from sandwiches, a picnic board and sharing plates through to more sophisticated specials. The crispy oriental duck salad and the bubble and squeak are mainstays, and influences range from Britain to the Med and Asia.

Old Warwick Rd,
LAPWORTH, B94 6JU
Tel.: (01564)782464
Website: www.bootinnlapworth.co.uk

2 mi southeast of Hockley Heath on B 4439; on the left hand side just before the village. Parking.

PRICES
Meals: £ 15 (lunch and early dinner)
and a la carte £ 23/40

MAP: 21

CLOSING TIMES
Open daily
booking essential

Purity Pure UBU, Marston's EPA and Sharp's Doom Bar

RED LION

Tasty home-cooking and country-chic bedrooms

With its flag floors and log fires, this 18C former coaching inn has the character of a country pub, and its stylish interior boasts a warm, modern feel. The seasonal menu offers classic pub dishes like homemade steak and Hook Norton pie, pan-fried calves' liver or fish and chips, with old favourites like rhubarb crumble or warm chocolate fudge cake for dessert. These are tasty, home-cooked dishes from the tried-and-tested school of cooking - so if you're after something a little more adventurous, try the daily specials board instead. Staff are pleasant and smartly attired; Cocoa, the chocolate Labrador, also gives a warm welcome. Bedrooms may be slightly on the small side but they are stylish and contemporary, with a good level of facilities.

Main St,
LONG COMPTON, CV36 5JS
Tel.: (01608)684221
Website: www.redlion-longcompton.co.uk

Between Chipping Norton and Shipston-on-Stour on A 3400. Parking.

PRICES
Meals: £ 14 (weekdays) and a la carte £ 25/31

5 rooms: £ 60/140

MAP: 22

CLOSING TIMES
Open daily

Adnams Broadside and Hook Norton Ales

STAG

Surprisingly contemporary village pub

Charles and Nigel may have won over the villagers before they even started, by distributing tasty home-baked bread to mark their arrival, but newcomers seem just as taken with this 16C thatched pub. Inside it's surprisingly contemporary, boasting a boldly coloured bar and two modern dining rooms: the first - adorned with deer antlers and animal heads - is cosy, beamed and wood-panelled; the second, overlooking the garden, boasts funky fabrics, large mirrors and dark Venetian blinds. The extensive menu changes with the seasons, offering generous, classically based dishes - maybe haddock fishcakes or pan-fried calves' liver - and the antipasti and charcuterie sharing plates are a hit. Service is efficient and copes well under pressure.

Welsh Rd,
OFFCHURCH, CV33 9AQ
Tel.: (01926)425801
Website: www.thestagatoffchurch.com

3.5 mi east of Royal Leamington Spa signposted off A 425. Parking.

PRICES
Meals: a la carte £ 23/42

MAP: 23

CLOSING TIMES
Open daily

Warwickshire Beer Co Darling Buds, Hook Norton Ales and St Austell Tribute

MALT SHOVEL (N)

A pub for all seasons

With its pretty blue and cream façade bedecked with ivy and hanging baskets, this is a pub for all seasons. In winter, you'll find a fire crackling in the grate in the rustic bar; there's a sizeable garden for when the weather's fine - and a covered terrace for when it can't make up its mind. The Mediterranean colour scheme means it feels sunny inside all year round; an impression enhanced by the cheery dispositions of the long-serving staff. People come here to dine rather than drink, and there's a separate, more formal restaurant in the converted barn. The menu offers plenty of pub classics but the Malt Shovel is also well known for its fish. Cooking tends to be traditional in style: just how the locals like it.

Barston Lane,
BARSTON, B92 0JP
Tel.: (01675)443223
Website: www.themaltshovelatbarston.com

Signposted off A 452 just south of Hampton-in-Arden. Parking.

PRICES
Meals: a la carte £ 24/39

MAP: 24

CLOSING TIMES
Closed Sunday dinner

Sharp's Doom Bar, Hook Norton Old Hooky and Black Sheep Best Bitter

ORANGE TREE

Cosy, rustic and contemporary by turns

'Hoof, fin, fur, feather and flour' is painted on both the front and back of this popular pub, giving some idea of what to expect: yes there is beer here but it's the food that really excites, and you'll find plenty of options under each heading, plus more under slightly less catchy ones such as 'grazing and sharing' or 'starters and salads'. Influences are global, so expect dishes like Mexican chilli beef, tandoori chicken burger or Thai crispy beef salad alongside the more traditional rib-eye, pizza, pie or risotto. This impressively smart pub has a unique style: cosy, rustic and contemporary by turns, with a bit of kitsch thrown in for good measure. You can eat anywhere, so have a wander round the various areas before settling on a seat.

Warwick Rd,
CHADWICK END, B93 0BN
Tel.: (01564)785364
Website: www.lovelypubs.co.uk

On A 4141 midway between Solihull and Warwick. Parking.

PRICES
Meals: £ 14 and a la carte £ 18/44

MAP: 25

CLOSING TIMES
Open daily
booking advisable

Purity Pure UBU and Greene King IPA

WOODBRIDGE INN (N)

Airy and open, yet with nooks and crannies galore

This modernised pub sits in a superb spot on the banks of the Severn, and is named after the timber bridge which originally spanned the river here. Rebuilt in iron in 1818, it is the second oldest iron bridge in the world – the oldest is a mile upriver, at the appropriately named Ironbridge. The pub's spacious interior has got 'Brunning and Price' written all over it: airy and open, yet with nooks and crannies galore, with rugs on wooden floors and interesting prints punctuating the walls. Menus list all the usual suspects like sausage and mash but it's worth going off-piste with choices like tandoori hake fillet with lentil and spinach dahl and cauliflower pakora. Arrive early in summer to get a river-view table on the terrace.

COALPORT, TF8 7JF
Tel.: (01952)882054
Website: www.woodbridge-coalport.co.uk

2 mi southeast of Ironbridge following the signs off B 4373. Parking.

PRICES
Meals: a la carte £ 22/45

MAP: 26

CLOSING TIMES
Open daily

Purple Moose Snowdonia Ale, Three Tuns XXX and Wood's Shropshire Lad

THE QUEENS

The look and the food are reassuringly traditional

Dating from the 16C, The Queens has been around nearly as long as the millstones in the wall dividing it from the brook. The pub might have been refurbished but its traditional look and feel remains – a conscious effort by the owners to respect the locals' preferences. There's a bar with some nice leather benches for drinkers, and three small rooms neatly laid for dining. Food plays a substantial role here: in true pub style you can get a hearty steak and ale pie but you'll also find the likes of steamed cod with Parma ham, tomatoes and black olives, showing the chef's passion for classical flavours. Dishes are attractively presented and more refined than their descriptions imply. Come in September for the village's annual scarecrow festival.

Queens Hill,
BELBROUGHTON, DY9 0DU
Tel.: (01562)730276
Website: www.thequeensbelbroughton.co.uk

Between Stourbridge and Bromsgrove off A 491. Parking.

PRICES
Meals: £ 19 (weekdays) and
a la carte £ 23/36

MAP: 27

CLOSING TIMES
Closed 25 December
bookings advisable at dinner

Marston's Pedigree, Ringwood Boondoggle and monthly guest ales

BELL & CROSS

Cooking by the England footie team's former chef

The Bell & Cross stands at what the locals call 'the old crossroads'. Colourful window boxes greet you at the front and round the back there's a spacious, well-kept lawn boasting lovely country views. The inside is made up of a series of traditionally decorated rooms; the cosy bar with its red leather banquettes and listed counter is particularly characterful. Football mementoes adorn the hall, harking back to the time when the owner cooked for the England football squad - but it's unlikely that they were given as much choice on their menus: there's sarnies, light bites and pub classics, and some more substantial dishes on the à la carte; not forgetting a set menu and some blackboard specials too. Influences range from Asia to the Med.

Holy Cross,
CLENT, DY9 9QL
Tel.: (01562)730319
Website: www.bellandcrossclent.co.uk

Between Hagley and Bromsgrove off A 491. Parking.

PRICES
Meals: £ 17 (weekdays) and
a la carte £ 20/34

MAP: 28

CLOSING TIMES
Closed 25 December and dinner
26 December and 1 January

Enville Ale, Wye Valley HPA and Purity Mad Goose

CHEQUERS

Extensive menus cover all bases

If football's your thing, then make for the "Players' Lounge" of this lightly washed roadside pub and sit among photos of the old England team and of Roger, the owner, who was their chef for 21 years. Despite the fact that rich burgundy colours and modern furnishings have been introduced, the exposed beams, the original wood and quarry-tiled floors and the fires blazing in the hearth maintain a cosy, traditional feel – furthered by a collection of timeless food items such as Colman's mustard, Lyle's golden syrup and HP and Worcestershire sauces displayed on shelves above the bar. Extensive menus offer a good selection of light bites and pub classics, while some more adventurous fish and offal-based specials are chalked up on the board daily.

Kidderminster Rd,
CUTNALL GREEN, Droitwich, WR9 0PJ
Tel.: (01299)851292
Website: www.chequerscutnallgreen.co.uk

3 mi north of Droitwich Spa on A 442. Parking.

PRICES
Meals: £ 17 (weekdays) and
a la carte £ 22/36

MAP: 29

CLOSING TIMES
Closed 25 December, dinner 26 December and 1 January

Wye Valley HPA, Marstons New World Pale Ale and Sharp's Doom Bar

BUTCHERS ARMS ✿

Unfussy yet sublimely flavoured dishes

This is a true rural inn, where the wooden beams are fringed with hop bines and farmers meet for a pint at the end of the day. It's run by a young couple - he cooks, while she takes care of front of house - and both the food and the pub itself have an admirable lack of pretension. There may be only one chef in the kitchen but what a chef! He grew up in France, with a French mother, and his culinary education began at an early age. He knows his braising from his blanching and his sorrel from his saffron; he knows where to obtain produce of the highest quality and uses it to create simple, yet sublimely flavoured dishes. The concise menu changes sometimes twice daily and dishes might include pork loin with truffle mash, red cabbage and crackling.

Lime Street,
ELDERSFIELD, GL19 4NX
Tel.: (01452)840381
Website: www.thebutchersarms.net

8.5 mi north of Gloucester by A 417 and signposted off B 4211. Parking.

PRICES
Meals: a la carte £ 39/51

MAP: 30

CLOSING TIMES
Closed 1 week early January, 1 week late August, Sunday dinner, Monday, lunch Tuesday to Thursday and bank holidays

Wye Valley Ales, Timothy Taylor Landlord and St Austell Tribute

WHITE HART

Careful cooking in a proudly run village local

Once a run-down old pub, the White Hart is now the pride and joy of owners Simon and Venetia, who have established it as a proper village local, where regulars watch TV from brown leather sofas and play on the games machine in the bar. If you're dining, head for the bright, contemporary dining room - or out into the garden on warmer days. Dishes are carefully prepared, classically based and rely on quality produce; you'll find light offerings such as baked camembert at lunch, along with some good value pub classics, while dinner features the likes of chicken, port and bacon pâté and loin of pork with champ potatoes and sage cream. Their annual beer festival features a barbecue and live music, and is a hit with locals and visitors alike.

HARTLEBURY, DY11 7TD
Tel.: (01299)250286
Website: www.thewhitehartinhartlebury.co.uk

4 mi south of Kidderminster, village signposted off A 449. Parking.

PRICES
Meals: £ 19 (lunch and early dinner)
and a la carte £ 20/37

MAP: 31

CLOSING TIMES
Closed 25 December and Sunday dinner

Purity Mad Goose, Hobsons Best Bitter and Wye Valley HPA

TALBOT INN (N)

Red-brick former hunting lodge

This red-brick 19C inn was originally built as a hunting lodge for the local estate, and the photos on the walls - and the hops hanging from the bar - attest to a time when it was popular with hop pickers here for the harvest. It's been refurbished top-to-toe but still retains its rustic character: a wood burning stove provides the focal point of the warmly decorated, welcoming bar and there's a dining room for a more comfortable meal, as well as a cosy lounge. Menus offer something for everyone, from pub classics like beer-battered fish of the day to locally shot game in season or ham hock with parsley sauce. Bedrooms provide contemporary comforts but avoid Rooms 1 and 2 as they can be noisy. Staff are friendly and try hard to please.

NEWNHAM BRIDGE, WR15 8JF
Tel.: (01584)781941
Website: www.talbotinnnewnhambridge.co.uk

3.5 mi east of Tenbury Wells on A 456. Parking.

PRICES
Meals: a la carte £ 22/30

7 rooms:
£ 65/115

MAP: 32

CLOSING TIMES
Open daily

Hobsons Best Bitter, Twisted Spire and Wye Valley Butty Bach

THE INN AT WELLAND N

Charming features and designer touches

With its minimalist modern sign, its landscaped garden and its decked terrace, it is clear on arrival that this country dining pub is a little bit different to the norm. Once inside, the designer touches continue; the designer in question being Gillian Pinchbeck, who together with her hands-on husband, David, has turned this place from wreck to "by 'eck!" Inside, it's light, open and stylish with plenty of charming features like flagged floors, beams and a wood burning stove. You'd be forgiven for thinking that dishes might be elaborate and overambitious, but no – there are plenty of pub classics as well as modern British dishes like slow-cooked shoulder of lamb or peppered loin of venison; all tasty, generous of portion and sensibly priced.

Hook Bank,
WELLAND, WR13 6LN
Tel.: (01684)592317
Website: www.theinnatwelland.co.uk

Between Wynds Pont and Upton-upon-Severn on the A 4104. Parking.

PRICES
Meals: a la carte £ 19/38

MAP: 33

CLOSING TIMES
Closed Sunday dinner and Monday

Wye Valley Butty Bach, Otter Bitter and Malvern Black Pear

YORKSHIRE & THE HUMBER

England

England's biggest county has a lot of room for the spectacular; it encapsulates the idea of desolate beauty. The bracing winds of the Dales whistle through glorious meadows and deep, winding valleys, while the vast moors are fringed with picturesque country towns like Thirsk, Helmsley and Pickering. Further south the charming Wolds roll towards the sea, enhanced by such Georgian gems as Beverley and Howden. Popular history sits easily here: York continues to enchant with its ancient walls and Gothic Minster, but, owing to its Brontë links, visitors descend on the cobbled street village of Haworth with as much enthusiasm. Steam railways criss-cross the region's bluff contours, while drivers get a more streamlined thrill on the Humber Bridge.

Yorkshire's food and drink emporiums range from quaintly traditional landmarks like the country tearoom and fish and chip shops proudly proclaiming to be the best in England, to warm and characterful pubs serving heart-warming local specialities.

North East
YORKSHIRE
North West
Yorkshire Dales National Park
Bishop Auckland
Middleton-in-Teesdale
W. Auckland
Newton-Aycliffe
Stockton-on-Tees
Billingham
Barnard Castle
Appleby
Brough
Darlington
Bowes
Eaglescliffe
Orton
Kirkby Stephen
Tebay
Richmond
Reeth
Northallerton
Leyburn
Sedbergh
Hawes
Bedale
Thirsk
Whernside
Kirkby Lonsdale
Ripon
Ingleton
Clapham
Boroughbridge
Settle
Threshfield
Knaresborough
Long Preston
Bolton Priory
Harrogate
Wetherby
Skipton
Gisburn
Tadcaster
Ilkley
Otley
Harewood
Clitheroe
Bingley
Keighley
Colne
Nelson
LEEDS
Padiham
Blackburn
Burnley
BRADFORD
Garforth
Castleford
Halifax
Accrington
Todmorden
Rawtenstall
Brighouse
Darwen
Dewsbury
Wakefield
Chorley
Rochdale
HUDDERSFIELD
Barnsley
Bury
Oldham
Holmfirth
MANCHESTER
Conisbrough
Ashton-under-Lyne
Stocksbridge
Rotherham
Glossop
Hyde
SHEFFIELD
Stockport
Peak
High Peak
Castleton
Whaley Bridge
Chapel-en-le-Frith
District
Dronfield
Wilmslow
Buxton
Staveley
Baslow
Macclesfield
Chesterfield
Wigan
Widnes
Runcorn
Ribble
Lune
Tees
Wharfe
Ure
Swale
PENNINE

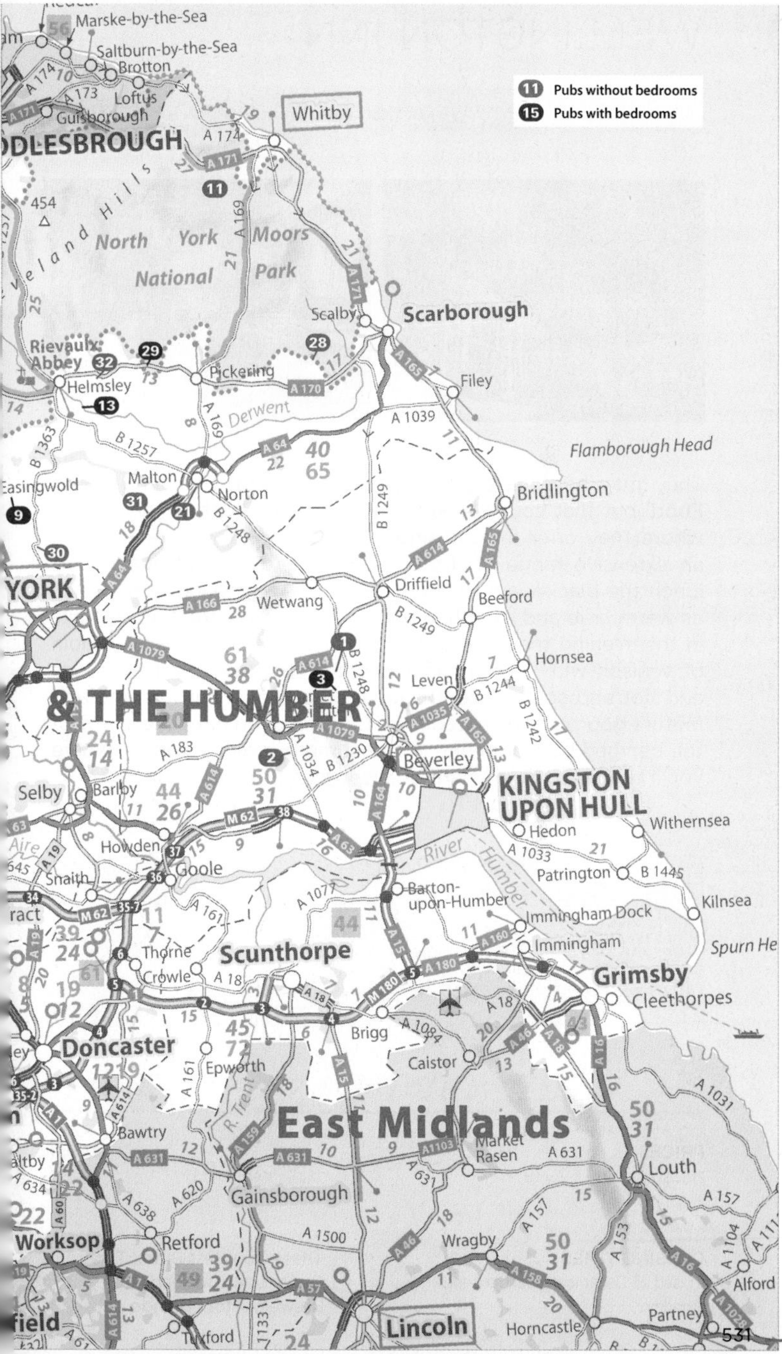
Pubs without bedrooms
Pubs with bedrooms
Marske-by-the-Sea
Saltburn-by-the-Sea
Brotton
Loftus
Guisborough
Whitby
DLESBROUGH
Cleveland Hills
North York Moors National Park
Scalby
Scarborough
Rievaulx Abbey
Helmsley
Pickering
Derwent
Filey
Flamborough Head
Malton
Norton
Easingwold
Bridlington
YORK
Wetwang
Driffield
Beeford
Hornsea
Leven
& THE HUMBER
Beverley
KINGSTON UPON HULL
Hedon
Withernsea
Selby
Barlby
Howden
Goole
Snaith
River Humber
Patrington
Barton-upon-Humber
Kilnsea
Immingham Dock
Immingham
Spurn He
Thorne
Crowle
Scunthorpe
Grimsby
Cleethorpes
Brigg
Caistor
Doncaster
Epworth
R. Trent
East Midlands
Bawtry
Market Rasen
Louth
Gainsborough
Worksop
Retford
Wragby
Alford
Lincoln
Horncastle
Partney
Tuxford

WELLINGTON INN

Well-run pub serving generous, flavoursome dishes

They may have called their company 'Warm Beer and Lousy Food' but that couldn't be further from the truth at the 'Welly', where they offer a good array of well-kept Yorkshire ales and an extensive range of dishes that capture the imagination. At lunch the blackboard 'Baaa...r Menu' lists appealing dishes such as warm crab and samphire tart or calves' liver and bacon, while in the evening there's a large à la carte offering the likes of loin of venison with parsnip boulangère or pork belly with scallops and hot and sour sauce. Dishes are generous, flavoursome and feature good quality ingredients. Eat next to an open fire in one of the beamed bars or in one of the numerous dining rooms, where you'll be served by a smart, efficient team.

19 The Green,
LUND, YO25 9TE
Tel.: (01377)217294
Website: www.thewellingtoninn.co.uk

10 mi northwest of Beverley just off B 1248. Parking.

PRICES
Meals: a la carte £ 25/39

MAP: 1

CLOSING TIMES
Closed 25 December, 1 January and Monday

Theakston Best Bitter, Timothy Taylor Landlord and Atom Brewery Atom Blonde

STAR

Menus proudly list local growers and suppliers

Owners Ben and Lindsay bought this once down-at-heel pub in the small village of Sancton over ten years ago and have since set about establishing and expanding it into the place you see before you today. There's a cosy, slightly rustic bar – its counter topped with homemade nibbles – where the locals like to come for a pint and maybe sausage and mash or a steak and ale pie. There are also two rooms with upholstered banquettes, smart wood-topped tables and plush carpets, which make up the restaurant; here you'll find a good value 'Yorkshire Lunch' menu and an à la carte offering hearty, boldly flavoured dishes which display a little more imagination. Every dish proudly lists the main ingredient's grower or supplier – all local, of course.

King St,
SANCTON, YO43 4QP
Tel.: (01430)827269
Website: www.thestaratsancton.co.uk

2 miles south of Market Weighton in centre of village on A 1034. Parking.

PRICES
Meals: £ 17 (weekday lunch) and a la carte £ 25/46

MAP: 2

CLOSING TIMES
Closed Monday

Black Sheep Best Bitter, Wold Top Best Bitter and Copper Dragon Golden Pippin

PIPE AND GLASS INN

Superb cooking uses top quality regional produce

Very personally run by its experienced owners - he cooks, while she looks after front of house - the Pipe and Glass Inn is a deservedly popular place. Grab a drink and a seat beside the log burner or head straight for a table in the contemporary dining room to enjoy food that's carefully executed, big on flavour and generously proportioned. Dishes are made with local, seasonal and traceable produce, and might include venison and juniper suet pudding or roast loin of red deer; desserts like the Pipe and Glass chocolate plate (subtitled 'Five reasons to love chocolate') continue the decadent theme. Luxurious bedrooms are equipped with the latest mod cons and have their own patios overlooking the estate woodland; breakfast is served in your room.

West End,
SOUTH DALTON, HU17 7PN
Tel.: (01430)810246
Website: www.pipeandglass.co.uk

5 mi northwest of Beverley by A 164, B 1248 and side road west. Parking.

PRICES
Meals: a la carte £ 22/52

2 rooms:
£ 135/170

MAP: 3

CLOSING TIMES
Closed 2 weeks January, Sunday dinner and Monday except bank holidays

Black Sheep Best Bitter, Great Yorkshire Brewery Two Chefs and Wold Top Wold Gold

CRAB AND LOBSTER

Traditional menu, decoration anything but!

From the moment you set eyes on this pub, you'll realise it's no ordinary place. Old advertisements and lobster pots hang from the walls, thatched crabs and lobsters sit on the roof and even the umbrellas are thatched. Inside it's just as quirky, with charming exposed beams hung with knick-knacks aplenty and all kinds of characterful memorabilia strewn over every surface. The menu, unsurprisingly, features plenty of seafood, with the likes of fish soup, fishcakes, fish pie, shellfish and lobster; alongside traditional British favourites such as cheese soufflé, pork cheek confit and crusted loin of lamb. Split between an 18C Georgian Manor and log cabins, the stylish bedrooms are themed around world-famous hotels; some boast private hot tubs.

Dishforth Rd,
ASENBY, YO7 3QL
Tel.: (01845)577286
Website: www.crabandlobster.com

4 mi southwest of Thirsk by B 1448 and A 168. Parking.

PRICES
Meals: £ 17 (lunch) and
a la carte £ 34/68

17 rooms:
£ 110/240

MAP: 4

CLOSING TIMES
Open daily

Copper Dragon Golden Pippin, Best Bitter and Theakston Best Bitter

BULL

Try the local meats and cheeses

The Bull is a member of the Ribble Valley Inns group - but don't expect some sort of faceless corporate brand - this is the bourgeoning pub company set up by Nigel Haworth and Craig Bancroft, co-proprietors of Lancashire's celebrated Northcote. They have led the way in promoting the specialities of their region and the Bull is no different. Expect real ales and local meats and cheeses, as well as traditional British dishes, rediscovered classics and the sort of puddings that make you feel patriotic. The Bull is an appropriate moniker as this pub is big and solid looking. It's at the side of Broughton Hall and is made up of assorted snugs and spaces, with beams, stone floors and log fires. It's cosy in winter and charming on a summer's day.

BROUGHTON, BD23 3AE
Tel.: (01756)792065
Website: www.thebullatbroughton.com

3 mi west of Skipton on A 59. In the grounds of Broughton Hall Country Park Estate. Parking.

PRICES
Meals: a la carte £ 19/40

MAP: 5

CLOSING TIMES
Closed 25 December

Thwaites Ales

RED LION

Stoutly traditional ferryman's inn

This appealing stone inn sits at the heart of a small rural community on the banks of the River Wharfe. It has a warm yet worn feel, which isn't all that surprising when you learn that it has cellars dating back to the 12C and a wood-panelled bar from its 16C ferryman's inn days. There's plenty of choice when it comes to where to sit - the cosy bar with its copper-topped counter, the laid-back lounge or the more formally dressed dining room. The choice of food is similarly wide, with a bar menu of pub favourites; an à la carte featuring local lamb in spring, East Coast fish in summer and game in winter; and a blackboard of daily specials. Bedrooms are traditional with modern overtones - those in the nearby manor house are the most contemporary.

BURNSALL, BD23 6BU
Tel.: (01756)720204
Website: www.redlion.co.uk

7 mi north of Bolton Abbey by B 6160. Parking.

PRICES
Meals: a la carte £ 21/41

25 rooms:
£ 60/158

MAP: 6

CLOSING TIMES
Open daily

Theakston Best Bitter, Copper Dragon Golden Pippin and Timothy Taylor Landlord

FOX AND HOUNDS

Run by a former Royal Marine!

It may be just a few minutes from the A1 but this traditional stone pub is a true country local. It's been in the same family since 1983 and is now run by hands-on couple Vincent and Helen. It's a fairly small place: to one side there's a stone-walled, open-fired bar; to the other, a neatly laid dining room with an array of equine paraphernalia, farming implements and blacksmith's tools filling the walls. Good-sized menus offer unfussy, home-cooked dishes; choose something from the daily changing blackboards, maybe ham hock terrine with piccalilli, followed by a satisfying steak and kidney short crust pie. Fruit and vegetables are from Snape, meats are from Bedale and fish, from Hartlepool. Local, organic and homemade products are also for sale.

CARTHORPE, DL8 2LG
Tel.: (01845)567433
Website: www.foxandhoundscarthorpe.co.uk

9 mi north of Ripon by minor road via Wath and Kirklington. Parking.

PRICES
Meals: £ 15 (weekdays) and
a la carte £ 21/42

MAP: 7

CLOSING TIMES
Closed first 2 weeks January, 25 December
and Monday

Black Sheep Best Bitter and
Theakston Best Bitter

YE OLD SUN INN

The locals are well looked after

The demise of many a post office has highlighted their importance in the community, but Ye Old Sun Inn is a good example of how significant a role the pub plays in local life. This family-run inn does it all: from selling homemade produce from its small deli to holding cookery demonstrations. It's also a great ambassador for regional suppliers, several of whom are name-checked on the menu. The open fires and rustic feel make this a very popular place with the locals, although race days at the Knavesmire bring a regular invasion of interlopers. The menus change monthly and are as seasonal as ever. Those not from these parts can take advantage of the three very smart bedrooms in the recently acquired house next door.

Main St,
COLTON, LS24 8EP
Tel.: (01904)744261
Website: www.yeoldsuninn.co.uk

3 mi northeast of Tadcaster by A 659 and A 64. Parking.

PRICES
Meals: £ 20 and a la carte £ 21/40

3 rooms:
£ 75/95

MAP: 8

CLOSING TIMES
Closed 26 and dinner 31 December

Black Sheep Best Bitter, Copper Dragon Golden Pippin and Rudgate Brewery Battle Axe

DURHAM OX

Family run, 300 years old and bags of character

Located in a sleepy little hamlet next to Crayke Castle is the 300 year old Durham Ox, a bustling family-run pub which boasts pleasant views up to a medieval church and over the Vale of York. You'll receive a warm welcome whether you sit in the carved wood-panelled bar with its vast inglenook fireplace or more formal beamed dining room; but when the weather's right, head straight for the rear courtyard, as this is definitely the place to be. The regularly changing menu features plenty of fresh seafood and Crayke game – and the grass-fed 40 day dry-aged steaks are their speciality. Set in converted farm cottages, the cosy bedrooms display original brickwork and quarry tiling; the suite is set over two floors and comes with a jacuzzi bath.

Westway,
CRAYKE, YO61 4TE
Tel.: (01347)821506
Website: www.thedurhamox.com

2 mi east of Easingwold on Helmsley rd. Parking.

PRICES
Meals: £ 18 (weekday lunch) and a la carte £ 20/40

6 rooms:
£ 100/140

MAP: 9

CLOSING TIMES
Closed dinner 25 December
booking essential

Black Sheep Best Bitter, York Brewery Guzzler and Timothy Taylor Landlord

BLUE LION

Game takes centre stage in season

Set in a delightful village, this former coaching inn boasts a rustic interior, pleasingly untouched by the minimalist makeover brigade. Dine in the charming flag-floored bar or in the high-ceilinged, wood-floored dining room; either way you'll sit at a polished wooden table in the glow of candlelight and enjoy unfussy, hearty, full-flavoured cooking of local produce. Dishes might include homemade pork pie, slow-cooked pigs' cheeks or roast wild venison, with game taking centre stage in season. The wine list is of particular note and offers a range of prices and plenty of variety by the bottle, carafe and glass. Bedrooms in the main house are furnished with antiques, while the rooms in the converted stable are more contemporary in style.

EAST WITTON, DL8 4SN
Tel.: (01969)624273
Website: www.thebluelion.co.uk

3 mi southeast of Leyburn on A 6108. Parking.

PRICES
Meals: £ 19/29 and a la carte £ 25/48

15 rooms:
£ 70/145

MAP: 10

CLOSING TIMES
Open daily
booking essential

Black Sheep Ales and
Theakston Best Bitter

WHEATSHEAF INN

Country feel with no-nonsense cooking

This late 17C inn is located at the centre of a delightful stone-built hamlet on the edge of the picturesque North Yorkshire Moors. There's a small garden and several rooms filled with framed prints and lithographs of hunting scenes, along with a delightful snug that boasts a lovely range - which acts as an open fire - and chunky tables crafted by one of the locals from thick slices of oak cut at the Castle Howard Estate. Menus offer a real taste of Yorkshire, utilising fresh produce from just outside the door, so you'll find the likes of lambs' kidneys, local steak, Whitby scampi and game shot within two miles, all accompanied by triple-cooked chips. It really is a family affair here, with mum cooking and her husband and daughter out front.

EGTON, YO21 1TZ
Tel.: (01947)895271
Website: www.wheatsheafegton.com

6.5 mi southwest of Whitby by A 171. Parking.

PRICES
Meals: a la carte £ 20/34

MAP: 11

CLOSING TIMES
Closed 25 December and Monday light lunch

Black Sheep Bitter, Timothy Taylor Landlord and Cropton Ales

CARPENTER'S ARMS

Stylish bedrooms overlook the Vale of Mowbray

Mentioned in the Domesday Book, Felixkirk's claim to fame is that it was once a local Commandery of the Knights Hospitallers of St John of Jerusalem. Dating back to the 18C, the Carpenter's Arms may not be quite as old, but it really is a good old village pub, so you'll often find local groups such as the bell ringers in. When it comes to dining, there's a choice of blackboard specials or dishes from the seasonal main menu, which offers everything from gammon or venison casserole to sea bass with ratatouille. Be sure to save room for pudding before the steep climb back up Sutton Bank; if you don't fancy the ascent, spend the night under a duck down duvet in a well-equipped, stylishly appointed bedroom, overlooking the Vale of Mowbray.

FELIXKIRK, YO7 2DP
Tel.: (01845)537369
Website: www.thecarpentersarmsfelixkirk.com

Signposted off A 170, 3 mi northeast of Thirsk. Parking.

PRICES
Meals: a la carte £ 22/41

10 rooms:
£ 125/175

MAP: 12

CLOSING TIMES
Open daily

Timothy Taylor Landlord, Black Sheep Bitter and Golden Sheep

STAR INN

Carefully executed, boldly favoured dishes

To fully appreciate the character of this thatched 14C pub, head for the main low-ceilinged bar with its open fire and photo-filled walls, then grab the kidney-shaped Mousey Thompson table for the best seat in the house; alternatively, try the rustic middle room or the brighter, more modern, brasserie-like restaurant with its chef's table. Carefully executed, boldly favoured dishes have a skilled, classical style with subtle touches of originality; they use the very best of local produce including fruit and veg from the kitchen garden and meats from their own pigs and chickens. Coffee is taken in the loft, with complimentary cheese and nuts. Stylish bedrooms come with unique features: one has a snooker table and another, a suspended bed.

High St,
HAROME, YO62 5JE
Tel.: (01439)770397
Website: www.thestaratharome.co.uk

2.75 mi southeast of Helmsley by A 170. Parking.

PRICES
Meals: £ 25 (weekdays) and
a la carte £ 32/55

9 rooms:
£ 150/260

MAP: 13

CLOSING TIMES
Closed Monday lunch except bank holidays
booking essential

Black Sheep Ale and Great Yorkshire Brewery Two Chefs

OAK TREE INN

Everything from bread to petit fours is homemade

Don't let the Brafferton Helperby sign confuse you – this did, in fact, start life as two even smaller villages; The Oak Tree being in the latter of the two. Younger sister to the Durham Ox and the Carpenters Arms, this is a place of two halves: there's a large bar, a tap room and two snugs, while in the old hay barn there's a smart dining room with large windows overlooking a terrace. The same menu is available throughout, offering hearty, generous dishes which use ingredients from small local suppliers; everything from the bread to the petit fours is homemade and combinations are familiar and comforting. If you're in a rush, pizzas and wines are also available to take away. Service is charming. Smart, modern bedrooms boast jacuzzi baths.

Raskelf Rd,
HELPERBY, YO61 2PH
Tel.: (01423)789189
Website: www.theoaktreehelperby.com

5 mi northeast of Boroughbridge on T-junction entering village. Parking.

PRICES
Meals: £ 15 (weekday lunch) and a la carte £ 25/34

6 rooms:
£ 100/140

MAP: 14

CLOSING TIMES
Open daily

Timothy Taylor Landlord and Black Sheep Best Bitter

ANGEL INN

Ever tried 'Yapas' (Yorkshire tapas)?

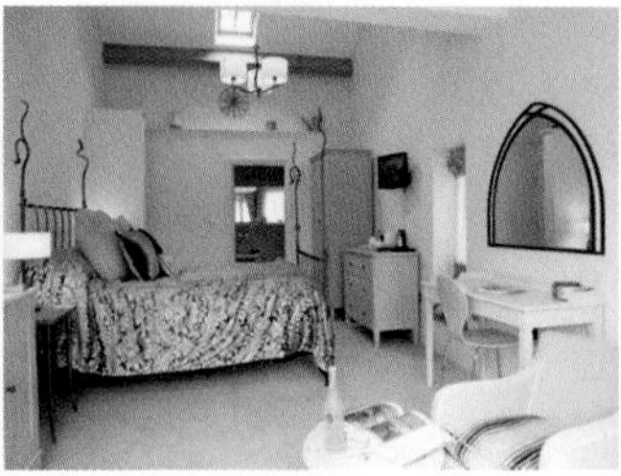

This 18C stone inn might be in a rural location but it's gained quite a reputation over the years. It's a characterful place, featuring old beams and roaring log fires, and the well-drilled team cope with the numbers proficiently. Bookings are only taken from 12-12:30 and 6-6:30pm; if you miss this, join the group of drinkers at the bar, waiting for their name to reach the top of the list. The seasonal menu offers an extensive range of hearty dishes crafted from local produce, alongside Yorkshire tapas and a good value midweek set selection; for a more formal experience, head to one of the smart dining rooms. Regular events include cookery classes and themed evenings. Bedrooms are found in the nearby 'Barn Lodgings' and 'Sycamore Bank'.

HETTON, BD23 6LT
Tel.: (01756)730263
Website: www.angelhetton.co.uk

5.75 mi north of Skipton by B 6265. Parking.

PRICES
Meals: a la carte £ 27/43

9 rooms:
£ 135/200

MAP: 15

CLOSING TIMES
Closed 4 days January
booking essential

Black Sheep Ale and Dark Horse Hetton Pale Ale

BLACK HORSE INN

Stylish bedrooms with designer bathrooms

Originally called 'The Salutation', this 18C pub was reputedly renamed after a highwayman rode away on his black horse with a local landowner's daughter. Inside it's been subtly modernised – it still has its original beams but now also has a smart flagged floor. Drinkers and diners sit alongside one another in the candlelit bar with its Welsh dresser and cushion-filled benches but there's a dedicated dining room too, with painted tables and high-backed chairs. The same menu is served throughout, ranging from sharing boards to flavoursome British classics that are a step above your usual pub fare; maybe Yorkshire game pie or oxtail casserole. Stylish bedrooms come with designer bathrooms; if the weather's good, head outside for a game of quoits.

Lumley Ln,
KIRKBY FLEETHAM, DL7 0SH
Tel.: (01609)749010
Website: www.blackhorsekirkbyfleetham.com

Midway between Catterick and Northallerton signposted off B 6271. Parking.

PRICES
Meals: £ 15 (lunch and early dinner) and a la carte £ 21/46

7 rooms:
£ 75/160

MAP: 16

CLOSING TIMES
Open daily
booking advisable

Black Sheep Best Bitter, Timothy Taylor Landlord and Yorkshire Ales Blonde

CHARLES BATHURST INN

The daily menu is inscribed on a mirror!

This characterful 18C hostelry is named after a local land and lead mine owner, and former resident. Sitting on the edge of the Pennine Way, high in the hills of Arkengarthdale, it boasts commanding views over the surrounding countryside and is so remotely set, that the only sound you'll hear is the 'clink' of quoits being thrown in the garden. Inside you're greeted by open fires, various timbered snugs and a charming dining room hung with old monochrome photos and sepia lithographs. Pub favourites are on offer at lunch, while the dinner menu - unusually inscribed on a mirror - offers more ambitious dishes such as scallops with chorizo or moules marinière, with plenty of fresh fish and game in season. Bedrooms are spacious and comfortable.

LANGTHWAITE, DL11 6EN
Tel.: (0333)7000779
Website: www.cbinn.co.uk

3.25 mi northwest of Reeth on Langthwaite rd. Parking.

PRICES
Meals: a la carte £ 21/35

19 rooms:
£ 81/125

MAP: 17

CLOSING TIMES
Closed 25 December

Theakston Best Bitter, Rudgate Ales and Black Sheep Ales

SANDPIPER INN

Takes pride in the provenance of its ingredients

A friendly Yorkshire welcome is extended to the Dale walkers who come to refuel at this stone-built, part-16C pub, situated just off the main square. Visitors can rest their blistered feet by the fire in the split-level beamed bar or plump for a seat in the more characterful dining room. A small enclosed terrace out the back provides a third alternative for when it's sunny but you'll have to come inside to read the blackboard menus, found hanging on the walls amidst the general clutter of decorative pictures, books and ornaments. Subtle, refined cooking offers a modern take on the classics, so expect dishes like ham hock terrine and piccalilli, pressed Dales lamb or slow-cooked Wensleydale beef. Two homely bedrooms are on the first floor.

Market Pl,
LEYBURN, DL8 5AT
Tel.: (01969)622206
Website: www.sandpiperinn.co.uk

In town centre. Limited parking available in the Market Place.

PRICES
Meals: a la carte £ 24/41

2 rooms:
£ 80/100

MAP: 18

CLOSING TIMES
Closed Tuesday in winter and Monday

Black Sheep Best Bitter, Rudgate Viking and Settle Signal Light

PUNCH BOWL INN

Traditional inn, deep in the heart of Swaledale

Set deep in the heart of Swaledale, this traditional 17C stone-built inn is a popular stop-off point for walkers, who refuel on classic dishes like duck liver parfait, braised local lamb shank or beef and red wine casserole; but don't go looking for a paper menu, since dishes are listed on mirrors in the bar. There's a selection of filled ciabatta at lunchtime, tasty nursery puddings like those of the sticky toffee or bread and butter varieties, and bi-monthly steak nights which prove popular with the villagers. Portions are generous and staff go about their business with a smile. Supremely comfortable bedrooms are decorated in a fresh, modern style; all of them have dramatic views over Swaledale, while the superior rooms are more spacious.

LOW ROW, DL11 6PF
Tel.: (01748)886233
Website: www.pbinn.co.uk

4 mi west of Reeth on B 6270. Parking.

PRICES
Meals: a la carte £ 20/33

11 rooms:
£ 99/140

MAP: 19

CLOSING TIMES
Closed 25 December

Black Sheep Ales, Theakston Best Bitter and Rudgate Brewery Jorvik Blonde

THE DUNSFORTH (N)

Menus offer admirable choice and value for money

There can be no sight more reassuring than a pile of Michelin Guides when you're about to order a meal! If you've spotted them, then you'll be enjoying the lively atmosphere in one of the fire-lit front rooms of this contemporary pub, but if it's a quieter, more intimate meal you're after, head instead to the smart restaurant with its hunting print wallpaper and stag's head. Menus offer admirable choice and value for money and, when it comes to the ingredients, seasonality and freshness are key, with meat from Boroughbridge, fish from Hartlepool and as much homemade as possible, from the freshly baked bread to the ice creams and petit fours. Dishes tend to have a modern twist but they do traditional too, if that's what you fancy.

Mary Ln,
LOWER DUNSFORTH, YO26 9SA
Tel.: (01423)320700
Website: www.thedunsforth.co.uk

4.25 mi southeast of Boroughbridge by B 6265. Parking.

PRICES
Meals: £ 20 and a la carte £ 28/48

MAP: 20

CLOSING TIMES
Closed Sunday dinner and Monday

Theakston Best Bitter and Old Peculier and Adnams Ghost Ship

NEW MALTON

Simple, honest and unpretentious

This 18C stone building has been serving the market town of Malton for many years, first as a pub, then a tea room and later, as a tapas restaurant - and now it's back as a pub again. There are three different rooms, all with open fires, reclaimed furniture and black and white photos of old town scenes, a style which is clearly a hit with the locals. The good-sized menu offers hearty pub classics with the occasional adventurous dish thrown in, and cooking is unfussy and flavoursome with an appealing Northern bias; the toad in the hole is particularly popular. Beers change regularly and food is served all day, every day; you're meant to order at the bar but if you catch one of the friendly team walking by, they'll happily save you the trip.

2-4 Market Pl,
MALTON, YO17 7LX
Tel.: (01653)693998
Website: www.thenewmalton.co.uk

In centre of town, ample on-street parking.

PRICES
Meals: a la carte £ 20/28

MAP: 21

CLOSING TIMES
Closed 25-26 December and 1 January

Wold Top Wold Gold, Hop Studio Blonde and Treboom Drum Beat

PUNCH BOWL INN

Ask for table 504 in the snug

You won't find Marton cum Grafton on your map because it's two villages which have slowly joined together over the years. What you will find is this delightful whitewashed inn, which part-dates from the 14C and is part of a burgeoning group run by experienced owners. It has a strange, almost crescent shape, with a small seating area in front, a lovely terrace behind and various little rooms with open fires and old beams; not forgetting a private room with wine glass chandeliers. The all-encompassing, seasonal menu features local produce and includes a seafood platter and a 'Yorkshire board', along with excellent fish and chips and a great rib-eye steak; from 5.30-7 they offer the 'Magnificent Seven' - 7 dishes at £7 each.

MARTON CUM GRAFTON, YO51 9QY
Tel.: (01423)322519
Website: www.thepunchbowlmartoncumgrafton.com

3.5 mi southeast of Boroughbridge by B 6265. In the centre of the village. Parking.

PRICES
Meals: a la carte £ 22/38

MAP: 22

CLOSING TIMES
Open daily

Timothy Taylor Landlord and Black Sheep Best Bitter

BUCK INN N

Creative, modern cooking from a keen young buck

With help from his father, young buck Matthew Roath has set up in business with his partner Samantha: he's hard at work in the kitchen, while she's out front making sure everything runs smoothly. You'll be offered a drink in the characterful beamed bar before being shown through to one of the two light and airy dining rooms beyond – choose the first, which is less formal, or dine in the bar. A collection of cookery books shows serious culinary intent and, indeed, the creative, modern dishes are well-constructed and tasty. Ingredients are staunchly local, with producers name-checked on the menu and game often exchanged for a few pints. The 'Market Menu', served weekday lunch and early dinner, offers particularly good bang for your buck.

MAUNBY, YO7 4HD
Tel.: (01845)587777
Website: www.thebuckinnmaunby.co.uk

7.75 mi northwest of Thirsk by A 61 and A 167. Parking.

PRICES
Meals: £ 17 (lunch and early dinner)
and a la carte £ 23/36

MAP: 23

CLOSING TIMES
Closed 26 December, 1 January,
Sunday dinner and Monday

Theakston Best Bitter and
Copper Dragon Golden Pippin

DAWNAY ARMS

Locally shot game from a native Yorkshireman

In the shadows of the impressive 18C Beningbrough Hall and Gardens, you'll find this handsome pub - its own garden leading straight down to the River Ouse. Step inside and you'll discover low beams, open fires and all manner of bric-a-brac, from old kitchen implements and horseshoes to a mincing machine and buffalo horns; and to the rear, the delightfully airy dining room has views across the terrace and garden to the river. The experienced chef - a native Yorkshireman - lets the seasons guide him and offers gutsy, well-executed British-inspired dishes such as crispy pig's head with black pudding or slow-cooked daube of beef. Game plays a huge part in the cooking and is locally shot. Portions are large, so two courses will probably suffice.

NEWTON-ON-OUSE, YO30 2BR
Tel.: (01347)848345
Website: www.thedawnayatnewton.co.uk

8 mi northwest of York by A 19 and minor road west. Parking.

PRICES
Meals: £ 19 (weekday lunch) and
a la carte £ 21/47

MAP: 24

CLOSING TIMES
Closed 1 January, Sunday dinner and
Monday except bank holidays

Black Sheep Best Bitter, Wold Top Angler's Reward and Timothy Taylor Landlord

GOLDEN LION

Atmospheric bar with over 65 different whiskies

This 18C stone inn sits overlooking the market cross of a historic village in the North York Moors National Park. With its low beamed ceiling, dark wood bar, church pew seating and welcoming wood-burning stove, it's the kind of place that the locals know and love; make for the atmospheric bar, which offers over 80 different whiskies and 15 gins. The cooking is traditional and satisfying, featuring filling dishes such as steak and kidney pie with suet crust or homemade chicken Kiev. The main selection stays largely the same but there's also a more ambitious weekly changing specials board to consider and be sure to save room for one of the tasty puddings with homemade ice cream. Modern bedrooms have heavy oak furnishings and good facilities.

6 West End,
OSMOTHERLEY, DL6 3AA
Tel.: (01609)883526
Website: www.goldenlionosmotherley.co.uk

6 mi northeast of Northallerton by A 684. Parking in the village.

PRICES
Meals: a la carte £ 20/39

7 rooms:
£ 65/100

MAP: 25

CLOSING TIMES
Closed 25 December, lunch Monday and Tuesday except bank holidays

Hop Studio XP, York Brewery Decade, Wall's Keepers Gold and Timothy Taylor Landlord

NAGS HEAD COUNTRY INN

Good range of Armagnacs dating from 1946

This rustic pub is set close to the A1 and has been run by the same quick-witted owner for over 40 years. It has a large garden, a small front terrace and a quirky interior, where over 700 framed ties hang on the walls of the open-fired bar. Stop here for a beer with the locals, before heading through to the dining area with its booths and hunting prints - or, if it's full, the large, Georgian-style dining room. The blackboard menu features all the classics accompanied by seasonal vegetables and a jug of gravy - the owner is also an avid shooter, so game season is the best time to visit. If Armagnac's your thing, there's a list of vintages dating back to 1946 and if you fancy staying the night, there are cosy bedrooms in the pub and annexe.

PICKHILL, YO7 4JG
Tel.: (01845)567391
Website: www.nagsheadpickhill.co.uk

7.5 mi northwest of Thirsk by A 61 and B 6267. Parking.

PRICES
Meals: a la carte £ 14/33

12 rooms:
£ 60/97

MAP: 26

CLOSING TIMES
Closed 25 December

Theakston Ales and Black Sheep Best Bitter

CROWN INN

Try a taste of every dessert with the 'assiette'

Tables out the front of this 14C inn make the most of its delightful position by the village green; don't be surprised to see a couple having a drink out here in the dark - although very lifelike, they are merely mannequins! All manner of bric-a-brac carries on the whimsical theme: look out for the grandfather clock, the stuffed stag's head and the fishing rods hanging from the ceiling. Menus offer pub classics like steak and ale pie alongside more ambitious dishes like 'Little Yorkshire Pig', comprising crisp belly pork, fillet medallions and black pudding; if you can't decide on a dessert, try them all with the 'assiette' of puddings. Well-appointed bedrooms come with feature beds, free-standing roll-top baths and plenty of extra touches.

ROECLIFFE, YO51 9LY
Tel.: (01423)322300
Website: www.crowninnroecliffe.com

1.5 mi west of Boroughbridge by minor road. Parking.

PRICES
Meals: a la carte £ 25/39

4 rooms:
£ 80/120

MAP: 27

CLOSING TIMES
Open daily

Timothy Taylor Landlord, Ilkley Brewery Gold and Theakston Best Bitter

ANVIL INN

Intimate dining room in a former smithy

As its name suggests, this charming inn was formerly a smithy, and much of the associated paraphernalia remains, including bellows, an open forge and the original anvil. In marked contrast - but blending in seamlessly - is the boldly coloured contemporary sitting room. Cooking is classical in essence, with the odd international influence, so expect crispy duck and pancakes alongside Shetland mussels or slow-roasted daube of beef. Local chef Mark prides himself on the use of regionally sourced produce; eggs come from the pub's own hens and the Stillington pork is a firm favourite. There are only seven tables in the intimate restaurant, so be sure to book ahead, particularly for Sunday lunch, which has become something of an institution.

Main St,
SAWDON, YO13 9DY
Tel.: (01723)859896
Website: www.theanvilinnsawdon.co.uk

10 mi southwest of Scarborough by A 170, turning right at Brompton onto Sawdon Ln. Parking.

PRICES
Meals: a la carte £ 25/39

MAP: 28

CLOSING TIMES
Closed 25-26 December, 1 January, Monday and Tuesday

Daleside Brewery Blonde Beer, Wold Top Mallard, Rudgate Ruby Mild

FOX AND HOUNDS

Hearty Yorkshire cooking and homely bedrooms

It's always a good sign if a pub has regulars: diners so au fait with what's on offer that they don't even need to look at the menu - and this pretty 18C inn has plenty. What keeps them coming back are the big portions of proper, hearty, Yorkshire cooking: pub classics like beer-battered haddock and chips or calves' liver; maybe some traditional slow braises or some brisket, and plenty of game in season. Customers not only return to eat but also to stay - in one of the spacious, homely, individually decorated bedrooms - with second generations of families now returning to experience the pub's excellent hospitality. Keeping all the balls in the air is Helen - who worked her way up from chambermaid to manager - backed up by a charming team.

Main St,
SINNINGTON, YO62 6SQ
Tel.: (01751)431577
Website: www.thefoxandhoundsinn.co.uk

Just off A 170 between Pickering and Kirkbymoorside. Parking.

PRICES
Meals: a la carte £ 24/44

10 rooms:
£ 59/170

MAP: 29

CLOSING TIMES
Closed 25-27 December

Copper Dragon Best Bitter and Black Sheep Golden Sheep

ROSE & CROWN

Delightful pub with a touch of glamour

This welcoming pub is found in a beautiful village, in amongst some delightful Georgian country houses. There's always a local or two to be found beside the log burning stove in the cosy bar, tucking into a gutsy classic like ham hock terrine or steak and shallot pie, while the elegant restaurant and airy conservatory are a hit with those after just a little more occasion. The atmosphere is relaxed, courtesy of the smiling owner and her friendly young team, and the hidden garden and super terrace are a must on sunny days. Menus offer plenty of choice, from tempting afternoon teas through to hearty classics like local asparagus with a free range poached egg and hollandaise, followed by halibut with wild rice and tomato and coriander salsa.

Main St,
SUTTON-ON-THE-FOREST, YO61 1DP
Tel.: (01347)811333
Website: www.theroseandcrownyork.co.uk

On B 1363 north of York. Parking.

PRICES
Meals: £ 18/28 and a la carte £ 25/37

MAP: 30

CLOSING TIMES
Closed first week January and Monday except bank holidays
booking essential

York Brewery Guzzler and Naylor's Velvet

CROWN AND CUSHION N

Local meat cooked on the charcoal-fired rotisserie

Two miles from Castle Howard, on the edge of the Howardian Hills, is this well-run 18C pub which makes a great start or stop-off point for the many walkers and birdwatchers that flock to the area. You can sip a beer by the fire alongside the locals in the Tap Room but the best place to eat is the lower rear dining area, which overlooks the semi-open kitchen – unless the sun's out, in which case head to the terrace with its country vista. The menu champions local meats and the kitchen's pride and joy is the charcoal-fired rotisserie known as 'Big Bertha'. This cooks meats and fish at 450 degrees, producing mouth-watering results and comes into its own with Sunday roast. Dishes are hearty, sandwiches are doorstops, and puddings are nursery style.

WELBURN, YO60 7DZ
Tel.: (01653)618777
Website: www.thecrownandcushionwelburn.com

6 mi southwest of Malton signposted off A 64. Parking.

PRICES
Meals: £ 17 and a la carte £ 26/40

MAP: 31

CLOSING TIMES
Open daily

Black Sheep Ales and Rudgate Battle Axe

PLOUGH INN (N)

Choose a seat in the cosy, characterful restaurant

Retirement is an opportunity to take some time for yourself, to relax, maybe get a pet or potter round in the garden... alternatively, you could buy your local pub, like the owners of this 16C inn. Having installed an equally local chef behind the stove, they are making village residents very happy; you might even spot them having a swift pint themselves at the end of the bar. Sit in the restaurant if you can - it's in the older part of the building, is hugely characterful, and is kept cosy by wood burners. Traditional dishes are the order of the day, so expect classics like fishcakes or chargrilled rib-eye steak, with game in season and desserts such as sticky toffee pudding. Prices are laudably low and service, friendly and relaxed.

Main St,
WOMBLETON, YO62 7RW
Tel.: (01751)431356
Website: www.theploughinnatwombleton.co.uk

Signposted off A 170, 4 mi east of Helmsley. Parking.

PRICES
Meals: a la carte £ 20/33

MAP: 32

CLOSING TIMES
Closed 25 December and Monday lunch

Black Sheep Best Bitter, John Smith's Bitter and Theakston Best Bitter

MILESTONE

It's all about homemade, local and organic produce

The owners of The Milestone are passionate about organic, locally sourced produce; they consider the quality of their ingredients to be the key to their success and don't believe in buying in things like bread, pasta and puddings, since they can make them in-house. Some of the hearty dishes on the menu like the lamb burger and the beef Bourguignon have become classics but the emphasis is on evolution and seasonality, so what's on offer changes frequently. Things never stand still here - they serve weekend brunch and takeaway sandwiches, and they even hold cookery demonstrations. Downstairs is spacious with understated décor, simple wood tables and banquettes, while the beamed first floor room provides a more formal dining space.

84 Green Ln,
SHEFFIELD, S3 8SE
Tel.: (0114)2728327
Website: www.the-milestone.co.uk

Between A 61 and River Don. Parking in Green Ln and Ball St.

PRICES
Meals: £ 14 and a la carte £ 17/38

MAP: 33

CLOSING TIMES
Closed 25-26 December and 1 January

Wentworth Ales and Kelham Island Best Bitter

WIG & PEN

Light lunches and elaborate modern dinners

The team behind the Milestone have moved closer into the heart of the city with this, its sister pub, which overlooks Paradise Square. The name comes from the legal offices which surround it, and the busy bar, with its high stools and sofas, is a magnet for office workers on their journey home. Those here to dine should head for the smarter area towards the rear, with its stylish feature wallpaper and wooden floors. Lunch offers sandwiches and a good value menu of light dishes like fishcakes or risotto, while dinner sees the ambition of the kitchen translated into elaborate dishes presented in a modern fashion; perhaps roast scallops with oxtail and crispy ox tongue, or loin of venison with celeriac purée, mulled pear and cocoa jelly.

44 Campo Ln,
SHEFFIELD, S1 2EG
Tel.: (0114)2722150
Website: www.the-wigandpen.co.uk

Just behind Sheffield Cathedral. On-street parking meters.

PRICES
Meals: £ 17 (dinner) and a la carte £ 19/29

MAP: 34

CLOSING TIMES
Closed 25-26 December and 1 January

Wentworth WPA and Kelham Island Ales

CRICKET INN

Food arrives in big, hearty portions

Hidden away in a delightful spot in the valley, next to the cricket ground, this is a proper pub in every sense of the word. The three rooms boast open fires and the walls are filled with cricketing paraphernalia, while the scrubbed tables are home to bottles of Sheffield's spicy Henderson's relish. Food comes in big, hearty portions, not for the faint-hearted, and there's something for everyone, from sandwiches and snacks like home-roasted pork scratchings, to things like cheese on toast or homemade fishcakes - as well as dishes such as steak and ale pie or slow-braised shoulder of lamb. 'Cricket Inn boards' come in ploughman's and fisherman's varieties, there's a little person's menu and some nice nursery style puddings finish things off.

Penny Ln,
TOTLEY, S17 3AZ
Tel.: (0114)2365256
Website: www.cricketinn.co.uk

6 mi southwest of Sheffield by A 61, A 621 and Hillfoot Rd. Parking.

PRICES
Meals: £ 15 (weekday lunch) and a la carte
£ 20/40

MAP: 35

CLOSING TIMES
Open daily

Thornbridge Ales

SHIBDEN MILL INN

Come for comforting favourites or gourmet dining

This is a pub of paradox: you're in the middle of a deep-sided valley in the quiet, unspoilt countryside, yet only a few minutes' drive from the centre of Halifax; it's popular with locals, yet people travel for miles to visit; and the menu promises 'Comforts and Favourites', like sausage and mash, as well as 'Gourmet Dining' with dishes like poached and sautéed wood pigeon. In a previous life this was a corn mill and the stream which used to turn the wheel runs alongside, adding to the tranquil feel if you're dining alfresco. Character is not in short supply either, with beamed ceilings, welcoming fires and lots of cosy corners. Staff are well-drilled and bedrooms, individually furnished; choose No. 14 if it's luxury you're after.

Shibden Mill Fold,
HALIFAX, HX3 7UL
Tel.: (01422)365840
Website: www.shibdenmillinn.com

Signposted off A 58, 2.25 mi northeast of Halifax. Parking.

PRICES
Meals: £ 14 (lunch and early dinner) and a la carte £ 27/35

11 rooms:
£ 95/192

MAP: 36

CLOSING TIMES
Closed dinner 25-26 December and 1 January

Moorhouse's Shibden Bitter, Little Valley Withens and Black Sheep Bitter

CROSS KEYS

A traditional inn serving hearty British fare

This traditional brick-built pub stands in a regenerated area of the city and was once the watering hole for workers of the 19C Round Foundry; the first floor dining room is named after James Watt, the inventor of the steam engine (although it's been said he stole many ideas from his inebriated workers!) It's a cosy, friendly place featuring flagged floors, old beams and exposed brick, along with welcoming wood-burning fires in winter - and it's always busy, so be sure to book. The cooking is hearty, tasty and British through-and-through: lunch sees a simple menu of sandwiches and pub classics such as cottage pie or chicken with pearl barley broth; dinner is more substantial, featuring the likes of chicken liver pâté and braised lamb shank.

107 Water Ln,
The Round Foundry, **LEEDS**, LS11 5WD
Tel.: (0113)2433711
Website: www.the-crosskeys.com

Just south of the River Aire in the Holbeck area. Metered parking adjacent.

PRICES
Meals: a la carte £ 23/34

MAP: 37

CLOSING TIMES
Closed 25-26 December and 1 January
booking essential

Kirkstall Prototype and Ilkley Dinner Ale

OLIVE BRANCH

Bustling pub offering unfussy, generous cooking

This roadside pub's rather bland exterior gives little indication as to what's inside: a central bar, four cosy rooms, plenty of character in the form of stone walls and exposed beams, and a chatty, bustling atmosphere. The menu offers lots of choice, with dishes like salad of Bury black pudding, crisp belly pork or Yorkshire Blue soufflé; cooking is straightforward and generous, and lets ingredients speak for themselves. The pub is particularly popular for its well-sourced steaks and holds steak nights every Tuesday; seafood isn't neglected either, with a daily blackboard menu and fish supper nights on Fridays. There's a secluded garden and terrace as well as comfy, modern bedrooms: take your pick from 'Duck', 'Topiary' and 'Serengeti'.

Manchester Rd,
MARSDEN, HD7 6LU
Tel.: (01484)844487
Website: www.olivebranch.uk.com

1 mi northeast on A 62. Parking.

PRICES
Meals: £ 20 and a la carte £ 22/45

3 rooms:
£ 60/110

MAP: 38

CLOSING TIMES
Open daily
dinner only and Sunday lunch

Nook Blond and guest ales

SCOTLAND

Scotland may be small, but its variety is immense. The vivacity of Glasgow can seem a thousand miles from the vast peatland wilderness of Caithness and Sutherland's Flow Country; the arty vibe of Georgian Edinburgh a world away from the remote and tranquil Ardnamurchan peninsula. And how many people link Scotland to its beaches? But wide golden sands trim the Atlantic at South Harris, and the coastline of the Highlands boasts empty islands and turquoise waters. Meantime, Fife's coast draws golf fans to St Andrews and the more secretive delights of the East Neuk, an area of fishing villages and stone harbours. Wherever you travel, the scent of a dramatic history prevails in the shape of castles, cathedrals and rugged lochside monuments to the heroes of old.

Food and drink embraces the traditional, too, typified by Aberdeen's famous Malt Whisky Trail. And what better than Highland game, fresh fish from the Tweed or haggis, neeps and tatties to complement a grand Scottish hike...

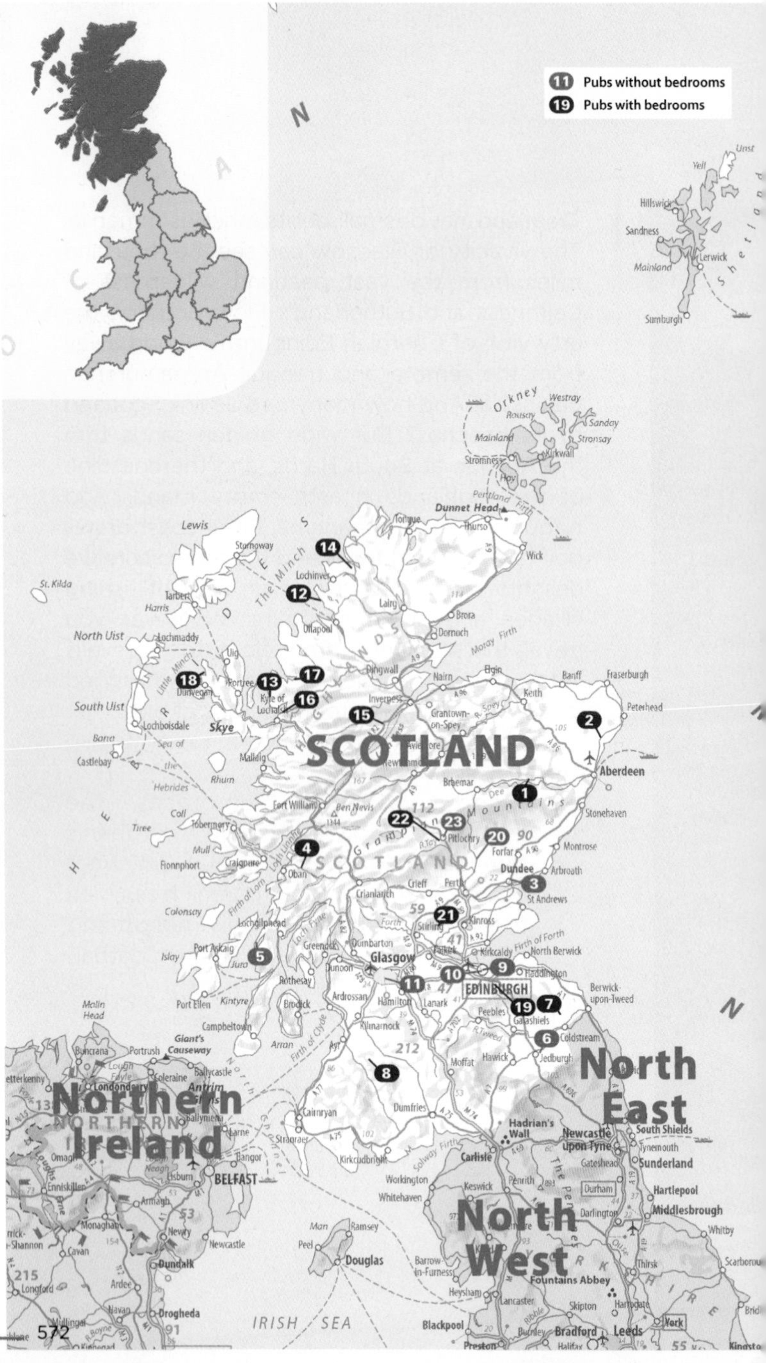

11 Pubs without bedrooms
19 Pubs with bedrooms
SCOTLAND
North East
North West
Northern Ireland
Orkney
Shetland
Lewis
Harris
North Uist
South Uist
Skye
St. Kilda
Stornoway
Tarbert
Lochmaddy
Lochboisdale
Barra
Castlebay
Dunvegan
Portree
Kyle of Lochalsh
Uig
Rhum
Coll
Tiree
Mull
Tobermory
Fionnphort
Craignure
Oban
Colonsay
Islay
Jura
Port Askaig
Port Ellen
Kintyre
Campbeltown
Arran
Brodick
Rothesay
Dunoon
Lochgilphead
Greenock
Dumbarton
Glasgow
Ardrossan
Hamilton
Lanark
Kilmarnock
Ayr
Cairnryan
Stranraer
Kirkcudbright
Dumfries
Moffat
Hawick
Jedburgh
Coldstream
Galashiels
Peebles
Berwick-upon-Tweed
EDINBURGH
Haddington
North Berwick
Kirkcaldy
Firth of Forth
Kinross
Falkirk
Stirling
Crieff
Perth
Crianlarich
St Andrews
Dundee
Arbroath
Forfar
Montrose
Pitlochry
Stonehaven
Aberdeen
Peterhead
Fraserburgh
Banff
Keith
Elgin
Nairn
Grantown-on-Spey
Inverness
Aviemore
Newtonmore
Braemar
Dingwall
Ullapool
Lochinver
Lairg
Tongue
Thurso
Wick
Brora
Dornoch
Moray Firth
Dunnet Head
Pentland Firth
Stromness
Kirkwall
Hoy
Mainland
Rousay
Westray
Sanday
Stronsay
Fort William
Ben Nevis
Mallaig
Grampian Mountains
The Minch
Little Minch
Sea of the Hebrides
Firth of Lorn
Loch Fyne
Loch Linnhe
Firth of Clyde
North Channel
Solway Firth
Unst
Yell
Hillswick
Sandness
Lerwick
Sumburgh
Giant's Causeway
Portrush
Coleraine
Ballycastle
Antrim
Londonderry
Buncrana
Letterkenny
Ballymena
Larne
Bangor
BELFAST
Lisburn
Omagh
Enniskillen
Armagh
Monaghan
Newry
Newcastle
Cavan
Dundalk
Ardee
Navan
Drogheda
Longford
Mullingar
IRISH SEA
Man
Ramsey
Peel
Douglas
Carlisle
Hadrian's Wall
Keswick
Penrith
Workington
Whitehaven
Barrow-in-Furness
Heysham
Lancaster
Blackpool
Preston
Skipton
Fountains Abbey
Harrogate
Bradford
Leeds
Halifax
York
Thirsk
Newcastle upon Tyne
Gateshead
South Shields
Tynemouth
Sunderland
Durham
Hartlepool
Middlesbrough
Darlington
Whitby
Scarborough

BOAT INN (N)

Carefully prepared, traditional dishes

Pubs the length and breadth of Britain serve traditional bar meals like fish and chips and steak pie - what makes the Boat Inn stand out is the care put into preparing these dishes. The menu is kept short and simple while portions are generous; the occasional international dish makes an appearance - perhaps a Thai beef salad - and there are freshly baked cakes on the counter. A train runs around a shelf in the bright front room, there's a cosy bar at the back, a smart private dining room called the Pine Loft and spacious bedrooms which come with their own kitchenettes. The pub's name comes from the ferry which used to cross the River Dee here and the inn is reputed to be haunted by the ghost of a passenger who perished on the crossing.

Charleston Rd,
ABOYNE, AB34 5EL
Tel.: (01339)886137
Website: www.theboatinnaboyne.co.uk

On B 968 just along from the village green. Parking.

PRICES
Meals: a la carte £ 18/27

8 rooms:
£ 70/105

MAP: 1

CLOSING TIMES
Closed 25 December and 1-2 January

Inveralmond Ossian and Cairngorm Trade Winds and Stag

COCK AND BULL

A fun place that doesn't take itself too seriously

The Cock and Bull is a quirky, atmospheric pub with a sense of fun befitting its name; check out the mural on the men's toilet door and the profusion of knick-knacks throughout. There's a choice of three rooms in which to dine: a cosy lounge with an open fire and low leather sofas, a more formal dining room and an airy conservatory. Wherever you sit, the menu's the same, and there's plenty of choice. You'll find classics like Arbroath smokie kedgeree or Cullen skink, alongside some more restaurant-style dishes such as confit pork belly or mushroom, watercress and ricotta tart; dishes are satisfying and everything arrives neatly presented. Some of the contemporary bedrooms are in a nearby annexe – a complimentary shuttle service is provided.

Ellon Rd,
Blairton, **BALMEDIE**, AB23 8XY
Tel.: (01358)743249
Website: www.thecockandbull.co.uk

On A 90 6 mi north of Aberdeen. Parking.

PRICES
Meals: a la carte £ 22/36

4 rooms:
£ 95/120

MAP: 2

CLOSING TIMES
Open daily

Burnside 3 Bullz

DROVERS INN

Freshly baked breads and local estate produce

Good cooking relies on good ingredients, so if the owner of a pub also has estates nearby that supply much of the produce, it's little wonder that the chef seems so contented. This remote Highland inn with its immaculate lawns was once a crofter's cottage. The bar with its open fires is a lovely spot but there's also a more formal dining room - to which the freshly baked breads add their wonderful aroma - and to the side, a lovely beamed room with a map of the area covering one entire wall. The well-priced menu makes particularly good use of the abundant local produce, such as game and venison from the shoots. Further value for money is provided by a wine list that eschews the usual 'mark-ups' and instead makes a uniform corkage charge.

MEMUS, DD8 3TY
Tel.: (01307)860322
Website: www.the-drovers.com

4 mi north of Kirriemuir by B 955 and minor road east. Parking.

PRICES
Meals: a la carte £ 24/39

MAP: 3

CLOSING TIMES
Closed 25-26 December

Inveralmond and Orkney Ales

TAYNUILT N

They serve their own bespoke lager on tap

For centuries, this inn has been a staging post on the main road to Oban; Coleridge and Wordsworth even enjoyed its hospitality back in 1803. These days it's run with pride and passion by the McNulty family and cooking is the main focus. Menus offer tasty pub classics with a twist: steak and triple-cooked chips is a favourite, while more adventurous dishes might include Gigha halibut with razor clams. The pub sits between Loch Etive and Loch Awe and its well-kept bedrooms are named after these and other Scottish lochs. It may be simply furnished but what it lacks in character, it more than makes up for in the warmth of its welcome. And there aren't many pubs who can claim to have their own bespoke lager on tap: pint of Taynuilt, anyone?

TAYNUILT, PA35 1JN
Tel.: (01866)822437
Website: www.taynuilthotel.co.uk

On main A 85 road through village, 12 mi east of Oban. Parking.

PRICES
Meals: a la carte £ 22/46

10 rooms:
£ 60/195

MAP: 4

CLOSING TIMES
Restricted opening in January

Loch Fyne Jarl and
Harviestoun Ales

TAYVALLICH INN

Extensive connections bring in top quality seafood

The Tayvallich Inn's sign shows the silhouette of a lobster, which gives a clue as to what this pub is all about. The chef knows a thing or two about seafood and you can expect to see plenty of locally caught fish and shellfish including langoustines, mussels, lobster and lemon sole - as well as scallops by the bucket load; but the menu also offers classic pub dishes like steak and chips and a popular curry of the day. The owners worked on nearby fish farms before taking over the reins here and make the most of their extensive connections to source the best produce possible. Dine in the bar, in the more formal dining area or out on the decked terrace, with its rustic style bench seating and picturesque views out over the bay.

TAYVALLICH, PA31 8PL
Tel.: (01546)870282
Website: www.tayvallichinn.com

12 mi west of Lochgilphead by A 816, B 841 and B 8025; on west shore of Loch Sween. Parking.

PRICES
Meals: a la carte £ 18/38

MAP: 5

CLOSING TIMES
Closed Monday November-March

Loch Ness Red Ness and Hoppy Ness,

ANCRUM CROSS KEYS N

Watch the chef at work

You just know that a pub's going to serve a good pint when the river at the bottom of the garden is called the River Ale! The fact that the man in charge also owns the nearby Scottish Borders Brewery has got to help - and judging by the number of locals in the rustic front bar of this 200 year old pub, they certainly seem to agree. But what about the food? Well, what really sets this place apart is the cooking - and we're not talking everyday pub grub. In the style of a modern city restaurant, menus list only the ingredients of a dish - 'seared mackerel, blood orange, olive powder, fennel pollen, red basil' - and dishes are carefully crafted and tasty with a refined edge. Sit in the larger of the dining rooms to watch the chef at work.

The Green,
ANCRUM, TD8 6XH
Tel.: (01835)830242
Website: www.ancrumcrosskeys.com

Between St Boswells and Jedburgh signposted off A 68. Parking around The Green.

PRICES
Meals: a la carte £ 18/36

MAP: 6

CLOSING TIMES
Closed Monday, Tuesday and lunch Wednesday

Scottish Borders Ales

WHEATSHEAF

Seafood from Eyemouth and meat from Border farms

Set in the heart of the village, overlooking the green, this substantial stone inn is far from your typical pub. Inside there are numerous sofa-filled rooms and two small dining areas - one linen-laid, the other with an attractive pine ceiling and furniture to match. The hands-on owners are extremely passionate when it comes to food and, in winter, they only serve lunch at weekends so that they can give dinner their full attention. The extensive evening menu offers ambitious dishes such as wood pigeon tartlet, followed by Scottish venison saddle or ballotine of partridge. Specials feature seafood from Eyemouth and meat comes from the surrounding border farms and is subsequently smoked on-site. Bedrooms are spacious, cosy and well-equipped.

Main St,
SWINTON, TD11 3JJ
Tel.: (01890)860257
Website: www.wheatsheaf-swinton.co.uk

In the centre of the village. Plenty of parking on the road.

PRICES
Meals: a la carte £ 23/42

14 rooms:
£ 89/159

MAP: 7

CLOSING TIMES
Closed 24 and 26 December
booking advisable

Stewart Brewing Edinburgh Gold and Holyrood Scottish Borders Foxy Blonde and Game Bird

SORN INN

Family-run pub serving international dishes

It's a real family affair here, with the father checking you in to one of the bedrooms and his son cooking your meals. The first clues as to the quality of food are the framed menus and the copy of the chefs' bible, 'Larousse' - and the cooking doesn't disappoint. The chef adopts an international approach, a result of his time spent on the QE2, so along with prime Scottish beef are dishes like wood pigeon with polenta and chicken with banana rice. There's plenty of flexibility here too: some dishes come in a choice of sizes and you can choose to have them either sitting in a high-backed leather chair in the restaurant or with your dog beside your feet in the pub. The blackboard specials are always worth a look and the lunch menu is a steal.

35 Main St,
SORN, KA5 6HU
Tel.: (01290)551305
Website: www.sorninn.com

In centre of village. Parking.

PRICES
Meals: a la carte £ 22/56

4 rooms:
£ 50/95

MAP: 8

CLOSING TIMES
Closed 6-16 January and Monday

Orkney Corncrake

THE SCRAN & SCALLIE

A place to share good food with the whole family

Found in the smart, village-like suburb of Stockbridge, this pub is the more casual venture of well-known chefs Tom Kitchin and Dominic Jack. It might seem an unusual name but 'Scran' means food and 'Scallie' means children, which reflects their desire for good food to be shared with the whole family. Pass through the heavy wood furnished bar to the dining room with its mix of rustic and contemporary décor; some walls are brick, others are stone, and some are boldly wallpapered and hung with old framed recipes. Extensive menus follow a 'Nature to Plate' philosophy, focusing on the classical and the local - and a map in the bar locates their suppliers. Where else can you start with sheep's heid broth and finish with jelly and ice cream?

1 Comely Bank Rd,
Stockbridge, **EDINBURGH**, EH4 1DT
Tel.: (0131)3326281
Website: www.scranandscallie.com

On the northwestern side of the city. On-street meter parking.

PRICES
Meals: £ 15 (weekday lunch) and
a la carte £ 19/54

MAP: 9

CLOSING TIMES
Closed 25 December
booking advisable

Harviestoun The Ridge,
Stewart Edinburgh Gold,
Isle of Skye Black Cuillin and
Orkney IPA

SHIP ON THE SHORE

This ship-like pub's speciality is fruits de mer

With its neat blue façade inset with ship's navigation lights and modelled on the Royal Yacht Britannia, this period building on the quayside looks ready to set sail. Inside, the walls are papered with European maritime charts, scrubbed wooden floors mimic a ship's deck and it's filled with nautical bric à brac. The kitchen follows a philosophy of 'sustainable Scottish seafood served simply with style', and 99% of the menu is just that. Classic dishes such as fishcakes and Cullen skink are mainstays and there are some more unusual offerings such as crispy curried squid with lime and mint yoghurt. What draws people from far and wide though, is their 'Fruits de Mer' platters. Champagne is the recommended drink; available by the bottle or glass.

24-26 The Shore,
LEITH, EH6 6QN
Tel.: (0131)5550409
Website: www.theshipontheshore.co.uk

On east side of river. On-street parking.

PRICES
Meals: a la carte £ 24/40

MAP: 10

CLOSING TIMES
Closed 24-26 December

Belhaven Best

THE FINNIESTON

Small and cosy, with seafood from local waters

This was once a conventional old boozer but an enthusiastic young team with a real passion for food and drink have resurrected it, and it now specialises in seafood dishes and gin-based cocktails. It's small and cosy, with an intriguing ceiling, a welcoming fire and lots of booths. The anchor motif on the glass reminds you where their strengths lie and the Popeye and Olive Oyl pictures on the toilet doors continue the theme. All of the seafood is from Scottish waters, with mackerel from Peterhead, langoustines from Troon and oysters from Cumbrae. Dishes are light, tasty and neatly presented, relying on just a handful of ingredients so that flavours are clear; if you have the fish and chips, 50p will be donated to the local Fishermen's Mission.

1125 Argyle St,
GLASGOW, G3 8ND
Tel.: (0141)2222884
Website: www.thefinniestonbar.com

On the west side close to Kelvingrove. On-street parking.

PRICES
Meals: a la carte £ 24/55

MAP: 11

CLOSING TIMES
Closed 24-26 December

No real ales offered

SUMMER ISLES (BAR)

A tiny pub with a tiny menu and big views

Set to the side of the Summer Isles Hotel, this tiny pub was originally an old crofters' bar and dates back to the mid-19C. Still popular with the locals today, it boasts two snug rooms filled with black ash tables, a large lawned area with bench seating and a small two-table terrace affording glorious views over the Summer Isles. Concise, daily changing menus have a strong seafood base, offering baguettes, salads and platters at lunchtime, supplemented by more substantial blackboard specials in the evening; although the star of the show has to be the plump, tasty langoustines, which are locally caught and best enjoyed with a chilled glass of Sauvignon Blanc. Comfortable bedrooms are available in the adjoining hotel.

ACHILTIBUIE, IV26 2YG
Tel.: (01854)622282
Website: www.summerisleshotel.com

15 mi northwest of Ullapool by A 835 and minor road west from Drumrunie. Parking.

PRICES
Meals: a la carte £ 20/38

13 rooms:
£ 125/240

MAP: 12

CLOSING TIMES
Closed November-March
bookings not accepted

An Teallach Ales

APPLECROSS INN

The freshest of seafood and a stunning seascape

Arrival at Applecross can involve a drive over the hair-raising, single-track Bealach na Ba, with its stunning views and hairpin bends; learner drivers and vertigo sufferers should travel the less scenic route along the coast road instead. This is an unpretentious sort of place, with a wood burning stove and an abundance of pine panelling. Service is friendly and the atmosphere, bustling; on sunny days, the terrace is unsurprisingly the most popular spot. Food-wise, the highlight is the freshest of seafood, often straight out of the sea and sometimes from within sight of the door; expect prawns, crabs and lobster from Applecross and oysters and mussels from Skye. Simple bedrooms in the next-door fishermen's cottages have marvellous sea views.

Shore St,
APPLECROSS, IV54 8LR
Tel.: (01520)744262
Website: www.applecross.uk.com

From Kishorn via Bealach na Ba or round by Shieldaig and along the coast road. Parking.

PRICES
Meals: a la carte £ 19/40

7 rooms:
£ 80/130

MAP: 13

CLOSING TIMES
Closed 25 December and 1 January
booking essential

An Teallach Crofters Pale Ale and Isle of Skye Hebridean Gold

KYLESKU (BAR)

Spectacular scenery and a homely feel

Breathtaking views of Loch Glendhu and the spectacular surrounding scenery make this inn an essential stop-off point if you're ever in the area. Friendly staff welcome guests and there's a cosy, homely atmosphere in the spacious fire-lit bar. Sup on local ale while you trade tales with walkers and cyclists, before settling down to eat seafood so local it practically swam in the door. Langoustines and fish come from the jetty in front of the bar and mussels are rope grown 200 yards away. Classic dishes might include salmon fishcakes or a fish pie, a satisfying bowl of soup or a platter of mature local cheeses; if you're after something a little more meaty, try a mature local steak. Eight comfortable bedrooms are upstairs in the hotel.

KYLESKU, IV27 4HW
Tel.: (01971)502231
Website: www.kyleskuhotel.co.uk

32 mi north of Ullapool by A 835, A 837 and A 894. On street parking.

PRICES
Meals: a la carte £ 16/43

8 rooms:
£ 65/120

MAP: 14

CLOSING TIMES
Closed November-February

An Teallach and Isle of Skye Ales

LOCH NESS INN

Dishes champion local produce

Considering its position, it would have been all too easy to make this inn a paean to all things 'Nessie' but thankfully, the only sign of the famous monster is in the pub's logo. The one place where the pub's location is justly celebrated is on the menu, so expect hearty, robust, flavoursome dishes which champion Scottish produce; perhaps Cullen skink, loin of venison or whisky-flambéed haggis. There are two main parts to the pub: the small Brewery Bar, home to locals and walkers fresh from the Great Glen Way; and the open-plan Lewiston restaurant with its wood burning stove and bright timbered beams. Service is sweet and well-meaning – and if you're after somewhere to lay your head, you'll find the bedrooms spacious and comfortable.

LEWISTON, IV63 6UW
Tel.: (01456)450991
Website: www.staylochness.co.uk

Between Inverness and Fort Augustus on A 82. Parking.

PRICES
Meals: a la carte £ 18/38

12 rooms:
£ 65/112

MAP: 15

CLOSING TIMES
Open daily

Loch Ness Brewery Ales
and Belhaven Best

PLOCKTON HOTEL

Menus keep things pleasingly local

With its distinctive black exterior, this one-time ships' chandlery is easy to spot. Owned and run by the Pearson family for over 20 years, it offers a warm welcome as well as stunning views over Loch Carron to the mountains beyond. Most of the action takes place in the wood-panelled bar, with its red leather banquettes, tartan carpets and wood burning stove; though if the weather's good, the front terrace fills up the fastest. Cooking is honest, fresh and hearty, with a strong Scottish influence, so expect Talisker whisky pâté, Plockton smokies, haggis and whisky or herring in oatmeal – and don't miss the Plockton prawns. Simple, comfortable bedrooms are split between the pub and an annexe; those to the front have wonderful views.

41 Harbour St,
PLOCKTON, IV52 8TN
Tel.: (01599)544274
Website: www.plocktonhotel.co.uk

5 mi north of Kyle of Lochalsh. Parking 50 yards away in village car park.

PRICES
Meals: a la carte £ 18/36

15 rooms:
£ 45/140

MAP: 16

CLOSING TIMES
Open daily

Highland Orkney IPA and Seafire, Cromarty Happy Chappy and Cairngorm Mountain Blue

TORRIDON INN

Perfect for those who enjoy outdoor pursuits

This is an easy place to miss, as from the outside it looks more like a Tourist Information Office than a pub, but it's well worth a visit, whether for a drink, a bite to eat or to take part in one of their many activities, from glen walks and kayaking to rock climbing and gorge scrambling. If these sound more like spectator sports to you, then simply sit back and enjoy the tranquil surroundings and glorious loch views from either the restaurant or the spacious, part-panelled bar decorated with stags' antlers and Ordnance Survey maps. The interesting menu and daily specials feature satisfying walkers' favourites and a few more elaborate dishes such as cheese soufflé or seared scallops. Simple, modern bedrooms are in the old stables.

TORRIDON, IV22 2EY
Tel.: (01445)791242
Website: www.thetorridon.com

1.5 mi south of Torridon on A 896. Parking.

PRICES
Meals: a la carte £ 21/36

12 rooms:
£ 110

MAP: 17

CLOSING TIMES
Closed mid-December-January and Monday-Thursday November, February and March

An Teallach Ben Damph, Cairngorm Trade Winds and Isle of Skye Red Cuillin

STEIN INN

The oldest inn on Skye offers wonderful loch views

With 'INN' emblazoned in bold letters on either end, there's no missing the oldest inn on Skye; a family-run establishment in an idyllic spot, with views to the Outer Hebrides. Sit on the grassy terrace or by the wood-burning stove in the cosy bar, with its exposed stone walls and nautical artefacts. The fishing boats bobbing along on the loch might well be bringing in the latest catch; local seafood dominates the menu and is what you should go for - perhaps some sweet fresh shrimps, half a lobster or some rollmop herrings for lunch, and Isle of Skye mussels or lemon sole for dinner. Bedrooms are simple and comfortable; they may not have TVs but with such a superb view - and over 90 whiskies on offer in the bar - who needs one?

MacLeod Terr,
Stein, **WATERNISH**, IV55 8GA
Tel.: (01470)592362
Website: www.stein-inn.co.uk

22 mi northwest of Portree by A 87, A 850 and B 886; on the shore of Loch Bay. Parking.

PRICES
Meals: a la carte £ 17/33

5 rooms:
£ 45/115

MAP: 18

CLOSING TIMES
Closed 1 January and 25 December

Caledonian Deuchars IPA,
Isle of Skye Red Cuillin and
Cairngorm Trade Winds

SUN INN

Superbly run pub with an extensive menu

This smartly refurbished pub, set on the main road from Edinburgh to Galashiels, started life in the 17C as a blacksmith's and only later became a coaching inn. It's a large place, consisting of two open-fired rooms with part wood and stone-faced walls hung with contemporary black and white photos of the area. Menus are extensive and feature good quality local produce, with suppliers listed on a blackboard. Lunch keeps things simple - you might find ham hock potato cakes, kipper pâté or liver and bacon - while dinner is more ambitious, with the likes of monkfish wrapped in ham, pig's cheek and black pudding or sea bass with saffron risotto. Completing the picture are smart, modern bedrooms boasting handmade furniture and Egyptian cotton linen.

Lothian Bridge,
DALKEITH, EH22 4TR
Tel.: (0131)6632456
Website: www.thesuninnedinburgh.co.uk

2 mi southwest of Dalkeith on A 7. Parking.

PRICES
Meals: £ 14 (weekdays) and
a la carte £ 20/39

5 rooms:
£ 75/150

MAP: 19

CLOSING TIMES
Closed 26 December and 1 January

Stewart Brewing Pentland IPA

DALMORE INN

A surprisingly stylish room hides within

With its whisky kegs out the front, it may look like a traditional pub, but cross the threshold and the Dalmore reveals a surprisingly stylish modern interior. Brightly coloured walls hung with photos of Scottish scenes are juxtaposed with old stonework; giant potted plants occupy the centre of the room; and a life-sized picture of a Highland cow greets you at the door. The cooking is good value, unfussy and full of flavour – everything is freshly prepared to order and they like to use Scottish produce wherever possible; you might find ham hock terrine or Arbroath smokie risotto, followed by venison and black pudding meatballs or a homemade burger topped with haggis. Service is warm, welcoming and well-executed.

Perth Rd,
BLAIRGOWRIE, PH10 6QB
Tel.: (01250)871088
Website: www.dalmoreinn.com

1.5 mi southwest of Blairgowrie on A 93. Parking.

PRICES
Meals: £ 10 (lunch) and a la carte £ 21/40

MAP: 20

CLOSING TIMES
Closed 25 December and 1-2 January

No real ales offered

TORMAUKIN INN

A friendly team lead the way

After a breathtaking drive along the A823, stop at the door of this characterful inn, where the owner and manageress will welcome you as if you're old friends. Cross over the threshold and a huge granite fireplace greets you; pass by it and you'll come to a dark beamed bar and a spacious, classically decorated dining room. The well-priced, carefully executed dishes are largely traditional - you might find home-smoked salmon or pressed terrine of game for starters, followed by steak and Guinness casserole or chicken stuffed with haggis; while tasty homemade breads and ice creams are offered at either end of your meal. Smart, tartan-floored bedrooms are spread between the inn, a stable block and a chalet; the former are the most comfortable.

GLENDEVON, FK14 7JY
Tel.: (01259)781252
Website: www.tormaukinhotel.co.uk

In centre of village on A 823. Parking.

PRICES
Meals: a la carte £ 20/39

13 rooms:
£ 50/80

MAP: 21

CLOSING TIMES
Closed 25 December

Harviestoun Ales and Kelburn Misty Law

INN ON THE TAY

Superbly located and offering great water views

As its name suggests, this smart, modern inn is located on the banks of the River Tay; head to the large dining room for superb views over the water, where you'll often see people rafting or canoeing. The bar menu offers the likes of scampi and chips or a burger with mozzarella and red onion jam, while the all-day menu is a little more ambitious, featuring dishes such as confit spring rolls or hot smoked salmon with beetroot and crème fraiche. If you're planning to stay the night, you'll find the bedrooms comfy and cosy; if you've not long to stop, pop in for coffee and a slice of homemade cake in the bar - try to bag one of the squashy sofas beside the log burning stove. The owners are cheery and welcoming, and the atmosphere is laid-back.

GRANDTULLY, PH9 0PL
Tel.: (01887)840760
Website: www.theinnonthetay.co.uk

5 mi northeast of Aberfeldy on A 827. Parking.

PRICES
Meals: a la carte £ 19/36

6 rooms:
£ 75/110

MAP: 22

CLOSING TIMES
Open daily

Inveralmond Ales

AULD SMIDDY INN

Satisfyingly hearty dishes follow the seasons

As you might have guessed, this building started life as a blacksmith's - before spending a short spell as a tea room and later finding its calling as a pub. A small but colourful garden stands out against smartly whitewashed walls and there's a large terrace and courtyard round the back. Inside it has a likeable simplicity, with polished slate floors and wood burning stoves; sit at the front beside the counter or in the rear room where the blacksmith would once have worked. In the summer, salads and fish dishes fill the menu; in colder months, the choice may be smaller but the portions certainly aren't, with hearty classics such as haggis, neeps and tatties or local steak, sausage and ale pie. They also hold a seafood festival twice a year.

154 Atholl Rd,
PITLOCHRY, PH16 5AG
Tel.: (01796)472356
Website: www.auldsmiddyinn.co.uk

At northern end of the main street. Pay and display parking nearby.

PRICES
Meals: a la carte £ 20/41

MAP: 23

CLOSING TIMES
Closed last week January-first week February and 25-26 December

Inveralmond Ales and Orkney Ales

WALES

It's nearly six hundred years since Owen Glyndawr escaped the clutches of the English to become a national hero, and in all that time the Welsh passion for unity has bound the country together like a scarlet-shirted scrum. It may be only 170 miles from north to south, but Wales contains great swathes of beauty, such as the dark and craggy heights of Snowdonia's ninety mountain peaks, the rolling sandstone bluffs of the Brecon Beacons, and Pembrokeshire's tantalising golden beaches. Bottle-nosed dolphins love it here too, arriving each summer at New Quay in Cardigan Bay. Highlights abound: formidable Harlech Castle dominates its coast, and Bala Lake has a railway that steams along its gentle shores.

Hay-on-Wye's four pubs and eighteen bookshops turn perceptions on their head, and Welsh cuisine is causing a surprise or two as well: the country teems with great raw ingredients now employed to their utmost potential, from the humblest cockle to the slenderest slice of succulent lamb.

Pubs without bedrooms
Pubs with bedrooms
LIVERPOOL
Liverpool Bay
Bootle
Wallasey
Birkenhead
Bebington
Ellesmere Port
Chester
Wrexham/ Wrecsam
North West
Wigan
St. Helens
Warrington
Widnes
Runcorn
Crewe
Nantwich
Whitchurch
Shrewsbury
Telford
West Midlands
Great Ormes Head
Llandudno
Colwyn Bay/ Bae Colwyn
Conwy
Prestatyn
Rhyl
Abergele
Holywell
St Asaph
Denbigh/ Dinbych
Mold/Yr Wyddgrug
Ruthin/ Rhuthun
Llangollen
Oswestry
Holyhead/ Caergybi
Holy Island
Isle of Anglesey
Amlwch
Llangefni
Beaumaris
Bangor
Menai Bridge
Plas Newydd
Caernarfon
Caernarfon Bay
Llanberis
Snowdon
Beddgelert
Snowdonia
Blaenau Ffestiniog
Betws-y-Coed
Llanrwst
Porthmadog
Criccieth
Pwllheli
Abersoch
Nefyn
Aberdaron
Lleyn Peninsula
Harlech
Bala
National Park
Dolgellau
Cader Idris
Machynlleth
Tywyn
Aberdovey
WALES
Welshpool/ Trallwng
Newtown/Y Drenewydd
THA CLIATH

Llangurig
Devil's Bridge
Llanrhystud
Aberaeron
New Quay
Synod Inn
Aberporth
Cardigan
Newport
Fishguard/
Abergwaun
Strumble Head
Pembrokeshire Coast National Park
St. David's Head
St. David's
Haverfordwest/Hwlffordd
St. Bride's Bay
Milford Haven/
Aberdaugleddau
Neyland
PembrokeDock
Pembroke
St. Govan's Head
Narberth
Whitland
Tenby/
Dinbych-y-pysgod
Saundersfoot
Pendine
Carmarthen Bay
St. Clears
Carmarthen/
Caerfyrddin
Crymmych
Newcastle Emlyn
Llandysul
Lampeter
Tregaron
Elan Valley
Rhayader
Llandrindod Wells
Builth Wells
Llanwrtyd Wells
Llandovery
Llandeilo
Llangadog
Sennybridge
Brecon
Black Mountain
Brecon Beacons National Park
Crickhowell
Talgarth
Black Mountains
Hay-on-Wye
Knighton
Kington
Presteigne
Ludlow
Tenbury Wells
Leominster
Bromyard
Hereford
Llanthony Priory
Pontrilas
Ross-on-Wye
Monmouth/
Trefynwy
Abergavenny
Raglan
Usk
Tintern Abbey
Coleford
Lydney
Chepstow
SEVERN BRIDGE
Kidwelly
Cross Hands
Ammanford
Burry Port
Llanelli
Pontarddulais
Pontardawe
SWANSEA/
ABERTAWE
Rhossili
Worms Head
Port-Eynon
The Mumbles
Port Talbot
Neath/
Castell-Nedd
Aberdare/
Aberdar
Merthyr Tydfil
Ebbw Vale/
Glynebwy
Tredegar
Bargoed
Maesteg
Mountain Ash
Rhondda
Pontypridd
Caerphilly/Caerffili
Cwmbrân
Pontypool
Risca
Bedwas
Newport/
Casnewydd
CARDIFF/
CAERDYDD
Bridgend/
Pen-y-bont
Porthcawl
Cowbridge
Penarth
Barry/
Barri
Severn Estuary
Avonmouth
Portishead
Clevedon
Clifton Bridge
Weston-super-Mare
Burnham-on-Sea
South West
Cheddar Gorge
Wells
BRISTOL CHANNEL
Lundy
Ilfracombe
Combe Martin
Lynton
Lynmouth
Porlock
Minehead

WHITE EAGLE

Stunning sea views from the terrace

Set in a small coastal hamlet on the peninsula, this pub boasts stunning sea views from its spacious decked terrace. From the outside it may look more like a restaurant but swing a right through the door and you'll find the regulars nursing their pints in the cosy bar. It's rightly popular, so you might have to wait for a table; fill your time by glancing over the display of the owners' business history - they also own Timpson Shoe Repairs. The monthly menu offers something for everyone and dishes arrive well-presented, in a contemporary style - whether it's the huge battered haddock and chips or pan-fried salmon with prawn and chorizo butter. Daily fish specials and regular themed weeks (maybe pie, sausage, Indian or Italian) feature.

RHOSCOLYN, LL65 2NJ
Tel.: (01407)860267
Website: www.white-eagle.co.uk

5 mi south of Holyhead by B 4545 and minor road south. Parking.

PRICES
Meals: £ 16 and a la carte £ 20/39

MAP: 1

CLOSING TIMES
Closed 25 December

Conwy Honey Fayre, Great Orme and Thornbridge Ales

Y POLYN

Welcoming to locals and visitors alike

The food is the focus at this small, rustic and pleasantly unfussy pub, which sits on a busy country road close to a stream and affords pleasant views. Mark, the owner, was previously an inspector with the AA, hence all the restaurant menus on display, which make quite a talking point. Pleasingly, he's just as welcoming to those on their first visit as to his trusty band of regulars. His wife Sue looks after the kitchen and her cooking is stout, filling and British at heart; the slow-cooked meats, fresh salads, satisfying soups and classic puds all hit the spot, both with the lunchtime couples and the more youthful crowd that gathers in the evening. Prices are kept realistic and the complimentary filtered mineral water is a nice touch.

NANTGAREDIG, SA32 7LH
Tel.: (01267)290000
Website: www.ypolynrestaurant.co.uk

6 mi east of Carmarthen by A 4300 on B 4310. Parking.

PRICES
Meals: £ 14 (weekday lunch)/35
and a la carte £ 27/34

MAP: 2

CLOSING TIMES
Closed Sunday dinner and Monday
booking advisable

Otley 01, 03 and Tomos
Watkin's Cwrw Braf

HARBOURMASTER

Nautical, New England styling and harbour views

With its vibrant blue exterior, you'll spot this place a mile off; not that the owners need worry about being noticed, as their reputation for good food and hospitality goes before them. As the name suggests, it once belonged to the harbourmaster and it offers lovely views out across the water. There's a bar-lounge with slate walls, a nautical New England style and an oval pewter-topped counter, as well as a modern dining room - make a play for 'cwtch', a table offering excellent harbour views. Choose between the bar menu or a more substantial evening à la carte supplemented by daily specials. Smart bedrooms, split between the house and a nearby cottage, are brightly decorated and well-equipped; some boast oversized windows or terraces.

Quay Par,
ABERAERON, SA46 0BA
Tel.: (01545)570755
Website: www.harbour-master.com

In town centre overlooking the harbour. Parking on street and around the harbour wall.

PRICES
Meals: a la carte £ 30/44

13 rooms:
£ 65/250

MAP: 3

CLOSING TIMES
Closed 25-26 December

Purple Moose Glaslyn and HM Best Bitter

Y FFARMERS

This really is the centre of the village

More than just the village pub, the passionately run Y Ffarmers is also the village hub. It's a characterful whitewashed building in a remote, picturesque valley, and was originally a farm and later a tax collector's office. With no village hall, life here really revolves around the place, which hosts everything from yoga classes and quiz nights to meetings of the local choir and bee keeping group. Turn right for the locals bar or left for the homely, open-fired restaurant, which opens out onto the garden. The concise, monthly à la carte offers a good range of satisfying, original dishes that are big on flavour. Most produce is from the valley, including locally grown organic veg, game from nearby shoots, and lobster and crab from Cardigan Bay.

LLANFIHANGEL-Y-CREUDDYN, SY23 4LA
Tel.: (01974)261275
Website: www.yffarmers.co.uk

7.75 mi southeast of Aberystwyth by A 487 and A 4120, turning right after Pant-y-crug. Parking in the village square.

PRICES
Meals: £ 12 (weekday lunch) and
a la carte £ 20/33

MAP: 4

CLOSING TIMES
Closed first week January, Monday, Tuesday and Sunday dinner

Evan Evans Cwrw Cayo, Wye Valley Butty Bach and Monty's Sunshine

Y TALBOT (N)

Sit in the bar rooms, where the action is

Y Talbot was originally a drover's inn and its oldest part dates back to the 17C; a hotel extension was added with the arrival of the railways in the 1860s and you can clearly see the join. While there's a modern restaurant in the Victorian part of the building, the bar rooms in the older part are where the action is, and the best place to sit. The chef has a classical culinary background, so expect well-executed, full-flavoured traditional dishes made with Welsh produce. The daily changing pie is a hit with the locals, as is the burger with Snowdonia cheddar, while the daily fish special reminds you you're not too far from the coast. Bedrooms are bright and modern: ask for one of the newest. Oh, and there's an elephant buried in the garden!

TREGARON, SY25 6JL
Tel.: (01974)298208
Website: www.ytalbot.com

In the centre of town. Unrestricted parking in The Square.

PRICES
Meals: a la carte £ 17/30

13 rooms:
£ 60/130

MAP: 5

CLOSING TIMES
Closed 25 December

Wye Valley Butty Bach, HPA and Evan Evans Bitter

PEN-Y-BRYN

Impressive bay views from the garden and terrace

You might need your sat nav, as even when you've located the right residential street, you could easily pass Pen-y-Bryn by. Looking more like a medical centre than a place to dine, it boasts impressive panoramic views over Colwyn Bay, especially from the garden and terrace. The spacious, open-plan interior is crammed full of pictures, bookcases and pottery, yet despite these and the oak floors, old furniture and open fires, it has a modern, laid-back feel. The extensive all-day menu offers plenty of choice, ranging from a classical ploughman's to more adventurous pheasant-based dishes; while during 'Beer and Bangers' weeks 12 varieties of sausage and over 20 beers are also offered. Large tables make it ideal for families or groups of friends.

Pen-y-Bryn Rd,
Upper Colwyn Bay, **COLWYN BAY**, LL29 6DD
Tel.: (01492)533360
Website: www.penybryn-colwynbay.co.uk

1 mi southwest of Colwyn Bay by B 5113. Parking.

PRICES
Meals: a la carte £ 20/51

MAP: 6

CLOSING TIMES
Closed 25-26 December and 1 January

Great Orme Welsh Black, Purple Moose Snowdonia Ale and Timothy Taylor Landlord

GROES INN

Characterful pub serving generous homemade dishes

Located in the foothills of Snowdonia, with the estuary in front and the mountains behind, the setting couldn't be more beautiful. Flowers greet you at the door and the characterful beamed interior is filled with pictures, copperware and china, all bathed in flickering firelight. If you're after nooks and crannies, there are several small rooms encircling the comfy bar, as well as an airy conservatory and an intimate dining room. The menu features British favourites in neatly presented, generous portions and everything is homemade. Specials are often a little more adventurous and feature fish from the nearby waters, lamb reared on the salt marshes or game from local estates. Bedrooms have lovely views; some boast balconies or terraces.

CONWY, LL32 8TN
Tel.: (01492)650545
Website: www.groesinn.com

3 mi south of Conwy on B 5106. Parking.

PRICES
Meals: a la carte £ 21/42

14 rooms:
£ 100/200

MAP: 7

CLOSING TIMES
Open daily

Great Orme Ales

KINMEL ARMS

They keep their own cows and grow fruit and herbs

This early 17C stone inn is hidden away in a hamlet by the entrance to Kinmel Hall. It's the type of pub that's not entirely sure if it wants to be a pub or a restaurant: true, there's a delightful open-fired bar with a slate-topped counter and low-level seating which hosts regular events for the locals; but there are also two spacious dining areas - one with chunky wood furniture and the other, with a more conservatory-like feel. Lunch sees classic pub-style dishes, while dinner steps things up a gear. They keep their own cows in the field over the road and even grow fruit and herbs in a small polytunnel. Stylish, contemporary bedrooms boast smart bathrooms and large kitchenettes - so you can enjoy your continental breakfast in your PJs.

The Village,
ST GEORGE, LL22 9BP
Tel.: (01745)832207
Website: www.thekinmelarms.co.uk

In the centre of village. Parking.

PRICES
Meals: a la carte £ 21/46

4 rooms:
£ 115/175

MAP: 8

CLOSING TIMES
Closed Sunday and Monday

Brecon 3 Beacons, Facer's Flintshire Bitter and Conwy Welsh Pride

GLYNNE ARMS

Choose classics or more original, ambitious dishes

This 200 year old coaching inn sits just across from the gates of Hawarden Castle and was once home to the Glynne family, hence its name. They're not the only family involved here though, as the descendants of PM William Gladstone (who own most of the village, including several farms and an interior design company), now have the Glynne Arms back under their wing. Their experience with interiors means that the pub's been smartly refurbished and has a slightly funky feel. Cooking follows in a similarly modern vein and presents some original, ambitious flavour combinations, but traditionalists aren't forgotten - there's a 'Family Classics' section, as well as steaks from the estate farms; and be sure to save room for one of the tasty desserts.

3 Glynne Way,
HAWARDEN, CH3 3NS
Tel.: (01244)569988
Website: www.theglynnearms.co.uk

In centre of the village. Parking

PRICES
Meals: £ 23 and a la carte £ 19/40

MAP: 9

CLOSING TIMES
Open daily

Facer's Splendid and Flintshire Ale

GLASFRYN

Sizeable pub offering plenty of choice

An early example of Arts and Crafts architecture, this glazed red-brick building was intended to be a judges' residence for the nearby courts but, never used, was turned into a farmhouse, before later falling into disrepair. It's a sizeable place, able to cater for a few hundred at every sitting, with some tables seating up to 20 at a time. Order at the large central bar and watch your order whizz past in the vacuum tube system on its way to the kitchen. Menus offer plenty of choice, from pub classics such as fish and chips to culinary classics such as plaice Véronique, with some lighter dishes alongside. Portions are generous, prices are sensible and service is surprisingly swift. The garden and terrace boast nice views over the town below.

Raikes Ln,
Sychdyn, **MOLD**, CH7 6LR
Tel.: (01352)750500
Website: www.glasfryn-mold.co.uk

1 mi north by A 5119 on Civic Centre rd. Parking.

PRICES
Meals: a la carte £ 21/31

MAP: 10

CLOSING TIMES
Open daily

Purple Moose Snowdonia Ale, Facer's Flintshire and Tatton Blonde

TAVERN

A place close to the chef's heart

Having worked in various locations around the country, chef Peter Wright jumped at the chance to buy a pub close to his heart - a pub in which his parents used to drink - when it came on the market. He has given the place a modern makeover and although the heavy tables and black and cream leather chairs may make it appear fairly formal, the menu is still very much in a hearty, comforting pub vein, offering the likes of half a pint of prawns and Welsh Black beef. The daily specials - particularly the grilled market fish dishes - prove popular, while the set "Chef's Choice" and 4 course tasting menus feature slightly more refined dishes such as assiette of seafood or Gressingham duck with parsnip purée, followed by peanut butter parfait.

Mold Rd,
Alltami, **MOLD**, CH7 6LG
Tel.: (01244)550485
Website: www.tavernrestaurant.co.uk

2.5 mi northeast of Mold, on A 494. Parking.

PRICES
Meals: a la carte £ 19/35

MAP: 11

CLOSING TIMES
Open daily

Hafod Brewery Ales

RIVERSIDE

Proudly Welsh, with a fresh, modern feel

If you fancy brushing up on your Welsh, head for this part-16C coaching inn with the name 'Glan Yr Afron' (Riverside) above the door, then make for the 'Cwtch' (cosy corner) with its welcoming wood-burning stove. The pub stands on the main road in the small village of Pennal, backing on to a tributary of the River Dovey, and despite various additions and its Grade II listing, has a fresh, modern feel inside - with one half of the room laid for dining and the other taken up by the bar. The friendly local team bring over tasty bread to nibble on while you study the menu, which features all the usual pub favourites along with some sharing boards. Cooking is no-nonsense, full of flavour and keenly priced, and the portions are suitably hearty.

PENNAL, SY20 9DW
Tel.: (01654)791285
Website: www.riversidehotel-pennal.co.uk

On A 493 between Aberdovey and Machynlleth. Parking.

PRICES
Meals: £ 13 and a la carte £ 18/34

MAP: 12

CLOSING TIMES
Open daily

Blue Monkey Infinity, Purple Moose Madog's Ale and Glaslyn

RAGLAN ARMS

Concise, constantly evolving menus

With fireside leather sofas, simply laid scrubbed pine tables and vases filled with fresh flowers, the Raglan Arms offers a wholesome cosiness. Dining happens mostly in the front of the room, although the conservatory at the back is popular with families at weekends. Menus change slightly at each service and are short and to the point, and the kitchen is clearly serious about food, using local produce wherever possible and employing a range of cooking styles. Dishes are unfussy and flavourful and might include warm local ox tongue, imam bayildi or Tamworth sausages and mash, while dessert could be a toffee and whisky parfait or a rhubarb and custard slice. The lunch menu offers good value, service is cheery and the wine list is a labour of love.

LLANDENNY, NP15 1DL
Tel.: (01291)690800
Website: www.theraglanarms.co.uk

In centre of the village. Parking.

PRICES
Meals: a la carte £ 24/35

MAP: 13

CLOSING TIMES
Closed 25-26 December, Sunday dinner and Monday

Wye Valley Ales

WHITE HART

A characterful interior steeped in history

The 16C White Hart became the property of Henry VIII as part of Jane Seymour's dowry and, a century later, during the civil war, Oliver Cromwell used it as his Monmouthshire headquarters. The characterful interior proudly shows off ornate Tudor plasterwork, a priest's hole and 11 fireplaces dating from the 1600s; if that's not enough, it's even referred to by TS Eliot in the poem 'Usk'. When it comes to dining, there's an adventurous à la carte of well-prepared, precisely presented dishes, along with a slightly simpler set menu; many dishes arrive on slates and most ingredients come from within a 10 mile radius. If you fancy staying the night, you may have to fight off the competition for the only room - a double with an adjoining single.

LLANGYBI, NP15 1NP
Tel.: (01633)450258
Website: www.thewhitehartvillageinn.com

2 mi south of Usk turning left after bridge over River Usk onto road signed to Llangybi. Parking.

PRICES
Meals: £ 20 (weekday dinner)/45 and a la carte £ 25/42

1 rooms: £ 95

MAP: 14

CLOSING TIMES
Closed Monday except bank holidays and Sunday dinner

Wye Valley Butty Bach and Ringwood Bitter

THE INN AT PENALLT

Proudly and enthusiastically run

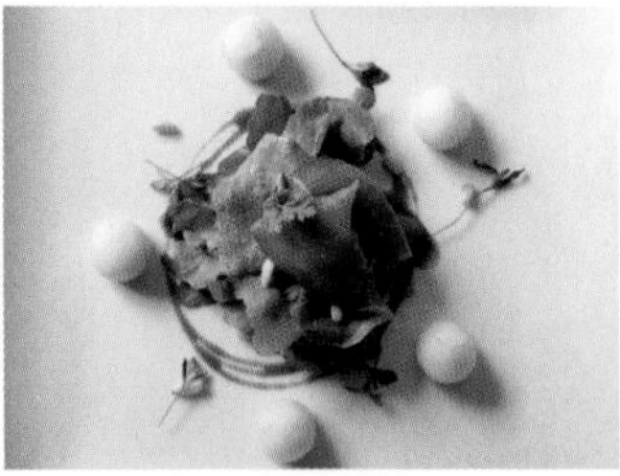

As enthusiastic owners go, Andrew and Jackie are up with the best of them. They bought the run down 'Bush Inn' back in 2009, spent 5 months refurbishing it and now it's their pride and joy. There's a choice of two rooms, both similarly styled in neutral hues and furnished with heavy wood; you'll find the locals gathered in the pubbier of the two, around the wood-burning stove, but for the best views, make for the comfy conservatory. Menus offer good-sized dishes with their roots firmly in the classics. Bread is freshly baked, the ice creams are homemade, and the majority of produce comes from within 40 miles. The beers are equally local and the Welsh whisky is also a big seller. Bedrooms are cosy, neat and tidy with modern facilities.

PENALLT, NP25 4SE
Tel.: (01600)772765
Website: www.theinnatpenallt.co.uk

5 mi south of Monmouth, off the B 4293 in village centre. Parking.

PRICES
Meals: £ 16 (weekday lunch) and a la carte £ 27/39

4 rooms:
£ 58

MAP: 15

CLOSING TIMES
Closed 5-22 January, Sunday dinner and Monday except bank holidays

Wye Valley Bitter and Butty Bach, Keystone Classic and Challenger

BELL AT SKENFRITH

An impressive choice of champagnes and cognacs

The Bell offers uncomplicated warmth: a seat in a comfy sofa by the inglenook, candles and meadow flowers on the tables and friendly, unobtrusive service. The weekly changing menu features hearty, classical dishes with the occasional ambitious twist; these might include rolled fishcakes or sirloin of Brecon beef with a mini steak and kidney pudding. Ingredients are allowed to speak for themselves, with local suppliers credited on the menu and much of the produce coming from their organic kitchen garden. Fruits of the vine are also taken seriously, with a large selection of half bottles and an impressive choice of champagnes and cognacs. Bedrooms are understated in their elegance, with super-comfy beds, fluffy towels and personalised toiletries.

SKENFRITH, NP7 8UH
Tel.: (01600)750235
Website: www.skenfrith.co.uk

12.5 mi east of Abergavenny on B 4521. Parking.

PRICES
Meals: a la carte £ 25/42

11 rooms:
£ 70/220

MAP: 16

CLOSING TIMES
Closed 2 weeks January
booking essential

Wye Valley HPA, Bitter and Butty Bach

FELIN FACH GRIFFIN

Attracts a great mix of customers

This terracotta-coloured former farmhouse in picturesque countryside is rather unique in that you'll find visitors aged from 1-100 and from all walks of life - which creates an almost bohemian atmosphere. Bright paintwork, colourful art and a scattering of magazines about the place provide a very 'lived in' feel and the atmosphere is extremely laid-back. The young staff interact well but just as importantly, have a good knowledge of what they're serving. Starters like local goat's curd with black olive purée or brawn with apricot chutney are followed by braised shin of Welsh beef or red mullet with salt cod brandade - and they're a cut above your usual pub grub. If you've eaten yourself to a standstill, pleasant bedrooms with comfy beds await.

Felin Fach,
BRECON, LD3 0UB
Tel.: (01874)620111
Website: www.felinfachgriffin.co.uk

4.75 mi northeast of Brecon by B 4602 off A 470. Parking.

PRICES
Meals: £ 21 (weekday lunch)/ 29 and a la carte £ 27/36

7 rooms: £ 100/168

MAP: 17

CLOSING TIMES
Closed 25 December and early January

Wye Valley Butty Bach, Brecon Six Beacons and Monty's Old Jailhouse

BEAR

Has stood proudly on this site since 1432

The well-maintained Bear stands proudly on the main street of this small town, its hanging baskets creating a riot of colour. Step through the front door into the hugely characterful lounge-bar with its shiny brass and open fireplaces and you can well believe it has been here since 1432. Diners can sit here or in the more formal restaurant; the latter may be more romantic but the former is undoubtedly the more appealing. The menu offers honest pub dishes like prawn cocktail, homemade faggots or braised Welsh lamb shank. The 'specials' add interest and a cheery young team provide swift, assured service, even when it's busy. Bedrooms are available in the main hotel: the most characterful feature exposed beams, four-posters and fireplaces.

High St,
CRICKHOWELL, NP8 1BW
Tel.: (01873)810408
Website: www.bearhotel.co.uk

In the town centre. Parking.

PRICES
Meals: a la carte £ 21/41

36 rooms:
£ 80/169

MAP: 18

CLOSING TIMES
Closed 25 December
bookings not accepted

Wye Valley Butty Bach, Brains The Rev. James and guest ales

HARP INN

Appealing menus of original dishes

Built to house workers constructing the medieval church, this 15C stone inn welcomes drinkers and diners alike. On a warm summer's day take a seat outside and make the most of the glorious view; in colder weather, head through to the charming flag-floored room with its warming open fire and beams hung with hop bines. 'Seasonality' and 'sustainability' are keywords here; breads, ice creams and crackers are homemade and everything else is locally sourced. Menus may be concise but dishes are original; you might find leek and ale rarebit, scrambled egg and home-spiced chorizo, or mackerel fillet with fennel spelt risotto - while the Welsh Black beef with triple-cooked chips has become a mainstay. Simple bedrooms come with wonderful views.

OLD RADNOR, LD8 2RH
Tel.: (01544)350655
Website: www.harpinnradnor.co.uk

Signposted south off A 44 east of Llandrindod Wells just before crossing the border into England. Parking.

PRICES
Meals: a la carte £ 20/34

5 rooms:
£ 65/105

MAP: 19

CLOSING TIMES
Closed Monday except bank holidays and lunch Tuesday-Friday - Restricted opening in winter

Wye Valley HPA, Hobsons Town Crier and Three Tuns XXX

THE PILOT

Hearty cooking and the heart of the community

You might assume that it has something to do with planes but 'The Pilot' is actually a reference to the mariners who guide ships safely into the Cardiff docks. This once rundown neighbourhood boozer has been transformed into a neat dining pub and it really has become part of the local community: regulars gather in the front room to watch the latest sporting events, while diners head to the rear, with its wood-burning stove and partial bay views. Ingredients are laudably local, with produce from the kitchen garden, nearby suppliers and even some of the locals' allotments. A good-sized blackboard menu mixes classic pub dishes with more adventurous offerings such as huntsman chicken or venison carpaccio, and dishes are hearty and honest.

67 Queens Rd,
PENARTH, CF64 1DJ
Tel.: (029)20710615
Website: www.knifeandforkfood.co.uk/pilot

5 mi south of Cardiff in residential area of the town. Unrestricted on-street parking.

PRICES
Meals: a la carte £ 19/32

MAP: 20

CLOSING TIMES
Open daily

Waen Festival Gold and Otley 01 and 010

PANT-YR-OCHAIN

Country manor house steeped in history

This is neither a typical rustic inn nor a 21C dining pub - but a classical country manor house in disguise. With Tudor wattle and daub walls backing a 16C inglenook fireplace, the place is steeped in history. Outside, mature gardens and well-manicured lawns stretch down to a small lake, and on a warm summer's day, lunch on the terrace or grass is hard to beat. In rainier weather, follow the polished quarry-tiled floors to the large central bar and choose from one of the numerous rooms surrounding it; some with ancient beams and exposed brick walls - all with nooks and crannies aplenty. The daily changing menu offers hearty, wholesome, all-day dishes, ranging from pies and casseroles to more interesting offerings such as hake with crab butter.

Old Wrexham Rd,
GRESFORD, LL12 8TY
Tel.: (01978)853525
Website: www.pantyrochain-gresford.co.uk

4.5 mi northeast of Wrexham by A 483 and B 5445. Parking.

PRICES
Meals: a la carte £ 21/60

MAP: 21

CLOSING TIMES
Open daily

Purple Moose Snowdonia Ale, Brunning and Price Phoenix Ale and Timothy Taylor Landlord

HAND AT LLANARMON

Cosy and welcoming with plenty of rustic charm

Set at the crossroads of two old drovers' roads, the Hand has been providing hospitality for several centuries and its current owners are continuing the tradition with flair, providing a warm welcome and hearty meals to travellers through this lush valley. There's a cosy bar, a spacious dining room and a pool room; and rustic charm abounds in the form of stone walls, open fires, ancient beams and quite a collection of taxidermy. The daily changing menu offers lots of choice, with plenty of wholesome pub classics like sausage and mash, steak and kidney pie or slow-braised lamb shank. Portions are generous, produce is local and the cooking, fresh and flavoursome. Cosy bedrooms have hill views and modern bathrooms; most feature a roll-top bath.

LLANARMON DYFFRYN CEIRIOG, LL20 7LD
Tel.: (01691)600666
Website: www.thehandhotel.co.uk

At the head of Ceiriog Valley northwest of Oswestry. Parking.

PRICES
Meals: £ 15 (weekday lunch) and a la carte £ 19/35

13 rooms: £ 45/128

MAP: 22

CLOSING TIMES
Closed 25 December

Joule's Pale Ale, Weetwood Cheshire Cat and Conwy Rampart

NORTHERN IRELAND

The presiding image of Northern Ireland for outsiders is buzzing Belfast, lying defiantly between mountain and coast. Its City Hall and Queen's University retain the power to impress, and it was within its mighty shipyards that the Titanic first saw the light of day. But the rest of the Six Counties demands attention, too. The forty thousand stone columns of the Giant's Causeway step out into the Irish Sea, part of a grand coastline, though Antrim can also boast nine scenic inland glens. County Down's rolling hills culminate in the alluring slopes of Slieve Donard in the magical Mourne Mountains, while Armagh's Orchard County is a riot of pink in springtime. Fermanagh's glassy, silent lakelands are a tranquil attraction, rivalled for their serenity by the heather-clad Sperrin Mountains, towering over Tyrone and Derry.

On top of all this is the cultural lure of boisterous oyster festivals and authentic horse fairs, while farmers' markets are now prominent all across the province.

2 Pubs without bedrooms
5 Pubs with bedrooms
Tiree
Tobermory
Mull
Craignure
Fionnphort
Loch Linnhe
Scotland
Firth of Lorn
Colonsay
Lochgilphead
Port Askaig
Islay
Jura
Port Ellen
Kintyre
Malin Head
Campbeltown
Giant's Causeway
Arran
Buncrana
Portrush
Lough Foyle
Coleraine
Ballycastle
North Channel
Letterkenny
Londonderry
Antrim Glens
Foyle
138
71
NORTHERN IRELAND
Ballymena
Donegal
N15
Larne
M2
Bundoran
Omagh
Lough Neagh
Bangor
1
3
4
5
BELFAST
N2
48
Lisburn
N15
Loughs
Erne
A4
73
Enniskillen
53
M1
2
Sligo
N16
Armagh
6
7
53
A1
N4
N17
142
Monaghan
Newry
Boyle
Carrick-on-Shannon
154
Newcastle
Cavan
Dundalk
N4
N2
215
Ardee
Longford
Roscommon
Navan
Drogheda
Ireland
IRISH
Mullingar
Lough Ree
R. Boyne
M3
M1
91
Athlone
55
Ballinasloe
Kinnegad
DUBLIN
M4
208
Tullamore
Shannon
N7
Birr
Dún Laoghaire
Lough Derg
M7
Naas
Portlaoise
Bray
Holyh
Roscrea
180
Glendalough
M9
M7
Nenagh
172
926
Wicklow
Carlow
250
M8

BILLY ANDY'S (N)

Generous portions of rustic cooking

It used to be the village store as well as a pub, and although the groceries are long gone, Billy Andy's still seems to be all things to all people, with drinkers, diners, overnight guests and music lovers all flocking here. There are two snug drinking areas, their walls filled with vintage posters; a wood burning stove and several open fires; and a pool table, a rustic dining room and a fine selection of whiskies - as well as four modern bedrooms, chatty staff and welcoming locals. Cooking is filling, with a strong Irish accent; expect Glenarm salmon, Finnebrogue venison, mature braised beef and rare breed pork. Desserts come in miniature so you can enjoy more than one; Friday is steak night and Saturday music sessions pack the place out.

66 Browndod Rd,
MOUNTHILL, BT40 3DX
Tel.: (028)28270648
Website: www.billyandys.com

5 mi southwest of Larne by A 8 on Browndod Rd. Parking.

PRICES
Meals: £ 16/19 and a la carte £ 18/33

4 rooms:
£ 40/80

MAP: 1

CLOSING TIMES
Closed 25-26 December and lunch Monday-Thursday

No real ales offered

PHEASANT

Children are well catered for

Set in the heart of County Lisburn, this sizeable creamwashed inn has a typically Irish feel, from the Guinness-themed artwork to the warm welcome and laid-back atmosphere. With its stained glass and dark wood, it has a somewhat Gothic style; the traditional open-fired bar is the place to sit when it's cold and the patio provides the ideal spot in warmer months. Internationally influenced menus showcase seasonal produce, with local seafood the speciality in summer and game from the nearby estate in winter. Children are well catered for too, with a dedicated selection of freshly prepared dishes, as well as toys and climbing frames. It's a popular place, so if you're in a group it could be worth booking the snug or the 'Gamekeepers Loft'.

410 Upper Ballynahinch Rd,
ANNAHILT, BT26 6NR
Tel.: (028)92638056
Website: www.thepheasantrestaurant.co.uk

1 mi north of Annahilt on Lisburn rd. Parking.

PRICES
Meals: £ 13 and a la carte £ 16/32

MAP: 2

CLOSING TIMES
Closed 12 July and 25 December

No real ales offered

POACHER'S POCKET

Robust, satisfying dishes - the beef is a hit

This neat, modern building is Danny Millar's second pub and follows in the footsteps of its older sister, the Parson's Nose. Set in the centre of a small village, its ethos is satisfyingly, 'local is best', so you'll find Irish Dexter beef alongside prawns and mussels from Portavogie or Strangford Lough. They are gaining a good reputation for their beef dishes, be it one of their hearty burgers which come in styles ranging from 'Classic' to 'Texan', or one of their grills, which usually include sirloin, rump, rib-eye and flat iron steak. Cooking is robust and satisfying, and only those with the largest of appetites will make it to dessert. If you fancy a bottle of wine or whiskey to take home, pop into their adjoining off licence.

181 Killinchy Rd,
LISBANE, Comber, BT23 5NE
Tel.: (028)97541589
Website: www.poacherspocketlisbane.com

3.5 mi southeast of Comber on the main road to Killinchy. Parking.

PRICES
Meals: £ 10 (weekdays) and a la carte
£ 18/32

MAP: 3

CLOSING TIMES
Closed 25 December

No real ales offered

GRACE NEILL'S

Reputedly the oldest pub in Ireland

Having first opened as the King's Arms in 1611, this is reputedly the oldest pub in Ireland and is still going strong. Renamed in the 1900s after a former landlady who would greet every visitor with a kiss, it consists of a small, snug original room – the place where smugglers once gathered to plot and scheme – and two large extensions; one beamed and one more contemporary in style. The large menu is satisfyingly classical and might feature Portavogie prawn cocktail or Strangford Lough mussels, followed by homemade burgers or local beef and Guinness pie; for those tight on time or money, lunch also provides a good value 'express' menu. Live music is a feature at the weekends and a guitar and tin whistle can always be found behind the bar.

33 High St,
DONAGHADEE, BT21 0AH
Tel.: (02891)884595
Website: www.graceneills.com

In town centre. Parking.

PRICES
Meals: £ 12 (weekday lunch)/18
and a la carte £ 18/39

MAP: 4

CLOSING TIMES
Closed 25 December

No real ales offered

PIER 36

Welcoming, family-run and overlooking the harbour

You couldn't pick a better spot for this family-run pub: it sits on the quayside overlooking the picturesque harbour and the lighthouse. But it's not just its location that marks it out; the hospitality here is pretty good too and the owners continually work to give their customers what they want - which explains why so many keep coming back. When it comes to the food, the menus are traditionally based and offer something for everyone. They purchase only the freshest seafood - so you can't go wrong with the local sole or mussels - and they also sell an impressive number of steaks, which is due, no doubt, to the fact that they hang and mature the meat themselves. Bedrooms are bright and modern, and some have great harbour and sea views.

36 The Parade,
DONAGHADEE, BT21 0HE
Tel.: (028)91884466
Website: www.pier36.co.uk

On the harbourfront. Parking in the street and at the rear.

PRICES
Meals: £ 10/17 and a la carte £ 18/41

6 rooms:
£ 50/99

MAP: 5

CLOSING TIMES
Closed 25 December

No real ales offered

PARSON'S NOSE

Proudly classical cooking - go for a fish special

The second venture for Danny Millar and Ronan Sweeney is this characterful Georgian inn, which started life as a private house built by the first Marquis of Downshire and dates back to the 18C. The rustic, open-fired bar displays a collection of brewing and distilling paraphernalia, while the dining room above overlooks the Queen's Lake in the grounds of the castle. Food is important here and those in the know will immediately get the culinary reference in the pub's name. Menus are unashamedly traditional and portions are generous; Dundrum oysters and mussels play a big part and the daily fish specials are always a hit - as is the slow-cooked Dexter shin pie. Puddings are classical and comforting, and the service, quick and efficient.

48 Lisburn St,
HILLSBOROUGH, BT26 6AB
Tel.: (028)92683009
Website: www.theparsonsnose.co.uk

In centre of the town. On-street parking.

PRICES
Meals: £ 10/23 and a la carte £ 16/33

MAP: 6

CLOSING TIMES
Closed 25 December
booking advisable

No real ales offered

PLOUGH INN

There's plenty of choice in where and what to eat

From its lush forest and glistening 40 acre lake to its impressive 17C castle and steep streets lined with antique shops, picturesque Hillsborough has plenty to offer, including the locally acclaimed Plough Inn. Having been trading since 1752, it's extremely well-established in the local community but it's not your usual kind of pub, as inside it's almost three establishments in one. The regulars can be found dining on pub classics in the dark wood bar or, from Thursday-Saturday, in the adjoining seafood restaurant, where the daily blackboard specials are a hit. The younger crowds tend to gather in the ground floor café-cum-cocktail-bar or in the trendy bistro above which offers an international menu. There are numerous multi-levelled terraces too.

3 The Square,
HILLSBOROUGH, BT26 6AG
Tel.: (028)92682985
Website: www.theploughhillsbrough.co.uk

At the top of the hill in the square. Parking.

PRICES
Meals: £ 12/24 and a la carte £ 16/33

MAP: 7

CLOSING TIMES
Closed 25-26 December

Hilden Ales

REPUBLIC OF IRELAND

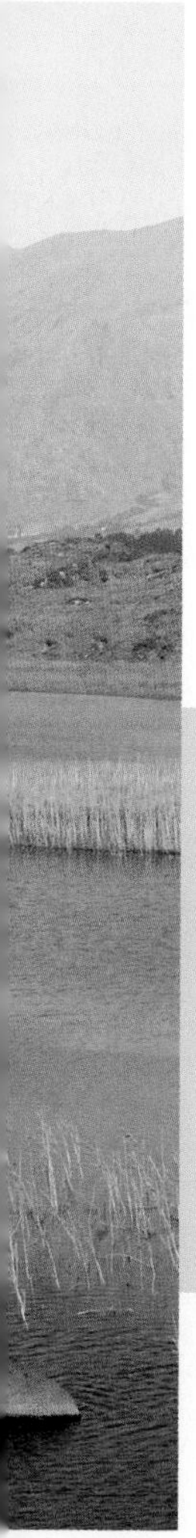

It's reckoned that Ireland offers forty luminous shades of green, and of course an even more famous shade of black liquid refreshment. But it's not all wondrous hills and down-home pubs. The country does other visitor-friendly phenomena just as idyllically: witness the limestone-layered Burren, cut-through by meandering streams, lakes and labyrinthine caves; or the fabulous Cliffs of Moher, unchanged for millennia, looming for mile after mile over the wild Atlantic waves. The cities burst with life: Dublin is now one of Europe's coolest capitals, and free-spirited Cork enjoys a rich cultural heritage.

Kilkenny mixes a renowned medieval flavour with a taste for excellent pubs; Galway, one of Ireland's prettiest cities, is enhanced by an easy, boho vibe. Best of all, perhaps, is to sit along the quayside of a fishing village in the esteemed company of a bowl of steaming fresh mussels or gleaming oysters and the taste of a distinctive micro-brewery beer (well, makes a change from stout...).

10 Pubs without bedrooms
15 Pubs with bedrooms
Fionnphort
Colonsay
Islay
Port Ellen
Malin Head
Giant's Causeway
Buncrana
Portrush
Coleraine
Lough Foyle
Letterkenny
Londonderry
Antrim Glens
R. Bann
Strabane
Donegal
Northern Ireland
Omagh
Bundoran
Belmullet
Enniskillen
Lisburn
Armagh
Achill
Ballina
Sligo
Monaghan
Newry
Boyle
Carrick-on-Shannon
Castlebar
Westport
Knock
Cavan
Dundalk
Lough Mask
Longford
Ardee
Clifden
Connemara
Lough Corrib
Roscommon
Navan
Drogheda
Lough Ree
Mullingar
R. Boyne
Galway
Ballinasloe
Athlone
Kinnegad
Aran
DUBLIN
REP. OF IRELAND
Cliffs of Moher
Ennistimon
Birr
Naas
Dún Laoghaire
Lough Derg
Portlaoise
Bray
Ennis
Roscrea
Glendalough
Wicklow
Kilrush
Limerick
Nenagh
Carlow
Listowel
Tipperary
Kilkenny
Arklow
R. Suir
R. Barrow
Cashel
Tralee
Dingle
Caher
Carrick-on-Suir
New Ross
Enniscorthy
Lakes of Killarney
Killarney
Mallow
Clonmel
Wexford
Cahersiveen
Fermoy
R. Blackwater
Waterford
Rosslare
Kenmare
Ring of Kerry
Cork
Dungarvan
Carnsore Point
Lee
Glengarriff
Cobh
Youghal
Bantry
Skibbereen
St. George's
St David's

MORRISSEY'S

Careful cooking shows respect for ingredients

As a boy Hugh McNally helped out at his mother's fish and chip shop; when he was older he worked at his grandparents' pub just across the road; and today that pub in the small coastal village of Doonbeg is his. It's been smartly refurbished, with banquettes along the walls, scrubbed wooden tables and walls filled with local artwork and books. There's also a decked terrace which overlooks the river and the castle ruins and is great for sunny days. The menu may be a simple affair but cooking is carefully done and shows respect for ingredients. Locally caught fish and shellfish feature heavily and the crabs in particular are worth a try. Bedrooms are smart and modern - two overlook the river - and they have bikes and even a kayak for hire.

DOONBEG
Tel.: (065)9055304
Website: www.morrisseysdoonbeg.com

In centre of village by the bridge. On-street parking.

PRICES
Meals: a la carte € 23/41

6 rooms:
€ 50/90

MAP: 1

CLOSING TIMES
Closed January, February and Monday dinner only and Sunday lunch

No real ales offered

VAUGHAN'S ANCHOR INN

Self-taught chef offering ambitious cooking

If you need to pick up some groceries in the picturesque fishing village of Liscannor, why not stop off at this family-run pub? Its cosy, pleasantly cluttered bar comes complete with a small shop selling everything from sea salt to birthday candles. The self-taught chef has travelled widely and has visited some of the world's best restaurants, so although lunch might feature traditional scampi and chips, the scampi will be made from langoustines and come in panko breadcrumbs and the chips will be homemade. Seafood plays an important role and will be on your plate just a few hours after it's landed; the seafood platter is a real hit - and how many pubs do you know that serve caviar? Smart bedrooms feature bright local art and colourful throws.

Main St,
LISCANNOR
Tel.: (065)7081548
Website: www.vaughans.ie

2 km from Lahinch by coast road, on main route to Cliffs of Moher. Parking.

PRICES
Meals: a la carte € 31/52

7 rooms:
€ 50/80

MAP: 2

CLOSING TIMES
Closed 25 December

No real ales offered

WILD HONEY INN

Classic dishes presented in a modern manner

With the Cliffs of Moher and the limestone landscape of The Burren on the doorstep, this roadside inn makes a great base for exploring County Clare; but it's also a great place to discover some good cuisine. From the outside, the three-storey building looks nothing like a pub - in fact, it started life as a hotel, and the garden was once the dance hall. It's a welcoming place, with a turf fire in the cosy bar and a peaceful guest lounge for those staying in one of the simply furnished bedrooms. When it comes to the food, they offer well-priced classic dishes presented in a modern way. They champion local produce, particularly seafood, and the kitchen shows respect for the natural ingredients, allowing their flavours to shine through. Bookings are not accepted

LISDOONVARNA
Tel.: (065)7074300
Website: www.wildhoneyinn.com

Just south of the village, on the Ennistimon rd. On-street parking.

PRICES
Meals: a la carte € 30/47

14 rooms:
€ 55/110

MAP: 3

CLOSING TIMES
Closed January-February, 24-26 December and restricted opening November-December and February-April

Galway Hooker

LINNANE'S LOBSTER BAR

Started life as a cottage, over 300 years ago

If you've not been before, leave plenty of time, as this tiny hamlet can be something of a challenge to find. Linnane's started life over 300 years ago as a traditional thatched cottage and is a simple but likeable place; roaring peat fires welcome you in the winter and the full-length windows are opened onto the terrace in summer. From the front it overlooks The Burren and to the rear you can watch the local boats unloading their catch on the small pier - some of which is brought straight into the kitchen. Unsurprisingly, they specialise in fresh fish and shellfish, with the lobster being a particular favourite. Some dishes are cooked simply, others, with a little more imagination, but all are tasty, well-prepared and sensibly priced.

New Quay Pier,
NEW QUAY
Tel.: (065)7078120
Website: www.linnanesbar.com

11 km northeast of Ballyvaughan following signs for Finavarra from N 67.

PRICES
Meals: a la carte € 22/52

MAP: 4

CLOSING TIMES
Closed Good Friday, 25 December and Monday-Thursday October-Easter

No real ales offered

POACHER'S INN

A neighbourhood pub that's a hit with the locals

It's not big, brash or colourful, but that doesn't mean the Poacher's Inn is lacking in a good old Irish pub atmosphere; in fact, if you're looking for the locals, this is probably where you'll find them. If you're in a rush, there are pre-prepared meals to takeaway; if you've time to stop, there's a whole array of menus to choose from. Lunch offers light snacks (the steak sandwich on homemade bread is particularly popular), supplemented by a good range of gutsy blackboard specials - the seafood dishes are the ones to choose. Dinner steps things up a gear and proudly showcases West Cork produce; maybe crab from Kinsale or fish from Skibbereen. Sit among framed maps and local prints in the wood-panelled front room or on stools in the cosy snug.

Clonakilty Rd,
BANDON
Tel.: (023)8841159
Website: www.poachersinnbandon.com

1.5 km southwest on N 71. Parking.

PRICES
Meals: € 25 (weekday dinner)
and a la carte € 25/45

MAP: 5

CLOSING TIMES
Closed Monday-Tuesday

No real ales offered

MARY ANN'S

Complete with a gallery of modern Irish art

You've little chance of missing this boldly painted pub or, for that matter, its larger than life owner. It's set in the heart of a sleepy village, up a steep, narrow street and the walk is sure to help you work up an appetite; if not, then while away some time in The Warren, the pub's art gallery, where the owner proudly displays his collection of modern Irish art. After this, head for the rustic bar, the linen-laid restaurant or, if the weather's right, the garden, where an enclosed dining area with gingham tablecloths and a mature fruiting vine provides the perfect suntrap. Menus are all-encompassing and offer plenty of choice; seafood is often a feature and there are usually several authentic Asian dishes courtesy of the Malaysian chefs.

Main St,
CASTLETOWNSHEND
Tel.: (028)36146
Website: www.westcorkweek.com/maryanns

Between Rosscarbery and Skibbereen south of N 71. On-street parking.

PRICES
Meals: a la carte € 26/52

MAP: 6

CLOSING TIMES
Closed 9 January-1 February, Christmas,
Mon-Tues October-March
dinner only

No real ales offered

AN SÚGÁN

Traditional throughout, with plenty of character

Offering charm aplenty and a real sense of history, this salmon-pink pub with its traditional shop front and memorabilia-filled interior is everything you could ask for. Run by a capable family team, it has established itself as something of a local institution so, along with the regulars, you'll find plenty of visitors too. Menus are traditional and largely based around the daily arrival of fresh, local seafood: lunch offers the likes of salmon and potato cakes or steamed Bantry Bay mussels, while dinner includes a selection of tasting plates and dishes such as Castletownbere scallops, flamed lobster or Ballyburden sirloin steak. Bedrooms are spacious and have bold feature walls; they are located in the old harbourmaster's house next door.

41 Wolfe Tone St,
CLONAKILTY
Tel.: (023)8833719
Website: www.ansugan.com

On the eastern side of town. Parking in the street.

PRICES
Meals: € 24 (weekday dinner)/38
and a la carte € 24/49

7 rooms:
€ 50/100

MAP: 7

CLOSING TIMES
Closed 25-26 December and Good Friday

No real ales offered

DEASY'S

Gloriously dated interior with a nautical feel

Hidden away in a picturesque hamlet, this appealing pub and its small decked terrace offer lovely views out across the bay. It's well run by a confident team but they aren't open regularly all year, so be sure to check the opening times before you go. The open-fired, stone-floored interior is gloriously dated, with mismatched wood furniture and a maritime feel courtesy of framed fish prints and old boat propellers hung on the walls. Dishes - chalked on the board daily - are dictated by the seasons and the latest catch brought in by the local boats; you might find roast monkfish or surf clams with braised pork belly and the Thai coconut fish soup is well worth a try. Puddings are, in the main, traditional, but they do a tasty panna cotta too.

Ring,
CLONAKILTY
Tel.: (023)8835741

3 km southeast, signposted off N 71 following signs for Ring. Limited parking.

PRICES
Meals: € 26 (dinner)/32 and a la carte € 31/47

MAP: 8

CLOSING TIMES
Closed 24-26 December, Good Friday, Sunday dinner, Monday and Tuesday dinner

No real ales offered

CRONIN'S

Run by the third generation of the Cronin family

Having been in the family since 1970, this good old Irish pub is now being run by the third generation of Cronins; you're still likely to find Mr Cronin Snr about the place, only this time on the other side of the bar. The keen team welcome one and all and being just a stone's throw from the harbour, that usually includes a yachtsman or two. The long bar is adorned with interesting artefacts, while the back room is filled with boxing memorabilia. During the week, they serve straightforward seafood dishes, while at weekends and midweek in summer, the restaurant is open for dinner, offering maybe scallops with leeks, fresh salmon tartare or their renowned shellfish platter. Produce is from nearby Oysterhaven and Ballycotton.

CROSSHAVEN
Tel.: (021)4831829
Website: www.croninspub.com

In the centre of town with free parking adjacent.

PRICES
Meals: a la carte € 18/40

MAP: 9

CLOSING TIMES
Closed 25 December and Good Friday

Blacks Kinsale Pale Ale, Trouble Sabotage and Eight Degrees Howling Gale

TODDIES AT THE BULMAN

Maritime-themed pub with excellent bay views

This pub is set in a great location, affording excellent views over Kinsale and the bay. Its décor is fittingly maritime themed, with an interesting mural of Moby Dick, and a carving of the famed Bulman Buoy it's named after hung on the ceiling. Scrubbed tables and open fires give it a rustic feel and pictures from yesteryear fill the walls. The cosy bar offers simple pub classics at lunch and it's also the venue for the regular live music nights, when locals and visitors alike can be found enjoying the craic; while upstairs, the well-travelled owner - formerly of Toddies restaurant - can be seen cooking carefully prepared, globally influenced dishes in the more formal dining room. Unsurprisingly, fresh, local seafood is the star of the show.

Summercove,
KINSALE
Tel.: (021)4772131
Website: www.thebulman.ie

East 2 km towards Summercove signposted to Charles Fort. Small free car park opposite.

MAP: 10

PRICES
Meals: a la carte € 34/51

CLOSING TIMES
Closed 25 December, Good Friday and Monday dinner

No real ales offered

CHOP HOUSE

Some dishes can be surprisingly elaborate

In a prominent position on the main interchange, just a drop goal from the Aviva Stadium, you'll find this imposing pub. Once a rather spit 'n' sawdust affair, it's been given a new lease of life by a local restaurateur - so much so, that dinner bookings are now advisable. For warmer days there's a small terrace; in colder weather head up the steps, through the bar and into the bright conservatory area. Lunchtimes see a relaxed menu of maybe beer-battered cod, wild mushroom tagliatelli or Landes chicken but to truly experience the kitchen's full talent come for dinner, where you'll discover the likes of North African spiced lamb breast with orange confit, raw tuna with teriyaki glaze or their speciality, 35 day dry-aged prime Irish steaks.

2 Shelbourne Rd,
BALLSBRIDGE
Tel.: (01)6602390
Website: www.thechophouse.ie

5min walk from Lansdowne Rd DART station. On-street pay and display parking.

PRICES
Meals: € 27/32 and a la carte € 30/49

MAP: 11

CLOSING TIMES
Open daily

O'Hara's Irish Pale Ale

MORAN'S OYSTER COTTAGE

Straightforward cooking and great hospitality

The name says it all: it's been run by seven generations of Morans; its speciality is oysters; and with whitewashed walls and lovely thatch, it's every bit a country cottage. Set in a tiny hamlet down winding country lanes, you'd never find it unless you knew it was there, and on a summer's day it'll soon become apparent that plenty of people do. The latest Moran to take the helm, Catherine, continues the family's philosophy of straightforward cooking and good hospitality. The menu barely changes - but then why change something that works so well? Throughout the year you'll find tasty prawns, mussels, crab, smoked salmon and lobster, along with daily baked brown bread; September - being native oyster season - is the best time to visit.

The Weir,
KILCOLGAN
Tel.: (091)796113
Website: www.moransoystercottage.com

5min from the village of Clarinbridge. Parking in road.

PRICES
Meals: a la carte € 28/46

MAP: 12

CLOSING TIMES
Closed Good Friday and 24-26 December

Galway Hooker

O'DOWDS

Run by the same family for over 100 years

The O'Dowd family have been dispensing gastronomic delights at this eye-catching blue-hued pub for over one hundred years. Sit in either the cosy fire-lit bar or the more spacious wood-panelled dining room to enjoy fresh, simply cooked seafood. Tender, sweet crab arrives straight from the shore, teamed with a glorious garlic butter to make the perfect meal; while the likes of brill, turbot and plaice are given the respect they deserve - simply lightly dusted with flour and then shallow fried. If you're coming for dinner, be sure to book ahead, and if lunch is your thing, then arrive early, otherwise you may find yourself watching enviously from the quayside as others tuck into home-baked soda rolls and steaming bowls of seafood chowder.

ROUNDSTONE
Tel.: (095)35809
Website: www.odowdsseafoodbar.com

On R 341 13 km from Clifden. Parking outside and on the quayside.

PRICES
Meals: € 22 and a la carte € 22/48

MAP: 13

CLOSING TIMES
Closed 25 December
booking advisable

No real ales offered

O'NEILL'S (THE POINT) SEAFOOD BAR

Generous portions of locally landed seafood

This smart pub has been run by the O'Neill family for over 150 years and, amazingly, several different generations are still involved. It stands in a great spot beside the Valentia Island car ferry terminal, with views of the sea and island, and has a pleasantly traditional feel, with family photographs, all manner of bric-a-brac and plenty of seafaring memorabilia. The menu offers generous portions of simply prepared, deliciously fresh, locally landed seafood. Lobster and crab are perennial favourites, salmon comes from the adjacent smokehouse and local fishermen bring their day's catch - which might include squid, monkfish or lobster - to the door. Unusually, they don't take credit cards and don't serve chips or puddings.

Renard Point,
CAHERSIVEEN
Tel.: (066)9472165
4.5 km west of Cahersiveen: follow the signs for the ferry. Parking.

MAP: 14

PRICES
Meals: a la carte € 34/42

CLOSING TIMES
Closed January-February
bookings not accepted

No real ales offered

QC'S

Cosy and characterful, with a nautical theme

Named after the owners, Quinlan and Cooke, this cosy little pub really delivers when it comes to character. Flagged floors, exposed stone walls and wood burning stoves feature, and there's a strong nautical theme running throughout, with oars, portholes and charts scattered about the place. Diners can eat either in the bar or in the pre-laid raised area towards the back. The menu is seafood-orientated, which comes as no surprise once you learn that the family also owns a local fish wholesalers. Cooking is fresh, unfussy and relies on classic combinations, with some more unusual choices appearing on the specials board; you'll find everything from fish and chips to sautéed squid with pesto. Spacious, modern bedrooms are just around the corner.

3 Main St,
CAHERSIVEEN
Tel.: (066)9472244
Website: www.qcbar.com

In the centre of town. Parking.

PRICES
Meals: € 21 (dinner) and a la carte € 26/48

6 rooms:
€ 65/110

MAP: 15

CLOSING TIMES
Closed 2 weeks November and Monday-Wednesday in winter
booking advisable

No real ales offered

BALLYMORE INN

Proud to use small artisan producers

Set in a small village close to the Aga Khan's stud, this pub's claim to fame is that Clint Eastwood and the late Larry Hagman have popped in on their way to the races. To the rear, a large bar screens sporting events and hosts live music, while to the front there's a spacious dining area with red leather banquettes, mosaic flooring and a Parisian brasserie feel. Lunchtime sees salads, homemade pizzas, stir fries and risottos, with some more substantial dishes appearing at dinner. The owner is keen to promote small artisan producers, so you'll find organic veg, meat from quality assured farms and farmhouse cheeses. Portions are generous but you won't want to miss the tasty bread or homemade tarts and pastries which feature at either end of the meal.

BALLYMORE EUSTACE
Tel.: (045)864585
Website: www.ballymoreinn.com

South of Naas on R 411. Parking.

PRICES
Meals: € 23 (lunch)/35 and
a la carte € 29/46

MAP: 16

CLOSING TIMES
Open daily

Trouble Brewing India Pale Ale and Ruddles Ales

FALLON'S

Save room for the tasty homemade puddings

Once half of the successful Fallon & Byrne food emporium in Dublin, Tom Fallon has taken his knowledge to the heart of Kildare, to share with the appreciative locals of Kilcullen. Satisfyingly, this is a proper bar, with a long wooden counter and a flagged floor - albeit one that's undergone a slight modernisation, courtesy of a boutique colour scheme and purple sofas - and at lunch the place is crammed with local office staff and ladies who lunch. Explore further, and you'll find a conservatory-style room at the back, while a linen-clad dining room provides a bit more formality in the evening. The menu offers plenty of choice, from a 'pie of the day' to grilled salmon with local black pudding, followed by tasty homemade puddings.

Main St,
KILCULLEN
Tel.: (045)481260
Website: www.fallonb.ie

At the Naas end of the main street. Parking.

PRICES
Meals: a la carte € 30/48

MAP: 17

CLOSING TIMES
Open daily

No real ales offered

OARSMAN

Traditional room adorned with various artefacts

With the River Shannon just 50m away and always a boatman or two inside, this pub's name is perfectly apt. Its double-fronted windows are filled with pottery, county flags and old artefacts, while a plethora of objects adorn the walls and an array of fishing tackle is displayed above the bar. This is a traditional pub through and through; family-owned, with rough wooden floors, old beams and stone-faced walls - and, unsurprisingly, frequented by the locals, especially at lunch. Snacks are available in the afternoon and there's a fairly substantial bar menu in the evening, while later in the week the comfy upstairs area offers dishes such as confit of Thornhill Farm duck or trio of Kettyle lamb. Cooking is simple and produce, laudably local.

Bridge St,
CARRICK-ON-SHANNON
Tel.: (071)9621733
Website: www.theoarsman.com

In the town centre. On-street parking meters.

PRICES
Meals: € 17 (weekdays)/55 and
a la carte € 23/46

MAP: 18

CLOSING TIMES
Closed 25-26 December, Good Friday and Monday

Galway Hooker and Eight Degrees Ales

FITZPATRICKS

Memorabilia and antiques feature inside and out

On the coast road to the peninsula, at the foot of the Cooley Mountains, you'll find this classical whitewashed pub overlooking Dundalk Bay. To call it characterful would be an understatement: this is a place where you can take in the whole of the Irish experience in one go. The car park and gardens are filled with colourful flowers planted in old bicycles, boots and even a bed; while inside there's a beautiful bar with brass rails, chock-full of memorabilia, including a fascinating collection of chamber pots and Victorian toiletries. The extensive menu features hearty, flavoursome portions of traditional dishes, with local steaks and seafood something of a speciality; come on a Tuesday evening for specials which are centred around lobster.

Rockmarshall,
JENKINSTOWN
Tel.: (042)9376193
Website: www.fitzpatricks-restaurant.com

9 km northeast of Dundalk following N 52 on R 173. Parking.

PRICES
Meals: € 28 (weekdays)/30 and
a la carte € 26/51

MAP: 19

CLOSING TIMES
Closed Good Friday and 25 December

No real ales offered

CROCKETS ON THE QUAY

Lively place - there's always something going on

This pub's vibrant orange exterior is matched on the inside by a lively atmosphere where there's always something going on, be it a poker night, a traditional Irish music session or a trivia quiz. Sports fans aren't forgotten either, with a pool table, TVs in almost every corner and two plasma screens in the garden. The place itself is rather dimly lit, but the light fittings that are located above each worn table really put the spotlight where it matters - on the food. Menus offer something for everybody, at prices to suit; fish and salads are popular in summer and the meaty game dishes and stews are a hit in the winter. Cooking is hearty yet refined and flavours are well-balanced. Bedrooms are currently too modest for us to recommend.

The Quay,
BALLINA
Tel.: (096)75930
Website: www.crocketsonthequay.ie

On the northeast edge of town by N 59 besides the River Moy. Parking.

PRICES
Meals: € 25 and a la carte € 23/41

MAP: 20

CLOSING TIMES
Closed 24-26 December and Good Friday
dinner only and lunch Saturday-Sunday

No real ales offered

TAVERN

Classic combinations and a great chowder

Most people come to the area to visit Croagh Patrick, the famous rock with a chapel perched on top, but this vibrantly painted pub has also put itself firmly on the map in recent years. With its designer colours, leather banquettes and quirky basket lampshades, it's the type of place that would fit right into a 'Country Living' magazine. In keeping with this style, staff are smart and attentive, and the kitchen produces an array of dishes with wide-ranging influences and a touch of refinement. Local seafood and meat arrive in classical combinations and the specials board lists the fruits of the latest catch. The chowder is award-winning, the chicken with chargrilled bacon is a perennial hit, and the daily cheesecake is an absolute must.

MURRISK
Tel.: (098)64060
Website: www.tavernmurrisk.com

9 km west of Westport on R 335. Parking.

PRICES
Meals: a la carte € 25/49

MAP: 21

CLOSING TIMES
Closed Good Friday and 25 December

No real ales offered

SHEEBEEN

Live music every Friday and Saturday night

This pretty whitewashed, thatched pub stands in a remote location in the shadow of the magnificent Croagh Patrick mountain and boasts lovely views out across the bay. On warmer days, grab a seat on one of the outside tables; when it's colder, head for the traditional snug, the rustic open-fired bar or the slightly more formal first floor dining room. The owner is passionate about keeping his pub honest and true, so along with the laid-back atmosphere and cheery groups of locals drinking Guinness, you'll find a selection of hearty, unfussy dishes on offer, including the likes of mussels, oysters and lobsters from the bay, and lamb and beef from the fields nearby. To top it all off, there are live music sessions every Friday and Saturday night.

Rosbeg,
WESTPORT
Tel.: (098)26528
Website: www.croninssheebeen.com

West of the town beyond Westport Quay. Parking.

MAP: 22

PRICES
Meals: a la carte € 23/37

CLOSING TIMES
Closed Good Friday, 25 December
and lunch weekdays November-mid March

No real ales offered

HARGADONS

Stone walls, sloping floors and character aplenty

Built in 1864 by a local merchant-cum-MP, this building started life as a grocer's (the original comestible drawers are still on display), before being acquired by the Hargadon brothers in 1909. To say it's characterful would be an understatement. There's a narrow passageway with booths; anterooms with oak-topped tables; thick walls hung with Guinness and Jameson's memorabilia; and a sloping stone floor designed to prevent flooding – there's even a lovely little "Ladies' Room" complete with its own serving hatch. Cooking is warming and hearty, offering the likes of Irish stew or bacon and cabbage, followed by tasty nursery puddings. They also have a good wine list, which makes sense when you see the large wine shop that adjoins the pub.

4-5 O'Connell St,
SLIGO
Tel.: (071)9153709
Website: www.hargadons.com

In the centre of town. Public parking nearby.

PRICES
Meals: a la carte € 19/29

MAP: 23

CLOSING TIMES
Closed Sunday
bookings not accepted

No real ales offered

LARKINS

Thatched pub in a charming lochside location

Set in a charming location on the shores of Lough Derg, this thatched whitewashed pub dates back around 300 years and is popular with the sailing set, particularly in the summer. As traditional inside as out, it boasts old flag and timber floors, a long wooden bar and original open fireplaces; and plays host to regular Irish folk music sessions and traditional Irish dancing groups. Throughout the day, the bar menu offers straightforward, unfussy dishes such as seafood chowder, homemade burgers or steak. In the evening, however, things step up a gear, with the likes of honey-roast duckling, herb-crusted fillet of cod or pan-fried lamb cutlets. Having come from farming backgrounds, the owners are passionate about sourcing local Irish produce.

GARRYKENNEDY
Tel.: (067)23232
Website: www.larkins.ie

9 km west of Nenagh by R 494 and minor road north. Free public car park opposite.

PRICES
Meals: € 20/35 and a la carte € 23/41

MAP: 24

CLOSING TIMES
Closed 25 December, Good Friday and Monday-Tuesday November-April

White Gypsy Ruby and Blond

FATTED CALF

Rustic pub with good links to local suppliers

With the Farrell family having finally hung up their glass cloths, this pub has been left in the safe hands of Feargal O'Donnell, who used to work in the kitchen of nearby Wineport Lodge. Aside from the name, the pub's changed little since he took over, with original Guinness and Gilbey's signs still adorning the attractive wood panels of the bar, and locals gathering around the TV and pool table in the snug. Having spent years working in the area, Feargal knows all of the best local suppliers, and his experience has definitely stepped the cooking up a gear. Dishes range from handmade sausages to local rabbit terrine, while tasty specials and bar snacks, such as duck rillette or black pudding on treacle bread, appear later in the evening.

GLASSON
Tel.: (090)6485208
Website: www.thefattedcalf.ie

On the N 55 in the centre of the village. Parking.

PRICES
Meals: € 25 (weekdays) and a la carte
€ 30/55

MAP: 25

CLOSING TIMES
Closed Good Friday, 25 December and
Monday except bank holidays

No real ales offered

LOBSTER POT

Carne's not-so-well-kept secret

If you're on your way to the ferry crossing at Rosslare or returning from a stroll along the nearby beach, this bold green pub is definitely worth calling in at. The interior is spotless and as soon as you see the staff in their smart waistcoats, you know they take things seriously here. Make for a cosy, characterful nook amongst the huge array of memorabilia and study the extensive menu of tasty home-style cooking, which offers a simple selection of light bites at lunch and a dinner menu exclusively for adults - as children must leave by 6pm. There are a few grills, but, as the name suggests, it's mostly seafood, with oysters and lobster cooked to order the specialities. But be sure to arrive early, as this is Carne's not-so-well-kept secret.

Ballyfane,
CARNE
Tel.: (053)9131110
Website: www.lobsterpotwexford.ie

Off N 25 following signs for Our Lady's Island. Parking.

PRICES
Meals: a la carte € 27/59

MAP: 26

CLOSING TIMES
Closed 1 January-10 February, 24-26 December, Good Friday and Monday except bank holidays

No real ales offered

BYRNE & WOODS

Arguably the second highest pub in Ireland

A smartly restored Morris Traveller stands outside what is arguably the second highest pub in Ireland, set up in the Wicklow Mountains. Built from stone, it looks older than it really is and, as its name may suggest, consists of two parts. 'Byrne' is a small, cosy bar with a stone fireplace and wood-burning stove - and is where you'll find the local drinkers and thrice-weekly live music sessions; while spacious, dimly lit 'Woods', is where the majority of diners head, characterised by dark wood furnishings, brown leather seating and a clubby feel. Cooking is fresh and straightforward, with lighter dishes on offer during the week, and the likes of pork belly with sage and apricot chutney or salmon with rocket pesto at the weekend.

Main St,
ROUNDWOOD
Tel.: (01)2817078
Website: www.byrneandwoods.com

On R 755 between Laragh and Killough. Parking.

PRICES
Meals: € 21 (weekday lunch)/
26 and a la carte € 24/45

MAP: 27

CLOSING TIMES
Closed 25-26 December

No real ales offered

INDEX OF **TOWNS**

M

N

INDEX OF **PUBS & INNS**

A

B

M

N

O

P

Q

R

CREDITS

P2: C. Joiner / age fotostock ▪ **P4-5:** Gloucester Old Spot, Piff's Elm Lazy Toad, Brampford Speke - Swan Inn, Swinbrook ▪ **P14:** FOTOSEARCH RM / age fotostock - Ron Bull / Alamy / hemis.fr ▪ **P239:** © R. Harding / hemis.fr ▪ **P59 :** © P. Packer / Sime / Photononstop ▪ **P185:** © J. Arnold / hemis.fr ▪ **P489:** © Flpa / hemis.fr ▪ **P404:** David Griffen, Cornish Arms, Padstow ▪ **P527:** © R. Maschmeyer / Robert Harding Picture Library / age fotostock. ▪ **662:** © Lluís Real / age fotostock

Thanks to:
Michelin would like to thank those pubs that provided us with their photographs.

Cover photographs:
Dundas Arms, Kintbury (Front cover) ▪ Beehive, Peterborough ▪ Feathered Nest, Nether Westcote.

MICHELIN TRAVEL PARTNER

Société par actions simplifiées au capital de 11 288 880 €
27 Cours de L'Île Seguin - 92100 Boulogne Billancourt (France)
R.C.S. Nanterre 433 677 721

Hannay House, 39 Clarendon Rd
Watford WD17 1JA
Tel: (01923) 205247
www.ViaMichelin.com
eatingoutinpubs-gbirl@uk.michelin.com

Dépôt légal octobre 2014
Printed in Italy 09-14

Typesetting: Nord Compo, Villeneuve-d'Ascq (France)

Printing and binding: L.E.G.O. SpA - LAVIS (TN) - Italy

YOUR OPINION MATTERS!

To help us constantly improve this guide, please fill in this questionnaire and return to:

Eating out in Pubs 2015
Michelin Travel Partner,
Hannay House, 39 Clarendon Road,
Watford, WD17 1JA, UK

First name: ....

Surname: ....

Address: ....

Profession: ....

< 25 years old ☐ 25-34 years old ☐

35-50 years old ☐ > 50 years ☐

1. How often do you use the Internet to look for information on pubs?

Never ☐
Occasionally (once a month) ☐
Regularly (once a week) ☐
Very frequently (more than once a week) ☐

2. Have you ever bought Michelin guides before?

☐ Yes ☐ No

3. If yes, which one(s)?

Eating out in Pubs ☐
The Michelin Guide Great Britain & Ireland ☐
The Green Guide (please specify titles) ☐

....

Other (please specify titles) ☐

....

4. If you have previously bought Eating out in Pubs, what made you purchase this new one?

....

....

5. If you buy the Michelin Guide Great Britain & Ireland, how often do you buy it?

Every year ☐
Every 2 years ☐
Every 3 years ☐
Every 4 years or more ☐

ABOUT EATING OUT IN PUBS :

6. Did you buy this guide:

For holidays? ☐
For a weekend/short break? ☐
For business purposes? ☐
As a gift? ☐
For everyday use? ☐

7. **How do you rate the different elements of this guide?**

NB: **1. Very Poor** **2. Poor** **3. Average** **4. Good** **5. Very Good**

	1	2	3	4	5
Selection of pubs	☐	☐	☐	☐	☐
Number of pubs in London	☐	☐	☐	☐	☐
Geographical spread of pubs	☐	☐	☐	☐	☐
Menu Prices	☐	☐	☐	☐	☐
Practical information (services, menus)	☐	☐	☐	☐	☐
Photos	☐	☐	☐	☐	☐
Description of the pubs	☐	☐	☐	☐	☐
Cover	☐	☐	☐	☐	☐
The format & size of the guide	☐	☐	☐	☐	☐
Guide Price	☐	☐	☐	☐	☐

8. **How easily could you find the information you were looking for ?**

....

....

9. **Please rate the guide out of 20 ..../20**

10. **Which aspects could we improve?**

....

....

....

....

....

....

11. **Was there a pub you particularly liked or a choice you didn't agree with? Perhaps you have a favourite place of your own that you would like to tell us about? Please send us your remarks and suggestions.**

....

....

....

....

....

....

....

....

....

....

Michelin Travel Partner
27 cours de l'Île Seguin
92105 Boulogne-Billancourt Cedex
France